PRELUDES

PRELUDES

✦

ESSAYS ON THE LUDIC IMAGINATION, 1961–1981

Christine Downing

iUniverse, Inc.
New York Lincoln Shanghai

PRELUDES
ESSAYS ON THE LUDIC IMAGINATION, 1961–1981

iUniverse books may be ordered through booksellers or by contacting:

iUniverse
2021 Pine Lake Road, Suite 100
Lincoln, NE 68512
www.iuniverse.com
1-800-Authors (1-800-288-4677)

ISBN-13: 978-0-595-35431-3 (pbk)
ISBN-13: 978-0-595-79926-8 (ebk)
ISBN-10: 0-595-35431-9 (pbk)
ISBN-10: 0-595-79926-4 (ebk)

Printed in the United States of America

For David L. Miller
who has been there all along...

Contents

Foreword

David L. Miller

Reading these early essays by Christine Downing on the ludic imagination brought forcefully back to mind an experience from thirty-five years ago, a painful experience that happened to me precisely during the years when Downing's essays were being composed.

In 1969, I had written a book on what I took to be the ludic imagination. It was called *Gods and Games: Toward a Theology of Play*, a book that is reviewed, not uncritically, but I now think appropriately, in Chapter Fourteen of the present work. My book included a brief commentary on the philosophical analysis of the notion of play by the Heidelberg philosopher, Hans-Georg Gadamer.

Not long after the book's publication, this famous German philosopher came to be a visiting professor at Syracuse University where I was teaching. Every Thursday afternoon, after his graduate seminar on Aristotle, he and I would go to a local country club bar to drink German beer and to talk. I had been told that he had read my book, and it is not difficult to imagine my growing anxiety when week after week went by without him saying a word to me about it.

Finally, after many torturous weeks—what seemed an eternity to a young professor in the thrall of a wise mentor!—he turned to the topic of my book. I was full of fear and trepidation, as it turned out that well I should have been. He said: "Professor Miller, you almost got the point!" I was crushed! What was wrong? It did little good for him to tell me that it was not entirely my fault. "English," he explained, "has a doublet for the idea: 'play,' the verb, and 'game,' the noun, are different words in English, whereas German says it with one and the same word, *ein Spiel spielen*, as does French, *jouer un jeu*." So, he explained to me that I had mistakenly thought that play has something to do with fun and games. "Very American," he said in a way that was not at all reassuring!

So what was the point of play? Gadamer asked me if I owned a bicycle. I said that I did. Then he asked me about the front wheel, the axle, and the nuts. He remarked that I probably knew that it was important not to tighten the nuts too tightly, else the wheel could not turn. "It has to have some *play* in it!" he announced in a teacherly fashion and, I thought, a little exultantly. And then he added, "...and not too much play, or the wheel will fall off. You know," he said, "*Spielraum,* 'play-room,' some room for play. It needs space." Gadamer, I believe, was trying to teach me what the author in these pages calls "psychic space," or "the psyche as space" (Chapter 20).

In reading this work thirty-five years later, I now see that Christine Downing already knew the point that I had almost understood. These essays are clearly not about play as unseriousness, not about fun and games, a point that should be abundantly demonstrated, for example, by the reference to the death camps of the Holocaust (Chapter 23). They are more about the space, the *Spielraum,* necessary for the wheel of life to turn soulfully. This "play room" is what both Buber and Heidegger refer to as the "between-realm" (see Chapter 4). It is not only demonstrated here by the fact that the author wrote these pieces when she was between thirty and fifty years of age, what the French, referring to "middle age" call *entre deux ages,* "*between* two ages." More to the point is the constant reference to the "between" in the chapters that follow. Here is only a partial list.

- between dreams & waking (Chapter 2)
- between I & Thou, self & other (Chapter 4)
- between past memory & future hope (Chapter 5)
- between literal & non-literal (Chapter 6)
- between belief & disbelief (Chapter 7)
- between play & seriousness (Chapter 9)
- between poetry & theology, secular & sacred (Chapter 10)
- between imagination & carnality (Chapter 14)
- between myth & reality (Chapter 15)
- between individual & communal (Chapter 17)
- between sanity & madness (Chapter 24)
- between age & youthfulness (Chapter 25)

It is as is said in Hindu theology, *neti neti,* "not this, not that," neither one nor the other, but the play between the two. This book is evidence that Christine Downing has thought this clearly and has lived this ludic spaciousness. It is not an apologia, not an attempt to persuade one that one ought to live in this way. It is rather a description that one likely does in fact, always and already, live this way whether one is aware of it or not. We live in this play, this interplay. We *are* between.

I had written earlier about this "between-realm" in Heidegger and Buber, but now, and especially in these essays, I think that it may be more true to the actual experience to imagine the "between" as an edge. It seems to me that these essays, themselves edgy in many respects, testify to life lived on an edge. When I say this I am thinking of "the razor's edge" of Hinduism's Katha Upanishad, of the edge of the "diamond sword of discriminating wisdom" of Buddhism, of the Cinvat Bridge of Zoroastrianism that is the knife-edge road to the other world, of the dangerous initiatory edge traversed by Altaic shamans in the spirit journey to the underworld, and of the saying by Jeremiah: "Each man who eats sour grapes, his teeth shall be set on edge."

I believe that the reader of this work may begin to experience such a psychic edge. If so, Christine Downing's essays will be felt to function as a possible prelude to the play of a truly ludic imagination, which, like Buber's "slow medicine," quietly enters the soul, working into the heart, awakening a secret melody to be noticed only later. Preludes, indeed!

Introduction

I had at first considered giving this collection the subtitle, *Early Essays*, but then realized this might lead the reader to expect *juvenilia*, whereas actually these pieces date from my thirties and forties, with the first being written just after my thirtieth birthday (as a graduate school paper) and the last as part of a celebration of my fiftieth. Nevertheless they are to me "preludes," dating from a time "before." Before the publication of *The Goddess*, before meeting River, before that decade when with a rush of writing energy I published seven further books: *Journey Through Menopause, Psyche's Sisters, Mirrors of the Self, Women's Mysteries, Gods In Our Midst,* and *The Long Journey Home*—a period in my life comparable to that still unbelievably short span during which Freud published *Interpretation of Dreams, Dora, Three Essays on Sexuality, The Psychopathology of Everyday Life,* and *Jokes and the Unconscious.*

Of course, this "before-ness" is not quite true after all, since I began working on the writing that eventually became *The Goddess* in 1975 and a large number of the papers I published in journals or presented at various universities and professional meetings eventually became part of that book. Beyond that, I decided early on that I wanted to cheat: to include as the first essay in this book something written shortly after the years it supposedly covers. "Dear Chris...Love, Christine" represents my view of precisely that period from a moment just beyond it.

The impulse to go back to the earlier time reminds me of Jung's returning in 1952 (at a time when he was just a little older than I am now) after the long years of work on *Mysterium Coniunctionis,* to the work of his early years, the work that precipitated and marked his break from Freud, *The Psychology of the Unconscious,* and reworking it radically to produce what we know as *Symbols of Transformation.* This kind of going back, this interest in discovering the continuities and discontinuities in our thinking, appears to be a natural project for one's later years—one I write about in the very last of the papers included here.

Unlike Jung what I offer here is not a reworking of the earlier material but simply a re-presentation of it. Well, I've cheated on that a bit as well. I've changed my "which"es into "that"s as my "spell check" demanded that I do (and noted in the process that almost everyone I quote makes the same mistake I still tend to make. Obviously my ear for language, usually quite reliable, is "off" here—but now I understand how it got misled!). I've changed the sexist language (all the "man" this and "man" that) that sounded so right *then* and sounds so off-key now. I've shortened a few pieces. I've reformatted (especially the footnotes) to give the whole a more uniform appearance. But essentially what is here is what I wrote then, not what I might write now.

Nonetheless, this collection of course reflects as much my present way of looking at things as it does the perspective of those earlier decades. For I have had to choose what to include and what to leave out. What is given here is perhaps a third or a quarter of what a "complete" early works might look like; it is only slightly more than half of what I had at first imagined including. After putting together my two anthologies, *Mirrors of the Self* and *The Long Journey Home,* I swore I would never again engage in such a project and had no anticipation, when I first began on this one, how similar in some respects it would be—particularly that it would entail the same painful necessity of selective omission.

There was also the issue of the best *ordering* of the book. For a while I played with a thematic pattern: gathering together the papers on dream, those on theology, or on Buber or Jung or Freud. But I quickly saw this wouldn't work, since so many of the essays might be put in this group but really just as well in another. Thus it quite soon became clear that the best arrangement would after all be a chronological one. And this then led me to see the continuities—my interest from the beginning of this period to its end and ongoingly today in dreams and metaphor, in literature and myth, in the Greeks and the Hebrews; my recognition of Freud and Jung, Buber and Mann as my lifelong teachers. It also made the discontinuities more visible. How engaged I was early on by the task of re-imagining theology (even more visible in the full listing of what I wrote in the mid1960s than is apparent in the choices included here). Also how (not surprisingly) in the period immediately preceding and following the completion of my dissertation on Buber's "theological imagination" I published many essays that grew out of that project and have written little that focuses directly on him since. How ever stronger Freud's influence becomes.

I had not realized beforehand the degree to which a gathering like this, if one conducts it oneself, is an *autobiographical* project—that in undertaking it one is both discovering and creating one's past and present self. So many of these papers evoke vivid memories of the life-context that helped inspire them or of the particular occasion at which they were first presented. The earliest, the paper on Dante, is imbued for me with memories of graduate seminars in the now-golden years of study at Drew. I remember that the acceptance for publication of the paper on Exodus was accompanied by an immediate invitation to me, a just minted Assistant Professor, to join the editorial board of the most important journal in my field—a sign of the readiness of the academy in the mid1960s to welcome a woman scholar, albeit no doubt in a token way. "Daydream" was presented at a session at the American Academy of Religion that marked a kind of Drew reunion. That same annual AAR meeting was the occasion of the first gathering of what became the AAR's Women's Caucus—a gathering that led to my being nominated to become the AAR's first woman president. I vividly recall how disappointed some of my feminist colleagues were by my choosing to speak on Freud and Myth in the presidential address I delivered three years later—though I am relieved that in the intervening years many of them have come to appreciate Freud's pertinence to the articulation of feminist concerns. "All Real Living is Meeting" opened the door to one of the most important friendships and loves of my life; the paper on Heinrich Böll's *The Clown* is a coded tribute to that relationship. I can see how liberating it was for me to move from the east coast to California in 1974: no more theology. As a tenured full professor I seem to have felt free to write about what really interested me in the language that felt most natural—which reminds me of Norman O. Brown telling us when he came to Drew just after having published his book on Freud about no longer feeling he had to write as a classicist about the things that classicists are expected to write about.

I understood that this autobiographical aspect would be more interesting to me than to my readers—and that I would need some criteria other than my own fascination to decide what should be included. Two seemed helpful. One: essays that would interest my present students at Pacifica, not because they'd learn about me but because of the continued contemporary pertinence of the essays themselves. Two (and this is not entirely distinct): those that might fit into the theme suggested by my subtitle: the "ludic imagination." I initially came up with this phrase because of its connection to "pre*ludes*" but quickly discovered how well it fit.

As I look over the listing of these essays there seems not to be one that doesn't focus on the imagination—and that doesn't try to honor its *ludic*, its playful and celebratory aspect. I see how this is true not only of the subject of these pieces but of their *form*. I've sometimes said that a stranger reading what I published in the 1960s would recognize the writer as bright and young and sometimes brash, but probably not as a woman. Maybe true, maybe not *as* true as I've supposed. I was surprised to see how all along I've enjoyed *playing* with voice. That in those relatively early more theologically focused essays I was (I see now) playing with, ventriloquizing, a theologian's voice, discovering what could and couldn't be said in it. Always pushing *theo-logos* in the direction of *theo-poesis*. I see how in some of early pieces published in the somewhat less distinguished journals (or never published at all) I had already found the personal voice that I think of as emerging only in *The Goddess*. I'm a little amazed at what I got away with, even at the rather formal meetings of the American Academy of Religion: how "Daydream" is spoken reverie, how "Theology as Make-Believe" is almost-psychedelic incantation. (I know it's really too long to have been included in its entirety, but I couldn't figure any way to cut it without distorting it.)

The book is mine, but it couldn't have come together without the dedicated help of others: Lesley Finlayson of the library at Pacifica Graduate Institute who scanned all the articles, Lori Pye who put hours into making sense of the gibberish that the scanning often issued in, Elaine Rother who agreed once again to ferry the book from my computer to the publisher. To them: my thanks.

1

"Dear Chris...Love, Christine"

Dear Chris,

I had a fantasy once, a year or so ago, in which we met and you embraced me, saying, "I'd like to grow up to be just like you." I wonder if you would say that if you really knew, really knew me, really knew all that has been part of my becoming the fifty-two-year-old woman now writing this letter.

I think of you often: twenty-eight, mother of five young children, about to begin graduate school. It's difficult to remember now all the ways that being twenty-eight then, almost twenty-five years ago, was different—perhaps especially for middle-class women—from being twenty-eight today. I have a daughter who is now almost as old as you; how different her life is from yours. I wonder if you and she would even know how to be friends.

Despite your ambitious and complex expectations for yourself, it would not have occurred to you to name yourself a feminist; the label had no contemporary currency. Despite your intense involvements with women while in college, the designation lesbian would have seemed utterly irrelevant to your experience. Though you saw your marrying as an undergraduate and immediately beginning to have a family as a conscious and personal choice (and as interestingly contrary to some of your adolescent dreams), it was certainly congruent with your time's conventions. Though I do remember how even then you understood "wife" and "mother" as roles you had happily undertaken to play, not as self-definitions. When at twenty-eight you felt ready to move beyond these roles, you certainly seemed imbued with much native confidence that whatever you might choose to do would be possible—you would have the requisite inner resources, and the world would respond welcomingly to your overtures.

My daughter, whom you knew only as an infant, has grown into a radiant, self-assured young woman, more clearly focused in her scholarly interests than you and with a more consciously developed sense of self. Though she values serious, committed relationships (she lived with her lover all through college) and

1

longs for a truly mutual, multidimensional, permanent liaison, she has a well-defined sense of personal boundaries. I cannot imagine her being swallowed up in any relationship; it seems evident that she has given priority to her dedication to her chosen discipline. When she finishes her doctoral degree in a year or so, she will already be a well-published, well-known figure in her field. Yet I sense her to have a much more tempered sense of her own limitations and of the outward possibilities likely to be available to her than you did, and a definite awareness of how those bounds are in part gender-related. It is a different time.

Still, you are alike in many ways—in your life-affirming energy, contagious enthusiasm, self-confident physical presence, intellectual acumen. Surprisingly, she would probably be more likely than you to appreciate these similarities, because she is more accustomed to turn to women for intimate friendship and to expect to find them her intellectual peers. I'm quite sure she would be interested in knowing how I'd tell my story to you.

It does make a difference to whom one tells one's story. I vividly remember how aware I became almost a decade ago, when I moved to California, to a strange city where I knew no one, that to the new people I met I was my stories. I seemingly had utter freedom to select, to omit, to change, to invent—yet actually each other person demanded a particular truth of me. Sandor Ferenczi once wrote a one-page paper about the significance of the choice of the particular other with whom one shares a particular dream. I tell you my dream because I believe it in some way to be about you; you listen because you believe it to be about me.

Thus I choose you for this telling of my story because I feel it to be about you. I choose you, the twenty-eight-year-old, rather than some earlier or later incarnation because I sense you to be at a juncture where you are deciding to become me or to become someone else. The possibility of your choosing some other, radically different life may exist more truly at this moment than at any preceding or subsequent time. I choose you because you'll be interested in the struggles, not just the successes; the inner aspect, not just the outwardly visible part; the personal dimension, not just the narrowly professional component. I choose you because you'll expect a particular kind of honesty, the kind I see you as having shared with our friend, Pat. What you'd be interested in, no curriculum vitae would communicate.

The name "Chris" so well conveys your particular kind of androgynous energy. Recently I have begun to prefer to be called "Christine," feeling myself ready now to accept the more feminine and somehow more whole connotations of the name I was given at birth but have never before been willing to claim. I'm not sure just when Chris became Christine; this letter is in part an exploration of that transition. I don't expect to find a particular moment when the change occurs—so for much that happens in the years that intervene between your decision to return to school and my writing of this letter, it may be more appropriate to say "we" than "you" or "I."

I wonder if I can imagine you any more clearly than you can imagine me. Oh, it's fairly easy, of course, for me to get the outward facts straight; but the inner meaning, the values, assumptions, questions, fears are more evasive. You are, at twenty-eight, about to celebrate the first birthday of your fifth child, your first daughter. You have just moved into a large, rambling house out in the country. It is all quite different from the life you'd once imagined for yourself, a life that would have had you at twenty-eight already an established writer of fiction, a sophisticated woman of the world with several fascinating lovers, maybe almost ready to choose one with whom to settle down. But the life you've actually chosen is genuinely fulfilling—the sexuality, the childbearing, the close friendships with other young women absorbed in the same challenges give you access to a discovery and validation of your feminine embodiment that you feel you might all too easily have missed.

But marriage isn't all you'd once hoped; there are intellectual interests and spiritual searchings that you find it impossible to share with husband, children, or the neighboring women. Quite early on and very painfully you recognized there was a part of you that felt radically unnurtured—until you met Pat, and luckily that was pretty soon, before your second child was born. Together you two read Jung, you began recording your dreams and working on them with one another's help. You began to write poetry and fiction; she returned to her sculpture. The two of you read the same books and discussed them passionately. You found language and courage to communicate to one another your uncertainties, ambivalences, restlessness, vulnerability, deep but elusive longings. Both of you believed that your searching wasn't simply a psychological matter; that it required some outward expression.

By the time you gave birth to your fifth child, you knew that you were on the verge of a new phase of life, though you had no picture of what that meant. During that first year of your daughter's life, you did some editing and research for a New York psychologist, you had a brief but intense affair. Both left you knowing, "That's not quite it, though I still don't know what is."

Was it just that year that you first read Buber's *Between Man and Man*? I remember that you had been encouraged to read *I and Thou* often before and had tried; but somehow had never gotten very far. This time you received what Buber had to say—that "all real living is meeting," that "I become I in order to say

Thou"—as a long-awaited complementation to Jung's emphasis on individuation, on the self. To bring these two perspectives together, experientially if not theoretically, seized you as a life task—though, again, what that might mean concretely remained a mystery.

I remember so vividly the evening you and Pat went to hear Esther Harding, the author of *Woman's Mysteries*, speak. You forgot so quickly the details of what she said, but the impression she made on you was ineradicable. You knew: "Here is a woman, not a nurturing mother nor a sexual playmate but a woman who clearly has her center in herself. She is as strong, as intelligent, as direct as the old-maid headmistress of my youth, her face as life-marked as the women in Grant Wood's portraits. But she conveys a gaiety, a wisdom of soul, an unquenched curiosity I have never marked in those other figures." Afterwards in Pat's kitchen, sipping coffee, you discovered that somehow in Harding's presence that evening you had each come to a radical decision. "I am going into therapy," she said; "I want to become an analyst." "I am going to graduate school; I want to write and maybe teach, but first there is so much I want to learn," you replied.

It was already midsummer, but you applied to the only school within easy commuting distance of your home. You didn't have a definite sense of a particular field of study you wanted to pursue. You'd been a literature major as an undergraduate but now wanted to include philosophy, theology, psychology—all the different ways in which we humans have tried to articulate and image what it means to be a human self. The catalogue of that single possible school suggested one could do that under the rubric "Theology and Culture." You had no idea that there may not have been any other school anywhere that offered such an interdisciplinary doctoral program. You had no idea that one didn't do graduate work in religious studies without first getting a seminary degree. You had no idea that women studied religious education, that only men studied theology. You really had so little idea of how lucky you'd been or of what you were getting into...

How I bless you for the naiveté and courage! How I'd like you to know what happened after that, how you became me!

As you began graduate school you certainly had very little in the way of defined long-range goals; perhaps we never have had. You were there, really, as part of a personal search, not out of professional ambition or economic need. You were there because you wanted a more directed course of study than the stacks of a suburban library could provide, because you wanted people to talk with about what you were reading and thinking, because you wanted respect-worthy criticism of your writing. You longed for contact with people competent to tell you where you were on target and where off, where what you had to say was a commonplace and where original.

It was your good fortune to find just the community of scholars for which you yearned—brilliant, dedicated teachers and bright, emotionally sensitive, warmly affectionate fellow students. The excitement of being in such a world was almost more than you could bear. The alternation between spending a morning studying Hölderlin in a way that called upon all your poetic and intuitive capacities and being required the same afternoon in a class on Karl Barth to think more logically, more rigorously, more quickly than ever before was almost enough to make one schizophrenic.

Luckily you went to school only one day a week. Though you had lots of studying to do in between, that was blessedly balanced by the hours devoted to sorting laundry, making bread, praising crayoned drawings, settling quarrels, reading bedtime stories. Only your oldest had yet started school and, of course, there was no daycare then. But your mother lived nearby; she was very proud of what you were doing and happy to play grandmother once a week. Your husband, too, seemed generously delighted by your new life and very willing to take on household chores and childrearing tasks. By the standards of today the division of family tasks was still very gender-determined, but I well understand how readily you assumed that it was your responsibility to do the food-shopping and to plan the meals, to oversee the cleaning and manage the family budget. You understood him to be helping you with *your* tasks.

This remained true later in that period when "you" gradually became "me," when we were both in some sense present. In our first years of teaching it was so important to us to coach a softball team and to teach Sunday school, to play Den Mother and P.T.A. president—as though it were all right to be not just a suburban housewife only if we didn't shirk the housewife's obligations. It was important to us to be known as a gourmet cook and expert seamstress, and as someone who juggled all this well and easily. Now I'm a little embarrassed at how long it took before we questioned the social expectations you took for granted—maybe just because it all seemed to work so easily for us. Even now I see our husband as having been quite remarkable in this easy acceptance of our new endeavors—and later of our financial independence, our having more recognition in our field than he had in his, even our love affairs.

Recently there has been much discussion of the role that mentors have played in the education of successful professional women. We certainly recognized that several of our professors took a special interest in us. We felt they appreciated and encouraged our intellectual gifts and regarded us as a vibrant, attractive young woman. But I don't believe you saw any one of them as having provided decisive direction or support—nor, in retrospect, do I. Indeed, I would say that our most important instructor was really Sigmund Freud (no more popular then among my Jungian cohorts than now among my feminist ones). Lou Salome once wrote of Freud that his was the father-face of her life (though they didn't meet until both were over fifty). For us his has been the teacher-face. We have read and reread, listened and talked back, and still learn more at each encounter.... Though no course on Freud was included in our graduate school curriculum, we knew we could no longer rest content with knowing only Jung's version of Freud and so persuaded one of our teachers to serve as tutor. We read through the entire corpus and much of the secondary literature as well; he read with us, book after book, and we met with him one evening each week to discuss and argue. (I remember also how week after week one of the other students sat in his car outside the professor's study window to protect us from being raped—his fantasy, not ours.)

I remember you had feared you might feel like "grandmother" because of starting graduate school so long after college; instead, because of years spent in seminary, in parishes, or earning money for further schooling, most of the other students were about your age. You were the only woman and reveled in that. The half dozen or so whom we came to know well all seemed half in love with us and yet also willing to include us as "one of the guys." They were not threatened by our brains or our ambition, or even by all those babies. They were a remarkable group of young men, able to show vulnerability, tenderness, confusion, hurt not only to us but also to one another. We and they were all at least somewhat Jungian and would have agreed that you were given (and took) an "anima" role. They welcomed our female presence as a support to their attempt to discover and cultivate their own "femininity." Long after they were dispersed all over the country, these men constituted our "kraas"—the community to which we would most spontaneously turn to share joy, anxiety, failure, the community to whom our writing was really addressed.

We had no female role models or colleagues and didn't even know enough to miss them.

You had wanted to go back to school in part as preparation for writing about the Buber-Jung dialogue. In the event we wrote our dissertation on Buber; our closest friend wrote his on Jung. We wanted very much to escape the constrictions of the traditional dissertation, to write with life and grace, to include not only our intellectual but also our emotional and existential response to Buber's writing. We were interested primarily in the interrelationship of form and content: how what Buber had to say forced him out of abstract, discursive theologizing toward poetry, folktale, drama. Our aim was not so much to prove a thesis as to explore the unfolding of a lifework.

Getting it written took longer than we'd expected. At first we had been wholeheartedly enthusiastic about being back in school, but after two years that eagerness had, to our great confusion, disappeared. I remember our being scheduled for a class presentation and finding we had nothing to say and couldn't bear any longer to be just a good reader, scholar, critic. We took a year off, officially to begin work on our dissertation. By then we had passed the qualifying exams with distinction, had been elected a Kent Fellow, and had received some recognition from distinguished scholars in our field, but weren't sure any more of how any of this connected with us. Our closest friend had taken a teaching position a thousand miles away; we missed him terribly. We wondered whether we wouldn't really rather just be a wife and mother "like everyone else." It was our youngest child's last year before kindergarten, and we wanted to spend it with her. I write about it lightly, but it was not an easy time for us.

In the late spring of that year we received a phone call asking if we'd be interested in a teaching appointment at the women's college of the state university. It was an ideal opportunity, *the* ideal opportunity—a good school only a half hour away from our home. We realized how much we'd missed *talking* during our year out of school, how much we longed for colleagues and students to talk with about what we were reading and thinking. That recognition led us to accept the job, even though we'd not finished the dissertation, even though we'd planned not even to consider teaching until our daughter was in first grade.

The first year of teaching was exhausting—and exhilarating. Students told us later they had never had a teacher as nervous as we were in our first few lectures. Material that we had expected would easily fill a week of classes (and should have) was used up in fifteen minutes; we found we no longer knew how to talk except in the technical theological language that had so bewildered us during our first weeks in graduate school; we wanted discussion and had no idea how to elicit it. We had been assigned courses we were entirely unprepared to teach. We were up till long past midnight every night and lost ten pounds that first semester. But we loved it; we felt that, though we had never consciously decided to become a teacher, we had found our true vocation.

It was a small department; the chair, who'd been there for years, was the only other full-time member. But this was the early sixties, when religion departments were beginning to attract students who in another era would have majored in psychology, philosophy, sociology, or literature—and we were ambitious and popular. The department grew quickly; an additional full-time person was added almost every year for the next six or seven. The curriculum also expanded, and we were soon able to teach courses that reflected our interdisciplinary interests: religion and literature, religion and psychology, myth and ritual. We felt the department was one that we and the chair had created together. He made it evident how fond he'd become of us (though we never talked about that directly and had no inkling of what that would one day engender).

You had done your graduate work in theology simply because that had made it possible for you to pursue your multidisciplinary interests. Naturally this led to a teaching assignment in a religion department, though we always felt a little uncomfortable there. We were at ease with what the actual teaching required but not with the public identification as a theologian, which seemed a misleading representation. We were never as pious nor as Christian as the label seemed to connote. Nevertheless these were years in which we tried to perform as a scholar in the theological field. We wrote on the exodus metaphor as constitutive for Hebraic faith, on literary amplifications of the Christ figure—always stressing the iconoclastic elements within the biblical tradition. We had no awareness that our claustrophobic response to the tradition might be rooted in its patriarchal androcentrism. Our critique was directed rather against its monotheistic, historicistic, and anthropocentric biases. I don't believe that reading what we published then would lead one to guess the author was female. Nor would we have wanted it otherwise. We would have seen no reason for our content, our style, or our conclusions to be different from what a male scholar might produce.

Our consciousness at that time was defined by what I would now call a heterosexual fantasy. We were happy that, though physically located on the campus of the women's college, ours was the only religion department in the university, so that our classes attracted as many men as women. We still felt comfortable with the Jungian notion that there are specifically feminine attributes and attitudes and specifically masculine ones, and that the task of individuation for both women and men is to bring the contra-sexual archetype to consciousness. Our ideal—for self and for the men with whom we were involved—was androgyny.

We felt our professional life was well balanced by the very different challenges and rewards of life at home with husband and children, and by our love affairs—which we understood as complementary to our marriage and unlikely to threaten it. Our life seemed stable and satisfying. But then it all fell apart. And so did the sense of a seamless continuity that has made it possible to speak so easily of "our" life. From this point onward it becomes necessary to use "I" rather than "we."

I fell in love more deeply than we had ever expected; my lover's wife learned of our affair and was shattered. I in turn had a serious breakdown as I came to terms with how badly I had wounded this other woman. I came very close to killing myself. I think that at this point what happened to me becomes something you might have deliberately chosen to avoid, could you have foreseen it. Though in some strange way perhaps you did foresee; I remember so clearly how often in your teens and early twenties you spoke, only half in jest, of your expectation that you would die before you were thirty-seven. In some ways you did. Strangely (not too strangely?) this breakdown occurred the year we'd been awarded an interdisciplinary fellowship which freed us from our teaching obligations. We had planned to go to Germany with our children and write a book. I did go to Germany and took our children, too, but did no writing—I spent most of that year in the underworld, not at all sure I would emerge. Sometime, perhaps at the beginning of spring, I began to heal.

It seems appropriate that I had gone to my motherland to recover and that recovery led to a loosening of the father-identification that had for so long bound me. When I returned to teaching in the fall of 1968, I felt as though I was entering an entirely new world. My re-established stability still felt very precarious; I felt fragile. I had no more career ambitions, hoped only to survive; teaching was a way of staying in the world of others. It was years before I wrote again or thought of myself as someone who had anything to say. (I got tenure during this time but on the basis of work we'd completed, though not necessarily published, earlier.) I returned to a world in which my new vulnerability was somehow appropriate. During the spring of 1968 while I was in Europe, student-led uprisings in Berlin and Paris were major events. I came home to discover that in America, too, students had begun to demand political responsibility and moral relevance from their universities and their professors. They wanted participation in shaping the curriculum; they wanted more experiential modes of teaching. They saw connections between the oppression of blacks and the oppressive war in Vietnam and their oppression as students. My female students were newly aware as well of their oppression as women, not only in concrete socioeconomic terms but by assumptions deeply ingrained in literature, philosophy, theology, language itself. They were also beginning to realize how this entered into their denigrating perceptions of themselves and of other women. My students were feminists; many were discovering they were also lesbians—that really valuing and loving themselves as women meant loving women. My students became my teachers—and in a sense my healers also, as they presented me with challenges that reawakened my life-energy.

Our adolescent children, involved by then in the peace movement, in rock music, in psychedelic drugs, were also teachers—as were the younger women I began to know who were just entering my field, women who looked to the women of my generation as role models but who really initiated *us* into the challenges of creating a genuinely feminist theology.

By the time of Cambodia and Kent State, I was visible on campus as one of the more radical faculty. I was not really aware of how alienated I had become from the department chair nor of the degree to which (in a time when university funding was suddenly tighter and when younger colleagues were no longer assured that each would in turn get tenure) the cooperative collegiality of our department had evaporated. The next fall a new instructor joined the department; he and I became close. We two and one other young man in our department were actively involved with the "radical faculty caucus." Our intimacy and our politics—to this day I don't know which was the weightier—were very upsetting to the chair to whom I'd once been so close. It took him several years, but he managed to get rid of all three of us—one of the men was not rehired when his probationary instructorship came to an end, the other was refused tenure. I had tenure and could have stayed, but preferred not to. Though all this was less shattering than the breakdown seven years earlier, I was again having to acknowledge how my own naiveté and recklessness had created havoc in the lives of others. I was also aware that in some definitive way a life phase was over and that leaving this university was a way of marking that transition.

In my personal life, also, it was time to move on. Our children were grown; I wanted to explore who I was apart from the roles of wife, mother, or even lover. I wanted to discover what it would be like to live alone, at least for a time. I was lucky enough to receive an invitation to come as visiting professor to a California university, and when I found I liked being there, arranged to stay on as chair of the department. My first year coincided with my term as the first woman president of the American Academy of Religion. This office came to me almost accidentally when (thanks to the efforts of the women's caucus) it was time for a woman to have this position, but my term became a kind of omen of the new blossoming that occurred when I moved to the west.

More than ever before, I felt I had come into my full power—as teacher, writer, woman—that I was doing exactly what I'd been born to do. I loved my teaching, not so much what I did in the university religion department but rather what I did in my role as adjunct instructor in a graduate clinical psychology program. I felt I had found my subject, my students, my voice. I was teaching Freud in a way that allowed me to pass on to others the gift I most valued from those years in graduate school. I was teaching future therapists about *therapeia*, about serving the wounded and vulnerable souls of their patients. I was teaching in a way that took advantage of all that I had learned through reading, friendship, failure, and joy.

I began to write in a way that brought together my personal experience and searching with my scholarly gifts and expertise—I now wrote because I *had* to. I wrote in order to make sense of my own life, and because I had something to say I believed would truly matter to others, though it wouldn't be "theology," wouldn't be published in the prestigious professional journals, wouldn't further my career. I began by writing about the Greek goddesses, then about sisters, then about menopause as a rite of passage.

More had shifted during that breakdown period than I immediately recognized. Chris became Christine. The androgynous understanding of self, according to which some of my attributes seemed feminine, others masculine, no longer fit. I now knew myself as female through and through, as much in my courage and intellectual capacity as in my gifts of empathy and intuition. I found my network had changed, that I now sent my drafts not to the men with whom I'd gone to graduate school but to women: former students and feminist colleagues all over the country, academicians, therapists, poets.

I've been here in San Diego nine years now; have just resigned as chair of the department and am once again on one of those leaves of absence from the academy that seem to become turning points. I have just finished my twentieth year of teaching. I've just completed menopause. I'm aware that if my life lasts as long as my mother's already has, I'm just beginning the second half of my adult life. It's strange, Chris, but in some ways I feel myself just as much on the threshold of a new beginning as you were at twenty-eight. I've gone back to school and gotten a graduate degree in counseling. I still want to teach—but less—and to be able to focus on teaching the things I really know and care about. I think I want to balance teaching more with the one-to-one work of therapy. Maybe it is time now to take on for myself that other half of Esther Harding's legacy, the half your friend Pat took on by choosing therapy when you chose teaching. Our lifelong fascination with the tension between Buber's stress on deep person-with-person interaction and Jung's emphasis on the search for self pulls me now to work with individuals in a way that teaching doesn't allow. Though I'm unsure. I know I'm not yet able to bring all that I know and am to this medium—as I can to teaching and writing. Of course, this is part of the attraction—to learn how to do something I don't know how to do. I've also been considering trying my hand at writing fiction. I know I want more time for quiet solitude and for reflective writing.

I want to live with the woman I love. The commitment to women becomes more and more central as the years unfold.

I think I've written you all this in part because I want your blessing on what I've made and will make of our life—but also because I want to thank you for your gift to me of hope and courage.

Love,
Christine

2

Such Stuff as Dreams are Made On

Dante begins his journey and his poem "full of sleep"; he ends with the vision of God. Dream and vision play a role both in his conception of life's journey, of how we come to an understanding of ourselves, and also in his conception of art. All of the "Inferno" could be regarded as a dream, a nightmare in which all is forever the same as with the Whippers in Kafka's *The Trial,* and all of the "Paradiso" as a vision, beyond our rational or moral comprehension. But in the "Purgatorio," the realm of action, history, conscious effort, there is an apparent distinction between dream and reality, unconscious and conscious, and it is one of the pilgrim's tasks to learn how to relate them. The pilgrim's three dreams constitute an integral part not only of the poem but also of the journey; each represents the particular stage of understanding at which the pilgrim has arrived. Each is as much a part of what he experiences and must learn to understand as any other episode of the canticle. The dreams are another mirror, another reflection of reality. The cause and the meaning of the dreams lies in the future, just as does the purpose and significance of the entire pilgrimage; they are meant to draw him on his way forward. The dreams have to be interpreted, they are always beyond the pilgrim's present understanding, intelligible only in terms of what is yet to come, but this is true of everything in Purgatory: its meaning lies outside it not within it. Each dream marks the transition from one day to the next and at the same time effects an inner movement in the pilgrim's understanding. The dreams are passive experiences, coming at night when we are of ourselves powerless; thus they represent our dependence on grace even in those waking hours when moral activity is required of us. The dreams serve as transitions and premonitions, and yet they must always still be incarnated. Dreams give a kind of knowledge that discursive waking thought cannot reach unaided, but this knowledge is useless unless the pilgrim "uses the waking hour when it comes."

We can only understand how dream fits into Dante's larger conception of poetic vision and human development, how it prefigures, epitomizes, and yet is incomplete, as we look closely at the three dreams in the "Purgatorio," noting how each is related to a particular stage of the pilgrim's journey and to what follows the dream, observing the progression in the series of dreams, and trying to understand that mode of consciousness beyond the alternation of dream and reality where contemplation is itself an action to which they point.

The first dream, in Canto 9, follows Dante's day in the beautiful valley of the Ante-Purgatorio, a place of nostalgia where the desire for the ethical work of the true Purgatory is not really felt. The sunset of this evening is described as the "hour that turns back the desire of those who sail the seas and melts their heart, that day when they have said to their sweet friends adieu." Chimes seem to *mourn* for a *dying* day. The night begins with the lunar aurora leaving her lover's arms, having to rise alone. Thus there are images of rising, but it is a concubine, a *false* dawn, that rises, a *sad* song that ascends into the air.

It is at this hour when the swallow sings of *former* woes that visions come which are almost prophetic. Dante's dream is not of the past but of the future. The mind wanders from the flesh not as from a lover's arms but as from a prison. Thus in dreaming the mind is a wanderer, as Dante the pilgrim is in the *Divine Comedy* as a whole. Yet both journeys are made possible not by his own activity but by that of another—in the dream by an eagle, an eagle suggestive to me of the vulture in Leonardo da Vinci's childhood dream and with the same homosexual connotations. For Dante the association is to Ganymede snatched to be raped by Jove. The cause behind this seizing is God's love; there is a recognition of this truth hidden in the false image of the nature of God's love associated with the level of understanding accessible in the Ante-Purgatorio. Within the dream Dante has a strong awareness of now being at the place where this experience of being carried upward to the fiery sphere by the eagle is meant to happen. The excessive brightness of this golden plumed eagle, his being terrible as lightning, seems to point forward to Lucia and to the naked sword of the Guardian Angel and on and on to the final beatific vision. Dante is carried up to the purifying flame that so scorches him that he is awakened.

This initial dream seems to prefigure the whole development which lies ahead for the dreamer, to present him not with a description of what he has already achieved but of the goal of his journey, a long journey which the dreamer must himself still actively and consciously make, a journey which actually begins with his recognition of the reality and relevance of the dream as an experience whose meaning must be sought. At this point the visionary flame scorches—when he finally passes through the flames that guard the terrestrial paradise, the very hem of his garment will be safe. In the dream he was completely passive; the effect of the flame is to wake him and he wakes to find himself in a new situation. Virgil tells him it is now time for him to put out all his strength.

This transition is repeated in several other images throughout the canto. In the passage from dream to waking an image of Achilles as a child being carried to safety by his mother appears, an image that again suggests that to this point Dante like a child has been carried but that as a man he must repeat the journey in a man's way. Since he left the straight way at the beginning of the "Inferno" there is no shorter way for him. Achilles is taken there "where the Greeks later made him depart." Dante wakes to find himself facing the sea, just as in the first canto of the "Inferno" morning finds him on the shore looking back at the dangerous water. He wakes freezing with terror; the dream has, indeed, struck him like that cold animal the scorpion and like a scorpion now incites him to action. But now it is morning; there is Virgil, his comfort, and the warming sun. Virgil is able to explain the dream in a way sufficient to remove its terror, to allow it to do the work proper to it at this moment. Virgil's explanation does not focus on the specific dream symbols but on the general sense of movement conveyed by the dream, the sense of being carried. He tells Dante that the dream presented symbolically an actual simultaneous outward event: while he slept Lucia had brought him to this place. "Then she and sleep together went away"—which suggests that the sleep which had overtaken Dante had really been sent by those guiding his entire journey. Virgil's explanation itself effects another change in Dante, "from fear to comfort." It frees him from care as sleep had freed him from confinement to thought. Now he is ready to follow Virgil up the rampart.

At this point Dante the poet asks the reader to observe well "how I exalt my subject, therefore marvel thou not if with greater art I sustain it." The dream was, indeed, an exaltation, a carrying up to the heights, but the real task of the journey is to get there and stay there; the real task of poetry is not just lyric flight but the sustaining of poetic vision even when confronted by the most mundane or prosaic reality. The meaning of the dream lies not in itself but in what it points to and leads toward. A dream is a symbolic action, something has really been effected through it, but this something must be completed by making the dream an integral part of the actual journey.

Virgil and Dante move on and see a gate, an entrance into purgatory itself, and a guardian who at first is silent as the dream is silent until interpreted. Dante opens his eyes still further, for now full consciousness is required, and he sees a sword reflecting light so brightly that he cannot keep his eyes fixed on it. The guardian warns them that unless they come with proper escort their proceeding upward might be to their hurt, as the flame had scorched Dante in his dream. It is only because of Lucia, because of what happened while Dante dreamt, that they are now permitted to move forward to the stairs. Now it is they who are to mount a series of steps, as at the beginning of the canto it had been Night. Dante is still brought up the stairs by Virgil but with his own good will. Dante does not understand all the symbols of this initiation rite any more than he had fully understood his dream, but it is enough to be able to use them. At this stage of the journey the appropriate action is sufficient interpretation. This entrance signifies the setting of a task: the washing off of the seven "P"s here marked on his fore- head. Dante is warned that "he who looketh back returns outside again." At the beginning of the canto the swallow sang of former woes, at its end souls who look forward to someday reaching paradise sing in praise of God. Dante's dream is not to be understood by his looking back at *it*, but by going forward. Its importance lies in the new consciousness and new activity it makes possible. Even in his apprehension of the song of praise, as in his understanding of the dream, "now the words are clear and now are not."

In Canto 15 we are given not a dream in the strict sense but an ecstatic vision in the middle of the afternoon, an experience that is nonetheless analogous to dreaming, is like being overcome by sleep or wine. Looking at this vision briefly allows us to understand a little more of Dante's use of dream and vision in the development of his poem and the movement of the pilgrim's journey. At the end of this vision the pilgrim says, "When my soul returned outwardly to the things which are outside it, I recognized my not false errors." The vision is not true in an outward sense and yet it is a reflection of reality. In an earlier part of this canto Virgil explains the multiple reflections of love that Dante cannot understand as long as he fixes his "mind merely on things of earth," for focus on literal meaning only draws darkness from light. Virgil is Dante's guide—still objectified, exter- nalized, at this stage of the journey—and yet so much a part of Dante that he sees the same vision; he doesn't look at Dante with merely outward eyes. He asks about the vision not so that Dante will tell him what he saw but so that Dante will understand that the meaning of the vision is that he have "no excuse for [not] opening his heart to the waters of peace which are poured from the eternal fount," and above all to encourage Dante to use his waking hour now that it has returned.

The first dream was much like the first step, "white marble so polished and smooth that I mirrored me therein," but the dream of the second night, pre- sented in Canto 19, is more like the second step, "rugged and calcined, cracked in its length and in its breadth." That first dream was a false dawn and yet a true premonition. This dream comes in that time before the dawn when the way for a "short time remains dark." This is a warning dream: the way forward is never assured. As Adrian suggests at the end of the canto the pilgrim may not tarry; there is a set time for the journey—just as at the end of the canticle Dante the poet speaks of the pages ordained for it. There a curb on art must be brought into play; here a disciplining of spirit is called for. In the first dream the mind wandered free from thoughts; in this dream the very thoughts ramble. Thought is transmuted into dream as the stuttering woman is transformed into a persuasive siren. But this is not yet a metamorphosis, a stable integration. It is premature because the only basis on which the reconciliation of dream and reality is possible is still lacking. This dream occurs at a time when the day's heat cannot warm the cold of the moon. Dante is deceived about the time, about where he is on his journey, when he believes that his look can transform "the stuttering woman, with eyes asquint, and crooked on her feet, with maimed hands, and of sallow hue," that it can loosen her tongue, set her straight, and color her face, as "the sun comforts the cold limbs which night weighs down." What the sun, God's love, might do, Dante's cannot. It can change his own perception but not the reality of that which confronts him. Dante's dream image may prefigure the transformations effected by love, but is as inadequate to embody the power of divine love as was Jove's love for Ganymede inadequate to represent the intervention of God's grace. In her song the Siren reveals that she leads mariners astray in mid-sea; even here in the middle of his journey Dante is not safe. She claims to have turned Ulysses from his wandering way and boasts of wholly satisfying those who live with her. But Dante knows from his time in the Inferno that Ulysses' wandering spirit was never put to rest until he was wrecked on the Mount of Purgatory. Could this mountain still wreck Dante? In the Ulysses canto in the "Inferno" Dante had worried lest his genius outrun Virtue; here again there is danger that he will overestimate the power of his own imagination. But again a lady, perhaps again Lucia, comes to Dante's rescue, this time within the dream itself. She calls on Virgil and he, too, is brought right into the dream—no longer as one who stands apart and sees what is really happening while Dante sleeps, nor as one who shares in the *seeing* of the vision, but as an actor in the dream itself. There is already movement toward that time when Dante will have made part of himself all that Virgil can teach him. Virgil uncovers the Siren's filthiness that her song cannot ultimately hide, as art cannot ultimately hide reality but seeks to include it. The song of the Siren is not Dante's own song, just as the song of the swallow in the first night's dream and the song of Leah are not, yet all are included in his.

Dante is shown the Siren's belly and its stench. This time the object of his love has her clothes torn off her as in the earlier dream his own clothes were scorched by flame. This belly is clearly no locus for a rebirth and yet through this dream a rebirth to another level of consciousness is nevertheless effected. When Dante awakes, Virgil immediately calls him to an opening that in this context must still have sexual connotations. Virgil forces Dante to look at the Siren naked just as the avaricious on the next terrace are made to look at the things of earth on which they had focused all their desires. As Dante, now awake, continues to ponder on the dream, to bend himself back to it, Virgil speaks about the dream only enough to show that he knows what it contained and to indicate that the important thing about it is how one frees oneself from the ancient witch. All that is required is that the pilgrim go on with his eyes directed upward toward the lure of the eternal King not downward to earthly symbols, even such earthly symbols as that of the papacy represented by Adrian at the end of the canto as he again reminds Dante, "Lift yourself up." Now Dante becomes like a bird spreading his own wings and we see that despite the initial impression left by this dream it marks a stage much further along on the pilgrim's journey. As he mounts to the fifth circle it is still desire that moves him, but there is now a clearer understanding of what kind of repast will satisfy that desire.

This repast, the sweet fruit which Virgil promises him, will be his the morning after Dante's third dream. At the beginning of Canto 27 in which this dream occurs there is a sunset of blood and flame that reminds us of the third step that had seemed made "of porphyry so flaming red as blood that spurts from a vein." The images are of the Creator shedding his blood, of Ganges scorched by a noon sun, of mulberry reddened with Thisbe's blood. This time the entire transition seems to precede rather than to follow the dream. The time has arrived for Dante himself to enter into the fiery sphere into which the eagle had carried him in the first dream, but his imagination and memory keep him rooted where he is. The authority of Virgil is put into question as never before. Virgil's appeal—"remember thee, remember thee…. Put away now, put away all fear"—is spoken in a tone which seems to say, Remember what I have done, for soon I can do no more. Virgil speaks of the *womb* of these flames, suggesting that here is the place of real rebirth. He encourages Dante to test with the hem of his garment the fact that this flame may be torment but not death—and, finally, he has to speak Beatrice's name. Nothing in the past can give Dante the desire to enter the flame, only the promise of what lies beyond. When Virgil smiles as at a "child that is won by an apple," we recognize that Dante does not yet fully understand the meaning of Beatrice, but that as with his understanding of his dreams, it is enough for now if he is motivated to perform the action now called for. Virgil's talk of Beatrice and a voice singing on the other side gets them safely through the fire and then it is time to prepare a bed for the night. When they settle down Dante pictures himself as a goat once agile and wanton now grown tame while ruminating, while digesting all that has happened. But clearly there is a contrast between a shepherd holding silent vigil by his flock at night in the open and Dante protected on both sides by a rock, with two shepherds for one goat! A contrast that suggests this might be a sacrificial goat, that these might be the preparations for an initiation rite. His dream comes in the hour when Venus "who seemeth ever burning with the fire of love" makes her first appearance—such a different image from the coldness and separation suggested by the images of the first night.

In the dream of this third night Dante beholds a lady, perhaps the lady of the voice which guided them through the flame, as it seems also to be the voice of Matilda in the next canto—for now the transitions between reality and dream are gradual and smooth. In this dream the interpretation is self-contained: Leah and Rachel appear as types of the active and contemplative lives. Here are two poles, but unlike the lady and the Siren of the preceding dream, the task now is not consciously to discriminate between them but rather to learn how to get both in focus, as Dante still finds himself unable to do with the griffon. When Dante wakes it is at the dawn "which rises gratefuller to wayfarers as on return they lodge less far from home"—which recalls the description just before the first dream of the homesickness which seizes those just setting out on a journey during their first night underway.

When Dante and his companions set out again, Virgil tells him that on this day his hungers will be satisfied and with every step Dante feels the pinions grown for his own flight. He no longer climbs the stairs, they speed beneath him. Virgil withdraws as guide for he has brought Dante as far as wit and art will go. Dante has now passed through the realm that the silver key of the Guardian had unlocked for him. Now Dante can take his own pleasure as his guide; his will is now "free, upright and whole": now he is crowned and mitered over himself. And Beatrice is soon to come.

This is the end of dream. In Canto 32 Dante falls asleep but there is no subject for dramatic poetry here, the poet says, except by passing on to when he awakes, because nothing happens. Dante sees now how grace and moral effort, passivity and action, dream and reality, are all part of the human journey—but that their integration can be achieved only in beatific vision.

3

What is Theology?

What is the meaning of the question "What is Theology?" Is this a question that can even be raised? Does one dare to raise it? Does one see how much is involved, how somehow this question puts the one who asks it in question? Yet can one "do" theology *without* asking it, as though we already "really" knew?

"Theology" comes from the Greek words *theos*, god, and *logos,* word; "god" and "speech"; God's speech. Is it God's word or human speech about God? The etymological roots of the word itself leave this ambiguous, as though the distinction suggested here were something that only arises afterwards.

Webster dissolves the ambiguity with the definition: "Theology: rational interpretation of religious faith." Theology is our word about faith, not just any kind of speaking about faith but *rational* language about faith. Is *this* the understanding of theology we all already have? For we act as though we not only already know perfectly well what theology is but also whether it is a good thing or a bad one, and we tend to make this a judgment on all theology as such. We neglect to ask whether there is some theologizing that tends to conceal rather than to bring into view the radical nature of the question: How can there be theology at all? Why is there, and how can there be, language about God, rather than silence?

Is it possible that to ask this question might be the primary theological task? Just as we are the beings who ask the question about the meaning of our own existence, so theology too must turn on itself and ask about the ground of its own possibility. To ask this question means to travel the road of asking it and, perhaps, to open up the realm where an answer might be found; not to *give* the answer but to *become* an answer-ing to it, to become one who *hears* the question and lives in response to it. For to theologize is itself an act of faith, faith in the possibility and relevance of our human speaking about God.

Faith as Response

The first question that arises is whether theology is a misunderstanding, an objectification, a betrayal of our encounter with God or whether it is something that grows out of a true apprehension of that encounter, as a continuation of it. Our understanding of theology, its legitimacy and its task, implies our whole understanding of the word of God, that is, of the relation of God to humankind.

Theology is a "rational interpretation of 'faith'"—not of God nor of religion but of *faith*. "Faith" seems to be another ambiguous wandering-around word. The medieval scholastics made a distinction between *fides quae creditur* and *fides quo creditur*, between what is believed and that by which it is believed, between God's word and our response. Yet this is less the differentiation between two things than the pointing to the two participants in a single event. Sometimes theology seems to forget this and to act as though it could speak of a God objectively known rather than as a subject addressing himself to another subject. But God as he is himself, abstracted from self-disclosure to us humans, is the god of the philosophers, of metaphysics, not the God of Abraham, of Isaac, of Jacob.

Or theology makes the opposite mistake, more fashionable today though so largely the *same* mistake, of thinking that its subject matter is human, subjective, religious experience. But because theology is a speaking about God and us in our togetherness, in the encounter, our response, our side of the event, is indeed part of the very subject matter of theology. We can in fact say that neither God nor humans are really known except in terms of the relationship between them: that it is their being toward one another as creator and creature, as speaker and hearer, that is for theology the most significant thing about both.

God as Speaker

"God's Word." "Our Response." Somehow I cannot seem to get away from metaphors drawn from the realm of language. Can it be that our word about God has its origin in the discovery that God is a self-disclosing, a speaking God? That ultimate reality cannot only be spoken about but that it itself already has a speaking character? And that this is the reason why these particular metaphors seem to push themselves forward?

It begins to appear that theology is, not just in its subject matter when it takes upon itself the explication of Biblical revelation but in its very impulse, grounded in the God of the Bible, the God who creates by saying "let there be light" and there is light, "let the earth bring forth living creatures" and it happens. This is the God who calls to particular persons and sends them forth to speak his word to others, to speak that word in their own language, and with acted-out, lived-out gestures: dramatized metaphors such as the yoke Jeremiah wore about his neck or Hosea's marriage; ultimately with a whole life become word, God's word.

The *word* that theology interprets is *heard*, not logically deduced—and, although as we shall see, theology is indeed, in a sense, a rational interpretation of faith, it is not a philosophical substitute for it. It begins with a hearing, with a word addressed to it, and endeavors somehow to convey this origin in its response. This word is truly a word, a word spoken in a definite place, at a specific moment, bearing a concrete message, containing an actual demand. It is not an "in-general," abstract truth but something that really takes place between god and humans, as event, as happening. It is here and now that God's word is heard: from the burning bush, at the entrance to the Temple, after the baptism by John.

Word of God as Event

The Greek-based word "theology" seems to blur our awareness of the difference between Greek and Hebrew forms of thought, and sometimes even to affect our understanding of the theological task. Thorlief Boman in his book *Hebrew Thought Compared with Greek* contrasts *logos,* the Greek word for ultimate reality, with *dabar,* the Hebrew word for ultimate reality.[1] Though each may be translated as "word," the understanding of ultimate reality is nevertheless quite different. *Legein* means "to gather" as well as "to speak," "to order, arrange"; so that *logos* for the Greek philosophers comes to mean coherence, rational order, *the* rational order underlying the manifoldness of the world of appearance and constituting its true reality. The *logos* is eternal, unchanging, and *therefore* divine. The divine in us is that in us that apprehends, participates in, and is thus an emanation of this rational order.

Dabar, on the other hand, means self-presentation in the presence of another. It is a speaking, acting, effecting word, a word that is also a deed like the word of creation or the word of commandment. It is not an emanation but a conscious, moral word, a word spoken *to* and calling for response, a word going from one to another, that implies distance between persons, not continuity or identity. *Dabar* is not God, but it is God as he reveals himself; it is his self-disclosure, that with which we are to be concerned. A theology of the word in this sense would thus be one that seeks to make the hidden-ness as well as the revelation of God apparent, to show that God's word is a self-disclosure of his mystery, that he cannot be fully known by us but chooses to present himself to us. It is also part of the Biblical understanding that God speaks to humankind through humans. The word of God is a word that passes from one human person to another. The Bible is interpretive proclamation. In these events, its writers claim, God guided us, supported us, and chastised us. This is *their* testimony, and yet it is God's word that is spoken here, is present here. The theologian hopes to keep the scriptures open as a place where God can be heard. In this he is like what Heidegger calls the guardian of art,[2] who responds to a work of art as art and not just as a thing, an object, and thus helps to keep it a work of art and so become, in a sense, co-creators. Thus the word of God is the word of God to us only if it is heard as such.

Word of God as Metaphor

Clearly "word of God" is a metaphor, or an analogy. But what is seeking to be expressed through this metaphor is precisely *the need for metaphor* in speaking of the relation of God to us. Metaphor is the bringing together of two things both of which remain themselves yet in their togetherness form a new being. (So that Jesus Christ as God/man is metaphor, metaphor become flesh.) This is what "word" means in the Bible; it means metaphor; it means the *covenant* of God with humankind. A metaphor has the dramatic oneness of a word with its answer. This one-ness, this covenant, this bringing-together, this relation "is an event and hence narration is the proper form to describe it."[3] So the *form* that Biblical testimony takes is most characteristically one that expresses this understanding of word as event, metaphor as symbolic *action:* the historical narrative of the Old Testament, and the parables, with their presentation of the events of daily life, in the New.

This theologizing that grows out of the Biblical rather than the Greek understanding of "word" will be theologizing that looks upon word as event and not as rational structure, that seeks to make us, too, recognize that God makes himself known in happenings, in history, not just in history as such, but in *this* event or that one. Father Lynch uses a comparison of the art of Dostoievski and Proust to present in a fresh and fascinating way his thesis about the relation between a truly narrative pattern, with its stresses in "therefore" and "consequently" and the Biblical understanding of the relation of the eternal and the temporal. He speaks of a "theological imagination," one that recognizes that the way to God is through human life, through the definite, the temporal, and the tragic, and one that in its awareness of our not wanting to be human, of our wish to come to God directly in a leap that denies time and our finitude, includes also the comic.[4] William Golding's novel, *The Spire,* could be read as a dramatization of the conflict between one who would mount directly to God and one who insists that in reaching toward God the possibilities and limitations of the particular earthly situation help chart our path, between Jocelin, the dean possessed by his vision of the steeple, and the master builder who insists that the watery substratum cannot support it, between the mystical and the theological imagination.

Word of God as Origin

The theological imagination is, then, an expression of faith in God as creator and revealer; it apprehends and affirms the "speaking-ness" of event and the "word-ness" of world. For it our human speaking takes place within a world that is God's word, God's speaking. What I am suggesting here is an *analogy* between our speech and God's activity. In an analogy the same word is used with reference to two different beings in such a way that its meaning is modulated by the relation between the two. When Thomists use analogies to ascribe predicates drawn from the natural world to God, they understand this relation to be that of creator to creature. The attribute, they say, belongs primarily to God but the predicate, the word we use for it, applies primarily to the creatures, to the phenomenal world, because we know it first. But the creature is like God, not vice-versa.[5] Thus the *word* "Speech" is one that we originally use with regard to the human sphere and then attribute to the divine, but the *origin-al* speaking is God's speaking, and our speaking is only possible because of it.

Analogies point to the way in which the creature is like God, is made in the image of God. Thus the analogy of speech suggests that the *imago dei* is our capacity for speech and that our vocation is response, like Abraham's answering, "Here I am." Martin Heidegger has called language "the house of our being." He quotes Hölderlin:

> Since we have been a conversation
> And have been able to hear from one another

And he points out the etymological relation between con-versation and turning to one another.[6] Language is thus that which we are able to communicate and so come into community.

The Broken-ness of Language

Yet language can also come *between* us in another way, as barrier, the way suggested in another story about tower building, the Biblical account of the tower of Babel. Before that "the whole earth was of one language and of one speech" but ever since, as the story goes, we have *not been* a conversation; our language is confounded and we do not understand one another's speech.

Martin Buber writes that the Baal-Shem, the founder of Hasidism, was a master of "a wisdom so rare among mortals that in each age only one single individual is its heir and guardian":

> The bearer of this wisdom could understand the language of all creatures. He perceived what the animals on the earth and in the air confided to one another about the secrets of their existence; indeed, even what the trees and plants spoke to one another was known to him. If he laid his ear to the black earth or the bare rock, the whispering of the creatures who shun the light and dwell in crevices and caves reached him.[7]

And the Baal-Shem could tell a story to a group of listeners so that it spoke to each as their own tale, awakened the secret melody of each person.

But for the others, in any age, all our speaking seems to involve a translation, a carrying across a barrier. Each of us has the feeling that our own "real" language is personal and private, though we label insane those who try to live within their private world, their own metaphorical structure, their own language.

Theologizing takes place within this broken-ness of language; it seeks to turn us to a common image for God, to make a particular event appear to another, too, as the word of God, as God's self-disclosure. So theology is a continuation of our response to God, an unfolding and a sharing. In essence and in origin theology is an answering. Must this not then be apparent in the way it is done? It springs forth as answering and intends to lead toward an answering, intends to bring us into an answering situation, to make us aware of being in one.

Making the event appear as living, still-speaking means finding the right metaphor, the living word. Because metaphors become clichés and images become idols, the task of the theologian can never be done once for all. We spend our time, as T. S. Eliot describes the poet,

> Trying to learn to use words, and every attempt
> Is a wholly new start, and a different kind of failure
> Because one has only learnt to get the better of words
> For the thing one no longer has to say, or the way in which
> One is no longer disposed to do it. And so each venture
> Is a new beginning, a raid on the inarticulate.[8]

Can we sound this likeness to the poet more deeply? W. H. Auden speaks of poetry as "response to sacred being," beginning in a compelled and awe-ful recognition that a phenomenon (two light dancing steps by a girl or perhaps two quiet steps by an old man) being wholly itself is laden with universal meaning, has an overwhelming importance. The impulse to create a work of art is felt when this passive awe is transformed unto a desire to express that awe in a rite of homage.[9]

Theologians in recent years have made much of the difference between history and nature. They characterize history as the realm of person and event, of the unique, the unpredictable, the irreversible. This distinction is considered to separate the Biblical view from Greek and Oriental views that regard the particular being or event as significant only as it represents what is universal or unchanging. History as the realm of change is, therefore, meaningless. Perhaps we need to overcome this distinction but in another direction, not by declaring it dissolved but by trying to step across it. Could we become aware not only of the uniqueness of human beings and of the event-ful-ness of the encounters between them, but awakened also to uniqueness, this-ness, word-ness in the created world, to be really present (as Buber describes) to this particular tree that is there before me now?[10]

In the Genesis story God creates by word but then leaves to us the task of naming, as though giving *its* word to each created being were our share in creation. Again I think of poetry. Auden says, "poetry pays homage by naming."[11] As if it were this that we are here for, to bring to speech that which without us is inarticulate:

> .... to be here is much and the transient Here
> seems to need and concern us strangely....
> .... Are we *here, perhaps* just to say:
> house, bridge, well, gate, jug, fruit, tree, window—
> at most, column, tower...but to *say,* understand this,
>   to say it
> as the Things themselves never fervently thought to be,
> Earth, isn't this what you want: invisibly
> To arise in us[12]

No, I haven't forgotten, theology is not poetry. Though I believe that theological speaking must, nevertheless, be done with at least remembrance of the kind of poetic naming, letting appear, about which Rilke muses in this elegy. The theologian's words, too, are spoken within this circle of being addressed, hearing, responding, by re-saying in our language so that others may hear.

Notes

1. Thorlief Boman, *Hebrew Thought Compared with Greek* (Philadelphia: Westminster Press, 1960) esp. 58-69.

2. Hans Jaeger, "Heidegger and the Work of Art," in Morris Phillipson, ed., *Aesthetics Today* (New York: World Publishing Company, 1961) 425.

3. Emil Brunner, *Truth as Encounter* (Philadelphia: Westminster Press, 1964) 88.

4. William F. Lynch, *Christ and Apollo* (New York: Sheed and Ward, 1960) esp. Ch. 1.

5. F. C. Copleston, *Aquinas* (London: Penguin, 1955) 129-136.

6. Martin Heidegger, *Existence and Being* (Chicago: Henry Regnery Co., 1949) 270.

7. Martin Buber, *The Legend of the Baal-Shem* (New York: Harper & Brothers, 1955) 185.

8. T. S. Eliot, *Four Quartets* (New York: Harcourt Brace, 1953) 16.

9. W. H. Auden, *The Dyer's Hand* (New York: Random House, 1962) 54-57.

10. Martin Buber, *I and Thou* (New York: Scribner's, 1958) 7.

11. Auden, *Dyer's Hand,* 57.

12. R. M. Rilke, *Duino Elegies* (Berkeley and Los Angeles: University of California Press, 1961) 67-71.

4

All Real Living is Meeting

Ever since I first read Martin Buber's *I and Thou* I have carried within me the memory of two phrases—"All real living is meeting"; "I become I as I say Thou"—two phrases which seemed to shape a knowledge which I recognized as true to my own experiencing. For the most creative encounters of my life have been those moments of shared presence with another to which Buber was pointing. In his early writings Buber seemed to focus in a somewhat romantic way on moments of instantaneous mutual recognition and affirmation, but then more and more clearly marriage becomes for him the paradigm for all "I-Thou" relationships. For in marriage the importance of continuity, of fidelity and trust persisting even in the moments (and they may be long "moments") when there is no immediate consciousness of encounter is made clear. Also, for Buber the sexual relationship between man and woman in marriage seemed an embodiment of the mystery of the other's otherness, which love affirms and cannot abolish. What I want to speak of here, however, is not this central relationship but the other relationships, the friendships with women and also with men, which arise alongside this one and without which our lives would be sadly narrowed and our marriages themselves impoverished.

For as that phrase of Buber's, "I become I as I say Thou," suggests, to be truly myself means to be able to turn to each one who meets me as *Thou,* as *you,* and not only to one; although the trust in that one's love for me may be what opens me for such meetings with others. I have come to understand that the meaning of friendships lies in the encounter itself and not only in my individuation, in what happens rather than in what results. I do not say "Thou" in order to become an I. The sharedness, what Buber calls "the Between," is what seems to me to lie at the center. Through our turning to one another we are brought into relation with what Paul Tillich speaks of as the "depth dimension," the meaningfulness, of life.

I have also come to believe that we must take more seriously than Jungians usually seem to the sexual element in interpersonal encounter. For to be a human being is to be an embodied creature, which means a sexual being, a man or a woman. Though we may agree that Freud too quickly reduces all meaning to sexuality, nevertheless it is important that we also recognize how his insistence that libido be understood as sexual rather than as undifferentiated psychic energy expresses his conception of the human being as a psychophysical unity. For we are sexual through and through, not simply in our bodies but in ourselves, and so our sexuality is part of all our relationships, though what it means and how it is to be expressed will be shaped by each particular relationship. Because the human way to meaning lies through the concrete and not through flight from it, we lose a rich aspect of friendship if we try to separate the spiritual from the bodily, if we seek to deny the ways in which the presence of sexual likeness or differentiation influences a relationship.

Our friendships with women, for those of us who are women ourselves, are expressions of that love for which the Greeks used the word *philia*; unlike the need-based, desiring love of *eros*, this kind of love is based on what is shared, on a common valuing and purposing. But the deepest friendships between women do not seem to grow from a sharing of an impersonal interest, an intellectual concern, as they often seem to between men, but from a sharing of feelings and emotional responses. The other women to whom we feel closest are those with whom we can speak of our most personal experiences, those in whose lives we can discern a common pattern, less in the superficial details than in the way of meeting that which comes to us. In such friendships we seem to be able to help one another sense an emerging rhythm and strengthen one another to move in time to that rhythm, to endure and to wait or to move forward. The depth of understanding, of communicable, articulable understanding, transcending even the understanding within a marriage, that is sometimes reached in such friendships seems to be the obverse of the sense of sameness, of there being less mystery, less otherness, than in any relationship with man no matter how intimate. Perhaps it is our confidence in this same-ness which also explains the fact that somehow such friendships do not seem to have to be tended as carefully: We are more able to trust that the other will be there ready for us when we turn to her again. Yet usually, in my experience, these friendships are a long time ripening; they grow slowly toward the complete sharing, rarely flash into being as a friendship with a man may. Without such friendship, without such sharing, we know we would go dry. A woman friend's love, which often takes the form of being a hard bed to us, as Nietzsche saw it must, which often presents itself as an almost unbearably challenging question, waters our growth, a growth which depends on our willingness to be met as the person our search for ourselves has uncovered. Yet (and perhaps this presents only the limits of my own experience) I think I would have to say that although I share my life with these friends (and there are only a few such friends, I would think, in any of our lives), I do not live it with them.

Most of us seem to feel confined by our culture (and by our culture's voice within us) to such friendships; the only really intimate relationships in our lives are with other women and with our mate, and perhaps a son or a father or a brother. Friendships with a man not related to us in such ways are usually ones that grow out of a shared interest and are confined to that interest; we are shy of letting the personal intrude. And of course we value such friendships partly for this very reason; we envy the ability men have to become absorbed in the intellectual, the abstract. They seem more in touch with an external reality, to move in a wider world; their conversation is free from that gossiping mimicry of intimacy that women may so easily fall into. So we let such friendships remain on *their* level, the *logos* level, are hesitant to bring *eros* (in Jung's sense), the more womanly way of relating, into the encounter.

Although we may pride ourselves on our liberal attitudes toward, for example, peace and civil rights, in this area we often seem very conservative, almost prudish. I wonder whether this prudishness may not have a theological basis, whether it may not stem from a false understanding of "spiritual." I know that as a theologian I may be suspected of looking at everything as though it were a theological problem; yet I do believe that we need to ask ourselves if we really take *incarnation* seriously enough. A year or so ago Tom Driver of Union Seminary published an essay called "Jesus and Sexuality." In it he shows how the Church, in denying sexuality to Jesus, is really denying humanity to him and approaching that heresy which looks upon his body as a disguise assumed by a purely spiritual presence. Driver goes on to question whether this denial does not also mean that the Church has failed to recognize that in Biblical Christianity (and Judaism) the power of sex has been demythologized: sex is neither, as in other religions, the ultimately fearful nor the ultimately desirable force, neither Satan nor God. It is a part of the given world, part of our created nature, given neither to be shunned nor to be worshipped but to be used responsibly.

I should like us to consider anew what we would mean by responsibility in heterosexual encounters, i.e. in friendships between men and women alongside of marriage. For I believe that the conventional rules of behavior do not always allow us to be responsible, to respond to that which encounters us, as a contextual ethic would do. Where the context is taken into account, responses are directed by situations and persons and not by abstract and therefore legalistic considerations. The most illuminating articulation of the situational understanding of morality with which I am familiar is Dietrich Bonhoeffer's essay, "What is Meant by Telling the Truth?" He says that being truthful means being true to the occasion and the relationship, finding the right word for the particular other whom we address and for the situation which we share. When I speak of this to my students I often try to help them see the different ways in which one would speak of sex in a classroom discussion, in a counseling session, with one's parents, on a date, within marriage. Yet despite these differences one would in each instance seek to be true to one's own experience and to the other who shared in it and also to the situation in which one now stands and speaks. Bonhoeffer gives the example of a young boy asked by his teacher before his classmates whether his father had once again come home drunk the night before. The boy stammers, "No" (although indeed his father had), because this was the only way he knew of defending his family's privacy against what he recognized to be the unjustifiable invasion of the teacher's question. We might do better, but the task is the same: to find the word that expresses our understanding of a particular Between in all its uniqueness. To be ethical, responsible, means being sensitive to the other and to our common situation, means finding the right expression for this personal relationship. By "right expression" I mean to include the language of the body as well as of the tongue; we seek to find the appropriate gesture as well as the right word in the strictly verbal sense. We aim to be faithful to the particular situation, to become conscious of its particularity, of what distinguishes this Between from all others.

Obviously this way of responding to encounters has hazards that a stereotyped response (or evasion) protects us from, but this is what response-ability means and demands. I like Gabriel Marcel's phrase, "creative fidelity," for it suggests the creative and recreative aspects of this understanding of faithfulness. "I become I as I say Thou." If we cannot be open to that which comes to us, we do not fully live our own lives. I think here of some lines from John Ciardi's poem, "I Marry You":

> To let our lives
> Out of our lives, and answer as they come
> Like dancers to the music, keeping whole
> By changing when it changes.

I do not at all mean to minimize the risks; since I am speaking from what I have begun to learn from my own life, I am speaking in part from what I have been taught by my mistakes, from error and failure and not only from joy. Yet when I say mistakes I mean not wrong relationships but irresponsibility in relationship.

I have become more and more sure that responsibility means consciousness and could almost adopt as my own motto that extra-canonical verse from the Gospel of Luke that Jung was so fond of quoting, "Blessed are you if you know what you are doing." Being conscious means being aware of one's own "magic" and one's susceptibility to the magic of others. By magic I mean the compelling power of our longing for completion when it leads us to see in a deeply desired other the realized image of the complement of our own being. Jung spoke of this magic, when a woman projects it on a man, as the workings of the *animus* and when a woman reflects it for a man, as the workings of the *anima*. It is so easy to be lured by this into a relationship that promises the fulfillment of all our dreams but which is instead the mirage that all magic worlds reveal themselves to have been when the spell is over. (Let us not forget, however, even in our disenchantment, that a mirage can only exist as a reflection of a reality.) This discovery is something that has to be lived through to be learned, otherwise we remain susceptible to its delusions long after we believe ourselves safely beyond their reach; perhaps, with wise help, it may not have to be lived out. From such a relationship we may, if we are lucky, learn much about ourselves, even though it included so little of genuine encounter, because so little of our real selves was involved. Through this experience, which may seem such a waste, we may have come closer to being persons who could now participate in a more genuine relationship. We have been brought to hope for a relationship that would be real, not based on the magic, one in which both participants would consciously seek to work through the magic, to be faithful both to the other and to themselves.

For there are friendships with men, with men besides the one who is our husband, in which we may reach a sense of together really touching a creative source which arises from the Between. Each such friendship is different; the challenge and the joy (and the pains) arise from trying to bring just this relationship to its meaning and shape. What do we two have to say to one another? What do we two have to give one another? In asking and answering we must seek to take into account who we two are, which means we must include those other relationships and responsibilities, especially of course our marriages, apart from which we are less than ourselves.

For such friendships there are no guidebooks; that is what creative friendship means. We have all, I am sure, experienced what (following *South Pacific*) we might call an "across the crowded room" encounter, in which there occurs a meeting of eyes, of persons, which takes us quite by surprise and yet which we know has happened, and for both. The question is, What do you make of it? It is so easy to respond conventionally—to ignore it and shake it off, or to fly into one another's arms. Both, in different situations of course, seem to be equally conventional responses, ones that evade the search for and the joy of finding the right unique expression. To evade this search in either of these ways, the prudent or the romantic, is to allow ourselves to be held captive by the myth that all close friendships between men and women mean, aim at (and probably hide), genital consummation. This is a social myth that easily becomes self-validating, as it inhibits us from testing its truth for ourselves. The joy of finding the peculiarly right expression is, I think, comparable only to the joy of poets at finding the right word that completes their stanza.

I am thinking now of a friendship which grew out of the delight of discovering in a conversation at the edge of a party that another had come to a way of teaching a particular course that I had thought uniquely my own. We found that we used many of the same rather out of the way books and hoped for the same kinds of responses from our students. The excitement was much like that of discovering a compatriot in a group assembled in a foreign land; it deepened as we became aware of how much of our journey toward this way of teaching, and so toward ourselves, could be shared and understood, how many were the levels at which we could feel in touch. But what has most deeply delighted me in this relationship is that we knew what to do with it and came to this knowledge together, and so naturally and simply: we found we wanted to work on a book which would present our approach. The parting hug becomes the embodiment of just this mutually conscious, mutually chosen, sublimation.

I am thinking also of a meeting with a man who seems to actualize the world-affirmative yea-saying which Nietzsche heralded, who embraces all that is present before him and brings it to life, so that for a moment you are part of that which is embraced. To fail to welcome those arms, to fail to respond to that warmth, would be to betray all one knows of open-ness and trust and joy. The meeting takes place in a golden hour that is betrayed only if you try to establish a continuity, to recapture the vanishing moment, for that would be to destroy the spontaneity that lies at the heart of his generous delight. One is only grateful that once one stood where this light fell and was warmed by it, and forever after one feels more alive.

Since I am a woman in an academic discipline where women are few, I quite often after a meeting or lecture find myself taking a walk with a man and talking with him, usually at first about what has just been said and our responses to it. But then we begin to share the more general responses and attitudes that lie behind these immediate ones. Sometimes I sense a search for a way to communicate something that has so long remained unspoken that the words have rusted together within and must be pried apart and dug up before they can be brought to light. And slowly the conversation turns to the wife and his longing to talk to her, to say these things to her, and his inability to do so because somehow, somewhere, the way has been lost. This has happened often enough and I have heard the same story from enough of my women friends to make me wonder whether such ruined hopes may not mean that our conception of marriage as an all-encompassing relationship asks too much of it and of us. The insistence on an exclusiveness which shuts all others out and on an inclusiveness which holds all of ourselves within comes in the end to prevent intimacy, to make us give up on a relationship in which not everything can be shared, to which not everything can be given. We have substituted for fidelity a totalitarian claim and no longer seem to know the difference. Yet the longing that this be the central relationship, that sharing go again below the surface levels of life together, is the dominant chord I hear in my friends' voices. I have learned so much about my own marriage from such interchanges, from hearing of marriage and its difficulties spoken of from the man's side, as sometimes it may have helped him to hear a woman's response. Sometimes, also, to have spoken of all this to one woman seems to help him find the words to say it also to the one to whom he most wants to say it. Ways of helping each other may open up which might so easily have been missed. Strange ways, sometimes, for among my closest women friends are one or two whom I first knew through their husbands' confidences.

It would not be honest, though, to speak of the widening and deepening of one's life that comes through open-ness to such friendships when they are given to one, without admitting that a relationship might grow so deep and strong, seem to create such a fulfilled meeting at all levels of one's own being and the other person's, that it would lead one to question one's marriage. A friendship might come which almost felt like a marriage. It had grown and ripened past betrayals and misunderstandings; you two had learned how to weather the seasons when the erotic element waned and then surprisingly reappeared; and you had felt the longing to bear this man's child, that often seems to a woman (at least to me) the touchstone of true love. This may happen and yet, I would like to say, even of this you need not be afraid. Even this may be met with responsibility, honesty, and fidelity. In a way I can hardly explain, one's commitment to one's marriage and one's love for one's husband may be strengthened through recognizing this other love as a life which might have been but which is not one's own, and through realizing the impossibility of leaving one's own life. It is a great joy to discover that one's marriage is a commitment which does not need to be shielded, that one can trust it as a pledge made with the core of one's being and renewed through a many-yeared living side by side.

There is that in each of us that longs for marriage and its stability and continuity and also that which is starved by exclusiveness. We need to find our own way of recognizing both of these longings as part of ourselves. But I cannot promise that it will be easy...

5

How Can We Hope and Not Dream? Exodus as Metaphor: A Study of the Biblical Imagination

This paper "essays" a literary critical approach to theologizing. What I want to do is to trace the role in the Old Testament of a particular metaphor, exodus, and at the same time to present the exploration of metaphor as the way of doing theology which grows out of an attentive reading of the O.T. itself. That is, like Walter Eichrodt, I seek to "plot our course as best we can along the lines of the O.T.'s own dialectic."[1]

In an essay on Hebrew humanism, Buber writes:

> When a great man speaks, he need not tell us about his character in order to reveal it to us. Language itself takes care of that. No matter what he communicates to us, the language he uses for this purpose expresses him and provides us access to him. Even language per se, the characteristic branch of word formation, the rhythmic flow of vowels and consonants, are the product of a special human pattern.[2]

He suggests here that to understand the Bible we need to understand the playfulness of its language, what R. P. Blackmur calls its "gesture":

> Gesture, in language, is the outward and dramatic play of inward and imaged meaning. It is that play of meaningfulness which cannot be defined in the formulas of the dictionary, but which is defined in their use together, gesture is that meaningfulness which is moving, in every sense of that word: what moves the words and what moves us.[3]

Buber seeks to make clear that this stress on form is based not on aesthetic but on theological, or more properly on biblical, grounds—on literary grounds in the sense that it is seen as demanded by the very character of the work being read, on the O.T.'s own understanding of the importance of language and word, of word as event, the particular event which happens. The claim is that, since here the selection and arrangement of words affect meaning, the O.T. asks to be read as we read poetry. In the O.T. the word is spoken in history; what happens between humans and God happens in the time and space of everyday, a particular day. It has a concrete form that is inseparable from its meaning, which is never simply an "abstractable" meaning. Just as it is impossible to disentangle the objectively historical from the biblical narrative, so also it is impossible to disentangle a biblical meaning from the narrative. It is not something one can also say otherwise; one cannot say it otherwise without making it other. The God of the Bible is the God of Abraham, of Exodus and Sinai, not an in-general God. Because the Bible presents this covenant of the absolute with the particular, form, shape, the particular matter, the how and where are an integral part of the what. This correlation between event and meaning suggests T. S. Eliot's "objective correlative,"[4] except that in place of a formula for an emotion we have here a form for a revelation. The event and its "meaning" are so "correlated" that the meaning can be fully "objectified" only through these events. Buber shows how important it is to notice form in its textural as well as its structural aspects, to recognize how even alliteration and pun are present not for the sake of "aesthetic embellishment" but to indicate significant relationship.

The present essay will, however, focus on the structural, on symbols that operate formatively throughout the O.T. What I hope to do is in many respects close to what Erich Voegelin attempts in *Israel and Revelation*: to read the O.T. as a symbolic form. Yet Voegelin seems to me to fail to do justice to the O.T. insofar as he is looking for a *philosophy* of symbolic forms and thus seems to prize the differentiated forms of philosophy more than the compact symbolism of myth. It seems to me that this Hegelian preference for the "logical" over the "mythological," for the logic of concept and proposition over the logic of image,[5] prevents at certain points a true understanding of the distinctive nature of the biblical imagination.

For in the O.T. the image making occurs always within the remembered context of three "texts" (although, typically, the context shapes the texts rather than vice versa):

Let us make man in our image, after our likeness [Gen. 1:26].

> So out of the ground [from which God had already formed man], the Lord God formed every beast of the field and every bird of the air, and brought them to the man to see what he would call them; and whatever the man called every living creature, that was its name [Gen. 2:19].
>
> You shall not make for yourself a graven image, or any likeness of anything that is in heaven above, or that is in the earth beneath, or that is in the water under the earth; you shall not bow down to them or serve them; for I the Lord your God am a jealous God.... You shall not take the name of your Lord in vain [Exod. 20:4-7].

Images are not to be gotten beyond, since man himself is the image of God, and thus a creator like God. Adam is a creaturely creator who gives names, creates images, and yet cannot breathe life into them. Our human images remain images, and this is as true of the philosopher's ideal as of the pagan's idol. Because the O.T. recognizes that human images are but words, names, it is consciously word play, metaphor. The commandment against images is central to this paper's exploration of the O.T.'s images, for "exodus" is the image of this commandment: exodus from the given security is what is called for from Israel again and again. As we shall see, the prophets' shattering of cherished concepts of God is such a call to "go forth."

What seems to be required for a reading of the O.T. is a *theology* of symbolic forms; that is, an approach to symbol that springs, not from the philosopher's view of symbol as inadequate because sensuously confused articulation of meaning, but from the biblical recognition of the binding of the meaningful as it may be seen by us humans to the sensuous and concrete. For what we have in the O.T. is a new form of word. As Amos Wilder notes in his *Language of the Gospel*,[6] a new truth demands a new language; to be at the limits of what can be said in a language, through the given symbols, is what renews language. Voegelin recognizes in the historical narratives of the Pentateuch "a new type of story that is neither myth nor pragmatic history." This new form in a sense creates its material; it absorbs various kinds of "content" and "transforms them according to its own principle of construction." Voegelin sees clearly that to study the O.T. means to examine paradigmatic events such as Sinai or Exodus, that is, single historical events which have become for the writers of the O.T. images of God's way with us in this world. We must recognize them as metaphors that have been elaborated so as to heighten the point rather than to increase the pragmatic accuracy.[7]

Walther Eichrodt, in his *Theology of the Old Testament*, first published in 1933, takes the absolutely essential first step toward such a theology of O.T. symbolic forms—a revolutionary one at the time—that opens a way we hope here to walk further along. He understands that O.T. theology must be done as literary criticism and not in terms of the structure of rationalistic concepts derived from Greek philosophy and imposed on a quite differently organized literature. He perceives that the Bible's unity is determined by its own central concepts and that to illumine its meaning means to take this structure seriously, rather than to abstract a propositional meaning from it. Therefore he proposes to substitute "covenant" for a "bloodless abstraction like ethical monotheism" and to show how it functions in this structural, meaning disclosing, and unifying way:

> The concept of the covenant was given this central position in the religious thinking of the O.T. so that, by working outward from it, the structural unity of the O.T. message might be made more readily visible.[8]

Eichrodt recognizes the peculiarity, the characteristically biblical nature, of this image: its historical aspect. "Covenant" refers to a process with a particular historical beginning,[9] the events of Sinai. To perceive the centrality of this concept is to see that what the O.T. is about is not God but the encounter between God and humankind in history, in event. The activity of God "can only be expressed in words in combination with the [human] response,"[10] can only be expressed by a word that represents this combination, this binding. Because covenant means just this, the binding together of God and human, it is the central symbol for the whole of O.T. theology, the structural key. We might even say that in choosing covenant as central metaphor, Eichrodt has picked out the O.T. metaphor for metaphor.

He aims at undertaking a "cross-sectional" analysis of covenant, rather than at tracing the historical development of the image.[11] The historical approach seems to him to presuppose a false evolutionary view that puts meaning only at the end of the development. But to my mind the history of the images, their continual reworking, is that through which complexity, irony, and depth are achieved. The historical development becomes in the O.T. what Robert Penn Warren calls the "earning of the insight,"[12] the testing of the vision.

Eichrodt begins with history, with the insistence that biblical knowledge of God is knowledge of God's acts in history, but he ends up adopting, or being stuck with still, an inadequate conception of history (and so of metaphor), one applied to the Bible but not really congruous with its own understanding. We begin to understand then why Eichrodt refers to the central image of his theology as a "concept." Does it not function for him after all in a rationalistic, logical way, as an eternal truth which simply *happens* to have been brought to the Israelites' awareness in a happening, but which is not itself "really" historical?

Eichrodt notes that the meaning of *berith* develops along two quite different lines of thought (or poetic association?), one leading to legalism and cult, the other to eschatological fulfillment.[13] He concludes that it is just this conjunction of the demands and the graciousness of God that alone gives the whole content of the O.T. understanding, although "it may indeed be true that the composite picture, this insight into the coherence of two at first sight divergent manifestations of the divine will, was not to be found, at any rate in this form, in ancient Israel."[14] And of course he is right; there is never a propositional reconciliation, but only that metaphorical bringing-together supplied by the redactor's arrangement.

Von Rad understands the O.T. history as remembered history, interpreted by faith, and seeks to distinguish the presentation of the Red Sea crossing or of the Joshua conquest from literal, objective history, and so to make us recognize that although the Bible presents these as historical events actually they function as images of faith. Israel's faith may indeed be grounded in a theology of history, but this is different from saying it is grounded in objective history. Thus von Rad, too, is quarreling with the nineteenth-century historians who thought that by getting to what had "really" happened one would get at the meaning. He believes that the O.T. history is really created by the historical imagination that uses certain images in order to create meaningful pattern out of otherwise meaningless succession. The commitment to these image patterns then shapes Israel's ongoing history, so that it is as true to speak of image creating history as of history creating image.

Von Rad pays attention to the metaphorical composition of the Pentateuch, which is based on a very few old motifs surrounded by organically developed clusters.[15] He seeks to discern the peculiarities of "the way in which faith perceives things,"[16] the patterns characteristic of a confessional presentation, the poetic techniques which enabled Israel "to express experiences met with in the course of history in such a way as to make the past become absolutely present."[17] Thus he sees clearly that what the theologian is presented with in the O.T. is poetry, not conceptual knowledge or objective history, is an imaginative literature—and that a proper understanding depends upon an approach that will recognize this. Von Rad knows that poetry here is no mere "esthetic pastime"; "historical poetry was the form in which Israel…made sure of historical facts, that is of their location and their significance."[18]

An adequate understanding of the biblical imagination will need to admit that the claim of an original and irremovable bond between event and image is central to the O.T.'s understanding of metaphor, but must then read the image work as image work, an imaginative effort undertaken by those conscious of participating in a historical task, of working with images constitutive of their people's past and now to be made active in their own present. The biblical writers knew that renewal means more than recollection and repetition, that it calls for their own lives, their own perspectives, new creation.

Because I follow von Rad in looking upon the primary historical motifs as poetic creations and not objective events, it seems legitimate to describe the redactor's system as metaphorical, rather than conceptual or historical. All that has developed as an organic expansion of the same symbol belongs together no matter when the expansion took place, because it is this expansion, this reinterpretation, that keeps the symbol symbolic, historical, meaningful for present existence. Israel's use of the ordering power of *ratio*, as von Rad says,[19] is applied to the ever renewed reflection on the meaning of historical events, to a boundless quest for the meaning of her history, a quest which in turn makes possible the living in history, the making of history, the exodus from past to future.

Eichrodt presents this ever-renewed reflection as it is applied to covenant. He shows how through reinterpretation it remains the image through which the biblical writers (and not only the historians among them) of many generations understand their relation to God. For the Yahwist this image makes it possible to see as historical the period before Sinai, an understanding which he expresses by retrojecting the covenant into the patriarchal period, thus demonstrating the formative power of symbol on history; through the symbol, the past events are ordered for the sake of present meaning.[20] Eichrodt presents the stages in the differentiation of the compact metaphor and the dangers of this "unpacking," of a translation into propositions or terminology.[21]

It is because covenant can become religious terminology, legalistic or cultic, that, as Eichrodt recognizes, the prophets do not use this image for the God-human relation when they are insisting on grace and the personal element in relationship, on love and loyalty and surrender.[22] Eichrodt perceives the danger, "once the *berith* has become the all-embracing symbol…and is no longer qualified by other images,"[23] of perversion of the covenant order into a cultic relationship.

II

What I want to do in the rest of this paper is to follow this lead by looking at one of those qualifying images, not of course as fully as Eichrodt does with covenant, but perhaps enough to indicate the relevance of the approach. There is no intent here to substitute as central the image of exodus for the one Eichrodt focused on; but rather to suggest that the images cannot all be reduced to one. Von Rad concludes that the O.T. contains "a number of distinct and heterogeneous revelatory acts" and "seems to be without a centre which determines everything and which could give to the various separate acts both an interpretation and their proper theological connection with one another."[24] Clearly, whatever unity the O.T. has is given to it through the interrelationships between many such biblical images. It is only by seeing the individual "histories" of these central images and their complex interweaving that we begin to get a sense of the O.T.'s peculiar structure.

The history of the exodus image can be traced from its original locus in rite, through its expansion in the various components of the historical narrative, to the prophetic effort to recapture its original meaning, which means in the end directing the image against itself. Yet it is of the highest importance to recognize that the decisive leap takes place at the beginning.[25] "For ask now of the days that are past...has any god ever attempted to go and take a nation for himself from the midst of another nation?" [Deut. 4:32-34]. Miriam's song in celebration of the miracle at the Red Sea is generally accepted as one of the oldest poetic couplets in the O.T. A close reading of the Pentateuch makes it clear that the memory of the Exodus was originally an independent motif preserved in a different tradition from that of the Sinai covenant. For instance, the ancient creedal recital in Deuteronomy 26 that focuses on the bringing out from Egypt and the bringing into the promised land entirely omits any reference to Sinai. In the oldest period, as the credo indicates, the Exodus "appears to have been given the rank of a unique saving event excelling all others. But this rank was later diminished through other theological ideas";[26] the Sinai covenant, the Davidic kingship, Solomon's temple. Yet despite such diminishment, the Exodus remains an independent and complementary image which the prophets, as we shall see, can make use of, instead of and in opposition to understandings of faith which depend upon the covenant image become graven image. That is, the prophets demand an exodus from covenant, a demythization of Israel's own image.

It seems well established that the narrative presentations of the Exodus are expansions of ancient cultic formulas—which means that the priestly contribution to the Torah, the one most concerned with cult and rite, though late, is symbolically correct in its insertion of the description of the first Passover celebration before the narration of the departure from Egypt. (Of course, this is also a very suggestive way of presenting the trusting quality of Exodus faith.)

Exodus is a biblical metaphor of deliverance, with affinities to the Platonic myth of the cave and the Indian Nirvana and Sunyata. These, too, point to what we have described as the exodus from Exodus, the misunderstanding that arises if deliverance is understood literally as transport to another realm. Thus the enlightened man returns to the cave, the Bodhisattva rejects heaven and thus finds himself in Nirvana; Sunyata means both the nothingness of the mundane and the Nothing that lies beyond. What distinguishes the biblical metaphor is obviously the indissoluble bond between meaning and event.

Yet before reading this off as deficiency (as indeed it must be for the philosopher), we need to recognize that this "failure" expresses Israel's understanding of truth as event, as happening rather than as always there, waiting to be unveiled, recollected. For Israel, the truth and its having happened at this time and place are not separable. Is this not also true for the poet's understanding of how truth is discovered? Metaphors spring from the recognition of meaning in concrete event; they are a saying that seeks to retain this binding of the universal and particular. Blackmur tells us that

> Symbol is the most exact possible meaning, almost tautologically exact, for what stirred the words to move and what the moving words made. Symbol stands for nothing previously known but for what is "here" made known.[27]

In a sense, all the reflections on Exodus that we find in the historical writing and in the prophets are still contained within the ritualistic purpose of the Passover, to recall to us the memory of this event, to restore to it its original meaningfulness; but the symbols which are presented so compactly in the ritual are expanded so as to permeate the whole life story of Moses.

The dramatization of the encounters between Pharaoh and Moses is the imaginative presentation of the conflict between cosmic-divine civilization and Yahweh. That we can easily see how the presentation of this conflict has been patterned on the conflict in later Israelite history between prophet and king is an indication of how that conflict between two orders which exodus represents is a conflict that persists in Israelite history. The Egyptian myth of the interregnum during which the son of the dead king must prepare himself in the desert for the conflict with the usurping uncle is an eternally recurring pageant within which the player must in turn play every role.[28] This time around, though, the conflict is in earnest, and when Israel emerges from the Red Sea as the Son of God, the Pharaoh has, from the point of view of O.T. faith, lost his standing as Son of God forever.

Yet we must not fail to note that though this is true, the O.T. does not hide that there is never a time in Israel's history when for many Israelites it is not true. At the Red Sea itself the people say, "Let us alone and let us serve the Egyptians. For it would have been better for us to serve the Egyptians than to die in the wilderness" (Exod. 14:12), and they continue their mumbling all the generation-long way to the Jordan. The request for the golden calf, for a god who will obviously go before them, symbolizes how even in the desert journeying God's presence is never objective, is always perceptible to faith alone, and how hard it is to be on the way without image. There is an event, the deliverance from Egypt, but that this is a saving event can easily in the desert become questionable. The Hebrews would rather have been pagans with an idol amenable to their wishes, for life in the wilderness means an experiencing of God's transcendence, of the God who is present but only as he wills to be present.

The O.T. recognizes this meaning in the Exodus story and highlights it by retrojecting it back into its accounts of primeval and patriarchal history; the motifs associated with the Exodus from Egypt are discovered as those through which meaning may be given to an assortment of myths and legends. The journey from security into the open is the journey of faith, the human journey, whose meaning is made clear in the drawing out of the Hebrews from Egypt into the desert but which is to be lived through in all times. The first man sent forth is Adam, sent from Eden not in trust but because of his reaching for a knowledge or knowing like God's; here the father of humankind is sent on the human way. But the direct commandment, "Go forth," is spoken in the Bible only twice, and both times addressed to Abraham.[29] The first time it demands a separation from the world of the fathers, from the known past; the second time from his son, from the promised future. In neither case is Abraham told where he is being sent, only (the first time) that it is out of the land of remembrance, only (the second time) that it is out of the land of expectation. Both times Abraham's response is given not in a word but by his going. Abraham like Moses remains in "a peculiarly empty space,"[30] remains in the desert, turned toward future, toward promise, toward God, having turned away from the past and the gods. Faith means such trusting even when the very image of promise and the seeming condition of promise's fulfillment, be it Isaac or Jerusalem, is threatened.

While the Hebrews wander on their way toward Canaan, the place of wandering is simply that which must be gone through in order to get to the promised land, to the real goal; it is the land of "the between," between Egypt, Sheol, the realm of death and the realm of true life. Yet for the prophets, who have seen the promised land become a nation like other nations and the Lord's anointed a king like other kings, the desert to which the Exodus from Egypt brought Israel becomes the symbol of holy ground. The place of Israel's birth as a nation becomes a symbol for Israel's rebirth as God's nation.

The prophets seek an image from which to attack the social and cultic order; their recall of the past is meant to serve as a call to the present. We need to recognize that their way forward is precisely the way through Israel's failure and disobedience, that the deepened understanding of the significance of the traditional images won by the prophets is a direct response to their idolatrization.

> The moral order of the upper classes was difficult to attack from the basis of free peasant order, because the peasants themselves had to be attacked on account of their cultic order. This attack with a double front, therefore, had a tendency to fall back on the order of the nomad society,[31]

on the period of wandering in the desert under Moses's leadership. This then forced upon the prophets the problem of differentiating the spiritual meaning of the desert existence from "a symbolism that enclosed it compactly in the ordering instructions for an association of nomad clans."[32] This differentiation required the efforts of generations of prophets. Since existence under God means justice and righteousness, love and humility, not legality of conduct, Exodus serves as the reminder that the divinely willed order can never be equated with any social order.[33]

Thus we find that the prophet Amos uses the Exodus as a metaphor for the right relationship between God and his people and yet at the same time insists that the Exodus is misunderstood if seen only as past and as promise and not also as future and demand. To show that ritualism is not what God wants, that he hates and despises Israel's feasts and solemn assemblies, Amos must say that these had not been part of the Mosaic order: "Did you bring me sacrifices and offerings the forty years in the wilderness, O house of Israel?" (Amos 5:25). God is the God of Exodus: "You only have I known of all the families of the earth" (3:2), and yet Israel must be taught not to make of Exodus a guarantee for the future which enables her to boast "Evil shall not overtake or meet us" (9:10). The day of the Lord will be one of judgment not vindication, a day of exodus from Israel's self-confident existence (5:8). "Israel shall surely go into exile away from its land"

(7:17) and this time it will really learn what a desert is: "not a famine of bread, nor a thirst for water, but of hearing the word of the Lord" (8:11).

For Hosea the time in the wilderness seems a time of honeymoon since which time Israel has played the harlot. "When Israel was a child, I loved him, and out of Egypt I called my son," but "the more I called them, the more they went from me; they kept sacrificing to the Baals, and burning incense to idols" (Hos. II:1, 2). Yet Hosea sees the loving forgiveness of Israel's God who will woo her back, and this wooing he imagines as a new exodus. The prophets seem to agree "that Israel's previous history with Jahweh has come to an end…that if Israel is to be saved, she must move in faith into a new saving activity of Jahweh, one which is only to come in the future."[34] The move toward this future is what the "new exodus" represents. For Hosea, the return to the wilderness means a complete ascesis from all religious and political symbolisms. Israel is called to turn away from the Baals and the kings and the foreign alliances in whom she has falsely put her trust, as once she left behind the Egyptian ordering (Hos. 3:4, 5). Then in the openness into which her returning brings her, God will come and "heal her turnings-away."

The image of Exodus does not function in the symbolic composition of Isaiah's prophecies, and yet Isaiah experiences an exodus that enters into the way in which the prophets who succeed him will use and interpret the image. For Isaiah is made to see the clash between God's will and the human realization, a clash unimaginable within a cosmological order like the Egyptian where what happens is what is divinely willed. This vision leads Isaiah to despair of a restoration of order and meaningfulness to history which would depend on human obedience and to image instead God's giving to Israel an ideal king in whose reign the earth would be "full of the knowledge of the Lord" (Isa. 11:9). He turns from the idea of a historical creation of order out of disorder toward an eschatological hope of order. To express this hope, he creates new images of Immanuel and the Prince of Peace (images which are transformations not of the memories associated with exodus or covenant but of those which recall the Davidic monarchy, although these images will become theologized in their turn as "messianic" images). Isaiah himself discovers the dangers in this way of imaging God's grace and sovereignty as a to-be-trusted-in future, for although he means by it to point to an order for history that Israel's lack of faith cannot abolish, he points to this order in such a way that it can be misinterpreted as literal information about the future. Thus the promise becomes powerless to stand as a demand over the present. His prophecy makes the heart of the people fat and their ears heavy; they hear, but do not understand. So he learns how every image can be received as idol and concludes that he must "bind up the testimony, seal the teaching among my disciples." The true understanding of order lives now only in the prophets and disciples who are in exodus from Israel as contemporary reality.

Jeremiah seems to have hoped at first that the restoration of the covenant represented by the Josiah reform would recall the people to their existence as an existence under God but "the past that was meant to be revitalized in a continuous present now became really a dead past; and the living word to which the heart was supposed to respond became the body of law to which the conduct could conform."[35] Because the covenant has been made into a substitute for God, Jeremiah comes to believe in the need for a new exodus, an exodus from this externalized covenant. For him, too, the time in the wilderness represents Israel's original faithfulness, but he realizes that that Exodus is of no help now:

> Behold, the days are coming, says the Lord, when man shall no longer say, "As the Lord liveth who brought up the people of Israel out of the land of Egypt." [Jer. 23:7].

So Jeremiah can call to his contemporaries to interpret the exile that confronts them as a new exodus and therefore as meaningful to those of faith and not an occasion for despair. This new exodus will lead to the making of a new covenant, one that cannot be externalized, for it will be written on the heart: for the imaginings of the human heart will be substituted for the image of God in us.

Even more clearly Second Isaiah uses the images associated with the Exodus to call for a turning from Exodus, a turning from the past to the future, from memory to hope. Yet still the hope can only be expressed through the historical image:

> Thus says the Lord who makes a way in the sea, a path in the mighty waters, who brings forth chariot and horse, army and warrior...Remember not the former things, nor consider the things of old. Behold, I am now doing a new thing; now it springs forth, do you not perceive it? I will make a way in the wilderness and rivers in the desert [Isa. 43:17-19].

Here the images from Miriam's song of victory are used to call for an exodus from Exodus; here the poet calls us to "wait without idols," to look toward the new thing now springing forth.

For the prophets seek to make Israel realize that it cannot be a question of faith in an image—be it covenant or even Exodus itself—but of an image of faith. They use an image, that of Exodus, to picture the life of faith as the one directed by the commandment, "Thou shall make no images," to call for an exodus from all images. Yet the prophets recognize that such an exodus can be called for only by using the image of the remembered Exodus and that this creates problems: Gideon is not the only iconoclast who ends up making an ephod. The image from history sends Israel into history without images. Although the image refers to a past event, it is an image that means deliverance from the past, from the secured existence which any established order, political or cultic, Egyptian or Israelite, becomes. The image of exodus is then that image through which Israel is reminded that faith remains faith, remains risk, means moving with trust toward promise.

Notes

1. Walter Eichrodt, *Theology of the Old Testament, Volume I* (Philadelphia: Westminster Press, 1961) 33.

2. Martin Buber, *Israel and the World* (New York: Schocken Books, 1963) 243.

3. Quoted by Robert W. Corrigan in William Arrowsmith and Roger Shattuck (eds.), *The Craft and Context of Translation* (New York: Anchor Books, 1964) 134.

4. T. S. Eliot, *Selected Essays: 1917-1932* (New York: Harcourt, Brace & Co., 1932) 124-25: "a set of objects, a situation, a chain of events which shall be the formula of that *particular* emotion" and appear as "artistically inevitable" because of "the complete adequacy of the external to the emotion."

5. Which I detect also in Ernst Cassirer and his "philosophy of symbolic forms," despite his recognition of the peculiarity of the mythic mode of representation.

6. Amos Wilder, *Language of the Gospel* (New York: Harper & Row, 1964).

7. Voegelin, *Israel,* 121. Cf. also "Saga and History" in Martin Buber's *Moses* (New York: Harper & Bros., 1958).

8. Eichrodt, *Theology I,* 17.

9. Eichrodt, *Theology I,* 14.

10. Eichrodt, *Theology I,* 15.

11. Eichrodt, *Theology I*, 28.

12. Quoted in Brooks, *Urn*, 194.

13. Eichrodt, *Theology I*, 66.

14. Eichrodt, *Theology I*, 69.

15. Von Rad, *Theology I*, 107.

16. Von Rad, *Theology I*, 108.

17. Von Rad, *Theology I*, 109.

18. Von Rad, *Theology I*, 110.

19. Von Rad, *Theology I*, 117.

20. Eichrodt, *Theology I*, 50.

21. Eichrodt, *Theology I*, 52.

22. Eichrodt, *Theology I*, 52.

23. Eichrodt, *Theology I*, 55.

24. Von Rad., *Theology I*, 115.

25. Voegelin, *Israel*, 316.

26. Voegelin, *Israel*, 316.

27. Blackmur, *The Lion and the Honeycomb* (New York: Harcourt, Brace & Co., 1955) 224.

28. S. N. Kramer, *Mythologies of the Ancient World* (New York: Anchor Books, 1961) 68ff.

29. Cf. Buber's essay "Abraham der Seher," in *Werke, Volume I* (Heidelberg: Lambert Schneider, 1952).

30. Voegelin, *Israel*, 398.

31. Voegelin, *Israel,* 181.

32. Voegelin, *Israel,* 182.

33. Voegelin, *Israel,* 449.

34. Von Rad, *Theology I,* 128.

35. Voegelin, *Israel,* 429.

6

It Pleased God By Foolishness to Save the World

Heinrich Böll is a problem to the critics; just as they think they have fit him neatly into a box labeled "social satirist" or "realist" or "Catholic"—oops he's out! and no matter how cleverly they juggle the categories there seems no way of catching him.

Böll's early novels focused on the plight of those who found themselves adrift in the confusions of postwar Germany and then left out of the later prosperity; they revealed the vacuity and absurdity of the clerical, political, and economic institutions which shaped the lives of the exploited, hopeless, somehow enduring little men. They were remarkable for the sureness of his depiction of the touch and smell of everyday life, the cutting edge of his satire, the controlled sympathy. It is not surprising that he was hailed as a social moralist, expressing his outrage at what had happened during the Nazi years and his almost greater pain at the falsity of the restoration that followed.

Böll has often been praised as a realist. The spare clarity of the prose (so often compared to Hemingway's) is for him more than a literary method; it is a moral act. "Does anyone know," he asks, "what it meant in 1945 to write even half a page of German prose?"[1] For Böll's generation the high words *had* lost all meaning; all that was left were the simple, everyday realities to be described as simply as possible. Böll is a master at rendering the taste and feel of things, situations, landscapes, moments. His Bonn is as vividly present to us as Joyce's Dublin or Thomas Mann's Lübeck. Readers of *The Clown* are unlikely ever to forget how carefully Marie Derkum replaces the top on the toothpaste or that cognac is not kept in the refrigerator. Böll seizes hold of just that detail which enables us to perceive not the typical but this particular moment, this specific thing. Böll could echo his Hans' words: "What I do best are the absurdities of daily life: I observe, add up these observations, increase them to the nth degree and draw the square root from them but with a different factor from the one I increased them by" (p. 95). There's an intensity to these observations that seems to light up the observed from within.

For we find we are not after all in the prosaic world of everyday. In *The Clown* Hans can identify smells conveyed through the telephone wires: the maid in his parents' home smells very nice, just of soap and a little nail polish, the man at the monastery smells strongly of cabbage and pipe tobacco, Hans' mother very characteristically smells of nothing. Something is happening here that cuts into the naturalism and that becomes more apparent in each succeeding novel. The given world is an absurd world whose character Böll depicts without any of the grotesqueries of Gunther Grass. What is the deed that breaks its spell?—a smile, a clown strumming a guitar, a burning jeep. The incursion of grace into the everyday world is not a natural event, it does not "really" happen and so it cannot be represented realistically. *The Clown* takes place during *Fasching*, Mardi Gras, when the conventional order is temporarily suspended. Does this mean that it would make more sense to look upon Böll as a religious novelist than as a realist?

Yet Böll has clearly said that although he is a Christian and an artist, he does not wish to be a Christian artist. He asks whether it is not possible to realize that one can be a Catholic as a negro is a negro, so that it just won't come off the skin, won't wash out any more.[2] His novels are deeply permeated by the atmosphere of Rhineland Catholicism but it would be mistaken to think of this as only texture, scenery, local color. For it often seems that the Church is the favorite object of Böll's art, of his satirical attack. Indeed, a review of *The Clown* in *America* represented its chief purpose as being to sneer and rip and claw at the Catholic Church.[3] Nor does the criticism touch only the clerical order; Böll is equally skeptical about the dogmas and ethics of the Church. What impels Böll's criticism is that same abstractness that he condemns in the economic and political world. As Hans says, the real problem is that "Catholics have no feeling whatever for detail" (p. 58), but talk about everything in terms of metaphysics and "abstract principles of order" (p. 65). Yet to note only the pervasiveness of the debunking attitude would still be to miss the most important way that Böll's Catholicism shapes his writing. To understand that, we must carefully watch the use of Christian language and symbolism in the action of his novel. One critic, trying earnestly to discover how Böll can possibly take his own Catholicism seriously, asks petulantly, "But when does he ever speak of God or the Cross, of hope, of resurrection, or justification?"[4] The answer of the careful reader must be: all the time but never directly. In Böll's novels the heroes are not saved at the last moment by a paradoxical dogma as Graham Greene's protagonists may be. The

Church does not save any more than Marxism does. In fact, Böll's heroes aren't saved at all—except in hope, which is to say, in metaphor. The hope, and the metaphors, are grounded not in belief but in a love of the world, a love toward creation.

I should like to suggest that it is just this love toward the world that expresses what is ineradicable in Böll's Catholicism: his open-ness to the sacramental. What holds together the social moralism, the literary realism and the Catholicism is this sacramental element that Böll himself calls his "esthetic humanism." His writing insists on the un-naturalness, the immorality, indeed the blasphemy of metaphysical abstraction and celebrates the immediate, the sensuous, the concrete. His social criticism seeks to tear off the masks of the prosperous not for the sake of revolution in the Marxist sense but for the sake of a return to the simple everyday verities. The simplicity of his language, the carefulness of his descriptions, seeks to make us able again to see things as they are, undisguised by the gloss of language. Form and content are here inextricably intertwined; it is the artist's loving, caring eye that redeems, renews. Böll attacks the Church because of its metaphysics but in its sacraments or, more accurately, its recognition of the sacramental, lies his hope. Because this hope is seen only as it shatters the everyday masks, as an incursion, a breaking-in of grace, it cannot be shown realistically or literally but only metaphorically, playfully, fantastically.

Böll's "feeling for detail" arises from his sense of the sacramental character of things but to awaken this awareness in us he also uses the Church's sacraments as explicit symbols of the sacramental—at the same time that he shows that when the Church separates the sacraments from the sacramental it blasphemes. I should like to look more closely at the structure of *The Clown* to show how what I have called Böll's sense of the sacramental gives shape to the clown's collection of moments.

To summarize the story: it tells of Hans Schnier, son of a well-to-do Bonn mining family, who grows up during the Nazi period, leaves school at age 21 with no talent for anything but doing imitations, a bitter disappointment to his family. Two months later he seduces a devout young Catholic girl whose father he admires and for five years they live together while he becomes successful as a traveling clown. Then she leaves Hans for a childhood sweetheart, now a "kind of Alcibiades of German Catholicism" (p. 110), who promises to marry her. Schnier is completely overwhelmed by her desertion. Unable to clown anymore, in utter depression, he returns to Bonn. There, alone in his apartment, he telephones his family and friends in an attempt to find some way of communicating his loss and recovering from it. At the end he puts on his white make-up, goes to the main railroad station, sits on its steps, guitar in hand, hat beside him, singing a verse he has just made up: "Catholic politics in Bonn, Are no concern of poor Pope John, Let them holler, let them go, Eeny, meeny, miny, mo" (p. 244).[5]

The entire action of the novel takes place in one evening; it begins with Hans' arrival at the train station in Bonn when it is already dark and ends a little after 9:30 the same night when he returns to the station and begins to sit on its steps. Yet Hans' memories and telephone conversations extend the scope and significance of his sense of betrayal, much as Herzog's letter-writing does. The story comes to encompass the Nazi period as well as the postwar German scene and like almost all of Böll's writing insists on the connection between this present and that past. Schnier's most successful act was called Arrival and Departure, "a long (almost too long) pantomime during which the audience confuses arrival and departure all the way through" (p. 2). Obviously this description would apply as well to the action of Böll's novel which begins and ends at the railroad station.

Böll began as a writer of short stories and this novel's structure recalls the short story's focus on the moment of turning, the critical or representative moment. In *The Clown* Böll focuses on the decisive moment in Hans' life and into that moment Hans brings many others, for "I am a clown and I collect moments" (p. 240). In *The Clown* we see everything only through the filter of Hans' associations and we know that sorrow and sentimentality color these memories. Yet Hans shows an objective honesty about his situation that leads us to trust his perceptions, even without our ever being given the opportunity to look from any perspective but his. He still cannot accept Marie's having left him, but he continues to show his respect for her new fiancé, Züpfner, who seems to him a Catholic "with a high degree of probability" (p. 66) and for Züpfner's dull schoolmaster father. When Hans errs, we come to believe he is not so much deceived as deliberately playing with fact. He pretends to himself that he was quite unprepared for Marie's departure, although actually there had been many warnings in all her discussions about marriage, about her desire for "catholic air," in his unwillingness to probe her "being taken ill abortively." At one level he must have known, for, we learn, his professional difficulties began not after Marie's going but just before. Hans admits that he is often the prey of his own imagination; that, for example, he has pictured his audience with Pope John so minutely that he almost believes it has actually taken place. "During those minutes I was with the Pope, saw his smile and heard his wonderful peasant's voice...Sometimes it happens the other way round: that something I really did experience seems to me untrue and not real" (p. 179). "At times I don't know whether what I have experienced tangibly and realistically is true, or whether my real experience is the true one. I get it all mixed up.... The fact that I remember the details so vividly is no guarantee" (p. 190). Hans' remembering is thus an imaginative recreation, yet we come to trust its essential truthfulness. As George Santayana said of the wearer of the comic mask:

> To embroider upon experience is not to bear false witness against one's neighbor, but to bear true witness to oneself. Fancy is playful and may be misleading to those who try to take it for literal fact; but literalness is impossible in any utterance of the spirit and if it were possible it would be deadly."[6]

For Hans is a clown. Many hints recall St. Paul's conviction that the servants of Christ must become fools that they may be wise, "For the wisdom of this world is folly with God" (I Cor. 3:18). And we cannot help but think of the juggler of Notre Dame and *his* Marie, and of Kierkegaard's declaration, "I ask nothing better than to be pointed out as the only one in our serious age who is not serious."[7] Hans respects Pope John as one of the few authentic Catholics in the world; "there was something of a wise old clown about him, too." (p. 176). For Hans being a clown is a full-time occupation in a way that seems difficult for most people to understand. "Even doctors have time off, and recently even priests. That annoys me, they have no business to and they should be able to understand that about the artist.... I have always argued with Marie as to whether the God in whom she believes takes time off or not, she always insists that he does, gets out the Old Testament and reads me the story of Creation: And He rested on the seventh day. I countered with the New Testament and said it was possible that the God of the Old Testament had taken time off, but the whole idea of a Christ taking time off was inconceivable to me" (p. 96).

As Suzanne Langer observes, the clown "has always been close to the gods...From the primitive exuberant religions that celebrate fertility and growth he tends ever to come into the ascetic cults, and tumble and juggle in all innocence before the virgin."[8] In her study of the fool Enid Welsford notes that the role of the clown in many ways parallels that of the tragic chorus: to offer critical, perceptive warning comments regarding the main action. The clown breaks open the established dichotomies of illusion and reality, wisdom and folly. He focuses on the bodily and fleshly; his humor is often coarse because directed at a false and vain rationality and spiritualism. The clown's humor, though often anti-ecclesiastical, is yet dependent on the underlying spiritual order.

> The King, the Priest, and the Fool all belong to the same regime, all belong essentially to a society shaped by belief in Divine order, human inadequacy,

efficacious ritual…. The fool in cap and bells can flourish only among a people who have sacraments, who value symbols as well as tools, and cannot forever survive the decay of faith in divinely imposed authority…. The fool had
his niche in a divinely planned order of society, to whose dependent, ephem-
eral, and often corrupt character it was his function to bear witness.[9]

For Hans Schnier clowning is not an incidental profession, and, although
there is pathos as well as comedy in his self-presentation, there is an affirmation of
an underlying though hidden order, the *komos* ode, the song of life. If there is
crucifixion, there is also resurrection. When Marie goes, Hans finds the puppet
strings broken, finds himself asking not "How be a poet in a time of dearth?" but
how be a clown in such a time. Hans knows that "the worst of all clown
sins….(is) arousing pity" (p. 255); he does not need his agent to tell him that
"there's nothing more depressing for people than a clown they feel sorry for" (p.
107). Hans once remarks that he found Kierkegaard "useful reading for an aspir-
ing clown" (p. 11). Kierkegaard was especially interested in that species of the
comic that includes pathos: "The pathos which is not secured by the presence of
the comic is illusion; the comic spirit that is not made secure by the presence of
pathos is immature." What humor does is to reconcile itself "to the pain which
despair seeks to abstract from although it knows no way out." Kierkegaard speaks
of the difficulty of finding an objective correlative of the religious individual since
the authenticity of his incognito demands that "there is absolutely nothing that
marks him off from others, absolutely nothing that could serve as a hint of his
secret inwardness." Yet he suggests that though one cannot conclude that a
humorist is a religious individual, nevertheless the outward appearance of a
humorist is an appropriate mask.[10] We sense that for Böll also Hans' clowning
(though it does not make him a Christ-figure in the conventional sense) may
make him a figure of the true Christian, as for W. H. Auden Falstaff's untiring
devotion to making others laugh becomes a comic image for a love that is absolutely self-giving.[11]

For Hans being a clown is not a mask that one takes off between performances. In every scene he finds it impossible to resist the clowning, the flippancy,
that his brother had always feared. When his father comes to the apartment for a
serious talk, he is distressed by the comical aspect lent the situation by Hans'
bathrobe and the odor of spilt coffee. Hans gets dressed and they begin talking.
His father asks him if he needs money and Hans shows him his swollen knee and
then points to his left breast (p. 141):

"And this," I said,
"Good God," he said, "heart."
"Yes," I said, "heart."
"I'll give Drohmert a call and ask him to come see you. He's the best heart specialist there is."
"You don't understand," I said, "I don't need to consult Drohmert."
"But didn't you say: heart?"
"Maybe I should have said soul, feelings, emotions—heart seemed to me the right word."

A few minutes later Hans is acting like a man who has just lost his sight in order to make a point that his father dismisses as soon as he perceives that the whole thing was only put on. Just before the father's departure, in a last vain attempt to return to the subject of money, Hans juggles with the one mark he has left.

Lynch says that the whole art of comedy "is to be an art of anamnesis, or memory, of the bloody human…as a path to God, or to any form of the great."[12] Aside from the phone conversations and the visit from Hans' father, most of the novel presents us with Hans' memories of the past and his imaginings of the future. He understands his role as that of remembering and reminding. Of course, what he mostly remembers is Marie and their five years together but also he remembers Nazism and the war. Hans' mother, who has made a career out of lecturing about the remorse of German youth, sighs when Hans reminds her of her dead daughter, "I suppose you can never forget that, can you?" "Forget? Ought I to, Mother?" (p. 25). Hans says (p. 184) that what upsets him is how people are

> so moved by all the remorse and loud protestations of democracy…they failed to grasp that the secret of the terror lay in the little things. To regret big things is child's play: political errors, adultery, murder, anti-Semitism—but who forgives, who understands, the little things?…The way Herbert Kalick, beside himself with rage, banged with his fist on our table, and looked at me with his stony eyes and said: "We've got to be ruthless, ruthless," or the way he grabbed Götz Buchel by the collar, stood him in front of the class and said: "Look at him—if that isn't a Jew!" I remember too many moments, too many details, tiny little things.

Remembering is important and Hans is struck by how many people, especially his father, advise him to "forget about the past," to "accept his situation."

Hans' concrete remembering protests abstractions. He is distressed by the Catholic group's comfortable discussion of the virtue of poverty; he loves Marie's father for never talking about honor. Hans speaks of his time as the era of prostitution: "People are becoming accustomed to the vocabulary of whores. I once met Sommerwild after one of those discussions ('Can Modern Art be Religious?'), and he asked me: 'Was I good? Did you like me?,' word for word the question whores ask their departing suitors. I almost expected him to ask 'Please recommend me to your friends'" (p. 242). He is distressed because his own father talks on TV—"about social obligations, about national consciousness, about Germany, about Christianity even, which he admitted he didn't believe in, and what was more, in such a way that you were forced to believe him" (p. 169). Hans tries to tell his father that as children they had all known they were rich and yet they had never had enough to eat. "Did you children ever lack for anything?" "Yes...that's what I'm trying to tell you: food" (p. 161).

But for Hans the issue between the concrete and the abstract, the sacramental and the metaphysical, is felt most sharply when he thinks of his life with Marie. He is convinced that his life with Marie is marriage and is deeply disturbed by the suggestion that without a civil and religious ceremony it isn't *really* a marriage. His deepest sadness and most anguished questioning come because Marie, due he feels to her Catholic education and the persuasiveness of "the group," cannot hold onto this recognition. From their first morning together, when Marie pours his coffee and butters his roll, Schnier has felt married to her. (And even as a schoolboy he had argued with his teacher that surely Brunhild was Siegfried's true wife.) When he goes home that first morning and tries to tell his brother Leo what has happened he stammers, "I was with a girl...with a woman—my wife" (p. 51). And so it seems obvious to him that in going to Züpfner now Marie is committing adultery. For Hans this adultery is not an abstract fact but something that becomes true precisely through the details. How can Marie bear to do the things, especially "the thing," with Züpfner that she had done with him? Hans finds that he is terribly afflicted by a disposition to monogamy: "There is only one woman with whom I can do everything that men do with women: Marie, and since she left me I live as a monk is supposed to live; only—I am not a monk" (p. 10). It seems to Hans that there is nothing they had done together that Marie could do with Züpfner "without seeming a traitor or a whore. She can't even spread butter on his toast" (p. 99). "Come to think of it, she couldn't even read the Bible with Züpfner without feeling like a traitor or a whore. She would be bound to think of the hotel in Düsseldorf where she had read aloud to me about Solomon and the Queen of Sheba till I fell asleep in the tub from exhaustion" (p. 109).

The contrast is always between an abstract and a concrete conception of marriage. He remembers how often in their conversations they had spoken together of their yet unborn children. They even discussed (p. 218f.) how they would dress their children:

> She was all for "jaunty, light-colored raincoats." I preferred parkas, since it seemed to me that a child couldn't very well play in a puddle in a jaunty, light-colored raincoat, while a parka was ideal for playing in puddles…Whether our children would actually be allowed to play in puddles was never completely clarified. Marie would just smile, be evasive and say: let's wait and see. If she was to have children with Züpfner she wouldn't be able to dress them in either parkas or jaunty, lightcolored raincoats, she would have to let her children run around without coats, for we had gone thoroughly into the matter of coats of all kinds. We had also discussed long and short pants, underwear, socks, shoes she would have to let her children run naked through the streets of Bonn if she didn't want to feel like a whore or a traitor.

Böll uses the affair between Hans and Marie, outwardly a sinful relation, as a sign of a trans-moral love. As Auden suggests:

> A direct manifestation of charity in secular terms is, therefore, impossible. One form of indirect manifestation employed by religious teachers has been through parables in which actions which are ethically immoral are made to stand as a sign for that which transcends ethics…If a parable of this kind is dramatized, the action must be comic, that is to say, the apparently immoral actions of the hero must not inflict, as in the actual world they would, real suffering upon others.
>
> Thus, Falstaff speaks of himself as if he were always robbing travelers. We see him do this once—incidentally, it is not Falstaff but the Prince who is the instigator—and the sight convinces us that he never has been and never could be a successful highwayman. The money is restolen from him and returned to its proper owners; the only sufferer is Falstaff himself who has been made a fool of. He lives shamelessly on credit, but none of his creditors seems to be in serious trouble as a result. The Hostess may swear that if he does not pay his bill, she will have to pawn her plate and tapestries, but this is shown to be the kind of exaggeration habitual to landladies, for in the next scene they are still there. What, overtly, is dishonesty becomes, parabolically, a sign for a lack of pride, humility which acknowledges its unimportance and dependence upon others.

Then he rejoices in his reputation as a fornicator with whom no woman is safe alone, but the Falstaff on stage is too old to fornicate, and it is impossible to imagine him younger. All we see him do is defend a whore against a bully, set her on his knee and make her cry out of affection and pity. What in the real world is promiscuous lust, the treatment of other persons as objects of sexual greed, becomes in the comic world of play a symbol for the charity that loves all neighbors without distinction (p. 202f.).[13]

But to ask a girl to bear the weight of such symbolism literally, "really" is to ask too much. And so, though Hans cannot understand Marie's leaving, we can. He has asked too much of her: "A Marie who would stay would be unbelievable."[14]

Hans sees himself to be fighting for Marie. Several times he asks what fighting for her might mean. At one level a duel seems most appropriate and yet any physical battle seems ridiculously inappropriate. Instead of fighting, all he actually does is clown, talk, remember. His opponent seems to be less Züpfner whom he respects than the whole social order, the world in the Pauline sense, the phoniness and abstraction of post-war Germany and especially the way this pervades the Church. The central event in the book is the confrontation with his father who represents this order, the well-meaning, decent father who is unable to break free. "He was not to blame, only stupid in a way which excluded tragedy" (p. 169). Recognizing what a superb piece of acting his father's representation of the committed businessman on TV is, Hans compliments him on his clowning, but his father does not have the ironic detachment to acknowledge the role-playing. For the first time Hans can thank his father for his gestures of courage in the Hitler times: for the way his father had put his hands on the son's shoulders when his school-teacher had brought him home for shouting "You Nazi swine"; for the way he had stood up for a friend's mother accused of espionage because she had crossed through the enemy lines to get some bread from her brother's bakery. But the one thing the father had really wanted to do for Hans during this visit, to make him a decent cup of coffee, does not happen. At the end of the book Hans again remembers these gestures of his father's and realizes anew how much alike they are, but the actual encounter is not really fulfilled, no catharsis occurs because of it. The father has done what he can but he cannot bring healing or salvation—not even coffee or money.

So if there is a turning-point, this is not it. As the phone call after his father's departure reveals, Hans is still in exactly the same situation as before, no Marie and only one mark to his name. But then in an impulsive gesture he takes that mark from his pocket and throws it out the window. Now he has *no* resources and it is this that is the climactic point. Lynch says that rock-bottom being cannot be hurt, that this invulnerability lies at the root of the hope of comedy; it is rock-bottom to which Hans has now brought himself. From this point on we move toward a comic resolution, that is, toward a happy ending. Note, however, that it is not the happy ending of "boy gets girl." Marie does not return; sex does not succeed.

Hans knows that in a sense tomorrow will be no different: "To tell the truth, tomorrow I'll still be injured, with no money, no bookings and no Marie—so it's not really urgent" (p. 237). Nevertheless he is deeply disappointed that his brother out of fear of an "exhortation" refuses to visit him that evening. Although he cannot explain it, Hans knows that the decisive time is today and so he continues preparing for his performance at the station. As he does this he thinks of his childhood friend, Edgar Wieneken. "The others believed in more than people, in God, in abstract money, in things like nation and Germany. Not Edgar" (p. 225). As he remembers this, Hans suddenly realizes his own faith in Edgar, his faith in "certain people," like Edgar's own faith and that, strangely, he too likes "the kind to which I belong: People. When one of my kind dies, I am sad. I would weep even at the grave of my mother" (p. 233). As the clown ponders this, we begin to see that though in this novel sex does not succeed, perhaps love does.

Marie will not come back nor does Hans "get over it" in the easy, false sense. There are only very subtle hints that the scene at the railroad station represents a happy ending. But as David Miller suggests, perhaps this is the only happy ending that "makes sense" in our time when we can no longer give credence to a literal, sociological happy ending. "Happy endings like the resurrection are incredible."[15] And perhaps the note of grace must be ineluctable at the level of plot. There sitting on the station steps is only ambiguous. Perhaps the *tranquilla* can be present only in the metaphors. The ending is clearly not a return to the Eden of the time with Marie but may represent what Auden calls the vision of the New Jerusalem:

> Our dream pictures of the Happy Place where suffering and evil are unknown are of two kinds, the Edens and the New Jerusalem. In their relation to the actual fallen world, the difference between Eden and New Jerusalem is a temporal one. Eden is a past world in which the contradictions of the present world have not yet arisen; New Jerusalem is a future world in which they have at last been resolved. Eden is a place where its inhabitants may do whatever they like to do, the motto over the gate is, "Do what thou wilt is here the Law." New Jerusalem is a place where its inhabitants like to do whatever they ought to do, and its motto is, "In His Will is our peace."

> In neither place is the moral law felt as an imperative…Nobody is born in New Jerusalem but to enter it, one must, either through one's own acts or by Divine Grace, have become good.[16]

It is only at the conclusion of the novel that we are let in on the metaphor that encloses the entire action. As Hans walks to the station he discovers it is carnival time. "That suited me fine. There is no better hiding place for a professional than among amateurs" (p. 246). How appropriate! For, as Cook observes, "In most rituals of fertility the comic play occurs at the same time as the Saturnalia."[17] But here the pagan note is transformed, for *Fasching* is the anticipation of Easter, the festival that marks the beginning of Lent. The *metaphor* of carnival in *The Clown* indicates a comic reunion (which the *plot* must be much more hesitant about). Since it is carnival time Hans now appears as the Lord of Misrule. The world is topsy-turvy—it is time for play. So Hans now plays out the traditional role of the Fool, as Enid Welsford perceives it, which is not to lead a revolt against the law but into the region where its writ does not run.[18] *Koinonia:* an order based on love and freedom, not law.

In the last pages of the book the motif of death and resurrection which had been hinted at throughout the novel becomes more prominent. Several times Hans had identified Christianity with those extraordinary and difficult to believe things: "resurrection of the body and eternal life" (p. 11, 65). Several times he speaks of believing that "the living are dead and that the dead live, not the way Protestants and Catholics believe it. For me a boy like George, who blew himself up with a bazooka, is more alive than my mother," and this is even more true of his dead sister Henrietta. Several times Hans' own death is suggested. The Kinkel's son tells Hans that the review of his most recent performance is not so much a panning as an obituary. Hans' agent tells him he seems to be committing artistic suicide. When Hans listens to Monika play the mazurka over the phone he recognizes this attempt at repetition as a kind of suicide and then says he feels terribly dirty and imagines he must stink "the way Lazarus stank" (p. 204). As he puts on his make-up before going back to the station he sees in the mirror the face of a suicide and then, as the white make-up goes on, the face of a corpse.

Hans can, at least with metaphor and mask, prepare for death. But a resurrection of this "man of sorrows" will be visible only to those with eyes to see. If comedy represents the return to the norm, it is not here the return to the world of "good sense," but to the norm of that extraordinary thing, the resurrection. Böll has been as indirect as possible in order to keep this from being a vision of cheap grace. He lets the former Hitler Youth leader, Kalick, tell Hans: "For every man there is a chance. Christians call it grace" (p. 187). Yet what can be said in a phony way may nevertheless be true—though it must be represented very subtly. The novel ends on a note of hope but not of certainty. Marie had once predicted that Hans would someday find himself in just this situation: "Marie was horrified when I bought a guitar a few months ago and said I would soon be singing songs to the guitar which I had composed myself. She thought this was 'beneath' me and I told her the only thing beneath the gutter was the canal, but she didn't understand what I meant, and I hate explaining a metaphor. Either you understand it or you don't. I am no exegete" (p. 30). Sitting on the station steps, Hans hopes that "people will be able to see that I was not a religious maniac who would spurn a modest donation" (p. 230). As the novel ends, the first coin falls into his hat and Hans goes on singing. As Mrs. Wieneken had told him years before, "If you can sing, you're still alive."

Notes

1. Quoted in *In Sachen Böll*, ed. Marcel Reich-Ranicki (Koln: Kiepenheuer & Witsch, 1968) 215.

2. Quoted in *In Sachen Böll*, 97.

3. *America*, Vol. 112, No. 7 (February 6, 1965).

4. Klaus Harprecht, "Seine katholische Landschaft," *In Sachen Böll*, 116.

5. The German text has: "Der arme Papst Johannes, hart nicht die CDU, er ist nicht Muller's Esel, er will nicht Muller's Kuh," *Ansichten eines Clowns* (Koln: Kiepenheuer & Witsch, 1963) 251.

6. George Santayana, "The Comic Mask," *Theories of Comedy*, ed. Paul Lauter (New York: Doubleday & Company, 1964) 417.

7. Soren Kierkegaard, *Concluding Scientific Postscript* (Princeton: Princeton University Press, 1944) 251.

8. Suzanne K. Langer, "The Great Dramatic Forms: The Comic Rhythm," in *Theories of Comedy*, 516.

9. Enid Welsford, *The Fool* (New York: Doubleday, 1961) 193, 299.

10. Kierkegaard, *Postscript*, 81, 464, 447.

11. W. H. Auden, *The Dyer's Hand* (New York: Random House, 1962) 206.

12. Lynch, *Christ*, 99.

13. Auden, *Dyer's Hand*, 202.

14. See essay by Irving Fetscher, "Menschlichkeit und Humor: Ansichten eines Clowns," *In Sachen Böll*, 275ff.

15. David L. Miller, "Ultima Tranquilla," a paper presented at the 1966 AAR meeting, Chicago.

16. Auden, *Dyer's Hand*, 409.

17. Cook, "Comedy and Tragedy," 488.

18. Welsford, *Fool*, 316.

7

Theology as Make-Believe: A Response to the Theology of Hope

We are here in that dim and treacherous realm between firm religious belief on the one side and make-believe on the other. Belief and make-believe have similar fertilizing effects upon human creativity. And in our time we are more at home with make-believe than we are with belief—or perhaps we have simply lost the sense of the distinction. Even the truths of science begin to look like partial metaphors; necessary (though sometimes contradictory) hypotheses, which guide and nourish the scientific imagination for a time, not adequate and final truth. Thus the whole problem of the Religious Myth is on the edge of an even darker mystery: that of the nature, even the possibility, of real faith in our time.

Francis Fergusson[1]

Or, following Johann Huizinga, *homo ludens*, culture as play, theology as make-believe. Belief is literalism and literalism is idolatry. Theology not as archeology but as eschatology. A theology of the last things, the future, the not-yet, a theology based not on experience but on hope and promise, can only be a theology of make-believe. For eschatology points to "a realm which has no shape at all but that which our images give it."[2] The future has no existence except in our anticipations, our hopes and fears, our images and dreams. As Jürgen Moltmann says, "The term eschatology is wrong."[3] Logic is beside the point: *eschato-poeisis*. "Turning and turning in the animal belly, the mineral belly, the belly of time. To find the way out: the poem"[4] (Norman O. Brown).

To hope is to dream. "Seeing that we have such hope, we use great freedom of speech" (II Cor. 3:12). In dreams begins fulfillment. To give existence to that which is denied and repressed in the world of experience, the world of the reality

65

principle—to give the unrealized hope, the unacknowledged dream, form—is creation, re-creation, reconciliation. To give shape to the dream, to bring it to poem, is to realize it. "A new heaven and a new earth."

To dream is not only to hope but to fear. "And behold, there was a great earthquake; and the sun became black as sackcloth, the full moon became like blood, and the stars of the sky fell to the earth as the fig tree sheds its winter fruit when shaken by a gale; the sky vanished like a scroll that is rolled up, and every mountain and island was removed from its place" (Rev. 6:12-14). To give shape to the chaos and the terror is to move toward subduing them, transcending them. R. W. B. Lewis: Even when comedy can no longer offer us a happy ending, its vision of the absurdity within the impending apocalypse is a "stay against hysteria," "rooted not quite in hope but in a hope about hope."[5] *Catch-22*. To give shape is an act of hope. To find the way out: the poem.

As model for the theologian not the Sisyphus whom William Hamilton chooses, "a man without faith, without hope, with only the present and therefore only love to guide him,"[6] but the Rebel, the Artist as Rebel: "No artist tolerates reality...but no artist can get along without reality. Artistic creation "rejects the world on account of what it lacks and in the name of what it sometimes is."[7]

A generation ago Martin Buber wrote, "When man can no longer say *Thou* to the 'dead' known God, everything depends on whether he can still say it to the living unknown God by saying *thou* with all his being to another living and known man."[8] Today we might say instead, "everything depends on whether he can still hope." Sam Keen: "The question of God is not the question of the existence of some remote infinite being. It is the question of the possibility of hope...To deny that there is a God is functionally equivalent to denying that there is any ground for hope."[9] (Though this leaves Ernst Bloch's question: "But why hypostasize the future as God?")

After the age of anxiety the age of hope, or of the hope about hope. For, as Gabriel Marcel observes, "except where the temptation to despair exists, there can be no hope."[10] Man exists as being-towardness, as toward the not yet, but not necessarily only toward death. Wolfhart Pannenberg believes that man as man raises the question of life *beyond* death;[11] for Ernst Bloch, "man is the creature who hopes, who phantasizes, who dreams about the future and strives to attain it."[12]

After the anatomies of anxiety, the horoscopes of hope: Gabriel Marcel's metaphysic of hope; William Lynch's psychology of hope; Moltmann's theology of hope. But if theology is make-believe, perhaps what we need is a *mythology* of hope. Not a catalogue of myth, not a tracing of hope in all its mythic incarnations beginning with what was left in Pandora's box when all else was gone. (Blessing or curse? Reality or illusion?) Not a mythology of hope in *that* sense, but mythology *as* hope. Hope as *mythopoeisis, eschato-poeisis*. The way out; the poem. A return to *mythos* but not a return to the dim and treacherous realm where the distinction between belief and make-believe is only beginning to emerge. Myth as made-believe, as make-belief. In place of original participation, final participation; in place of idolatry, play. Myths and dreams as anticipations not memories; myths as images of hope not nostalgia, the mythic as image of hope.

Mythology as hope: In *The Hero With A Thousand Faces* Joseph Campbell limns the monomyth, "the one shapeshifting yet marvellously constant story,"[13] in which the hero sets out from the world of the past and the common day toward the promised land and the unknown future. "Now the Lord said to Abram, 'Go from your country and your kindred and your father's house to the land that I will show you.'" For Bloch what fires the human spirit in all presents is the promise of a homecoming.

> All seems familiar, even the hastening greeting
> Seems the greeting of friends, each face seems congenial.
> To be sure! It is the native land, the soil of the homeland,
> That which thou seekest is near, and already coming to meet thee.
>
> (Hölderlin[14])

In his *Anatomy of Criticism* Northrop Frye seeks to show that all literary genres derive from the quest myth whose meaning is the vision of a world in which all antitheses are resolved, the mingling of the sun and the hero, the realizing of a world in which the inner desire and the outward circumstance coincide.

> Song, as you explain it, is not passion,
> not striving for some end at last attained;
> song is Being. Easy for gods to fashion.
> But when shall we *be*? And when will he bend
> the earth and stars upon our being? Youth,
> it is not that you are in love; although
> the voice bursts your mouth open, you must find
> how to forget your rash song. That will go.

It is another breath that sings the truth.

A breath round nothing. A gust in the god. A wind.

(Rilke[15])

To hope is thus to set forth from the world of the known myths toward the unknown myth. The meaning of myth lies in the vision of fulfillment. "Abraham and Orpheus, be with me now…" (Delmore Schwartz[16])

Campbell's study of mythology issues in *Creative Mythology*. As Fergusson remarks, "Myths generate new forms (like the differing children of one parent) in the imaginations of those who try to grasp them."[17] Johannes Metz's call for the development of theology as eschatology is an appeal for "Creative Hope." The "theology of the future" is not to become a subterfuge for holding on to the theology of the past. To paraphrase Marx on Feuerbach, "Not new interpretations of theology but a transformation." A theology shaped by the future, by vision, by imagination. Theology as make-believe.

An eschatological theology. Not about the eschaton or others' interpretations of it. Not simply to apprehend the rebirth of images which gave shape to St. John's Apocalypse but to participate in such a rebirth. A theology of the last days. Hope itself as an eschatological gift: "May the God of hope fill you with all joy and peace in believing, so that by the power of the Holy Spirit you may abound in hope" (Rom. 15:13).

A Joachimite theology. A theology which bursts forth from the charged tension between present and future. Not from the hidden identity between the present and the time of fulfillment as in *gnosis*. Not from the point of view of a future already realized as in apocalyptic. Not from an eventless interim of passive waiting for a wholly transcendent future. But a theology written at the moment of transition—from the now pregnant with future, shaped by vision. A now full of the presence of presentness and the futurity of the future, a present transformed by the future acting upon it, not a future which is wholly beyond. Ernst Fuchs calls it a time between the times, the last hour of the world and the first hour of the kingdom, a time which is chronologically impossible but is nevertheless not reducible to a mathematical point, for it is a time-*for*, a time for response to what is on the way, a time for hope.[18] As Ernst Kasemann insists, interpretations of Jesus' eschatology as realized or as futuristic both miss the point. For primitive Christianity, also, eschatology does not swallow history nor is eschatology (except in Luke) swallowed by salvation history; the Gospels arise precisely as ways of presenting the paradox of the identity between the created and the exalted Lord.[19] Moltmann insists, "From first to last, and not merely in the epilogue, Christianity is eschatology, is hope, is forward looking and forward moving, and therefore also revolutionizing and transforming the present."[20] To be seized by the already-approaching character of the future is always to be a revolutionary. Consider Jesus, Joachim, Marx. A now determined by the promise of something new. A theology of eschatological vision, of creative hope. Theology as make-believe.

The theology of expectation as arising to express *our* sense of the nearness of the future, our fears and hopes of the unknown which approaches. A theology which knows the same fears as those that give birth to the modern literary apocalypses: *The Day of the Locust, The Sotweed Factor, Catch 22*. A theologizing that recognizes with Philip Rahv that the contemporary "craze for myth" may represent most of all the fear of history,[21] but which believes that myth may provide an overcoming and not merely an escape. The theology of hope not simply as an exercise of biblical scholarship but as an expression of the present "reanimating of those great and ancient archetypes by which Western man has periodically explained to himself...the most spectacular of his expectations and terrors,"[22] a reanimation visible also in our literature, our art, our dreams. A theology which knows the same fears and arises as a response to the rebirth of the same archetypes. "Abraham and Orpheus, be with us now..."

But the theological imagination is not the same as the apocalyptic imagination. Apocalypse is not hope. "Superficially" the apocalyptic visions "may resemble the nature and the processes of hope. In fact, they are a brilliant and exuberant counterfeit of hope. But on examination they prove to be the very reverse of hope. They are based on a hidden despair of coping with human reality, or they are based on the bad taste of this reality...They are a form of 'hope' that proposes the impossible rather than the possible."[23]

Buber says that "Wherever man shudders before the menace of his own work and longs to flee from the radically demanding historical hour, there he finds himself near to the apocalyptic vision of a process that cannot be arrested..."[24] Saul Bellow's Herzog: "We must get it out of our head that this is a doomed time, that we are waiting for the end, and the rest of it...Things are grim enough without these shivery games....We love apocalypses too much."[25] Robert Alter sees in Herzog's continual "attempts to counterpose against the great, killing abstractions of modern intellectual life the concrete particulars—poignant, saddening, ludicrous, sordid—that constitute the individuality, the vividly recollected specialness, of one man's life" and in Herzog's "expressed hope for human value in an infinite and indifferent universe" a reflection of that imagining proper to prophetic eschatology.[26] Lynch poses the theological imagination against the gnostic; Buber the prophetic imagination over against the apocalyptic.

The theological imagination is not the same as the apocalyptic imagination. The difference is analogous to the difference R. W. B. Lewis discerns between Hawthorne's allegorical imagination and Melville's metaphorical imagination. Melville's method meant beginning with the actual, often with the personally experienced, and then "enlarging by the resources of art toward fullness and beauty," whereas Hawthorne begins with the general and then seeks "for the concrete terms by which he might embody it."[27] The prophet's metaphors are not analogies, not based on the idea of a rational order of the universe that can be represented adequately by a network of rational analogies. They serve to point not to the eternal but to the not-yet and so their images are events, represent the meeting of the old with the approaching future, are a new word, a not-until-now word to point to the not-yet.

The prophetic imagination. Prophecy and typology. A rebirth of images. Images created not *ex nihilo*, but like the phoenix born of the ashes of other images: Resurrection. The theology of the future, not any future but the promised future. Eschatology and typology: without typology eschatology is gnosticism—or historicism—or apocalypse; without eschatology typology would be idolatry. A past and a future related through promise and hope, through memory and anticipation. A theology of hope arises out of the typological imagination which understands revelation as presence and promise.

To think typologically is to be free of the oppositions upon which Moltmann insists: epiphany *or* eschatology, the God of presence *or* the God of promise who is always before us; events as unique *or* recurring, sequence as linear *or* cyclic, the past as history *or* symbol. To take on again the typological imagination is to see history as figures not causes, events as images. The relation between what was and what is yet to be is not simply that of historical sequence; what is as important is the similarity of form between the remembered event and the anticipated one. The latter is understood as the fulfillment, the fuller actualization of all that is latent, implicit, potential in the earlier, as its hidden meaning. Typology insists on the radical difference between past and future, present and fulfillment, but at the same time holds that the future fulfillment is expected not beyond time but in time and is already at work. Figure and fulfillment each belongs in its historical context; the significance of each in its historical place is deepened by the recognition of the tension between promise and fulfillment which typological interpretation lifts into view. The relation is metaphorical; each event remains unambiguously itself and yet bringing the two together creates a dramatic unity like the oneness of a word with its answer.

The events of the past are seen not as mere anticipatory shadows whose significance would dissolve with the fulfilling appearance, for they have been transformed into images of hope through which the past is not left in the past but continues its working, into images through which men have hoped, have reached into the future. The thread of promise and fulfillment, of fulfillment which is then understood as sign of new promise leading toward eschatological fulfillment is what holds the events of history together. Hope is tied to history through creative memory. As von Rad shows, prophetic eschatology sweeps away the false security, the idolatrous hope based on the saving events of the past, but is charged with the expectation of something soon to happen, the comingness of a new saving event. The break with the past goes so deep that the new state cannot be understood as a continuation of what went before. The decisive factor in Israel's history lies in some future event, the old bases of salvation are null and void, *and yet*: "the specific form of the new thing which they herald is not chosen at random; the new is to be effected in a way…analogous to God's former saving work. Thus Hosea foretells a new entry into the land, Isaiah a new David and a new Zion, Jeremiah a new covenant and Deutero-Isaiah a new Exodus."[28] There is a tremendous shift of hope from the past to the future and yet nevertheless even in this new hope a connection with the past. The images of fulfillment are created out of memories. The old which no longer has power to generate hope may still generate images of hope.

Typology can recognize epiphany and interpret it eschatologically because it recognizes in moments of presence the vision of an unvanishing fulfillment. It can recognize uniqueness *and* recurrence because its sense of same and other is less coarse than ours. The prophetic notion of salvation as recreation cannot be grasped by interpreting it as either cyclic or linear. The mythic is not exhausted by the myth of the eternal return; there is also the myth of the new beginning. (Heraclitus: "the way up is the way down" *but* "you never step into the same river twice.") As Harold Watts suggests, the two models seem to be as intimately related in ways that vex and elude as that other pair of logical incompatibles, comedy and tragedy.[29] Marcel: "Might we not say that hope always implies the super-logical connection between a return and something new?"[30] Norman O. Brown: "Revolution is not a slate wiped clean but a revolving cycle. Even newness is renewal."[31] Wolfhart Pannenberg: "The arrival of what is future can be thought through to its conclusion only with the idea of repetition (which does not exclude the new), in the sense that in it the future *has* arrived in a *permanent* present."[32] Fulfillment is different both from an end to time or its endless repetition and can perhaps only be imagined through a metaphorical conjunction of line and circle: a *new* time. "Abraham and Orpheus, be with me now…"

Memory, like anticipation, is imaginative. For the typological imagination even the past becomes unfixed, is seen not as over, but as full of potentialities and hopes, understood in the light of what is yet to come. Thus for Joachim the interpretation of history becomes prophecy, the right understanding of the past depends on the proper perspective for the future. As Moltmann says, "It is not our experiences which make faith and hope, but it is faith and hope that make experiences."[33] Hope's relation to the future is thus entirely different from prediction's, for the hard facts that could serve as "causes" are dissolved or made fluid. Christianity, as Metz points out, "honors the poverty of its knowledge about the future"[34] because it believes radically in the not-yetness of the future. Hope is not a rational calculation of what must happen nor a sentimental optimism, not a spiritualized private salvation from history nor an idolatrous trust in a *deus ex machina*. Its trust in the openness of the future, its vision of a happy ending, allows it to see possibilities in the past which an "objective" history couldn't. Hope creates new possibilities precisely because it is, as Lynch observes, a "sense of the possible" or a sense for possibilities. "If we wait till all the evidence is in before we trust, we will never trust—because it is trust that gives the evidence its structural existence."[35] Pannenberg finds a contradiction between Ernst Bloch's appeal to the potentialities of the present and Bloch's emphasis on the *novum* in the future: "If the future is already latent in those potentialities and latencies…it would no longer descend upon everything that has been and that is with the suddenness and incalculability of the new."[36] But this is to miss the sense in which the *potentialities* of the present are themselves still to be *made*. What we couldn't hope for on the basis of the visible possibilities, we hope for nevertheless. As Buber says, we cannot learn the limit of what is attainable in a desired direction except through going in that direction.

The insistence that the past is factor *or* symbol destroys the possibility of eschatology. For if history is understood only causally, the past becomes determinative of the future and in place of the inbreaking of the new and surprising only the working out of immanent possibility.

> It has all been filed boys, history has a trend,
> Each of us enisled, boys, waiting for the end.

> (Empson[37])

But if the past is understood only symbolically, allegorically, then the future, too, is de-historicized. Fulfillment is either spiritualized, eternalized, as in gnosticism, or the future is seen as the negation of the past whose form can be imaged not from a midpoint in history but only *a posteriori*, from the end, as in apocalypticism. In both cases there is no creative relation between the present and realization, hope is not creative but esoteric. The future is wholly new; nothing is "*aufgehoben.*"

For the apocalyptic imagination revelation means only a breaking of seals and a lifting of veils, the uncovering of a pattern of events determined in the long ago past. Apocalyptic's images are intended only to unveil the future not to help shape it; imagination is not understood as response-ability, as man's way of responding to the undetermined future. "Apocalyptic knows nothing of an inner transformation of man that must precede the transformation of the world and co-operate with it."[38] The apocalyptic imagination does not recognize the correspondence between inward and outward transformation, the correlation between consciousness and world. Only inward, subjective, transformation may be illusion, hocus-pocus; but only outward transformation is despair turned inside out.

Where the prophetic imagination perceives images the apocalyptic sees ciphers whose meaning is esoteric, subjective, and arbitrary, but univocal. It elaborates its images through logical speculation rather than in "obedience"; it plays with possibility, with omnipossibility. History as cryptogram not poetry; event as mystery not image. Knowledge of the future is not really imaginative but calculative, a decoding. But as Marcel repeats so often, "hope is a mystery not a problem.... 'I hope' cannot ever be taken to imply: 'I am in the secret, I know the purpose of God or the gods, whilst you are a profane outsider'...Such an interpretation...does not take into account all that there is of humility, of timidity, of chastity in the true character of hope."[39] The past is understood only as a sourcebook of images, for the realization of the future means its negation. The apocalyptic imagination is radically dualistic, foresees a complete break between the present age and the one to come. Because it tends to understand its vision of the future literally, apocalypse often issues in exact predictions as to the hour and shape of the coming eon; the vision that begins in despair also collapses in despair as its god fails to appear on schedule.

Prophecy's metaphors, on the other hand, are so over-determined that its hopes are not exhausted by disappointment or fulfillment; its images are recognized as images, not understood literally, and so are open to re-interpretation, re-creation. Hope is expressed in images but the hope is not in the image. Belief is literalism and literalism is idolatry. The prophetic imagination is ready to let go of its images of the future because the truly beyond is also beyond our imagination; nevertheless it is only through the imagination that can we move toward it. The story of the sacrifice of Isaac, the image of the promised future for Abraham, suggests that if we are ready to make the offering, "the Lord will provide."

Both Moltmann and Pannenberg criticize the theology of the generation that preceded theirs for its transcendentalist views of eschatology: Barth for understanding the eschaton as a supra-temporal beyondness and not as the coming future; Bultmann for reducing history to historicity and eschatology to the goal of individual existence. Yet even in Pannenberg and Moltmann we may discern a remnant of transcendentalism which fails to fully grasp the paradoxical tension between present and future that belongs to prophetic eschatology. In Pannenberg because he minimizes the opposition between historical and apocalyptic, in Moltmann because he overemphasizes it.

For Pannenberg that revelation can only be grasped from the perspective of eschatology means that God's divinity will not be revealed until the coming of the Kingdom. "God is God only in the manner that the future has power over the present."[40] He can therefore be known only from the future, from the end of history which means here not, as in Bultmann, history's being broken off, but its completion, its become-wholeness. Pannenberg sees in apocalypse recognition of the providential purpose which links all history, a positive continuation of Old Testament history. He thus stresses in apocalypse not its dualism but its cosmic universalism, its inclusion within the eschatological perspective of the whole of history. He sees no radical disjunction between eschatological event and historical event. An eschatological event is simply a radically new historical event, one for which past history provides no analogy; thus, for Pannenberg even the Resurrection is historical. The Resurrection is proleptic: "The future is still hidden from the world but revealed in Jesus Christ."[41] Pannenberg maintains that the Christ-event can be expressed only in the language of the apocalyptic tradition,[42] by which he seems to mean that it must be understood in relation to the apocalyptic horizon of expectations, that its meaning also can be understood only from the end. Pannenberg's eschatology seems thus to forsake the historical location, to become *theoria,* speculation, to deny the significance of the present. To know God seems to mean to know his plan. Yet Pannenberg wants to say that "the power of the future does not rob man of his freedom to go beyond anything that is present" and indeed calls him to go "beyond what he is and beyond the conditions he finds in the world."[43] Yet the question remains whether for Pannenberg eschatology means only that reality is not yet visible, whether for him the power of the future over the present really leaves no room for the power of the present over the future.

But Moltmann by stressing the radical disjunction, the contradiction, between present and future, the newness of the new, sometimes seems to approach too closely the dualism of apocalypse. He understands the difference between the apocalyptic and the prophetic, recognizes the determinism, the immutability, the never-transcended dualism, the apparently non-historical perspective, of apocalypse, but appreciates in apocalyptic its concern for the whole human and cosmic world and believes that primitive Christianity adopts the same cosmic horizon. This emphasis of apocalyptic seems to him an important correction of the tendency to concentrate on the God-self correlation in a way which makes of the world the self-sufficient world, the *alternative* to God. Christian hope must, he believes, rediscover the world as God's world, as a world full of possibilities. He also values in apocalyptic its sense of the radical difference between fulfillment and all that precedes it, all that is even imaginable beforehand. Otherwise the future is not God's future but is determined by man, by his "talent for dreaming" and acting on his dreams. Moltmann's interpretation of creation *ex nihilo* and of resurrection from the dead stresses this absolute newness[44] in a way which seems to allow little room for the active role of a present directed toward the future in the creation of future, despite his recognition at other points along the way of how hope may create history.

I believe that though primitive Christianity may adopt many of the images of apocalypse, it does not take on the apocalyptic imagination. Bultmann says that Jesus "rejects the whole content of apocalyptic speculation, as he rejects also the calculation of the time and the watching for signs" that he "absolutely repudiates all representations of the Kingdom which human imagination can create."[45] Yet Jesus' parables are full of images of the Kingdom, which differ from apocalyptic images because what the parables represent is not the Kingdom as such but its coming-ness.

Typology maintains the difference between fact and hope, reality and wish, the present and the promised; eschatology announces that this separation is not the last word. As Kant saw, man cannot accept that it is; he must imagine the integration though it cannot be "known," cannot be proven, can never be deduced from the facts. The gap is overcome in vision now, in poetry, in myth. Eschatology is a vision of reconciliation, the reunion of circumstance and inward desire, the integration of the reality principle and the pleasure principle. "Abraham and Orpheus, be near, be near..."

Bloch perceives that Kant saw the indestructibility of the idea of the uncondi-tional, the not-determined, in us. Kant's questions "'What ought I to do?' and 'What may I hope?' have no place in this world of reality. In spite of this they are not nonsense, but rather the highest sense, the only thing which makes sense."[46] But Moltmann seems to ignore the third *Critique* and therefore believes that Kant brings about "an ethical reduction of eschatology" and furthermore a reduc-tion which makes the eschatological perspective completely irrelevant to the world of experience.[47] That is, Kant leaves the gap between knowledge and desire, nature and freedom, experience and hope—in fact, radicalizes it. But this is to stop short of the *Critique of Judgment* and its attempt to establish the unity of experience. Here Kant recognizes the relationships between hope and the future and the imagination. Esthetic perception, the feeling of pleasure, emerges as the center of consciousness. We respond with a feeling of pleasure to the per-ception of pure form when the imagination sees the object suspended from its links to the worlds of theoretical and practical reason, released as free being, unity, completeness, beauty, fulfillment. Because artistic form is an intuitive demonstration of the reality of freedom; art symbolizes that to which no sense perception can correspond. The reconciliation is imaginative, make-believe.

For Freud, also, imagination, fantasy, is the mental activity that retains the reality principle, that continues to speak the language of the pleasure principle. But as Lynch sees, Freud could not succeed in envisioning the reconciliation of the wishing faculty of the libido and the organizing faculty of the ego because he was in touch only with the world of repressed wishes for the inappropriate and the unreal.[48] The imagination, however, exists even apart from repression; it is an independent mental process with its own truth: "the reconciliation of the individ-ual with the whole, of desire with realization, of happiness with reason." As Her-bert Marcuse stresses, "While this harmony has been removed established reality principle, phantasy insists that it can and must become real, that behind the illu-sion lies *knowledge*. The truths of imagination are first realized when phantasy itself takes form, when it creates a universe of perception and comprehension—a subjective and at the same time objective universe. This occurs in art." (The way out: the poem.) "In its refusal to accept as final the limitations imposed upon freedom and happiness by the reality principle, its refusal to accept what can be, lies the critical function of phantasy…. That the propositions of the artistic imag-ination are untrue in terms of the actual organization of the facts belongs to the essence of their truth."[49] Fantasy protects the aspirations for the integral of man and nature which are repressed by reason.

As Marcuse to Freud, so Bloch to Marx, and both to Feuerbach: Projection, wish-fulfillment, fantasy, are the source not only of illusion but also of critiques of the reality principle, are not always expressions of a repressed alienation but sometimes instruments of reconciliation. Fantasy, make-believe, not as escape but as the way to fulfillment. Make-believe as hope's self-projection, creative expectation, an anticipatory reaching toward the future. To relegate real possibilities to the no man's land of utopia is the work of the reality principle. Faith as wish-fulfillment, projection —no longer unconsciously but self-consciously. "To perform the act of figuration consciously.... *that* is imagination."[50] Faith not as belief, but as made-belief, make-believe. "Theology by design"; "Theology as Hypothetical"; "Creative Hope"; "Creative Mythology"; Theology as make-believe.

Through fantasy to the real. Or, "imagining the real." Buber uses the phrase for a meeting with another into which no false images creep, a "bold swinging" into his life in which I attempt to make present his wholeness and uniqueness, his as yet unactualized potentialities.[51] Thus, to imagine the real is to make present the fulfillment of the factually given. Through fantasy to the real. "A non-repressive reality principle." Marcuse calls on us to learn to look upon the images of fantasy as referring not to mankind's badly conquered past but to the unconquered future, to a civilization in which the antagonism of the sensuous and the ordered is reconciled. An unrepressed fantasizing does not produce chaos but form, a new form, a new reality principle: the order of art, "purposiveness without purpose," springing from an erotic exuberance, a delight in the free play of released potentialities.[52] Through fantasy to form. "St. John simply yields himself to the images.... In a long concatenation of images, each fixes the sense of the others, and is itself determined by them. If we appreciate the connection rightly, we feel the new image emerging out of the hidden mind under the evocation of the images already in place."[53]

Through fantasy to the real; to fantasy from the real. The theological imagination. The prophetic imagination. True images, Buber tells us, arise as response, proceed not from subjectivity but from encounter. Bloch also believes that fruitful fantasy issues from a correspondence between the not-yet-conscious, the creative imagination, and the not-yet-come-into being of the object. "Man as active, subjective factor must be in harmony with the objective movement of reality. He must listen to this movement in an almost musical sense."[54] Marcel suggests that to hope means to promote this process from within. A realizing imagination attends to detail, to the concrete, the finite, the particular, the painful and difficult, the absurd and the tragic.

"Imagining the real" means for Moltmann a Christological imagination. A non-utopian theology is not aroused by the idea of possibility; it is not openness toward coming events as such but to the promised future, to Christ and his future. "Without the knowledge of Christ, hope would become merely utopian, a leap forward into empty air."[55] "He is our hope" (Col. 1:27). Moltmann seeks to elaborate what a Christology understood from the perspective of eschatology means. He understands the resurrection as a *promissio* which leads to the Church's *missio*. The resurrection points beyond itself but is itself something new, not just the "meaning" of the cross. It is not that in Christ everything has really already happened but that the results are not yet all in view, nor that fulfillment is wholly future. Hope cannot be reduced to historicity, individualistic liberation from history, nor to history, the working-out of immanent possibility. Christ's future is something which really has not happened yet, although the resurrection is a promise which transforms hope into confidence. The parousia of Christ is the presence of what is coming towards us, so to speak an arriving future...(It) is a different thing from a reality that is experienced now and given now. As compared with what can now be experienced, it is something new. Yet it is not for that reason totally separate from the reality which we can now experience and have now to live in, but, as the future that is really outstanding, it works upon the present by awakening hopes...The *eschaton* of the parousia of Christ...causes the present...to become historic by breaking away from the past and breaking out towards the things that are to come. "The Christian expectation is directed to no other than Christ who has come, but it expects something new from him, something that has not yet happened so far."[56]

Imagining the real: a correspondence between the not-yet-conscious and the not-yet-transformed world. The monomyth: the hero sets out from the world of the past, "dies to the world and comes to birth from within."[57] Yet though the myth sends us out from the world of the fathers back upon ourselves, back upon the inward sphere of our own becoming, the way is not wholly solitary. At the end of the journey, "all seems the greeting of friends." Homecoming. Myth is always overdetermined, always has also a social and a cosmic meaning. Hope, Lynch tells us, is relative, relational, and "must rediscover the other half of itself the outside world."[58] Hope not only imagines, it imagines with, from this mutuality something new and free is born. Myth is the sphere of dream awake and the waking, as Heraclitus said, have a world in common. Buber interprets this to mean that each soul has its logos "deep in itself, but the logos does not attain to its fullness in us but rather between us." "Since we have been a conversation and have been able to hear from one another..." (Hölderlin).[59] The new arises not out of the unshared dream but out of conversation; conversation "does not know in advance just where it will end. It takes its cues from others."[60] Fruitful conversation depends on the "surprising" role of the other. In talking together as in working together there are agnostic elements, "but in so far as it lets itself be determined by the logos it is a common battle and produces the common: out of the extremist tension, when it takes place in the service of the logos, arises ever anew the harmony of the lyre."[61]

In dreams begins responsibility. "The waking have a world in common." "I rebel; therefore we exist" (Camus). To go forth, like Stephen Daedalus, for the millionth time to forge out of the smithy of his soul a new conscience for the race. Conscience, consciousness, a knowing together. Johannes Metz: "What the Christian knows about the future he glimpses only through awarenesses which accompany 'being for others.'"[62] And so Metz calls his theology of hope, *political* theology, a theology essentially related to the world as society. The future as the presence of shared hope. Delmore Schwartz's poem "The First Morning of the Second World":

> Suddenly and certainly I saw how surely the measure and treasure of
>   pleasure is
> being as being with, belonging
> Figured and touched in the experience of voices in chorus.
> Withness is ripeness,
> Ripeness is withness,
> To be is to be in love,
> Love is the fullness of being.[63]

Creative hope. Creative expectation. Marcel: "To expect is in some way to give."[64] The community of hope. The sharing of dreams. Not the mutual cancellation of dreams as in Lawrence Durrell's *Alexandrian Quartet*, but a hidden harmony as in Joyce Cary's trilogy. The harmony of the lyre.

Creative hope. Creative Mythology. Theology as fantasy, no longer unconsciously but self-consciously. Final participation. Theology as make-believe. "Not a movement from *logos* back to *mythos*, but a movement ahead to *mythos*."[65] Marcuse: the imagination is simultaneously, retrospective and expectant. "It looks not only back to an original golden past but also forward to still unrealized but realizable possibilities."[66] Homecoming. Slochower: the promise of myth is fulfillment.[67] Campbell: a "making use" not of one mythology only but of all the dead and set-fast symbologies of the past will make possible the anticipation and activation of the creative imagination out of which new myth may unfold. A making-use like that of Mann's *The Magic Mountain* and of Joyce's *Ulysses*, the two novels which Campbell reads by way of mythic association all the way through *Creative Mythology*: "Musically developed and manipulated motifs of explicit mythological association, echoing and re-echoing, serve in both novels to reveal within all, within each, the image whole that on the waking plane is apparently in pieces."[68] To such a making-use of the old which no longer has the power to generate hope but may still generate images of hope, theology is also called. "Myths generate new forms in the imaginations of those who try to grasp them." A theology of the future. A theology of hope. Theology as make-believe.

"Old father, old artificer stand me now and ever in good stead."[69]

Notes

1. Francis Fergusson, "'Myth' and the Literary Scruple" in John B. Vickery, ed., *Myth and Literature* (Lincoln: University of Nebraska Press, 1966) 144.

2. Austin Farrar, *A Rebirth of Images* (Boston: Beacon Press, 1949) 17.

3. Jürgen Moltmann, *The Theology of Hope* (New York: Harper and Row, 1967) 17.

4. Norman O. Brown, *Love's Body* (New York: Random House, 1966) 56.

5. R. W. B. Lewis, *Trials of the Word* (New Haven: Yale University Press, 1965) 227-235.

6. William Hamilton, "Thursday's Child," in Thomas J. J. Altizer and William Hamilton, *Radical Theology and the Death of God* (Indianapolis: The Boggs-Merrill Company, Inc., 1966) 87.

7. Albert Camus, *The Rebel* (New York: Random House, 1956) 253.

8. Martin Buber, *Between Man and Man* (New York: The Macmillan Company, 1965) 168.

9. Sam Keen, "Hope in a Posthuman Era," in Martin E. Marty and Dean G. Peerman, eds., *New Theology No.5* (New York: The Macmillan Company, 1968) 87.

10. Gabriel Marcel, *Homo Viator* (New York: Harper & Brothers, 1962) 38.

11. Wolfhart Pannenberg, *Grundzüge der Christologie* (Gerd Mohn: Gütersloher Verlagshaus, 1964) 79.

12. Harvey Cox, "Ernst Bloch and 'The Pull of the Future'" in *New Theology No. 5,* 193.

13. Joseph Campbell, *Hero With a Thousand Faces* (New York: Meridian Books, 1956) 30.

14. Hölderlin, "Homecoming," from the translation used in Martin Heidegger, *Existence and Being* (Chicago: Henry Regnery Company, 1949) 239.

15. Rainer Maria Rilke, *Sonnets to Orpheus,* trans. C. F. MacIntyre (Berkeley: University of California Press, 1960) 7.

16. Delmore Schwartz, *Selected Poems* (New York: New Directions, 1967) 73.

17. Fergusson, "Literary Scruple," 140.

18. Ernst Fuchs, *Studies of the Historical Jesus* (Naperville, Illinois: Alec R. Allenson, Inc., 1964) 158.

19. Ernst Käsemann, *Essays on New Testament Themes* (London: SCM Press, Ltd , 1964) 15-47.

20. Moltmann, *Theology,* 16.

21. Philip Rahv, "The Myth and the Powerhouse," in Vickery, *Myth,* 111.

22. Lewis, *Trials,* 206.

23. William F. Lynch, *Images of Hope* (New York: New American Library, 1965) 17.

24. Martin Buber, "Prophecy, Apocalyptic, and the Historical Hour," in *Pointing The Way* (New York: Harper & Row, 1963) 203.

25. Saul Bellow, *Herzog,* quoted by R. W. B. Lewis, *Trials,* 212.

26. Robert Alter, "The Apocalyptic Temper," in *Commentary*, Vol. 41, 6 (June 1966) 65.

27. Lewis, *Trials*, 39.

28. Gerhard von Rad, *Old Testament Theology, Vol. II* (New York: Harper & Row, 1965) 11.

29. Harold H. Watts, "Myth and Drama," in Vickery, *Myth*, 75-85.

30. Marcel, *Homo*, 67.

31. Norman O. Brown, "A Reply to Herbert Marcuse," in *Commentary*, Vol. 43, 3 (March 1967) 83.

32. Wolfhart Pannenberg, "Appearance as the Arrival of the Future," in *Journal of the American Academy of Religion*, XXXV, 2 (June 1967) 118.

33. Moltmann, *Hope*, 120.

34. Johannes Mertz, "Creative Hope," in *Cross Currents*, Vol. XVII, 2 (Spring 1967) 178.

35. Lynch, *Images*, 24, 107.

36. Wolfhart Pannenberg, "The God of Hope" in *Cross Currents*, Vol. XVIII, 3 (Summer 1968) 288.

37. From a verse by William Empson used as the epigraph for Leslie A. Fiedler, *Waiting for the End* (New York: Stein and Day, 1964).

38. Martin Buber, "Prophecy," 204.

39. Marcel, *Homo*, 35.

40. Pannenberg, "God of Hope," 290.

41. Wolfhart Pannenberg, "Redemptive Event and History," in Claus Westermann, ed., *Essays on Old Testament Hermeneutics* (Richmond: John Knox Press, 1964) 314.

42. Pannenberg, *Grundzuge*, 93.

43. Pannenberg, "God of Hope," 290, 294.

44. Moltmann, *Theology,* throughout but cf. esp. 85.

45. Rudolf Bultmann, *Jesus and the Word* (New York: Charles Scribner's Sons, 1958) 39.

46. Ernst Bloch, "Man as Possibility," in *Cross Currents,* Vol. XVIII, 3 (Summer 1968) 277.

47. Moltmann, *Theology,* 46f.

48. Lynch, *Images,* 111.

49. Herbert Marcuse, *Eros and Civilization* (New York: Random House, 1962) 130, 135.

50. Owen Barfield, *Saving the Appearances* (London: Faber & Faber, 1958) 147.

51. Martin Buber, *Knowledge of Man* (New York: Harper & Row, 1965) 81.

52. Marcuse, *Eros,* 134.

53. Farrar, *Rebirth,* 18.

54. Bloch, *Man,* 280.

55. Moltmann, *Theology,* 103.

56. Moltmann, *Theology,* 227, 229.

57. Joseph Campbell, *Creative Mythology* (New York: The Viking Press, 1968) 578.

58. Lynch, *Images,* 19, 24, 146.

59. Martin Buber, "What is Common to All," in *Review of Metaphysics,* Vol. X, 3 (March 1958) 367.

60. Franz Rosenzweig, "The New Thinking," in Nahum Glatzer, *Franz Rosenzweig* (New York: Schocken Books, 1961) 199.

61. Buber, "Common," 375.

62. Metz, "Creative Hope," 177.

63. Schwartz, *Selected Poems*, 154.

64. Marcel, *Homo*, 58.

65. Walter H. Capps, "An Assessment of the Theological Side of the School of Hope," in *Cross Currents*, Vol. XVIII, 3 (Summer 1968) 331.

66. Marcuse, *Eros,* 134.

67. Harry Slochower, "The Use of Myth in Kafka and Mann," in Vickery, *Myth*, 355.

68. Campbell, *Creative*, 677, 659.

69. James Joyce, "Portrait of the Artist as a Young Man," in *The Portable James Joyce* (New York: Viking Press, 1949) 525.

8

Guilt and Responsibility in the Thought of Martin Buber

In undertaking to present Martin Buber's understanding of responsibility and guilt, one must emphasize how important it is to pay attention to the form of his writings, to care for his way of speaking. Because guilt is for Buber the failure to speak, or a false speaking between persons, we must seek to learn from his example what he means by authentic speech and by genuine response. Buber's turning to tale and novel, legend and drama, to translation and imitation, as well as to more scholarly modes of exposition, suggests that Buber recognizes the search for the right form, for the right words and images and structure, as part of the theological task. In several of his introductory passages he has sought to describe how the way of saying and the full understanding of what is to be said are discovered together: the writing of *I and Thou* must wait until he receives the right word; his chronicle *For The Sake of Heaven* is put aside for a quarter of a century until its form has so ripened that the actual writing seems almost a copying. Ben Shahn has defined style as "the shape of one's specific meanings" that cannot be imitated or taught any more than "a tone of voice or a personality."[1] This implies that the way to an understanding of Buber's meaning must lie through attention to his way of shaping content, to what Kenneth Burke would call his "strategy," his "art."

In one of his early books Buber records a Hasidic rabbi's words about the mystery of communication:

> At times my words enter like a silence into the hearers and rest in them and work later, like slow medicines; at times my words do not at first work at all in the man to whom I say them, but when he says them to another, they come back to him and enter into his heart in great depth and do their work in perfection.[2]

85

Like Rabbi Nachman, Buber has wished his words to work in his hearers, has hoped they would take them to that place in themselves "where there is water and the reeds and grasses grow" and where they might reroot themselves. Buber seems always to wish that he could tell a story as the Baal Shem the founder of Hasidism used to so that each of his listeners could recognize in it their own story:

> Under the touch of [his] words, the secret melody of each person was awak-
> ened, the ruined melody that had been presumed dead, and each received the
> message of his dispersed life, that it was still there, and was anxious for him. It
> spoke to each, to him alone, there was no other; he was everyone, he was the
> tale.[3]

Rabbi Nachman's recognition that sometimes understanding comes only when we ourselves undertake the retelling is what Buber himself experienced not only with his reshaping of Hasidic legends but also in his Biblical studies and in his attempts to speak of "the life of dialogue." Because he knows this he helps us recognize that his telling is fulfilled when we his hearers become speakers in turn and take our place in the chain of narrators—not as simply echoes of his words, but as responders to them, for retelling means making present again the newness, the living speaking-ness of the word. By bodying forth its power to create response Buber himself found that a simple translation of the Hasidic legends would not do, that his own blood and spirit was called for, that somehow the more independent his narration became the more faithful it seemed to be.

Buber recognizes that if the exchange of thought between himself and us is to be a living interchange it will be dramatic, for the words that move between persons embody the mystery and tension of word and answer:

> Essential to drama is the fact that two men never mean the same things by the
> words they use; that there is, therefore, no pure reply; that at each point of the
> conversation therefore, understanding and misunderstanding are interwoven.[4]

All conversation is thus, like translation, an attempt at communication across language barriers. As a child Buber used to play a game with himself which began with his trying to translate a word or phrase from one language to another; he would find it in the other language but would discover also that something had been lost. In his game he would imaginatively create a dialogue between two who spoke different languages—perhaps German and French, or Hebrew and Latin—and thus experience the gap between what one said and what the other from his language's way of thinking could receive. Here we have an abyss discovered long ago and a game still to be played: a game which means taking seriously that the word is spoken in the between, into the shared situation.

A living interchange of thought depends on the word being a spoken word, being address and not simply proposition, meaning the other and their common presence. "The importance of the spoken word," Buber says, "is grounded in the fact that it does not want to remain with the speaker. It reaches out toward a hearer, it lays hold of him, it even makes a hearer into a speaker, if perhaps only a soundless one."[5] Meaningful communication depends on the listener's otherness, on his "surprising" role. Language is a system of possible tensions, which ceases to be living language, becomes fixed and frozen, when it no longer means something personal to the two trying to communicate by way of it. Though their understanding of the concept under discussion (as "guilt" and "responsibility" are the concepts before us) may be very close, for each it will have a different "aura," different personal connotations, unless they "join in betraying the logos for logical analysis."[6] It is the ambiguity of the word that constitutes living language and makes conversation fruitful. There is something to hear from the other just because we don't already mean the same thing. Buber, therefore, aims at a philosophizing that would work through these ambiguities rather than seeking a language purified of them. For Buber as for Franz Rosenzweig a "new thinking," the method of speech bound to time and taking its cue from the other, is to replace the method of thinking which proceeds from the abstract and the propositional. Buber recognizes that there were already intimations of this in Heraclitus and in Plato:

> It is to this that the seventh Platonic epistle points when it hints at the existence of a teaching which attains to effective reality not otherwise than in manifold togetherness and living with one another, as a light that is kindled from leaping fire.[7]

Buber understands his own sharing to be philosophical because in it he has sought to transform his unique experience into a universal which might point us to the equivalent event in our own lives, to bring his personal experiences and insights into the world common to all. He says that his basic intention has been to bear witness to an experience and to show it to be one accessible to all in some measure, in some form. In this he believes himself close both to Socrates and to Descartes' *Discourse on Method*. The universal, the concept, serves as a bridge; the focus is still on the two unique events, the one in his life and the one in yours. And sometimes, as in *For the Sake of Heaven* and the Hasidic tales, even the bridge has had the concrete, unique form that characterizes the universal of art. And there are times, as for Buber in writing *I and Thou*, when all one "can do is to indicate indirectly certain events in man's life which can scarcely be described…and in the end…to appeal to the witness of [the hearer's] own mysteries—buried, perhaps, but still attainable."[8] At other times Buber's own experience, his own way to the insight, seems to be the only way of pointing to it; these experiences themselves and not just their universalized form belong to the telling. In his interpretation of Biblical and Zoroastrian mythic images of good and evil Buber writes:

> We are dealing here, as Plato already knew, with truths such as can be communicated adequately to the generality of mankind only in the form of myths…Everything conceptual in this connection is merely an aid, a useful bridge between myth and reality…[Man] listens to the myth of Lucifer and hushes it up in his own life. He needs the bridge.[9]

The conceptual detour thus serves for Buber to make man recognize the relevance of the experience embodied in the myth to his own existence; the bridge opens us to hear the myth as a word spoken to us about us.

Thus when Buber in his William Alanson White lecture on "Guilt and Guilt Feelings" adopts the generalizing language of philosophy to say, "Man is the being who is capable of becoming guilty and is capable of illuminating his guilt,"[10] he is not seeking to define guilt theoretically or abstractly but rather to speak of guilt in such a way as to make you recognize your own guilt and responsibility. In doing this we find him including the example of a life history and a discussion of two novels. To develop his point he must turn to the concrete and unique, to that which unfolds in time.

Yet his discussion throughout this essay remains philosophical in another sense that is very important to him. Although he mentions both the legal plane and the plane of faith he concerns himself here with clarifying the meaning of guilt on what he calls the plane of conscience, the human interpersonal sphere. Because he seeks to illuminate the facticity of our human existence and not to explain it through the idea of God, Buber holds his sharing to be philosophical rather than theological. And although his interpretation of guilt is phenomenologically based, he wants to distinguish it clearly from a psychological analysis that would reduce guilt to guilt feelings. For him, as for Paul Tillich, guilt is ontological as well as pathological; its place is not the soul but the relationship between the self and the human world. "Existential guilt occurs," Buber says, "when someone injures an order of the human world whose foundations he knows and recognizes as those of his own existence and of all common human existence."[11] Guilt is not to be explained away as simply the consequence of the fear of punishment; conscience is not simply the internalization of familial and social taboos, as Freud claimed. Rather, such taboos are themselves the expression of early humankind's recognition "of a primal fact of man as man—the fact that man can become guilty and know it."[12]

Therefore Buber seeks for a way of showing us, of bringing us to recognize, that guilt is truly known when we recognize it not as something that takes place only within the person but between person and person, as an occurrence, as dramatic event. Thus in his novel *For the Sake of Heaven* he presents the conflict between two understandings of human responsibility dramatically, as a conflict between two Hasidic leaders that leads to a climactic confrontation, to catastrophe and failure, and then to death for both of them. The scene is 19th-century Poland at the time of the Napoleonic wars which one of them seeks to fan and through Kabalistic ritual to transform into the apocalyptic wars of Gog and Magog. The Seer of Lublin seeks to bring redemption through magic compulsion, by striving to heighten that darkness and conflict which must precede the ultimate victory of the light; the Yehudi, on the other hand, preaches the need for an inward turning and knows that the way to redemption leads though repentance and hallowing. As his friend Bunam says:

> Truly it does depend on us; not on our power but on our repentance; not until man despairs of himself and turns to God with the entire force of that despair will help be given him.[13]

The Yehudi's understanding of human responsibility as meaning guilt and repentance is here dramatically set against the Seer's search for the power to make use of evil which he regards as a mysterious external force. The Seer discovers the evil in his obsession only on his deathbed when he hears the words, "Thy will is not my will."

Yet even within the novel Buber shows that we really only come to an understanding of evil and guilt as we know it from our own inner experience, as our own condition. As the Yehudi says:

> It does not suffice me to know the truths concerning the evil that is in the world. The evil in the world is mighty; evil has power over the world. And I certainly gain no experience of evil when I meet my fellow-man. For in that case I can grasp it only from without, estrangedly or with hatred and contempt, in which case it really does not enter my vision; or else, I can overcome

it with my love and in that case I have no vision of it either. I experience it when I meet myself. Within me, where no element of strangeness has divisive force and no love has redeeming force.[14]

Buber seems to use his portrait of the Yehudi's two marriages to present us with a clue to that guilt which the Yehudi must have experienced when he met himself and which taught him the meaning of repentance.

Since the Yehudi has stressed the importance of the inward encounter we are not surprised to find Buber looking for a way of understanding guilt which is not as reductive as the psychologist's and yet begins with our own experience. To provide us with knowledge such experience must however have reached a high degree of objectivity. Therefore, Buber believes it is necessary to depend on memory, "to proceed from the viewpoint of a man looking back over his life who has achieved the indispensable distance from even those amongst the remembered inner and outer occurrences which for him are bound up with the actuality of evil but whose memory has not lost the no less requisite force and freshness."[15] Such remembering is different from that which takes place in psychoanalysis because here there is no attempt to penetrate behind the memory to a repressed reality but only to recall an occurrence as reliably, concretely, and completely as possible, unreduced and undissected. This, Buber proposes, is the method proper to philosophical anthropology. Unlike the psychologist who risks transforming the psychic process through self-observation and also shrinks events to their psychic size, the philosophical anthropologist is concerned with the whole body-soul person. He

> renews in reflection the memory of what happened to him in a certain life-context from "within" and from "without" and also grasps the remembered share of other men in the common situations. Such integrative making-present of human existence reflects the recognition that man becomes man in the presence of the other.[16]

The philosophical anthropologist does not become an observer of his or her own life through a division of consciousness but must be willing to let anger rage without trying to gain a perspective. Rather we must depend on memory and recollection like great writers who

> in their dealings with other men do not deliberately register their peculiarities and so to speak, make invisible notes, but deal with them in a natural and uninhibited way, and leave the harvest to the hour of harvest.[17]

Then around these remembered experiences, these writers build up and crystallize their knowledge of human existence, a knowledge that they will often find they can convey only through example. What is to be said cannot fully be detached from the "teaching event." Again and again Buber will say: "I can answer it adequately only by confession"; "From my own unforgettable experience I know well…" As he wrote in *Daniel,* our knowledge always comes to us bearing a sign, an image out of a place and a moment and the seal of a life-experience, a sign which continues to cleave to this knowledge. By sharing our gathered knowledge we seek then to awaken in another his or her self-reflection and thereafter to help them advance from their own experience to a more comprehensive knowledge of existence. At the same time we will find our own knowledge supplemented and deepened by the unique and individual experiences of the other, by what we could learn from no one else but this particular person. Thus the way to an understanding of guilt lies in self-reflection and in communication, lies precisely in seeking to overcome that lack of honesty and unity with oneself and that failure to enter into authentic relation which for Buber constitute guilt.

We must speak of our own life, must throw (*ballein*) the personal image, the remembered guilt, to the other so that it may become symbol (*syn-ballein*); the other must catch it, for the receiving is part of this speaking-out event. Of course, the personal examples which we share are the most paradigmatic ones, drawn "from the province where things succeed, are rounded off, are in fact exemplary."[18]

Thus when Buber speaks of original guilt as remaining with oneself, there seems always present the sign, the image of the place and the moment in which this knowledge came home to him, in which he was shockingly brought face to face with his own guilt, the event which he reports in *Between Man and Man* as "a conversion," the meeting with the unknown young man after a morning of religious enthusiasm for which Buber fails to be really present in spirit. We might say that the movement from this event that took place in the autumn of 1914 to the completed writing of *I and Thou* is a movement from the compact to the differentiated. *I and Thou* is the unpacking of the metaphor, the bringing of the event into the world of word and thereby transforming and "realizing" it, so that the meeting which, after all, did not happen then may be brought to happening now.

It is important for us to see that unlike Buber's earlier mystical experiences with the linden tree and the piece of mica which he reinterprets in *I and Thou* as examples of dialogical encounters with the natural world, here it is the relationship that is not established, the abyss between persons that is not overcome, which leads to insight, to the recognition of the overwhelming significance of conversation with the other. Here guilt reveals the meaning of responsibility, of the call to us to respond with the whole of our being, with full presentness. At first I had thought the order in my title, although right euphoniously was otherwise wrong; now I see that one learns the meaning of responsibility from the concrete failure to relate. As George Fox puts this same insight, the light that shows us our sin heals. The failure is thus experienced as bearing within it not just judgment but also knowledge and a call—a summons to share the knowledge learned here.

The visit from the young man is for Buber what Freud would call a traumatic event, one which remains numinous just because it was not lived out, because it failed. It remains in the past as still living, still gathering "affects" about it; but because his imaginative memory could weave together past and present, the past could later be brought into the present with renewing power, as in Proust, rather than as a compulsive patterning. The memory was brought out of the private world into the interpersonal world not through psychoanalytic transference but through creative remembering. Such philosophical anthropological remembering is very like the process of artistic creation. Time is irreversible, and therefore guilt is not eradicable, as the young man's almost immediate death in the war made Buber realize. Thus the only way forward is through the recognition and admission of guilt and failure. Buber recalls Kafka's parable "Before the Law" and Joseph K's failing to understand that the confession of guilt would cause the door to spring open. That this is an event that is still to be completed means for Buber that it is to be fulfilled through speaking of it to another. For, of course, it is just his being able to speak to another that had been put in question.

It seems to be as imperative for Buber to share this remembered failure as it is for Jean-Baptiste in Camus' *The Fall*—and like Jean-Baptiste, Buber seeks to make you recognize in his story a mirroring of your own. But Jean-Baptiste's confession, like that of Stavrogin in Dostoevski's *The Possessed*, which Buber discusses in his essay on guilt, though true is fictitious. He seeks to dissolve his guilt by showing it to be something all of us share and for which therefore no single one must stand responsible. For Buber the remembering is a way of persevering in his knowledge of the identity between his present self and the self who was thus guilty in the past. The sharing is intended as an act of reconciliation, as working towards a newly won genuine relation with the one now addressed. This visit is for Buber a "symbol of transformation" drawn not from the world of dream or vision or myth as in Jung's examples but from event, from "the world common to all."

As this episode shows, for Buber guilt is not being there for the other; it is the failure to enter into relation, to respond as we are able; redemption from our guilt comes through confession and the re-establishment of relation. There is, however, another event in Buber's life that he has also spoken of as a decisive turning-point and which illuminates another aspect of what guilt means to him. In "My Way to Hasidism" he tells how a passage from the testament of the Baal Shem liberated him from the *olam ha-tohu,* the world of confusion, in which he had lived since shortly after leaving his grandfather's house:

> The whirl of the age took me in. Until my twentieth year, and in small mea-sure even then, my spirit was in steady and multiple movement, in an alterna-tion of tension and release, determined by manifold influences, taking ever new shape, but without center and without growing substance.[19]

The Baal Shem's words about arising from sleep as a new man worthy to cre-ate freed Buber from this indecision and directionlessness. This passage flashed toward him as his moment of self-discovery and also bore for him a summons to proclaim, a task. Thus for Buber being given direction and unity and being called to witness, to share, were but two sides of the same event. In *Good and Evil* Buber speaks of the way of whirl in which he had once been caught as evil imagining, as play with possibility:

> In the swirling space of images through which [man] strays, each and every-thing entices him to be made incarnate by him; he grasps at them like a wan-ton burglar, not with decision, but only in order to overcome the tension of omni-possibility.[20]

He understands the guilt of Adam and Eve to have been of this kind, not a decision between good and evil but an almost dreamlike lassitudinous failure to decide, a falling into evil and guilt.

To be disintegrated is then another form of being guilty—guilty toward the self one is intended to be, called to be, because one is flooded by the chaos of potentialities, distracted by fantasy, the imagery of possibilities:

> Evil is lack of direction and that which is done in it and out of it as the grasp-ing, seizing, devouring, compelling, seducing, exploiting, humiliating, tortur-ing, and destroying of what offers itself. Good is direction and what is done in it; that which is done in it is done with the whole soul, so that in fact all the vigor and passion with which evil might have been done is included in it.[21]

Thus Buber says here that one can only do good with the whole unified soul, as in *I and Thou* he said that one can only say *Thou* with the entire being. I am guilty, then, if I fail to become myself—though I become I so that I may say *Thou*. I am guilty also if I make my life subservient to "seeming," to the images I produce in others. I am guilty if, like Garcin in *No Exit*, I proceed not from what I am but from what I wish to seem, and so let myself be represented by a ghost, hide behind the mask of my *persona*. Buber wants to help us recognize that the call to us to become ourselves is already an address to us, a claim on us, so that here also, guilt means the failure to respond to a legitimate claim or address. He believes that there is a presentiment planted in each of us of "what is meant and purposed for him and for him alone."[22] In seeking to awaken us to this it seems unimportant whether we understand this as the Creator's call to us or as the archetype of individuation—so long as we understand that it is demanded of us, entrusted to us, that we fulfill this intention. On his deathbed, the Hasidic Rabbi Susya is reported to have said: "When I come to be judged I will not be asked, 'Why were you not Moses?' but rather, 'Why were you not Susya?'" The helper for Buber, be he Hasidic *zaddik* or psychoanalyst or educator, is the one who senses this unrealized unity and is able to help the other gather him or herself. This purpose presents itself to us in concrete situations in which we must decide for chaos or for direction. In speaking of two such situations in his own life Buber has sought to uncover the basic structure of this occurrence which we all encounter innumerable times.

For Buber we are beings who are capable of becoming guilty and capable of illuminating our guilt. He seeks to awaken us to this capability that is but the hither side of another human ability—response-ability. There is a twofold movement in human life, distance and relation. Distancing is the presupposition but not the source of establishing relationships. To fail to reach across that which lies between persons is to be guilty of not being fully a person, or as Buber put it in *I and Thou*: without *It* we cannot live, but those who live with *It* alone are less than human. He hopes to stir our will to be confirmed as what we really are and to perceive our fellow humans as what they really are, as whole and unique. The gift for such interhuman confirmation that lets no false images creep in between the one and the other Buber calls "imagining the real." It does not mean looking *at* the other but "a bold swinging" into the life of the particular real persons who confront me, whom I attempt to make present in just this way, in their wholeness and uniqueness.

Dostoevski's Kirilov believed that the death of God would free us from our sense of guilt, and so, to prove his freedom from the fear of death and thereby liberate us, he killed himself. Buber has sought to show that guilt does not depend on our fear of earthly or heavenly retribution, that it arises from our recognition of having injured that order upon which all common human existence is based. Therefore he can speak of guilt as an objective fact without having to introduce the idea of God. He believes that even when we can no longer say *Thou* to the dead known God, if we can still say *thou* with all our being to another living and known person, if we know ourselves as *able* to say this and yet fail to say it, we will still know guilt. Guilt, as Buber sees it, is incurred between persons through their failure to turn to one another as persons.

We humans are for Buber beings who are capable of guilt but not beings who *are* guilty. In Adam's disobedience Buber sees no "must-sin" and hence no original sin. Thus, even when Buber considers guilt on the plane of faith, and not only now on the plane of conscience, we humans are responsibly involved in the reconciliation as well as in the sin. Buber knows what it is to have "one over against him who receives his confession, answers it, 'forgives' him,"[23] but he believes that the Pauline understanding of grace undervalues the role of us humans as God's helpers. It seems to him to spring from a misinterpretation of the dialogical relation between humans and God as one of cause and effect. Buber does not believe we can divide redemption into a part that is dependent on us and another part that is dependent on God; nevertheless, in the meeting between God and human both human action and God's grace are reality. The world, says the Talmud, was created for the sake of human beginning, for the sake of the turning. To be created in God's image means for Buber to be created as response-able.

Because what Buber seeks to do is to awaken us to the capacity for truly going out to the other which he believes lies buried in each of us, his own way of trying to speak to us is an integral part of what he has to say. And so, therefore, is our way of hearing and responding. He seeks to awaken in us the knowledge of what it is to be a person in a world of persons.

In his *Tales of the Hasidim* Buber includes a blessing which one of the Hasidic rabbis is said to have pronounced at the circumcision of the son of a friend, a blessing which includes these three spheres in which we may become guilty: "May you not fool God, may you not fool yourself, and may you not fool people."[24]

Notes

1.   Ben Shahn, *The Shape of Content* (New York: Vintage Books, 1960) 142.

2. Martin Buber, *Tales of Rabbi Nachman* (New York: Horizon Press, 1956) 30.

3. Martin Buber, *The Legend of the Baal-Shem* (New York: Harper and Brothers, 1955) 152.

4. Martin Buber, *Pointing the Way* (New York: Harper and Row, 1957) 63.

5. Martin Buber, "The Word That is Spoken," in *Modern Age*, Vol. V, 4, 354.

6. Buber, "The Word," 356.

7. Martin Buber, "What Is Common to All," in *The Review of Metaphysics*, Vol. XI, 3, 376.

8. Martin Buber, *I and Thou* (New York: Charles Scribners Sons, 1958) 127.

9. Martin Buber, *Good and Evil* (New York: Charles Scribners Sons, 1953) 116, 117.

10. Martin Buber, *The Knowledge of Man* (New York: Harper and Row, 1965) 146.

11. Buber, *Knowledge,* 127.

12. Buber, *Knowledge,* 126.

13. Martin Buber, *For the Sake of Heaven* (New York: Meridian Books, 1958) 113.

14. Buber, *Heaven,* 57.

15. Buber, *Good and Evil,* 122.

16. Sydney and Beatrice Rome, eds., *Philosophical Interrogations* (New York: Holt, Rinehart and Winston, 1964) 59.

17. Martin Buber, *Between Man and Man* (New York: Macmillan, 1965) 125.

18. Buber, *Man and Man,* 36.

19. Martin Buber, *Hasidism and Modern Man* (New York: Horizon Press, 1958) 52.

20. Buber, *Good and Evil,* 92.

21. Buber, *Good and Evil,* 130.

22. Buber, *Good and Evil,* 132.

23. Buber, *Knowledge,* 137.

24. Martin Buber, *Tales of the Hasidim: The Later Masters* (New York: Schocken, 1962) 155.

9

Abraham And Orpheus Be With Me Now

"Abraham and Orpheus Be With Me Now…"

Weeks ago I chose this line from a poem by Delmore Schwartz to serve as my title because it suggests that belonging-together of faith and imagination that I hoped to explore. I had originally intended to let these words do their work while I went ahead and developed the theme without directly alluding to them. I thought I knew what I wanted to say and how. But then towards the end of last week I found myself discovering references to Orpheus in almost every book I picked up—as though I were being told: That line isn't just ornament, it's the thread leading into the heart of the labyrinth itself. "Trust the images—follow where they lead." So then I thought, perhaps I better read that poem again. Therefore last Friday night I went to the neighbor who had borrowed my copy of Delmore Schwartz's *Collected Poetry* to recover the book. But though we looked everywhere in her house, we could not find it. Her husband and mine joined the search but to no avail. Neither looking nor thinking seemed to do any good. Finally Janice said, "Maybe we should consult the *I Ching*. I wanted to ask you to show me how to use it anyway." So we tossed the coins and were directed to the Hexagram Hsien, "Attraction," composed of the trigrams for pool and mountain. The oracle read: "Though they are opposite in character, a mutually responsive feeling enables them to be together. The stubborn and the joyous are conjoined. The holy sage stimulates, man's heart and the whole world is thenceforth at peace." No word about where my book might be, but still I felt a confirmation of the focus on Abraham and Orpheus, perhaps as important as any the poem might have given—because more playful.

Abraham and Orpheus—the man of stubborn faith and the man of joyous song—opposite in character but somehow conjoined.

Playfulness is perhaps better demonstrated than talked about. I realized how deep the Quaker suspicion of play penetrates when I discovered in myself the temptation to speak of it seriously, discursively, literally and so to speak idolatrously. Better to let Abraham and Orpheus manifest a different way of being in the world, a different relation to the divine, than that of the ascetic, works-oriented performance principle that hold us under its sway. In place of Prometheus and Sisyphus, the accepted culture-heroes, Abraham and Orpheus—a faith that expresses itself in laughter and in song. Perhaps they can teach us how to recover a sense of the radical freedom that faith brings—the willingness to release our tight grasp, to let go and let be—and the joy.

Perhaps from them we can learn how to take up the inherited images of faith in a way that allows them to function as images again—which brings them livingly out of the past, not analyzed, dissected, dead—but resurrected. That makes them into song. Laurens Van der Post speaks of taking images into that place in ourselves where there is water and where the reeds and grasses grow. Martin Buber has spoken of recreating the Hasidic tales out of his own blood and spirit. If we understand the process to which these two are pointing, we know how these images from the past can become as close to our own experience as the images of our own dreams. Francis Fergusson tells us that one of the most striking properties of myths is that they have the power to generate new forms (like the differing children of one parent) in the imaginations of those who try to grasp them. There is no one true version. The myth of Oedipus is embodied in Sophocles's trilogy but also in Seneca, Dryden, Anouilh and Freud. The figure of Moses provides a focus for Israel's imaginative remembering over many generations. The beginning point may be historical but the many-layered elaboration of the significance of the originating event reshapes the past and brings it meaningfully into ever new presents. Belief and make-believe are closely related.

As Andrew Lang once wrote:

> Among the lowest tribes we usually find just as in ancient Greece the belief in a deathless Father, Mother, Maker, and also the crowds of humorous, obscene, fanciful myths that are in flagrant contradiction with the religious character of that belief.... For the present we can only say that the religious conception uprises from the human intellect in one mood, that of earnest contemplation and submission, while the mythical ideas uprise from another mood, that of playful and erratic fancy. The two moods are conspicuous even in Christianity. The former, that of earnest and submissive contemplation, declares itself in prayers, hymns, and the dim religious light of cathedrals. The second mood, that of playful and erratic fancy, is conspicuous in the buffoonery of miracle plays, in the burlesque popular tales about our Lord and the

Apostles, and in the grotesque sculptures on sacred edifices. The two moods are present and in conflict through the whole religious history of the race.

But how often the mood of playful fancy has been repressed and how one dimensional, how disembodied, faith may then become. One of the unfortunate results of the fixing of the biblical canon is that it inhibits the free retelling of the story, suggests that there is *a* right way of telling the story. Rudolf Bultmann shows what the closing of the canon did to the Jesus tradition, how it prevented the gospel form from developing into a literary genre by arbitrarily cutting off its development. Yet in the nineteenth century histories of Jesus which sought to accommodate the biblical Jesus to a liberal theology and in the Christ figures of some contemporary literature we can see how the Christ image may nevertheless be reincarnated in our imagination. A living faith seems to depend on images which still have such power over us. Otherwise we live in a time between the gods, a time when the old gods have died, become idol-objects, and the new have not yet made their presence known. Hosea tells us that when faith has become literal trust in a contractual covenant, Israel must return to the wilderness and "dwell many days without king or prince, without sacrifice or pillar, without ephod or teraphim." Only then will she be prepared to return and seek the Lord. The images of God must themselves be allowed to be with us as they will be, not as we want to fix them. That, as Yahweh told Moses, is what it means to have a living God.

We often forget how freely the ancient Israelite historians and prophets took up and reworked stories and traditions borrowed from surrounding cultures. Their work displays a syncretism that we tend to shy from, a demythologizing and a remythologizing. This freedom demonstrates their recognition of these images and myths as metaphors, not idols filled with a fearful sacred power that might contaminate. Even the sexual imagery of the despised Baal cults can be taken up in the service of Hosea's prophecy. The Jewish legends collected by Ginzburg, the folk versions of the same episodes recounted in our Bible, show how these myths were taken into the Israelite imagination and continually renewed. The story of Abraham has been told and retold by the Talmudists and the authors of the medieval Kabala, by St. Paul and by Kafka. Kierkegaard revealed its power over him in *Fear And Trembling* where his "let's pretend" revisions of the story of the sacrifice of Isaac illuminate all the more clearly the peculiar nature of the faith of the biblical patriarch.

The Old Testament shows us that *mythos*, symbolic narrative, reveals meanings irreducible to *logos*, conceptual abstraction. To tell what the Old Testament means by faith is to retell the story of Abraham. It is not to say "Abraham, Abraham" as piously as possible and invoke thereby a conception of faith derived elsewhere, nor is it to replace the story with a definition—that would be to commit the heresy of paraphrase. There can be no literal relation to Abraham. Paul shows his understanding of this in his "Letter to the Romans" where he writes that the heirs of Abraham are not the adherents of the law but those who share his faith, a faith which means letting go all assured knowledge of God. Only he who is pulled to retell the story once again participates in its meaning.

The story begins with Abraham being called away from the world of the fathers: "Go from your country and from your father's house to the land that I will show you." So Abraham goes, leaving behind all that is known, ordered, established and ventures towards the unknown, trusting in a promise whose fulfillment lies many generations ahead. "And Abraham went"—unlike Lot's wife, without even looking back. Because he trusts when there are no signs, he is called righteous, one who knows how rightly to order his life—on the basis of his trust, not on the basis of works or accomplishments. Yet the narrative includes many episodes which recount how Abraham messes things up when he tries to arrange them, when he manipulates them, tries to make them come out right, when he gets anxious. Abraham is no more the man of perfect faith than Job is the man of perfect patience. He tries to protect himself from a Pharaoh's jealousy (and later from Abimelech's) by telling Sarah to say she is his sister not his wife and only succeeds in creating needless complications. When he and Sarah despair of ever having the promised child, they arrange for Sarah's handmaid Hagar to bear Abraham a son, only to find that again they have created a situation that makes Sarah wildly jealous, that brings deep grief to Abraham, and that leads to Hagar's and Ishmael's being sent into the desert. (What fun the legends have in elaborating this tale—in inventing episodes that will absolve Sarah, or in imagining a later reconciliation between Abraham and Hagar.)

Like Job, Abraham contends with a God who doesn't conform to his sense of meaningfulness; he rebels against absurdity, argues against the vengefulness of God in the Sodom and Gomorrah episode. To go forward in trust is not the same as going forward in resignation. There is a real struggle on Abraham's part, a sense of responsibility for a just ordering. In the open, in the wilderness where Abraham finds himself after the departure from his father's house, nothing is ever sure and Abraham has to experience this over and over again. A God you seem to know surprises you—the whole basis of the relationship is put in question.

Yet there are joyous surprises too. Both Abraham and Sarah laugh at the thought of having a child in their old age—and so when Isaac is born he is the child of laughter. He is called "He laughs" and represents joy and fulfillment and how funny life sometimes is. But then Abraham is called to take this much-loved son and offer him as a sacrifice on a mountain in Moriah. He is called now to leave the world of the son, of a glimpsed future, to give up Isaac who for him is an image of God, of God's trustworthiness—and he goes—thereby manifesting his willingness to go through that, not trying to make sense of it yet trusting that sense would be made. But Isaac is saved and so is laughter—that laughter which sustains in the wilderness, in that time-between in which Abraham lives out his life.

This laughter brings Abraham close to Orpheus and to Orpheus' brother, Nietzsche's Zarathustra who came, so Nietzsche tells us, in order to teach us how to laugh.

Orpheus is the singer who awakens the secret melody of each person, the musician with magic in his notes. There is a gentleness to Orpheus and in the music his lyre sings. He brings peace through song not force—like David and like Isaiah's Prince of Peace. His music is the music of Apollo—it is soothing, calming, the notes bring purgation, catharsis. As Rilke tells us:

> Orpheus sings…
> Animals from the silence, from the clear
> now opened wood come forth from the nest and den,
> and so it came to pass that not from fear
> or craftiness were they so quiet then
> but to be listening.

But there is another, more Dionysian, aspect to Orpheus. He has confronted the underworld in order to rescue his mate Eurydice and met its threat with song. He too has dared the unknown, the confrontation with nothingness, protected not by Abraham's absurd faith but by song. It is only when he loses trust in his music that he looks back and loses Eurydice. Later Orpheus is himself torn to pieces by Dionysus' jealous maidens—a death so like Dionysus' own as to suggest a mythic identification between the two.

We can understand then how Orpheus comes to be seen as one who knows the secrets of Hades, one who knows how to meet the terrifying, absurd, unknown, untamed. We recognize why in the sixth century he is made the prophet of a mystery religion, one who has power to intercede with the powers below for those who live by his precepts. Like Abraham he is made into one who teaches the rite of initiation and the founder of a book religion. As though the wisdom of song or of laughing trust could be codified!

Orpheus the divine singer becomes one who knows the true origin of things, who underwrites a cosmogony different from Hesiod's in which Night is the primal principle, Zeus swallows the earlier gods and all is reborn, recreated out of him. Humans are created from the smoking remnants of the Titans who have just feasted on Dionysus, Zeus' son. The Orphics played with the inherited mythology, used the same mythical material but infused it with new meaning. In the climactic myths of the *Phaedo*, the *Gorgias* and the *Republic* Plato, who clearly did not take the Orphic traditions literally, nevertheless conveys his serious regard for them:

> We must ever maintain a real belief in the ancient and sacred stories, those that proclaim that our soul is immortal and has judges and pays full requital for its deed as soon as man has left the body behind. Now to maintain that these things are just as I have said will befit a man of common sense—but this or something similar is true about our souls and their dwelling places.

Not only Plato took over the Orphic mythology.... There is a ceiling painting in the Domitilia catacomb in Rome that has Orpheus not Jesus at its center; there are many early Christian representations of Orpheus as the good shepherd, as the Davidic psalmist. It was understood then that the Greek image and the Christian could be playfully conjoined. Orpheus' peace-bringing song is but another manifestation of the joy-bringing word of Jesus. Jesus in his parables preached of a future that fills not empties the present—and meanwhile, as Abraham experienced, much is happening that is cause for laughter. Existence is song, Rilke wrote in his *Sonnets To Orpheus:*

> Song as you explain it is not passion
> Not striving for some end at last attained
> Song is being. Easy for gods to fashion.
> But when shall WE BE?
>
> Orpheus and Abraham be with me now...

10

God Made Man Because He Loves Stories: Martin Buber's Retellings of the Hasidic Tales

For Martin Buber the search for theological understanding presented itself as a search for forms. We miss what is important to Buber unless we pay heed to his reaching for a way of speaking. His turning to tale and novel, to translation and imitation, suggests how much form matters to him. Often in the introductions to his books he describes how the way of saying and the full understanding of what is to be said are discovered together: the writing of *I and Thou* must wait until he receives the right word; *For the Sake of Heaven* is put aside for a quarter of a century until its form has so ripened that the actual writing seems almost a copying. Buber expresses his consciousness of the inseparability of form and meaning in his essay, "The Word that is Spoken":

> Every authentic poem is also true, but its truth stands outside all relation to an expressible What. We call poetry the not very frequently appearing form of words that imparts to us a truth which cannot come to words in any other manner than this one, in the manner of this form. Therefore, every paraphrase of a poem robs it of its truth.[1]

His lifework exemplifies his effort to bring poetry and theology closer together. His search for words that will not remain between the walls growing layer by layer like decaying leaves is a search for a more imaginative theology; he hopes for a rebirth of the theological imagination.

Buber's interest in the imagination extends back to his very earliest writings but it is only gradually that he appreciates that a theological imagination must be a verbal imagination, a celebration of *logos*, of the primal wedding between meaning and speech, in which words and not simply visual images would participate in a playful pointing to the divine. From the image-makers of the Bible he learns that images are not added on to experience but that the imagination participates in the original perception and in the preserving memory. Because we humans are given a word to answer and not simply to repeat, faithful response must be imaginative and creative. The theological imagination seeks not to clothe but to body forth events, to express their eventfulness, their speaking-ness. Buber's care for words, for their sensuous, gesturing play, expresses his care for the living word.

Because in Buber the search for form is recognized as part of the theological task, we are prepared to discover form and content, mode of formulation and theological understanding, changing together. Attention to the form of his works therefore also means attention to the form of the life work as a whole. When we read Buber's works "in order" we discover a circling back again and again to images and events first introduced in the earliest books. These images are brought into the new present not through simple repetition but through re-interpretation. Thus Buber's meeting with the linden tree is for him unforgettable, though at first he speaks of feeling its bark as his own skin, then in *I and Thou* of its being bodied over against him, and finally of its waiting for him in order to become green.[2] This spiraling movement becomes visibly structural in *I and Thou* where a few soon-announced motifs are repeated again and again like a refrain more richly burdened at each reappearance. In a more subtle way it is also the form of the lifework as a whole, a form whereby the whole life may be carried livingly into the present, a form of translation.

In our present essay we wish to focus on one manifestation of this movement, the development of Buber's interpretation of Hasidism and particularly the relation between his earlier and later translations of the Hasidic legends. At all periods Buber looked upon the tales rather than the more theoretical and homiletic formulations as the most authentic source of Hasidic teaching; nevertheless there is a remarkable difference in his understanding of these tales at the beginning and end of his career, a difference reflected in his very different versions of them. As Buber becomes more conscious of the tension between responsible and fanciful elaboration, he no longer understands translation as an unfolding of images but rather as an attempt to let words burst forth from event. This change in the form of his retelling parallels his transition from mysticism toward a theology of address and response.

Although Buber is the most well known interpreter of Hasidism in our time, he has been severely criticized for an emphasis on the tales that purportedly leads him to a modern subjectivist and world-affirmative interpretation of Hasidism. Gershon Scholem, the contemporary expert on the history of Jewish mysticism, believes that Buber's disregard of the significance of kabalistic lore as a creative impulse in Hasidism and of the strictness of the Hasidic relation to the Torah has falsified his picture of Hasidism. He blames this distortion on Buber's dependence on just those sources that lie most open to misinterpretation, the tales.[3] Yet in his own book, *Major Trends in Jewish Mysticism*, Scholem (though admittedly more interested than Buber ever has been in relating Hasidism to the history of Jewish mysticism and to seeing it as a stage in a process which also includes Lurianic Kabalism and Sabbatianism) characterizes Hasidism much as Buber does. He recognizes that "this burst of mystical energy was unproductive of new religious *ideas*, to say nothing of new theories of mystical knowledge" and that, therefore, the new element must be sought "in the experience of an inner revival." He recognizes that the leader, the *zaddik*, is set apart by his character rather than his learning; he repeats a Hasid's confession, "I did not go to the 'maggid' of Meseritz to learn Torah from him but to watch him tie his boot-laces." Most significantly, he concludes:

> When all is said and done it is this myth that represents the greatest creative expression of Hasidism. In the place of the theoretical disquisition, or at least side by side with it, you get the Hasidic tale. Around the lives of the great Zaddikim, the bearers of that irrational something which their mode of life expressed, legends were spun often in their own lifetime…To tell a story of the deeds of the saints has become a new religious value and there is something of the celebration of a religious rite about it. Not a few of the great Zaddikim…have laid down the whole treasure of their ideas in such tales. Their Torah took the form of an inexhaustible fountain of story-telling. Nothing at all has remained theory, everything has become a story.[4]

It is to this inexhaustible fountain that Buber has sought to bring us. As Walter Kaufmann suggests, here the question of historical accuracy may not be quite the right one. What we are given is what Buber heard in Hasidism, though it is true that others have not heard it quite so. That he added nothing does not mean that he gave back what he found. Through cutting and polishing, Kaufmann believes, Buber has in his later translations brought these tales to their fulfillment; they cannot be improved by shortening; he has given them their definitive form.[5] But the way toward the discovery of this definitive concentrated form was by no means a direct one and it is its turnings that we intend to trace here.

Buber's earliest retellings of the Hasidic tales arose out of the experience of being personally addressed by some words from the testament of the Baal-Shem, the founder of Hasidism: "He takes unto himself the quality of fervor. He arises from sleep with fervor for he is hallowed and become another man and is worthy to create and is become like the Holy One, blessed be He, when He created His world." Buber had turned to a study of Jewish mysticism (after a deep immersion in Christian mystical literature) during a period when he had become aware of an abyss between himself and his own true being, of being lost in the whirl of omni-possibility, "determined by manifold influences, taking ever new shape, but without center and without growing substance." He had sensed that the way toward self-discovery must for him lead through self-discovery as a Jew. The advent of the Baal-Shem's words was for him the moment of self-discovery and at the same time the discovery of a task. Thus from the very beginning Hasidism meant for Buber a release from the arbitrary. The image of the man worthy to create works creatively on him and leads him into his own creating, to the first writing that seems genuinely his own. He begins by seeking to retell Hasidic tales and legends so as to re-present the creativity of the Baal-Shem and of Rabbi Nachman.

Buber found these tales in a form in which folk-fantasy had already been at work upon them and he discovered that a new forming, not just simple translation, was called for. Buber speaks of his work with the tales first told by Rabbi Nachman, one of the later Hasidic masters, as a "re-creation," not a translation but a retelling "with full freedom out of his spirit as it is present to me...Even the new pieces that I inserted express my unity with the spirit of Rabbi Nachman: more adequately than the direct disciples, I received and completed the task, a later messenger in a foreign realm."[6] What makes Buber feel of "one spirit" with Nachman is that he in his time had consciously been a renewer as are Buber and Perez and Kafka in theirs. All give new shape to the old themes and take on themselves the responsibility for renewal. It should, however, be noted that although Buber's retelling is a re-forming, it is so in a very conservative sense. There is not in his retelling of Nachman's tales the radically new sense of how one tells a story, of how myths are to be brought into the present, that we find in Joyce's *Ulysses* two decades later. Nor does Buber present the Hasidic stories, as does Perez, as parables of the distance between himself, the modern intellectual, and the inherited pieties.

Buber is at first repelled by the Hebrew in which much of the Hasidic teaching is recorded, by its "ungainliness," "unshapeliness," almost as though he were applying the standards of Renaissance painting to Byzantine mosaics or to Picasso. For the awkwardness and abruptness which disturbed Buber may, in fact, characterize the Hebrew language and express its understanding of reality. Erich Auerbach's decades later comparison of the literary style of the *Odyssey* and of the Genesis story of Abraham's sacrifice of Isaac is relevant here.[7] As he shows, in the *Odyssey* there is a leisurely progression of events with uninterrupted connections, fully externalized descriptions with everything taking place in a uniformly illuminated foreground. In the Abraham story there is no place description, only the voice coming out of hidden-ness and Abraham's answering "Here I am." This response presents Abraham's psychological situation, his being-there before God. Then there is the journey whose whole meaning lies in the moment toward which father and son are going. Buber hears the difference already, just as he has recognized that for the Jew the ear is more important than the eye, time more than space,[8] but he does not yet appreciate it. His conception of retelling is still a very painterly one, the *nachbildung* of a *vorbild*. At this time it is the rhythm, the unique qualities of the language he is translating into,[9] that are the governing, guiding ones. Actually, however, most of Nachman's tales had been preserved not in Hebrew but in Yiddish, that "tenderly blunt, melancholy and bitter idiom in which the young Nachman spoke to God and was not answered." The Yiddish language, "suited to the picaresque or the lyric,"[10] more leisurely, more spacious, more intimate, was much more congenial to Buber. Yiddish was "a language of great plasticity, neither set nor formalized, always in a rapid process of growth and dissolution; it was a language that intimately reflected the travail of wandering, exile, dispersion; a language drenched with idiom.... a blend of speech so persistently complex and ironic—really a kind of underground speech—so as to qualify severely the very values it was dedicated to defend."[11] In translating from Yiddish to German, Buber sought to surround this everyday speech and rhythm with a new elegance and dignity. He was able to retain the possibility of an accumulation of sensuous impression, the plasticity and the wandering quality but not—in these first versions—the self-reflective irony.

Buber speaks of his disappointment with his first attempts at translating two of Rabbi Nachman's fairytales because they seemed to make only more visible the distortions he had found in the stories as transmitted. In his collection of Yiddish tales Irving Howe includes a translation of one of Nachman's stories that shows what these tales are like apart from Buber's reshaping. This story is much more didactic, more forcedly paradoxical, more stripped to the narrative bone, than any of Buber's versions except perhaps "The Steer and the Ram," the first on which Buber worked which he was willing to include in the original 1905 version of *The Tales of Rabbi Nachman*. Buber found the story's dependence on an allegorical understanding of the Jewish prayer shawl an image so uncongenial that he left it out of the 1927 edition because "its content had become too strange."[12]

Buber discovered that he had to tell the stories from out of himself, "as a true painter takes unto himself the lines of the models and achieves the genuine image out of the memory formed of them." At this time he frequently uses the analogy with painting to describe his work. He speaks of wanting to recreate the form distorted "through the confusion of lines and the muddying of the pure colors."[13] Some of the tales seem indeed to be more like pictures than like narrative representations of event. For instance, "The Master of Prayer" puts into images the kabalistic teaching about the scattering of the Shekinah (God's presence in the world). There are lovely descriptions for each of the ways that God is present in the world, for each of the values that humans have chosen to regard as ultimate. Redemption is "opening the ways" that go between the different lands in which these values rule and thus the reunification of the Shekinah.

Many of these stories present a contrast between two ways of being in the world, between people governed by two opposed impulses, but these are fairytales and so the opposition is always played out on an externalized level. The focus is not on inner reflection nor on dramatic conflict but on the patterned relationship working itself out. As in Jung's model of the psyche, the assumption is that the opposing poles are essentially complementary. They are related through being joined in one event, one story, and thus what is conceived as basically a timeless pattern is shown as a temporal unfolding. "The Clever Man and the Simple Man" is a version of the classic tale of the brilliant young man who went out into the world and mastered all its arts and of the simple one who stayed in the village as a rather clumsy cobbler yet was nevertheless joyous and in good spirits from morning until evening. Then each is called by the king whom neither sees. The simple man, once he is convinced that it is not a jest that he should be called, responds and becomes prime minister. The clever one doubts, is sure that the message could not possibly be intended for him, wonders whether the message is really from the king, begins to believe that perhaps there is no king at all. Sure enough, although he searches all through the kingdom, he is never able to find anyone who has ever seen the king until he comes to the simple man who sees him daily. "What makes you think," jeers the clever man, "that he with whom you speak is actually the king?" We are reminded here of Kafka, of K's desperate attempt to get in touch with the castle or of the Chinese Emperor's message to his humble subjects, but there is not here the same stress on the hopeless, inescapable paradox of faith. Kafka presents the world surrealistically, as it appears to someone anxiously searching for meaning in a world without coherence, a world of disorder and senseless repetition, a world of nightmare. The world of these early retellings of Buber's is more that of the daydream.

Buber began with the tales but in bringing them to us he prefaces his book with several introductory chapters. He needs exposition to interpret the meaning of the tales because in his retelling they have become more image or melody than word. He sees that poetic form and prosaic content need each other but has not here managed to integrate them. The introduction begins with a chapter on Jewish mysticism and its relation to the ecstatic wisdom of Eckhart, Plotinus and Laotse. The mystic's prayer, Buber writes, is not from I to Thou but God himself speaking the innermost word within. This is the event, God's speaking within; the external word is only its garment. Rabbi Nachman said, "I have in me teachings without clothes, and it is very hard for me until they clothe themselves."[14] The metaphor is already to be found in the *Zohar*: "Thus had the Torah not clothed herself in the garments of this world, the world could not endure it. The stories of the Torah are thus only her outer garments, and whoever looks upon the garment as being the Torah itself, woe to that man."[15] This conception of word is at this time Buber's own. Word is a form for wordless meaning rather than a response to an address. The original event is not really a word event. In prayer, Nachman says, the external words are meant to crumble to ashes so that only the will and fervor ascend. In these tales Buber again and again refers to the true voice of a person as a wordless melody. The "Master of the Word" is the one found singing to himself, not addressing a crowd of people; when he stops, the song was "around him and lived in all places and yet was always different and new, for each of the things sang it in his own way. The things and beings relayed the song; the air itself became a singing mouth and bore the melody into the worlds."[16] The *nigun*, the melody, not the words, is the essence of the song. In his retelling Buber sought to reproduce the *nigun*. Like Jung when he interprets dreams, Buber begins with the image in its visual aspect rather than with the verbal report on it and with the shape of the entire story rather than with separated out of context elements. Often in reading we sense that though the directing line has come from the source, what we have is like a watercolor done from a black and white sketch. At this time Buber applauds the Hasidic enthusiasts who dare to join their rambling dreams to the given text, although later he will come to be suspicious of any kind of arbitrary elaboration. In Buber's retelling, Nachman's teachings are not only clothed but well-dressed. The stories have been made charming but there is little sense of Nachman's voice, of his style, little that is particularly Jewish in rhythm or aura or point. Buber's poeticization which presents symbol as image and event as pattern seems quite soon even to him an apprentice's achievement.

Buber's next book, his 1908 *The Legend of the Baal-Shem*, also has its source in the traditional legends, but what Buber sought to do here was not to retell stories that the Baal Shem had himself told but rather from the tales told about him to reconstruct the inner process of the master's life. Again Buber had begun by translating and again found that more was required: the stories did not become any more winged in translation than they had been in the crude and clumsy original. He discovered that the more independent his narration became, the more "faithful" it seems to be:

> And therefore although by far the largest part of the book is autonomous fiction composed from traditional motifs, I might honestly report of my experience of the legend: I bore in me the blood and spirit of those who created it and out of my blood and spirit it has become new.[17]

Retelling means making present again the newness, the living speaking-ness of the word: "I stand in the chain of narrators, a link between links; I tell once again the old stories and if they sound new, it is because the new already lay dormant in them when they were told for the first time."

Although he is still writing within the spell the Hasidic legends have cast over him, Buber feels that he has in this second attempt resisted the temptation of a "poetic" recreation; there is here a felt limit on the freedom of retelling, a sense that "alien," too personal, elements are forbidden:

> The existing material was so formless that I was tempted to deal with this as with some kind of subject-matter for poetry. That I did not succumb to this temptation I owe to the power of the Hasidic point of view that I encountered in all these stories. But within these limits, which forbid the bringing in of alien motifs, all freedom remained.

Buber refers to this retelling as an epic one. In epic there is meaningfulness beyond the personal; what happens here concerns human destiny as such; narrative and deed arise out of an historical and a supernatural background. But Buber makes no attempt (except somewhat in the expository introductory section) to represent the "real" life in its world historical connections nor even to suggest the local atmosphere of the *shtetl* setting. "I only desire to convey the relation to God and the world that these men intended, willed and sought to live.... I build up his life out of his legends which contain the dream and longing of a people."[18] In a sense then this is still a "poetic" telling, one that reconstructs the life using only the subjective pattern of significant associations and not the objective structure of verifiable biographical and historical events; it does not focus on the inseparable intermixture of the two dimensions. Buber does not yet seek to reconstruct the intended occurrence of each individual story as he does decades later in *The Tales of the Hasidim* nor ask "What event in real life could have been experienced in such a way as to lead to this interpretation?" as he does in his *Moses*.[19]

In *Nachman* the tales were thought of as "clothing" to the teaching, now they are its "body," they embody it, body it forth. Buber calls what he is presenting here "myth" and speaks of myth as that which has at all times vitalized and yet also endangered Jewish religiousness. He sees Judaism as the fight against myth, not the victory over it, but precisely the conflict. He makes a distinction between legend, the form that myth takes within Judaism, and myth as it is elsewhere:

> The legend is the myth of the calling. In it the original personality of the myth is divided. In pure myth there is no division of essential being. It knows multiplicity but not duality. Even the hero only stands on another rung than that of the god, not over against him; they are not the I and the Thou. The hero has a mission but not a call. He ascends but he does not become transformed. The god of pure myth does not call, he begets; he sends forth the one whom he begets, the hero. The god of the legend calls forth the son of man the prophet, the holy man.
> The legend is the myth of I and Thou, of the caller and the called…The legend of the Baal-Shem is not the history of a man but the history of a calling.[20]

"The myth of the I and the Thou"—"familiar as a word that you always have at hand and believe you know—although it has never occurred to you to regard it."[21] Here, as often again, it seems as though Buber had quickly set down a phrase that he will understand more and more as his life continues.

For Buber the distinction between legend and myth is decisive; as he comes to a deeper appreciation of its meaning he sees that the difference is also a formal one: the Hasidic legends cannot be expressed with the austerity appropriate to Buddhist myth nor with the intimacy of the Franciscan tales. Buber's search for the appropriate form for the myth of the calling is continued in *I and Thou*, in his *Tales of the Hasidim*, and in the chronicle, *For the Sake of Heaven*. However, in *The Legend of the Baal-Shem* Buber failed to find a form which would express the peculiar character of legend. Despite the introduction, the adventures of his hero fall into the pattern of the "monomyth" described by Joseph Campbell in *The*

Hero with a Thousand Faces and could indeed be interpreted along the lines of the Jungian myth of the self in search of the Self.

Buber begins his narrative with the words addressed to the Baal Shem by his dying father when he was yet much too young to understand them. The words were words of warning: that in the beginning, at the turning, and at the fulfillment, he would be confronted by the Adversary within and without, "in the shadow of a dream and in living flesh," And words of reassurance: "your soul is an ore that no one can crush and only God can melt."[22] The remaining stories are the report of this prophecy's fulfillment, of the Baal-Shem's encounters with the Adversary and of his deepening understanding of the truth of his father's words. He remembers those words for the first time when he is yet a child leading some younger children to school in order to protect them from a werewolf. The words return with meaning and so with strength-giving power. He finds that evil, the dark heart of the werewolf, has to be touched and thus released from its suffering. The next morning a poor possessed charcoal burner is found lying dead with great peace on his face. It reminds us of the Grimm fairytale of the princess and the toad in which the princess must touch the toad that lies in bed beside her and, admitting her horror, throw it against the wall before it can be released and transformed into the fairy prince.

In *The Legend of the Baal Shem* Buber sought to present not just the stories the master told but the man himself as word, not fairy tales but the legend of a mythic hero whose life is a response to a calling and who knows that the word is more than something you take into your mouth. It is rather "as if you entered into the word…The word is an abyss through which the speaker strides."[23] The Baal Shem lives in a world of word. He is able to understand the language of all creatures; his words come to listeners, "in whom an answer slowly awakens and warms itself by listening."[24]

In one episode, called "The Revelation," the Baal Shem, now about thirty, is an innkeeper in the Carpathians. One day he recognizes that he stands in the midst of waiting: the peaks look down on him and wait; the springs look up at him and wait. Soon after a rabbi who has stopped at the inn becomes the witness of creation. He tries to drive off after a short rest but almost immediately finds himself in the midst of a great whirl. All the things of the world seem dislodged from their places and lost in confusion, and even within himself there is turmoil and darkness. Then the innkeeper appears, makes his way through the chaos and restores order and direction. The second morning the rabbi hopefully sets out again but this time he encounters not chaos but rigidity and determinism. Heaven is a brazen, heavy shell and all the things of the earth grow imprisoned and sickly in their places; he feels himself also transfixed in an inescapable prison. Again the innkeeper appears. This time he is able to "melt the shell of passivity" and the rabbi finds he can freely return to the inn. On the third day the rabbi experiences the "abyss." Everything lies in silent agony. "All things were enveloped by the abyss and yet the whole abyss was between each thing and the other." Then the helper comes once more and through his touch the things are joined and see and know and grasp one another. "They saw each other through his eyes and touched one another through his hand. And since the things came to one another, there was no longer an abyss, but a light space of seeing and touching." During the remaining three days the rabbi too becomes part of the waiting, and when the seventh morning comes he and the innkeeper celebrate the holy Sabbath together.[25]

The Tales of Rabbi Nachman and *The Legend of the Baal Shem* were both written before the First World War, before *I and Thou*, before Buber's translation (with Franz Rosenzweig) of the Hebrew Bible into German, long before the books of biblical commentary. Forty years later, after Buber's move to Jerusalem, during the Second World War, he returned to his work of retelling Hasidic legends. In his 1946 preface to *Tales of the Hasidim* he writes: "Along with much else I owe the urge to this new and more comprehensive composition to the air of this land. Our sages say that it makes one wise; to me it has granted a different gift: the strength to make a new beginning. I had regarded my work on the Hasidic legends as completed. This book is the outcome of a beginning."[26] At this time Buber returns to artistic modes of communication not only in these *Tales* but also in a chronicle novel and a mystery play. These works express his understanding of a theological imagination that can be distinguished from the fantasizing imagination that he has come to reject more and more deeply. Buber is convinced that religion cannot be demythologized, that an objectifying theology inevitably leads to the "eclipse of God." He now understands the work of the imagination not as a shaping of visual images but as a responding in words that wed speech and meaning to one another. Where in his earlier retellings he had expanded, he now concentrates—in order to allow meaning to burst forth from event. The mythical no longer means a poetic unfolding; it does not even any longer mean the myth of the calling, the myth of dialogical relationship, so much as it means the myth of the turning, of *tsuvah*, of dramatic reversal.

Buber relates the aim of his new retelling to the central theme of his later years: "I was concerned…with restoring immediacy to the relation between man and God, with helping to end 'the eclipse of God.'" He says that his undertaking was neither a literary project nor a work of detached historical scholarship but "derives from the desire to convey to our time the force of a former life of faith and to help our age renew its ruptured bond with the Absolute."[27] Buber believes that "Hasidism has its word to speak in the crisis of Western man," a word which might heal "the sickening of our contact with things and beings," which might remind us of the purpose for which we are here on earth. He knows that he himself cannot speak as a Hasid, that his own relation to Jewish tradition is wholly different; he recognizes also that he carries Hasidism into the world "against its will": "Hasidism wishes to work exclusively within the boundaries of the Jewish tradition and to concern no one outside of them" but he had found something "that hid itself in Hasidism" that "would, or rather should, go out into the world."[28]

In most cultures, Buber says, the legend developed side by side with the literary form of the short story, whereas the Jewish legends were not given a literary form until our own time. In explaining why, he implies a criticism of his own earlier versions: "The inner tempo of the Hasidim is frequently too impassioned, too violent for the calm form of the literary tale, a form which could not contain the abundance of what they had to say. And so the Hasidim never shaped their legend into a precious vessel; with few exceptions it never becomes either the work of an individual artist or a work of folk-art; it remains unformed." Buber is now highly critical of the kind of expansion and coloring that the Grimm brothers had found permissible in their rendering of German folk stories. Although he still finds it expedient "to begin by giving up the available form (or rather formlessness)" of the extant tales, Buber now seeks to "reconstruct the events in question with the greatest accuracy" and "in a form suited to the subject-matter." He has learned that the more "naked" his telling is, "the more adequately it fulfills its function."[29] His new versions are anecdotal, highly condensed narratives in which events are reported so as to culminate in a significant saying; they report actions of the *zaddikim* that lead into dialogues in which the *zaddik* conveys his teaching.

Perhaps we can most clearly appreciate the kind of cutting and polishing which Buber now finds appropriate if we contrast his retelling with that of a translation in the scholar's sense, Louis I. Newman's *Hasidic Anthology*. Some idea of the difference is implied by the very ordering of the books: Newman's contains more aphorisms than anecdotes, and arranges both aphorisms and tales alphabetically under such categories as: the After-Life, Borrowing and Lending, Circumcision, Diligence, Exile and Redemption. Buber has arranged the tales in order to illuminate the individual characters of the *zaddikim* and to recreate the pattern of their lives. Buber's versions tend to be more compact, more sharply pointed. Buber tells us that Rabbi Bunam "is said to have once addressed his pupils thus: 'I wanted to write a book called Adam which would be about the whole man. But then I decided not to write it.'"[30] Newman renders this thus: "Said Rabbi Bunam: 'It was my intention to write a treatise under the title "Man." It was to require merely a quarter of a page, and the whole meaning of the term "man" was to be included therein. But after consideration, I changed my decision, lest my treatise might lead to false commentaries.'"[31] Even more striking is how much more moralistic Newman's versions often are:

Newman:	Before the Besht became renowned, it chanced that once he lacked money for the Sabbath. At sunrise on Friday, he went to the house of a stranger, knocked on the door, and then took his departure. The man awakened, dressed hurriedly, and ran after the Besht. When he approached the Besht and observed his poor raiment, he asked: "If you came to me to obtain aid, why did you go away?" The Besht replied: "When a man is born, his sustenance is born with him. It is merely his imperfections that cause his livelihood to await the persuasion of his efforts before it comes to him. Since each man's imperfections are different in scale, the amount of effort required is also different. I believed that my life, removed from worldliness, entitled me to gain my needs with but little effort; hence I knocked at your door. After I had made this effort, I felt confident that God would aid me, and it makes no difference to me whether help comes through you or through another person."
Buber:	It happened in the days of the Baal-Shem's youth, that one Friday he had nothing at all in the house to prepare for the Sabbath, not a crumb, not a penny. So early in the morning, he tapped at the window of a well-to-do man, and said: "There is someone who has nothing for the Sabbath," and walked on. The man, who did not know the Baal-Shem, ran after him and asked: "If you need help, why do you run away?" The Baal-Shem laughed and replied: "We know from the Gemara that every man is born with his livelihood. Now, of course,

the heavier the load of one's sins, the greater effort one
must make to get the appointed livelihood to come.
But this morning I felt scarcely any weight on my
shoulders. Still there was enough to make me do a little
something—and that is just what I did."[32]

Most characteristic of the difference between Buber's telling now and that of
his own earlier efforts is the contrast between "The Revelation" as recounted in
The Legend of the Baal-Shem and the episode now entitled "The Baal-Shem
Reveals Himself." Here again we have the story of the rabbi who stops at the inn
and is detained against his will to stay for the Sabbath. Again the Sabbath eve is
the one on which the Baal-Shem receives the message that the time of self-con-
cealment is over. But now in place of those strange experiences of whirl and
prison and abyss that restrain the rabbi, there is only a broken wheel and similar
everyday obstacles to force him to stay on until Friday comes. There is nothing to
arouse the rabbi's wonder at his host; the guest is asked to pronounce the bene-
diction over the wine lest his host "give himself away by the fervor he knew he
could not conceal." But in the middle of the night the guest awakens and sees a
great white light that shines out from the hearth. Although there is now none of
the earlier elaboration of this vision, no word of a bluish light which incessantly
changed color nor of an unmoving white light which surrounds the master's
head, the effect is the same: the rabbi recognizes whom he has seen.[33]

What we note in these tales is their austerity, how often they have been
reduced to the simplest interchange:

> "What was most important to your teacher?"
> "Whatever he happened to be doing at the moment."
>
> "I have no key to open you."
> "Then pry me open with a nail."
>
> When Mendel was in Kotzk, the rabbi of that town asked him: "Where did
> you learn the art of silence?" He was on the verge of answering the question,
> but then he changed his mind, and practiced his art.[34]

The concentration *of* words is at the same time a concentration *on* words, on the saying that arises from the event:

> Rabbi Elimelekh's servant once forgot a spoon for Rabbi Mendel who was a guest at Rabbi Elimelekh's table. Everyone ate except Rabbi Mendel. The zaddik observed this and asked: "Why aren't you eating?"
>
> "I have no spoon," said his guest. "Look," said Rabbi Elimelekh, "one must know enough to ask for a spoon, and a plate too, if need be." Rabbi Mendel took the word of his teacher to heart. From that day on his fortunes were on the mend.
>
> Rabbi Moshe of Kobryn said: "When you utter a word before God, then enter into that word with every one of your limbs."
>
> One of his listeners asked: "How can a big human being possibly enter into a little word?"
>
> "Anyone who thinks himself bigger than the word," said the zaddik, "is not the kind of person we are talking about."[35]

Often we are reminded of Kafka's parables. Kafka's Abraham "who was prepared to satisfy the demand for a sacrifice immediately, with the promptness of a waiter, but was unable to bring it off because he could not get away, being indispensable" is so like the rabbi of Apt who postpones again and again until it is too late, always for the best of reasons, his visit to the rabbi of Naskhizh, for whom everything, "teaching and prayers, eating and sleeping, is all of one piece." Kafka's "Before the Law" ends with the doorkeeper telling the man: "No one but you could gain admittance through this door, since this door was intended only for you. Now I am going to shut it." The Hasidic "Story of the Cape" tells of a woman who comes to the maggid of Kosnitz with her longing for a son and is told how his mother's willing gift of her one fine thing, her good cape, had led to his own birth: "'I, too,' cried the mother, 'will bring you a good cape of mine so that I may get a son.' 'That won't work,' said the maggid. 'You heard the story. My mother had no story to go by.'" Mendel's silence suggests Kafka's servant who cannot understand much less answer the questions put to him by the stranger in the tavern and so apologetically rises to leave but is told: "Stay, that was only a test. He who does not answer the questions has passed the test."[36] The relationship goes deeper than these parallels in dramatic situation; it reaches to the inner tempo of the poetry. Both Buber and Kafka bear in themselves the blood and spirit of those who created the Hasidic tradition and each has made it new out of his own blood and spirit; each found that in the age of the eclipse of God a tightening, an intensification, a dramatization was demanded.

In *Tales of the Hasidim* Buber includes an anecdote about one of the Baal-Shem's disciples writing down all of his master's teachings. When the Baal-Shem discovered this book, he studied it for a long time, page by page, and then said, "In all this there is not a single word I said. You were not listening for the sake of heaven...so your ears heard what I did not say."[37] Perhaps this anecdote will serve as a preface to the "chronicle" Buber wrote during the Second World War, *For the Sake of Heaven.* What led him to compose a full-length fictional narrative was his search for an inter-relating form for "an enormous coil of stories of inter-related content" that he had come upon in his work on the Hasidic tales but which demanded a different method, not just the juxtaposition of anecdote with anecdote nor a theoretically conceived connection. What was called for was a delineation of the outer and inner dramatic patterns and, though these were very fragmentary, the filling in could no longer be done with the old freedom but only through obedience to what was demanded by the events and characters them-selves. Buber tells us that the theme of the book had already seized him during the last year of the First World War but it is only now in the new "atmosphere of telluric crisis" that it comes to ripeness, that is to form, that it announces its inner completion.[38]

Even fictional creation now means to Buber a bodying forth of what confronts him rather than of his own response to it. What he seeks to convey is the shape of dramatic necessity, of form as what Francis Ferguson calls the "*moto spirital.*"[39] Now it is the incidents and characterization that create the form; there is no longer any room for poetic ornamentation. The form of this novel is dramatic in Ferguson's sense; its action is definable by a verb expressing the purpose. As Chekov's *Three Sisters* can be summed up "To go to Moscow," so *For the Sake of Heaven* can be rendered "To bring redemption in our time, God willing." This chronicle is dramatic also in the sense articulated by Buber in his 1925 fragment on "Drama and Theatre": "With the mere antagonistic existence of the persons that proclaims itself dialogically, the dramatic is essentially present; all action can only unfold it."[40] Here the drama arises out of the conflict between the Hasidim of Pshysha and of Lublin, between the Yehudi and the Seer, between redemption prepared through the inward turning and the way of magic compulsion. To present "the cruel antitheticalness" of existence this conflict represented meant penetrating "to the kernel from both sides."[41] *For the Sake of Heaven* succeeds as drama, as the dialogues in Buber's 1913 book, *Daniel*, never begin to, just because here Buber has succeeded in this penetration. This is not just theology in fictional guise; it is event. The characters live for us because they live for Buber as persons, not as self-created aspects of self. True, each represents a point of view, indeed, a theological point of view, but it is one he lives by—and thus one which gives him life—perhaps more life than Naptha or Settembrini of Thomas Mann's *Magic Mountain* have, for they live only by their hope that Hans might live by their ideas. The opposition between the Yehudi and the Seer is not an esthetic contrast but a genuinely ethical conflict. The differences between them are not just theoretical but existential. Therefore the confrontation between them must be eventful and not just dialogical.

The Seer and the Yehudi are in conflict about the relation between symbol and reality. The Seer seeks to use his powers to end this eon and bring in another; the Yehudi through hallowing, to transform this world. This is again the conflict so often described by Buber between the apocalyptist and the prophet, the contrast between the artist who creates a world out of his own soul and the artist who seeks to praise and rescue the things of the earth. Indeed, the severest critics of Buber's interpretation of Hasidism have praised his own faithfulness to the given, to his sources, in this novel. Rivka Schatz-Uffenheimer wonders whether Buber really knows what he has put in the Seer's mouth, so authentically Hasidic does it seem to her. In the picture of the Yehudi, also, she finds Buber has been true to his sources rather than his inclinations, so that even in Buber's presentation the description of the Yehudi's death marks his return to Hasidism, the rejoining of Pshysha to Lublin. Despite the necessary exaggerations of a novel, the reader, she finds, has here been brought to the true earth of Hasidic Judaism: the circle of Lublin has been given flesh and blood.[42]

The action centers on Lublin throughout but to the participants it seems as though the outcome of the Napoleonic wars were being decided in this provincial city. The atmosphere of telluric crisis is created in such a way as to include our world and its wars as well. The events on the battlefield are only surface happenings; their meaning is being determined in the Seer's house of study; the reality is not the war but the symbolical ritual drama enacted by the Hasidim. This novel is about a "turning" as *The Legend of the Baal-Shem* had not been at all; there we were still in the realm of the picaresque, of development perhaps but never of the turning. Here the tension is wound more and more tightly. As it deepens we recall the last lines of *I and Thou*:

> In each new aeon fate becomes more oppressive, turning more shattering. And the theophany becomes ever nearer, increasingly near to the sphere that lies between beings, to the Kingdom that is hidden in our midst, there between us. History is a mysterious approach. Every spiral of its way leads us both into profounder perversion and more fundamental turning. But the event that

from the side of the world is called turning is called, from God's side, redemption.[43]

Turning, the biblical *tsuvah*, the redirection of one's heart to God, is for Buber the central event in human life. The world was created for the sake of this beginning, for the sake of such reversal. That is why in *For the Sake of Heaven* the action must build up to such a climax. As the novel moves toward the turning, it focuses more and more on the conflict between the Seer's and the Yehudi's understandings of how the turning, the turning of the world to God, is to be brought about. They agree that it will come as a light after darkness. For the Seer this means a rejoicing in Napoleon's victories as perhaps the beginning of the wars of Gog and Magog. For the Yehudi it means trust even when we believe ourselves lost. Both agree that the beginning must come from the human side. The Seer believes this means "we must strive to heighten earth's conflict." The Yehudi and his friends reply: "Truly it does depend on us; not on our power but on our repentance; not until man despairs of himself and turns to God with the entire force of that despair will help be given him." The climax comes through a confrontation that neither had sought. Despite their fundamental opposition, each respected and loved the other; the conflict comes to a head only because it is blown up by the Seer's jealous disciples. The Yehudi cries in fear: "How can you know what you're doing by fanning this evil?" and is told: "It is too late in time to think of the individual soul."[44]

The central moment comes in connection with a celebration of the Seder during which each of the participants was to fix his entire soul upon the coming of redemption during each part of the ceremony and to do so according to very special attitudes and aims as directed by the Seer. The Yehudi and his friends agreed to participate since the goal was that which "from the beginning was the aim of their common and passionate desire: the coming of redemption, come as it may." But all is lost because everywhere disturbances took place. In Kalev the rabbi recited the *Haggadah* in Hungarian; in Tschernobil the *Afikoman* was not to be found. Everywhere disturbances took place, but especially in the Yehudi's home in Pshysha. The Seer's attempt has failed: "It was on the day after that Pesach night that Napoleon Bonaparte set forth from Paris upon that decisive campaign which put an end to his dominion."[45] The cause of failure is seemingly completely accidental: the celebration in Pshysha had been delayed by a squabble between the Yehudi's wife and his mother. So there is failure and then, shortly after, death for both the Yehudi and the Rabbi. The Yehudi willingly dies to bring the Seer a message from heaven because "if one is permitted to bring a message from the world of truth, it is bound to be a message of truth." The night before he dies the Seer suddenly cries out in a strong voice: "For My plans are not your plans, neither are your ways My ways, is the saying of the Lord." As the Maggid had said, "Everything points to the coming of redemption, but otherwise than we are inclined to think."[46]

At the end of *For the Sake of Heaven* the Yehudi and the Seer have each in a sense converted the other. But they are both dead; the Messiah has not come; the way of magic coercion has failed. Now, and this is clearly *our* now, we are on another spiral of the way; in our eon fate has become still more oppressive; the turning would be even more shattering. "We await a theophany..."

> When the great Rabbi Israel Baal Shem-Tov saw misfortune threatening the Jews it was his custom to go into a certain part of the forest to meditate. There he would light a fire, say a special prayer, and the miracle would be accomplished and the misfortune averted. Later, when his disciple, the celebrated Maggid of Mezritch, had occasion, for the same reason, to intercede with heaven, he would go to the same place in the forest and say: "Master of the Universe, listen! I do not know how to light the fire, but I am still able to say the prayer" and again the miracle would be accomplished. Still later, Rabbi Moshe-Leib of Sasov, in order to save his people once more, would go into the forest and say: "I do not know how to light the fire, I do not know the prayer, but I know the place and this must be sufficient." It was sufficient and the miracle was accomplished. Then it fell to Rabbi Israel of Rizhyn to overcome misfortune. Sitting in his armchair, his head in his hands, he spoke to God: "I am unable to light the fire and I do not know the prayer; I cannot even find the place in the forest. All I can do is to tell the story, and this must be sufficient." And it was sufficient.

Notes

1. Martin Buber, "The Word That Is Spoken," *Modern Age*, V, 24 (Fall 1961) 358.

2. Martin Buber, *Daniel* (New York: Holt, Rinehart and Winston, 1964) 54; *I and Thou* (New York: Charles Scribners Sons, 1958) 8; *The Knowledge of Man* (New York: Harper & Row, 1965) 15.

3. Gershon Scholem, "Martin Buber's Hasidism," *Commentary*, XXXII, 4 (Feb. 1964) 19.

4. Gershon Scholem, *Major Trends in Jewish Mysticism* (New York: Schocken Books, 1961) 327, 338, 344, 349.

5. Paul Arthur Schillp and Maurice Friedman, eds., *Martin Buber* (Stuttgart: W. Kohlhammer Verlag, 1963) 581.

6. Martin Buber, *Hasidism and Modern Man* (New York: Horizon Press, 1958) 59, 57, 62.

7. Erich Auerbach, *Mimesis* (New York: Doubleday, 1953) 1-19.

8. Cf. Buber's introduction to *Jüdische Künstler* (Berlin: Jüdischer Verlag, 1903).

9. Whereas in his "verdeutschung" of the Hebrew Bible he seeks to reproduce in German the peculiarities of the original.

10. Irving Howe and Eliezer Greenberg, editors, *A Treasury of Yiddish Stories* (New York: Meridian Books, 1954) 32, 10.

11. Howe, *Yiddish Stories*, 231-233.

12. Hans Kohn, *Martin Buber: Sein Werk und Seine Zeit* (Köln: Joseph Melzer Verlag, 1961) 305.

13. Buber, *Modern Man*, 61.

14. Martin Buber, *Tales of Rabbi Nachman* (New York: Horizon Press, 1956) 29, 30.

15. Gershon Scholem, ed., *Zohar* (New York: Schocken Books, 1963) 121.

16. Buber, *Nachman*, 142.

17. Buber, *Modern Man*, 63.

18. Martin Buber, *The Legend of the Baal Shem* (New York: Harper & Brothers, 1955) vii, ix, x.

19. Martin Buber, *Moses* (New York: Harper & Brothers, 1946) 16.

20. Buber, *Baal Shem*, xiii.

21. Buber, *Daniel*, 102.

22. Buber, *Baal Shem*, 52.

23. Buber, *Baal Shem*, 39.

24. Rainer Maria Rilke, *Duino Elegies* (Berkeley: University of California Press, 1961) 51.

25. Buber, *Baal Shem*, 62-72.

26. Martin Buber, *Tales of the Hasidim: Early Masters* (New York: Schocken Books, 1961) xii.

27. Martin Buber, "Interpreting Hasidism," *Commentary*, VI 3 (Sept. 1963) 224, 218.

28. Buber, *Modern Man*, 38, 40, 22.

29. Buber, *Early Masters*, vi, vii, viii, ix.

30. Martin Buber, *Between Man and Man* (New York: The Macmillan Company, 1965) 118.

31. Louis I. Newman, *Hasidic Anthology* (New York: Schocken Books, 1963) 230.

32. Newman, *Anthology*, 513; Buber, *Early Masters*, 45.

33. Buber, *Early Masters*, 46 ff.

34. Buber, *Later Masters*, 173; *Early Masters*, 277, 301.

35. Buber, *Early Masters*, 125, 169.

36. Franz Kafka, *Parables and Paradoxes* (New York: Schocken Books, 1963) 41, 65, 183; Buber, *Early Masters*, 166, 286.

37. Buber, *Early Masters*, 56.

38. Martin Buber, *For the Sake of Heaven* (New York: Meridian Books, 1958) ix, xi.

39. Francis Ferguson, *The Human Image in Dramatic in Dramatic Literature* (Garden City: Doubleday, 1961) 98-105.

40. Martin Buber, *Pointing the Way* (New York: Harper & Row, 1963) 64.

41. Buber, *Heaven*, x.

42. Schillp and Friedman, *Buber,* 296-301.

43. Buber, *I and Thou*, 119, 120.

44. Buber, *Heaven*, 108, 113, 255f.

45. Buber, *Heaven*, 276, 280.

46. Buber, *Heaven*, 280, 309, 293.

11

Daydream

"One does not dream with taught ideas…"

That line from Gaston Bachelard echoes even within the dream. Within the dream there are no teachers, only fellow dreamers: not only Bachelard but also Freud and Jung, and Eliade and Heidegger, Rilke and Anais Nin, Stanley Hopper and Richard Underwood, Hermann Hesse, Joseph Knecht and Joseph, the son of Jacob. They are present in my dream, neither forgotten nor remembered but simply there, as voices that speak, in the form of phrases and lines that are alive within my own psyche. Their images and mine are deeply interfused. For I find myself belonging to a league of dreamers close brother to that League of Spiritual Wayfarers which set out on their journey to the east a generation ago. We play with one another's images and through our musing together hope to create the art and rituals whereby we may bring others into the sphere of dream awake. Long ago the Muses were responsible for connecting the realm of waking consciousness with the hidden realm of vision; today it falls upon us dreamers. In the playspace of daydream we are not isolated from one another as we are when we dream in sleep. We meet in a world given shape by the shared images. From within that world we call to others. We call from within the dream, gently, gently; we call by telling about the dream, by daydreaming about daydreaming…

For the dreams of day are different from the dreams of night.

When the Chinese sage awoke he was confused: was it in dream that he had been a butterfly or was that reality and this the dream? As daydreamer I know: I am woman and butterfly; I am Psyche.

The dreams of day are as different from the dreams of night as is the happily dancing butterfly from the roughly wakened moth.

But the story of Psyche really begins at night and with the rude awakening, begins when the wax from Psyche's candle rouses the consort whom she had known only in the dark and fearfully, and awakens in her the longing for more conscious relationship. She awakens from his dream no longer content to be his anima and wonders what she must do to become herself a dreamer. It is only later, only after she has accomplished the labors imposed on her, that Psyche can meet Eros in the daylight, the daylight of daydream, and out of their intercourse become pregnant with their daughter, Pleasure.

When Freud speaks of Eros it is mostly of the Eros still involved in the dark underworld, the Eros who nightly engages in battle with Thanatos. In the dreams of night the conflict goes on; the battle between the god of love and growth and creation against the god of death, repetition, and aggression is endlessly repeated.

In the dreams of day there is new birth. The offspring of the meeting between Psyche and Eros when they meet in conscious love is a female child. Daydreams too are feminine in languages that care enough to notice: *reverie, songerie, Traumerei*—able to give birth in their turn to new daydreams.

Daydreams are born in a place between the world of day and the world of night. They come upon us, as Bachelard observed, in moments when one feels something in oneself which is going to sleep and something which is awakening. Daydreaming finds us at the moment of transition, suspended. To daydream is to be in the between, to be nowhere, to be in the nowhereland, in Utopia. But in daydream we make this nowhere point a world, a world created by metaphor and vision. The daydream does not take place at the boundary between dream and waking thought but rather erases that boundary. The daydreamer knows that to overcome the artificial separation of conscious and unconscious modes of thought requires that we be awake from sleep—and yet dream on.

In the dreams of night we are abducted to foreign lands often disguised to look familiar and homelike but irredeemably uncanny. The space within which daydreams happen may appear new and outlandish but it is always home and daydreaming is always homecoming. We live in a time when we have been taught that you can't go home again; but you can—though only as an adult. Daydreaming is not a return to the infantile, a yielding to oceanic feeling; it is active imagination.

Daydreaming is psyche-delic, mind-expanding; in it both modes of psychic functioning, the conscious and the unconscious, the directed and the spontaneous, the verbal and the visual, conjoin. The daydream is the embrace of masculine and feminine aspects of the self; it is androgynous existence.

And where the dreams of night condense images and fuse many into one, the dreams of day take delight in endless multiplication, reflection, metamorphosis. There is an almost infinite reservoir of dream material, all that has ever entered my world, not only yesterday or in earliest childhood but at any moment along the way, which I arrange not to convey a secret message but to create happiness. As long as the wisdom of the night is smuggled surreptitiously across the border it will be compactly wrapped, aphoristic. Daydreams suggest an economy of affluence, largesse, of wish unstintingly indulged.

For daydreams express the dreamer's wholehearted wish to continue imagining, not the conflict between our longing to stay asleep and the rebellious claim to be heard of other long denied and forgotten desires. In the dreams of night there is a struggle between the anarchic impulses of the Id and the conservative repressiveness of the ego that issues in a compromise formation. Dreams express ambiguity, discord, drama; they represent distortion, dream*work*. Daydreams are constructed out of love not fear, as play not work, and therefore assume a very different shape (a shape which our night dreams too may take when we learn to play with them, though the beasts of night are never wholly tamed).

In daydream there is display not disguise, intercourse not battle, conception not victory. Because there is no need for disguise in construction, because we can avow the shaping wish, there is less need for plot, for what Freud called secondary elaboration. Where there is no conflict, there is no need for a narrative, dramatic elaboration and thus there is allowance for a self-indulgent delight in the image itself. In daydream there is no forced condensation, no need for one image to substitute for another, there is space and time for both. Because in daydream there is a conscious recognition of the connections between one image and another, an appreciation of metamorphosis, we have metaphor not cipher. The daydream means new creation, the child, Pleasure. In both the dreams of night and those of day we are freed from the linear time of waking life; in night dream all times are compressed into one, in daydream time is opened up. Moments in the present become gates into the past not masks for it. Here there is nothing that might be called residue, all is sublimed.

Daydreams feel like our own creation. We are not spectators or helpless performers ignorant of the role assigned us, but ourselves the active shapers. There is a mysterious anonymity about the subject of our night dreaming that not only Bachelard but also Rieff and Ricoeur have remarked upon and which we, too, must sometimes have felt; but in our daydreaming it is clearly our familiar ego that dreams and that moves about within the dream as hero, yet an ego different from the practical one of everyday life, a psychedelic hero whose aim and chief delight is beauty and play.

In daydream we self-consciously take on the heroic, mythic role and thus retain a humorous perspective. In us as in Thomas Mann's Joseph the mythical has become subjective, taken up by the active imagination. Freely and joyously we celebrate our fresh incarnations of the typical and recurrent; because the mythic identifications are conscious, they are playful, festive, comic.

Freud looked mostly at the dreams of night where we, all unconsciously, repeat the ancient myths, especially the tragic myth of Oedipus. He saw unceasing conflict, mitigated only by moments of negotiated ceasefire. This immersion in the tragic element led him to invoke in his own writing the virtues tragedy affirms: insight, skepticism, and courageous endurance.

But daydreams seem more like fairytale than like myth, constructed not to give language to a darkly hidden truth but to entertain and delight. Myths seem heavy with sacred archetypal meaning, while fairytales seem insignificant, only products of a light and profane hour. But the comic vision of an ultimately happy ending is not so easily dismissed. There is that in us which recognizes it as the truer, though more hardly won, perspective. The god of night is Dionysos who presided at the birth of tragedy; above his shrine at Delphi is built the temple to Apollo, god of the daylight dream. As Rilke muses, "Where two heartways meet..."

Daydreams are dreams of happiness. Freud speaks of daydreams as the expression of unsatisfied wishes and suggests that happy people never daydream. Yet even he sees how daydreams attach themselves to moments of fulfillment (not frustration) in our childhood and project future fulfillment. It is only about the present that he is wrong, though his recognition of the relationship between the play of children and the daydreams of adults should have guided him more truly. He sees expressed in the play of the child the child's wish to be grown up and discovers again and again in dream the adult's wish to be a child again. What he misses is that the daydream grows out of another wish, the wish to be growing up, in transition, the desire to recover the openness of the child's world. This is very different from the return to the child's world that happens in the dreams of night. There we return over and over again to the fixed scenes of trauma, like the Whippers in Kafka's *The Trial,* forever frozen into the same posture—the moments of trauma that determine our present. But daydreaming returns us to a past that is still open, in motion, changeable, reshapeable. In daydream we re-imagine our childhood not only remember it, as in Hesse's novels the remembered Calw becomes the re-imagined Gebersau. For daydream the return to childhood means the return to hope, happiness, beginnings. It is the gift of a long childhood that releases us humans to think symbolically, perhaps we dreamers who are not poets dream of a sharing even playfully in the first place; but we are separated from the child's playfulness as from its sexuality by the period of latency. It is as important that we rediscover play as that we learn to recover our polymorphous sexuality. In daydream the experiences of childhood function symbolically not just as linear causes of our present but as still alive moments, still pregnant with many futures that we happily imagine. These childhood events do not shape our present unbeknownst to us but knowingly we make with them a more richly dimensioned present. In daydream we do not become children again but the child and the adult in us discover how to play together.

To discover how to play together: that is what it is all about. The ego that shapes the daydream is different from the ego of everyday but still ego, still that in us that is social, turned toward others. Daydreams concern our lives with others, our ambitions and our eroticism—but in a world without failure or hate, where no one succeeds at the expense of another and all loves are returned. I long to incorporate others into my play not just as figures of my dream but as fellow imaginers, fellow dreamers, fellow players. For the dreams of day can be shared wholly differently from the way we communicate the dreams of night. We are not restricted to reporting on them afterwards; we can speak out of them while they are still in process. We can include the other not as interpreter but as fellow dreamer. For we need no interpreters. Daydreams are not easily forgotten; we are not ashamed of them. They do not need to be explained or decoded. They do not need to be brought into consciousness for they are already there. In daydream we reach for a wider consciousness, a true knowing together.

This is the new consciousness that Stephen Daedalus felt called upon to forge. He longed for the poets' power to entice us into their dreams. Poets recreate their dreams and make them available to us. Language becomes the medium of vision; image is transposed into word; word-play and word-creation the paradigm of all play and creation. But perhaps we dreamers who are not poets dream of a sharing even more complete, less verbal and less retrospective, more full-bodied and more immediate.

First, though, we must practice dreaming, as the poets do, in broad daylight. Freud knew that our daydreams were our most cherished possessions but that most adults concealed their daydreaming, made of it their most closely held secret. To have secrets is important for a child in process of shaping a self, but an adult no longer needs such concealment—that is preliminary. For the adult to give up his shame, the shame of still being a player, with images and longings if not with blocks and dolls, is as important as transcending our shames about sexuality. It is no more shameful for the adult still to harbor the playing child than for the child to prefigure the sexual adult. Freed of the need for secrecy, we enjoy our daydreams without shame. Daydreams are to be welcomed, loved and named.

When they are concealed and solitary they are more like night dreams than they need to be, because pushed into an artificial darkness.

Freud believed that when ordinary daydreamers share their fantasies they bring no pleasure, but repel others or leave them untouched. Only the poets' artistry and the "forepleasure" it yields persuade us to heed the dreams they share with us and enjoy them unashamed. It is as if forepleasure were not also true pleasure, as though we were charmed into the dream by its esthetic beauty against our wishes. Yet the meaning of daydreaming is simply that it brings pleasure and happiness. The daydream is true wish fulfillment—we do not look outside the dream for some other, more real, fulfillment. The future that the dream creates is not a linear future beyond the dream but joyful expansion of the moment within which the dream happens. It is just this delight in delight, this sense of fulfillment, that we hope to express.

For daydreams are to be shared, inhabited together. Just because they are our most cherished possession we yearn to know how to give them to those we love. We share our night dreams, too, of course. Geza Roheim says we do so to assure ourselves that we are safely back in the world of others and yet retain some talisman of the frightful, beautiful passage through the dark. Sandor Ferenczi suggests that we relate our dream to the person it seems to be about and that he listens because he understands it to be about the dreamer. But we can participate in one another's daydreams so that they are not about one or the other of us but about us, our fellowship. When I call you into the dream I call not as a guide who offers to take you in and bring you safely back, but as a lover who hopes to live there with you. To share in the creation of a world constructed of images, to get inside one another's imagining, is an intimacy deeper than intercourse. You enter my dream as you enter my body, my intercourse. You enter my dream as you enter my body, your thrusting penis. But I also experience your womb and my penis. We are each hermaphrodite; our love is fourfold, complete.

Daydreams lead us out of our self-enclosed world toward a truly social existence. If kept secret, daydreams too can be regressive and isolating, imprisoning us in the private world of personal obsessions; but shared they lead forward into a new future. Our night dreams make manifest that we participate in archetypal patterns of fear and desire, that at bottom we all have the same dream. But we experience one another's daydreams as harmonious with our own yet not their double, and make as much as we can of the surface variations. In the interpenetration of images we discover signs not of a universal destiny but of a common future.

Freud helped us to repersonalize the dreams of night, to see them as our own creation, clues to new personal growth and integration. As we begin to dream together about our common future, we resocialize daydreaming. "Big" dreams, tribal dreams, provide not privatized escapes from a disintegrating world but a vision of a new social order. Each crisis in life, personal or social, needs to be dreamt upon; no culture comes into being until it has first been envisioned in dream. In daydream we create a world out of metaphor and image, we create Utopia, the nowhereland. In daydream we find ourselves in the place between, in the period of transition midway through a rite of passage. We have left off the off the old patterns of socialization; here we relate on the basis of images not roles. The new pattern of socialization that lies on the other side of the rite has no shape as yet; its order will emerge out of our dreams. Daydreams give us the possibility and hope of re-ordering the world to give pleasure, of founding a world on metaphor, memory and hope. Daydreams are always about the future.

Daydreams are always about a future that is already here. When we dream awake it is most truly about and for the present; we daydream for the delight of dreaming as such. We dream ourselves and what we see, and each is image of the other. So for Anais Nin Tangiers reveals itself as image of her inner city and as she writes of its labyrinthine mysteriousness she becomes its image as well.

Daydreaming is embodied, sensual dreaming; it is dreaming with the whole body. In daydream I learn how to dream that which is there, present, now—to see it in a different way, with a different kind of consciousness. I am open to all its meanings, not only those that grow out of my needs, conscious or repressed, but all possible associations. In daydream I am attuned to its secrets not my own, to its polymorphousness. I see with the imagination, not with eyes closed but with eyes newly opened; I let that which is there function symbolically, associatively, not only literally or linearly. "Things as they are are changed upon the blue guitar..."

In daydream I see not only with my eyes but with ears and fingers and mouth. I transcend the fetishism of the visual as I experience the polymorphousness of psychedelic dream. We transcend the fetishism of the genital as together we experience the metamorphoses inspired by the dreams of day. Daydreaming together is much like tripping together, where any touching is cosmic but coitus seems comic. Comic too seems the busy pretentiousness of the everyday ego, the tragic seriousness of the figures of the dreams of night. Comic but lovable—we welcome them into our daydreaming.

I am woman and butterfly; I am Psyche. When I have intercourse with Eros, the god of love and ever more comprehensive relationship, in the playspace of daydream, Pleasure is born.

The dreams of day are different from the dreams of night. In them the child and the adult within play together, the man in me and the woman in me embrace. Daydreams create a world founded on metaphor and vision, a world re-ordered to give shared pleasure. The daydream is true wish-fulfillment; we do not look outside the dream for some other, more real, completion. To participate in one another's daydreams is an intimacy deeper than intercourse. We who belong to the league of dreamers call you into the playspace of daydream, call by telling about the dream, call by daydreaming about daydreaming…

References

Bachelard, Gaston. *The Poetics of Reverie*. Boston: Beacon Press, 1971.

Brown, Norman O. *Love's Body*. New York: Random House, 1966.

Freud, Sigmund. "The Relation of the Poet to Daydreaming," in *Delusion and Dream*. Boston: Beacon Press, 1956.

Hillman, James. "On Psychological Creativity," in *The Myth of Analysis*. Evanston: Northwestern University Press, 1972.

12

The Three "Incarnations" in Hermann Hesse's Magister Ludi

"In the beginning was the myth." So runs the first line of Hermann Hesse's first successful novel, *Peter Camenzind*. In the end is the legend. The final section of Hesse's last and most ambitious novel, *Magister Ludi*, is entitled "The Legend of the Magister Ludi." This section is followed by an appendix containing the posthumous writings of Joseph Knecht, the novel's protagonist, including several further short legends gathered together under the subtitle, "The Three Lives" (or "Three Incarnations," depending on which translation you consult). I intend in this paper to explore the relationship of these three tales to the novel proper and to Hesse's lifework and to consider what Hesse might intend by this movement from myth to legend.

Martin Buber has defined legend as the myth of the I and the Thou, the myth of the caller and the called, the self and the other. We shall return to this aspect later. He also writes of legend as mythisized history: history apprehended with the imagination, event understood as revelation, seen as prefigurative. It is in this sense that the chronicler of *Magister Ludi* understands his project. "History's third dimension," he tells us, "is always fiction." The epigraph attached to his account suggests how necessary it is for the truly conscientious historian to speak of things whose existence is neither probable nor demonstrable—for to treat them as existing brings them a step closer to the possibility of being born. Imaginative projection helps to create history. Thus Hesse's projection of an imagined alternate society, Castalia, has the same intended function as Joseph Knecht's projection of alternate lives. Castalia exists in the imagination, not in the past or the future; it is a wholly esthetic realm—a realm whose most serious occupation is play: Magister Ludi.

Hesse has often suggested that we humans are truly ourselves only when at play. Several of his early artist heroes are secretly troubled by their ability to imitate nature but not to play with her as the true masters do, but Joseph Knecht is the Magister Ludi, the master player from whom (so Hesse suggests in one of his poems) Hesse himself learned to play.

The chronicler seems less aware of how much he himself has been infected by the spirit of play that pervades the life-story he has set out to tell. He is uneasily aware that his project seems to run counter to the prevailing usages in Castalia, that there is a prejudice against history and biography in the pedagogical province. There is a cherishing of the ideal of anonymity, an idealization of those "who have gone beyond all original and idiosyncratic qualities to achieve the greatest possible integration into the generality," a reverencing of those "who have tragically sacrificed themselves for the general whole."[1] He hopes to represent Knecht as such a hero and asserts the appropriateness of interest in the individual, in his name and face and gestures, in the case of such a truly exemplary man. Knecht does not fit himself to the examples provided by his predecessors: rather he himself becomes example. Yet the chronicler fails to recognize how much his own project derives from Knecht's deeply suspect interest in the world of history and politics. The life-story that he tells tells us more than he himself knows, just as the life-stories that Joseph Knecht composed during his mid-twenties contained more than he understood at the time.

These "Lives" which the chronicler appends to his narrative account of Knecht's life (along with some poems Knecht had written during his late adolescence) were written after Joseph's formal schooling was completed, when he (like the other elite students) was free for several years to choose his own fields of study and research. The only obligation was to compose each year a special kind of stylistic exercise called a "Life." Each such "Life" was to be a "fictitious autobiography set in any period of the past the writer chose. The student's assignment was to transpose himself back to the surroundings, culture and intellectual climate of any earlier era and to imagine himself living a suitable life in that period" (*Ludi*, 99).

The three "Lives" are presented in *Magister Ludi* as written by Joseph Knecht during the appropriate period of his education, but they were not originally written by Hesse with this setting in mind. All three were published separately years before the novel was completed at a time when Hesse's conception of the whole book was very different. "The idea that originally fired me," Hesse writes, "was the notion of reincarnation as the vehicle through which to express stability in change, the continuity in tradition, and the life of the spirit generally. And then one day, many years before I actually started writing, I visualized a particular but supra-temporal life history: I imagined a man who in several incarnations experiences the great epochs of human history."[2] "The book was to contain several biographies of the same man, who lives on earth at different times—or at least thinks that he had such existences" (*Ludi,* xii).

Originally also, as the first introductory chapter still suggests, the focus was to be on Castalia, on the Order; the novel was to be a celebration of the fusion of intellect and imagination represented by Magister Ludi. But under the pressure of the barbarism represented by Nazi Germany Hesse reconceived the novel so that it embodies not only that celebration but also a critique of Castalia's utopian spirituality. The "Lives" had been composed before Hesse had envisioned the defection from the Order that occurs toward the end of Knecht's life and so it is not surprising that they do not directly anticipate that move. Yet, as Knecht is supposed to have composed them at a time in his life when he also did not foresee his departure from Castalia, this seems wholly appropriate.

Meanwhile Hesse had also come to see that his imaginary society could be made visible only through a central personage and so Knecht who originally had been only one member of the series steps into the center: the other lives are presented as issuing out of his creative imagination. Thus the "Lives" themselves are reincarnated, placed within a different structure, given a different role and meaning.

As Hesse came to a clearer sense of form, he recognized the need for a central consciousness that could imaginatively construct (or reconstruct) the series of lives: the connections between them are meaningful only if they are made conscious. Thus the "Lives" are made part of the Castalian educational program. Indeed writing such "incarnations" was the only acceptable creative outlet in the Castalian educational program (Knecht's poems had been secret and to that degree subversive creations) that otherwise was almost entirely focused on preservation and cultivation. The creation of imaginary pre-existences was for Knecht as for most of the students much more than a mere scholastic exercise. His "Lives" were the "expressions of wishful thinking," "exalted self-portraits"; they revealed the dreams and ideals of the writer (*Ludi,* 100). The chronicler suggests that the three extant such lives composed by Knecht that he reproduces are "possibly the most valuable part" of his book (*Ludi,* 101).

These exercises were regarded as a "game for the imaginative faculties," a playful reincarnation of the ancient Asian doctrine of reincarnation and transmigration. "All teachers and students were familiar with the concept that their present existence might have been preceded by others, in other bodies, at other times, under other conditions. To be sure they did not believe this in any strict sense;

there was no element of dogma in the idea…. They learned to regard their own persons as masks, as the transitory garb of an entelechy" (*Ludi*, 110).

To understand the function of this exercise it may help to consider some things Herbert Fingarette has to say about reincarnation, about "the language of many selves," and about the connections between psychoanalytic and karmic ways of describing self-transformation. Fingarette makes clear that it is only the power of remembering past lives that creates the continuity between them. To be liberated is to know that "my present life is only one of a set of lives. These lives are in certain respects entirely separate: their social, geographic, and physical characters may be quite unrelated to one another. Yet they form an interdependent series by virtue of a peculiar continuity: *karma*, 'Action.' This karmic continuity is a psychomoral one."[3] Knowledge of one's former lives brings liberation from karmic bonds. So for Knecht decisively to "transcend" (as he puts it in one of his early poems) means consciously appropriating former ways of being in the world which would otherwise still have unconscious power over him. Thus he must know the other "Lives" as his own.

Writing the "Lives," like psychoanalysis, as Fingarette understands it, "reveals the Self in greater depths, reveals it as a *community* of selves. The genuinely startling thing…is not simply the discovery that these other archaic selves exist, nor even that they have an impact on the present. What startles is the peculiarly close, subtle, and complex texture of the threads which weave these other selves and the adult conscious self into a single great pattern." Fingarette goes so far as to say, "The vicarious living of other lives is not merely a desirable experience; it is essential. There can be no development into a *human* being without the incorporation into the total Self of a variety of lives and part-lives. The more these are fully lived, the more rich and deep a Self."[4]

Because the "Lives" are thus a way to self-knowledge it is not surprising that many of the students come at some level to believe in the truth of their fictional incarnations. For such fictions give us, as Freud knew, "the plurality of lives which we need. We die with the hero with whom we have identified ourselves; yet we survive him, and are ready to die again just as safely with another hero."[5] As these alternate lives enter into waking consciousness they become part of a more richly-dimensioned self. Multiple incarnation is effected through the imagination. Knecht knows his "Lives" to be his own creations and yet to issue from something other than his rational conscious self: they embody more about himself than he yet wholly comprehends. These "Lives" have power because they have been sensuously imagined, experienced as vividly as the drug-induced visions in Pablo's Magic Theatre in Hesse's *Steppenwolf.*

Indeed the hope of overcoming time and death and ego that underlies the composition of the "Lives" is a recurrent theme in Hesse's writings. There are references to reincarnation or resurrection in several of the earlier novels: in *Beneath the Wheel* Hans' death is connected up with the pastor who has the reputation of not even believing in resurrection. In *Gertrud* Kuhn struggles with the book on theosophy his childhood teacher lends him, is attracted by the notion of karma but can't take it literally and so finds no solace in it. In *Demian* Pistorious and Frau Eva convey to Emil the metaphorical power of religious imagery like that associated with the doctrine of karma. In the "Treatise on the Steppenwolf" there is mention of how Indian literature is free of the fiction of an ego—the heroes of the Indian epics are not individuals but whole reels of individuals in a series of incarnations.

In several of Hesse's novels there are faces that suddenly reveal an archaic pre-human heritage: Klein sees this in Teresina. Emil sees in Demian a face bearing the scars of an entirely different history, the life of an animal or tree or planet, and sees the same face emerging in his own painting and in his dreams. Steppenwolf feels it in himself. Klingsor's last painting, the self-portrait, contains the faces of men and women, youths and sages, and the faces of a more remote history: animal, vegetable, stone. This is the same face Govinda sees when he looks at Siddhartha during their last encounter.

Many of Hesse's heroes are attuned to recurrences, prefigurations. As Klingsor puts it, there are always birds that fly ahead, always harbingers and omens. These intimations of repetition are fearful to Klein until as he is drowning he finds himself able to let go the invented crutch of time. Siddhartha, too, is initially troubled by his son's repetition of his own rebellion but then learns that if one can see the pattern, suffer it to the end, it need not recur. Liberation depends on consciousness. Simultaneity, plurality, repetition, do not themselves bring release, as the Steppenwolf found. Seriousness, literalism, Goethe tells him, insists on taking time too seriously; laughter and play release.

So as a theme reincarnation appears throughout Hesse's writing, even though it does not become a structural device until *Magister Ludi*. Yet in Hesse's earlier novels we have many a Klingsor asking, why time? why this idiotic succession of one thing after another? why not a roaring, surfeiting simultaneity? And many a Klein hoping to be able to glue together the broken porcelain snuffbox, to order the fragments of his life, many a Pistorious aware that every god or devil that ever existed, exists as latent possibility, wish, alternative within us though we are mostly unaware of it. In those novels we find Hesse searching for formal means by which such simultaneity might be expressed.

First, as I have suggested, he uses the form of *myth*. In *Peter Camenzind* there is an invocation of the theme of eternal recurrence at the beginning of the tale when Camenzind speaks of the people of his village—each playing his part in turn, disappearing and being replaced by other old men who inhabit the same cottages and bear the same names; at the story's end Peter returns to the village and knows that as he grows old he in his turn will take his father's place and play his small role in the village.

Hesse's novels are filled with mythological prefigurations. There is Mother Eve in *Narcissus and Goldmund* and Orpheus in Klingsor's dream but it is in *Demian* that we are most aware of this device as we note the function of the references to Cain, the Prodigal Son, to Jesus at Gethsemane and to Nietzsche.

Often there are dreams through which past and future merge into presentness, though less objectively than in the consciously contrived fantasies embodied in Knecht's "Lives." Peter Camenzind dreams of a purely animal existence. In *Demian* there is Emil's dream of a homecoming in which his mother and Demian and his own painting interfuse in a premonitory vision of Frau Eva. Narcissus dreams of his forgotten childhood and lost mother.

Sometimes the splits in the self, the multiplicity of inner lives, are externalized in alter egos or archetypal projections. Again this happens most powerfully in *Demian* where we have not only the ego/self relationship of Emil and Demian but also Emil's encounters with shadow, anima, Wise Old Man and Great Mother—and where the ambiguity as to whether these figures have only inward or also outward reality is masterfully maintained. But the same kind of encounter occurs between Hans Giebenroth and his friend Hermann Heilner in *Beneath the Wheel*. Teresina serves as a looking glass for Klein just as Hermione does for the Steppenwolf. At the end of the *Journey to the East* Hermann sees his own image flow into Leo's as the double figurine of his vision reshapes itself.

The relation of Narcissus to Goldmund is not that of ego to self or to the anima but of two complementary aspects of the psyche: consciousness and the creative unconscious. Narcissus sees in Goldmund the lost half of his own nature: It is not our purpose to become one another; it is to recognize each other, to learn to see the other and honor him for what he is: each the other's opposite and complement. Thus where Klein needs to struggle free from Wagner, where Demian must die, Hermione be killed, Hermann become one with Leo, Goldmund's death leaves Narcissus bereft.

Because Knecht can give concrete embodiment to his other selves he does not need to suffer their unconscious power over him or project them on others. The "Lives" make projection unnecessary.

There are structural devices which serve this same purpose of providing release from the limitations of a single ego as protagonist and which demonstrate how central a theme this is in Hesse's fiction. There is the river in *Siddhartha* that is everywhere at the same time and for which only the present unshadowed by past and future exists—and which Siddhartha's face comes to mirror. There is the League in *The Journey to the East* whose members wander through space and time, meet figures out of myth and classical literature, persons important in ancient and modern history, personal friends and characters from other of Hesse's fictions. There is the Magic Theatre of *Steppenwolf* in which all unacknowledged fantasies are imaginatively enacted—which is explicitly named in the chronicler's history as a precursor of *Magister Ludi*.

And there is, of course, the Glass Bead Game itself. The essence of the game is the reduction of all human knowledge to abstract timeless essences that can then be played with simultaneously. Knecht himself has a mystical experience of the power of the game to overcome transitoriness. He was studying a dead language and suddenly realized that despite the decay and death of that language, it had not been lost: its youth, maturity and downfall were preserved in our memory and could be reconstructed as part of the game. Yet at the same time he senses the inadequacy of the game's abstractness and decides upon the consuming project of reconstructing the contents of one game: translating it back from the language of the game into its original languages, recovering its original concreteness.

Knecht is here confronting the same question about the limits of the power of art voiced by many of Hesse's artist heroes. Klingsor cannot answer when he is asked, "Is your painted July which you have there in your portfolio enough for you? Have you abolished time? Are you without fear of the autumn, the winter?" And the musician Kuhn is deeply aware of how unable he has been to make song and sweet music of his own life.

The literary artist can live many lives through his art more directly than painter or musician. As the "Treatise on the Steppenwolf" confides, the characters of a poem are to be regarded not as separate beings but as various aspects of the poet's soul. Knecht, too, is an artist, a maker of poems and legends, though one who sees his central role not as self-expression but as education. Knecht is the last of Hesse's own incarnations—which he now sees as a repetitive series. Knecht is Hesse's consummate protagonist, created to transcend those repetitions: the adult version of all those earlier adolescents.

Hesse is wholly conscious that his fictions have served as *his* "incarnations." When working on *Narcissus and Goldmund*, he wrote:

> I am now at work on something new and a character is emerging who for a while will serve as a symbol and bearer of my life experience, thoughts and problems. The emergence of these mythical figures (Peter Camenzind, Knulp, Demian, Siddhartha, Harry Haller and so on) is the creative center from which everything else flows. Almost every book I have written has been a spiritual biography. Central to each are not stories, entanglements, and tensions, but monologues in which a particular person's relation to the world and to himself is put under the microscope.

It was only in retrospect however that Hesse discovered how each story is a repetition of those that preceded:

> All these pieces were about me, reflected my particular path, my secret dreams and hopes, my own bitter griefs. Even those books in which I had honestly thought while writing them to portray destinies and conflicts that were not mine in fact sang the same song, breathed the same air, and interpreted the same destiny—mine.

But the goal had always been to win free of this obsession with the subjective:

> If one regards writing as a form of personal confession, then art must be seen as a long ever-changing, winding path whose object is to express the personality, the ego of the artist so completely and so exhaustively that by the finish this ego is, as it were, so exposed and exhausted as to be burned out and speechless.[6]

In a sense, of course, Hesse is embodied in every one of his characters, especially in the protagonists who so often have names with the same initials as his own, but he also often (like Alfred Hitchcock) writes himself in as a minor spectator character as well: the librettist in *Gertrud*, Knulp's companion, Klingsor's friend TuFu, the Elder Brother in the Chinese Garden at the outskirts of Castalia. And in his books there are also incarnations of his friends and colleagues, of philosophers like Nietzsche and Burckhardt whose influence he so deeply respects, and incarnations of characters from his own other fiction and of Goethe's Wilhelm Meister and Kafka's Josef K.

One could compose a true Master Player's game by trying to gather together all the connections among Hesse's books, all the places, figures, themes, situations which recur from one book to another, and to see in what ways *Magister Ludi* can be understood as a transcending. In retrospect one may discover the karmic continuity, see in the early works the germ that ripens here.

Some of the Most Important Motifs

Home and Mother: All Hesse's heroes seem to come from a town much like Calw. Mothers are the source of life; they signify the connection to home that has usually been lost. The protagonists are often motherless children: Peter Camenzind feels freed by his mother's death to leave but makes no lasting connection in the outside world. Hans in *Beneath the Wheel* is a motherless child. Demian represents the need to replace the natural mother with the archetypal one: Frau Eva. Goldmund, because of his loss of his natural mother is like Emil engaged in a search for the mother image, Eve. Narcissus sees that dreamers and poets take their being from the mother. At the end of the novel Goldmund asks Narcissus: "How can you die without a connection to the mother?" The deepest dream in Hesse's fiction is the dream of homecoming, of return to the mother: all journeys have that shape.

School, World of Men, Fathers: In *Beneath the Wheel* it is said: "Maulbronn stamps its students forever"; and indeed it is reincarnated as the Mariabronn of *Narcissus and Goldmund,* and as Escholz, Mariafels, and Castalia itself in *Magister Ludi*.

Escape: Always in the novels there is the need to escape. HH can in *Wheel* though Hans can't—and so HH, then like Knecht, becomes a legend. Goldmund does, though he returns to Mariabronn broken, and Narcissus never can. Knecht is much more affirmative of the world of the male order; he even becomes a Father himself. Yet eventually he has to leave that world. Indeed his departure is prefigured more clearly in Hesse's earlier books than in his own "Lives." Hesse didn't know when he started *Magister Ludi* it would turn out like that—a reader might have guessed.

The East: Very often the East is presented as the symbol of a land to escape to. There is the trip to China projected at the end of *Rosshalde*; *Siddhartha* is Hesse's own imagined journey to the East. There is the book of that name; there is Knecht's visit to the Chinese sage.

Women and Men: The females in Hesse's fiction are always evanescent, committed to someone else. Often there are lower class male friends who play the role of tempters, shadow figures. The male bond is important and often takes the shape of an esoteric circle: a group of artist friends, the league, the players of the game.

Vocation: The notion of service continually reappears: from Peter Camenzind's devotion to St. Francis through Leo, the servant who is secretly the leader.

Death: Again and again there is death, especially by drowning. Peter Camenzind's friend, Hans Giebenrath, Klein, Klingsor all drown. Pierre in *Rosshalde* dreams of a watery death; Siddhartha is absorbed by the river. From Boppi in *Peter Camenzind* and again from the Music Master in *Magister Ludi* we learn of an *ars moriendi*, are told that death can be reconciliation, homecoming.

All these themes and motifs are taken up again in the account of Knecht's life. The lives of Hesse's earlier heroes are just as much Knecht's other lives as are those which he himself composes. Knecht, too, is a motherless child, though he seems not to miss her consciously, to have sublimated the sense of loss into an attraction to the world of concreteness and historical responsibility. He seems hardly aware of the region outside Castalia as representing home and yet is pulled back nevertheless. He never returns in memory, in nostalgic longing, yet does in reality. He, too, is an outsider, made so by his initiation into the order, but feels in harmony with that election.

Unlike Demian and all the other earlier heroes Knecht experiences no adolescent struggles, does not have to wrestle with shadow, anima or mother. He is happy at Eschfels and at Mariabronn, can battle worthily with antagonists like Plinio, is content with the impersonal sex made available to the elect students; accepts his place in an all male world, dies consciously, willingly, not accidentally or in flight. He sees his life as a perpetual transcending, a progression from stage to stage, as a series of incarnations, new beginnings and new deaths, acts of awakening and acts of parting, each stage as a theme needing to be developed and then dismissed, as a natural line albeit not the straight line of a geometry exercise. As he leaves Castalia he sees his present journey as the same as that of the walking tours of his youth: all that had been could recur and many new things as well. He feels himself especially close again to the youth who had written the poem "Transcend" and who had composed the "Lives." The "Lives" had, of course, been written before Knecht consciously knew of his eventual defection from the Order and so there are no overt prefigurations of that departure, though we can see presentiments of the later decision very early on in his story as the chronicler tells it. For instance, Knecht remembers that even at Escholz, when a pupil was dismissed, he sometimes wondered whether that might be not a cause for suffering but a positive step forward; as though those boys had been brave enough to take a plunge, to take things seriously. He learns from the Music Master a love for the sensuous aspect of music, not just the distilled abstracts used in Magister Ludi. He feels the partial truth hidden in Plinio's coarse, exaggerated accusations about the sterility of Castalia during their school-age debates, and years later finds himself still dreaming of those debates and the old conflict between ethics and esthetics which they embodied. His adolescent poetic musings were already a conscious though minor act of rebellion.

The "Lives" represent his own attempt to give expression to the dreams and ideals that animated him at the end of his student years, and seem to focus on the dialectical interplay between students and teachers, servants and masters, sons and fathers.

"The Rainmaker," the first of Knecht's "Lives," is the story of an orphaned boy growing up in a matriarchal culture who is accepted as an apprentice by Turu the Rainmaker, the most set apart member of the tribe. The story is deeply pervaded with a sense of always, of continuity and repetition. The narrator often suggests that in the young Knecht there dwells, though still in germ, all the anxiety and curiosity and craving for understanding of which the human soul is capable. But what the boy develops is a kind of intimate sensuous knowing very different from that inculcated in Castalia: an intuition of a hidden center to the vast net of associations his imagination presents to him: an ability to eavesdrop on the secret relations between clouds and storms and the phases of the moon. Eventually when Turu dies, Knecht becomes the Rainmaker in his turn and then Turu reappears as the son who is destined eventually to be his successor. When Knecht first confronts his own apprentice he experiences the strangeness of this recurrence and reversal of his own relation to his Master. Joseph Knecht (in a moment that hasn't happened yet when he writes the story) will during his daydream musing when the Music Master is dying feel this same alternation between identification with the old man and the boy, now revering, now revered, now leading, now obeying—and comes upon a moment when he is both, simultaneously Master and small pupil. The Rainmaker comes to experience betrayal and later a crisis in the life of his people which demands his own self-sacrifice. Here there is no break with the old customs but a yielding up to them, the kind of self-surrender Joseph Knecht associates with his taking on the role of Magister. The Rainmaker's death represents a keeping faith with the future and particularly with the only way that leads into the real future, his son—as Joseph Knecht's own not yet known death will signify his commitment to the future embodied in Tito.

In the story about "The Father Confessor" we seem to have some premonitions of the friendship later to develop between Knecht and Father Jacobus. For here too a mature man who had exhausted a particular way of being in the world, whose way has stopped working for him, meets another who is able to suggest to him a new pattern of life, more active, more interventionist. Dion Pugil is not only Jacobus but also Plinio (who ultimately provides Knecht with the situation in which he can enact his new beginning). In the story Famulus must start all over again, as servant, as son and then as successor. The good death of Dion Pugil, his radiant childlike smile, seems prefigurative of the Music Master's death. Despair, Knecht seems already to intuit as he writes, can be the awakening of new life, though it may be this very foreknowledge that keeps him from ever being really thrown by despair.

The third incarnation, "The Indian Life," is the story of a young Indian boy, born as heir to the throne but sent off because of palace intrigues to be brought up by simple herdsmen. During his youth he meets a yogi sitting quietly deep in the forest who impresses him deeply, but he is pulled back into the world, becomes enthralled by a beautiful young woman who betrays him and whose lover he then murders. In his subsequent flight he comes upon the yogi again, stays with him but finds no release; he is still restless with longing for Parvati. He prepares to leave and as a last gesture goes to fetch a gourd of water for the yogi—and there by the stream falls into a trance in which he experiences with lifelike vividness all that would/will happen if he recovers Parvati. When he awakens he discovers this was all fantasy, all *Maya*, and resolves to stay with the yogi as his servant—though he sees that that life too is *Maya*. But the fantasy is not, by being recognized as such, reduced to nothingness: the images remain. This story is Joseph Knecht's celebration of what can be learned through fantasy, through imaginative incarnation, and what it means to decide to live one's own life—knowing that it too is *maya*, is play.

So Knecht much later can leave Castalia, seeing his life there as a game completed, as a game that is no longer play. He leaves with only a toy flute in hand, leaves as still the playful magician Plinio had always discerned him to be.

Knecht's departure and his death were not overtly prepared for in the "Lives" but there is preparation nevertheless. The "Lives" help us better understand his readiness to participate in Tito's festive celebration of the beginning of their relationship. He appreciates the youth's danced offering of himself to earth and water, and feels compelled to answer the summons to enter that water, to offer himself. In the "Lives" he already knew that stories must end with new beginnings.

Yet we may still feel some dissatisfaction, believe that Hesse would not have known what else to do with Knecht—that he can imagine the departure, will it, but is unable to conceive the life on the other side, the life in the world. What is visible in the "Lives" Knecht can appropriate because he has made it, but he seems to have no way of appropriating the lives embodied in Hesse's earlier fiction—and so he is an adult who has never truly been an adolescent, never suffered through what those earlier heroes did. His transcendence seems empty, abstract. He cannot really breathe outside Castalia. And only outside Castalia could he truly live as legend and not only as myth. This is suggested even in the novel itself: the section called "The Legend" tells about Knecht's life after he leaves the Order; the three "legends" of course also occur on other territory. Hesse had wanted to create a hero who ends by doing something new, not by returning to the age-old pattern as Peter Camenzind had, and within the order Knecht is indeed venerated as someone who has reshaped the pattern. Knecht does not have to tell his own story, it matters enough to others so they will tell it. He has affected some *thou*'s, some others: especially Tito and the chronicler. But he has not found a way of living beyond Castalia. Hesse had felt called to create a life that would answer to the new situation represented by the world threatened by Nazism—which meant giving up the world he had created and loved, the world of myth, the world of Castalia, for the world of history. He sought here to break out of the pattern of his own repetitions, to leave the world of adolescent yearning for the world of adult fulfillment—but he and Knecht can do that only as resolution, only as gesture.

So there is dissatisfaction, and yet also, at least for me, a beauty and power suggested by a line of verse from one of Knecht's earliest poems:

> In all beginnings dwells a magic force
> For guarding us and helping us to live.

As I read *Magister Ludi* and particularly the "Lives" I participate myself in multiple incarnation: I experience the story of the Rainmaker as his, and as Josef Knecht's who lived through him, as the chronicler's who clearly lives through Knecht, as Hesse's, and as my own. And I am called back into the imagination of myself in an earlier incarnation, when I at 24 (the age Knecht was when he composed the Lives) first read Hesse. I am pulled into the life of my son Eric, now deeply in tune with Hesse's poetry though put off by the prose, himself now as old as Knecht was when he wrote his poems. And I feel also the bond with Knecht as he becomes the Magister Ludi, the master of his game, at age 41—my own age now. And I begin to wonder already what I shall do when my game is no longer play...

Notes

1. Hermann Hesse, *Magister Ludi,* translated by Richard and Clara Winston (Bantam Books, 1970) 3, 4, 5. The German title is *Das Glasperlenspiel,* "The Glass Bead Game" but alas, both translations I own use the "Magister Ludi" title. Henceforward references will be included in the text under the rubric *Ludi.*

2. Bernhard Zeller, *Portrait of Hesse* (New York: Herder and Herder, 1971) 141.

3. Herbert Fingarette, *The Self in Transformation* (New York: Harper Torchbooks, 1965) 177.

4. Fingarette, 181, 190.

5. Fingarette, 187.

6. Zeller, 115, 100, 99.

13

Symptoms and Symbols: Edward Whitmont's Symbolic Quest

One moves through Edward Whitmont's book as one follows the path of that labyrinth from the floor of Chartres Cathedral reproduced on its cover; one goes from the periphery to the center only by covering the total plane surface of the circle. The book is not, as its subtitle might imply, another introduction to Jungian psychology, but rather a search for a symbolics that at the same time seeks to awaken the symbolic function in its readers. That is why it focuses on "therapy" only in the final chapter, although *therapeia* (from the Greek word meaning "attend to, worship") is the focus throughout. Whitmont believes that the repression of the search for transliteral meaning, for symbolic understanding, is as powerful in our time as was the repression of sexuality in the preFreudian Victorian world. He hopes to show us a way of attending to our experiences that will bring us in touch again with numinous reality. The book requires the working together of writer and reader as clearly as the therapeutic encounter depends on the work of both analyst and patient (client? analysand?—we need a better word).

As I went through the first few chapters my response seemed to be mostly that of intellectual appreciation shadowed by a few emphatically marked reservations. But I came to realize that my yes-es and no-es had in them a personal as well as a more scholarly component and I began to wonder about what in me underlay these responses. I began then to apply the symbolic quest to my own reading. I was intrigued to see how close together lay that which I most applauded and that of which I was most critical and understood that these particular conjunctions must have some special meaning for me.

I was particularly impressed with Whitmont's presentation of the complex interrelation of persona, shadow, anima/animus, ego, Self. He recognizes the danger of idolatry in forgetting that Self and shadow and the rest are *metaphors*.

148

He knows that all "psychological terms and theories that are taken for established facts become hindrances rather than aids." This appreciation of the metaphorical is also evident in his masterful use of dreams as pointer. Often pages of explication are shown to be but another way of saying what a dream conveys in a few closely interwoven images.

Whitmont regards Jung's teaching us how to engage the partial personalities that live within us in a inner dialogue, how to receive and befriend the strangers within, as his most important contribution to our understanding of the psyche. His own descriptions of what it means to confront an archetype as a *thou*, "as it speaks *to* us rather than *through* us to others," of how one can learn to treat the anima "like a problematic partner…with attention and consideration but also with discipline and experimental interplay and challenge" are among the most important elements in his book. One knew all that already, but somehow *this* description of it serves as a call to undertake the dialogue anew.

These things in the book I was deeply impressed by. Yet there were also the reservations and they seemed colored with a not wholly appropriate emotional animus. Why? As I pondered this, I began to see more clearly the difference Whitmont makes so much of between a "symbolic" and a "symptomatic" analysis. (Though one of the things I initially protested was just this duality. It seemed so unfair to Freud. As indeed it is. But perhaps it bothered me less because of that than because I needed to appreciate its more immediate relevance to me. "New life always approaches in suspect form.") I began to see that the emotional component in my response did not need to mean only symptom, hang-up, distortion—it might also conceal a forward-pointing call. (I'd still say "not only/but also," whereas Whitmont seems more often to say "not/but" and so to neglect what is so important in depth psychology's analysis of the symbolic: that the symbol dissimulates *and* manifests, *hides* and *reveals*.) Obviously my "no-es" were part of what pulled me into the book, engaged me with it, were not simply the protests of a detached scholar. I saw that I wasn't called upon to stifle them but rather to learn what heeding them might mean. The primary motif of my protests seemed to be a defense of Freud vis-à-vis Jung, which hurt. It was almost like having to witness an unbearable conflict between one's parents and finding oneself standing up for the father even though one really knew that was not a way that led to reconciliation. Upon reflection I understood this as an expression of that tension between the mythic and the literal that forces us toward the symbolic and discerned within the tension a double task. One, personal, inward: a recognition that I didn't want to respond as the analytical intellectual but that this kind of emotional response wasn't desirable either, that I needed to take the conflict to a different place, to understand it symbolically as a call to the integration of the thinking and feeling in me, a balancing of what Whitmont prefers to call the yang and the yin. And an outward task: a discovery that perhaps the integration of Freud and Jung that I see as so timely now is *my* responsibility, not Whitmont's.

The book had become a partner, pulling me toward a new relation to self and also to another, represented by the book itself: a book that seems to know so well what it is about, that speaks so wisely, so affirmatively, of the inevitability and importance of projection:

> The personal encounter is indispensable for actualization and for the realization of our innate potential. Human fulfillment, maturing development and individual realization cannot take place through introverted analytical withdrawal alone; they require the encounter of an *I* with a *Thou*. But neither can the encounter lead to true relatedness unless it occurs simultaneously with an introspective inner search.

It seems to me that it is here that Whitmont has most clearly gone beyond his teacher, Jung, not just as many good students do by being able to say something more clearly, more logically, less ambiguously (and so, alas, often less richly, more literalistically), but in going beyond the Buber-Jung controversy over the primacy of the relation to self and the relation to the other. Whitmont doesn't solve the dilemma theoretically (which is perhaps not possible anyway) but simply demonstrates that he is past it, as over and over again he voices his knowledge of the importance of the relation between the I and the thou, not only the internal thou's of the archetypes but also those of actual embodied human others. His distinction between the urge to involvement and relatedness represented by what Jung called the Eros concept (but which he prefers to speak of as "Yin") from what Buber meant by encounter is of signal importance:

> The Eros aspect of Yin is not one of understanding but only of contact and merging.... Full human I-Thou relatedness cannot simply be called an Eros function, as it has usually been presented in the writings of analytical psychology; it arises out of the interaction of Yang and Yin in their double polarity of love and challenging aggressiveness, of creative understanding and emotional gestation. It requires distance and separateness no less than involvement.

Whitmont's care for others is expressed also in his insistence on the necessity and rightness of the steps we take along the way toward maturity: the development of the persona, the differentiation of the superior function. He shows how important it is that the dialogue between ego and Self be dynamic, as though the ego were a partner chosen by the Self and "given full responsibility with his particular functioning (awareness, understanding and choice)." He emphasizes the need to test in real life the hints and messages from the unconscious. He stresses too the continuing need for relatedness to that in the archetypes that forever remains numinous and transcendent, "beyond analysis," that continues to express itself in ever new forms and thus connects us to the limitlessness of the psyche. How absurd it would be to try to dry out this ocean!

Yet within this affirmation is a recognition of the importance of no-saying and conflict that I had not expected from a Jungian. (My deaf-spots begin to reveal themselves.) The I, Whitmont says, grows through learning self-denial (and thus ego, persona and shadow grow in step with one another) and later as the Self enters the stage:

> Conflict with oneself appears to be a basic, constant and inevitable element of life-functioning, perhaps *the* most basic. Our whole development pattern is structured in such a way that conflict with and dissolution of what once has been established are unavoidable; our original ego development makes us fear and oppose that which life puts in our way as the goal of our search.

I had also not expected from a Jungian such emphasis on embodiment, incarnation, nor the development of this emphasis in a way much closer to what Freud is trying to say through *his* symbols of the sexuality of the libido, his image of Eros, than Whitmont seems ready to acknowledge.

The symbolic quest brings us to a reconciliation different from a happy ending or "solution" to our problems. We discover that what is at first felt as an impossible deadlock may turn out to be an initiation into symbolic experience. The conflict may bring forth what Jung called the reconciling symbol.

> What is experienced only in terms of a personal impasse can seem quite hopeless until and unless it receives a general human meaningfulness by being recognized as one's individual and perhaps as discordant share in, or variation of, an eternal mythological motif.

This directs us once again toward the parallel between the personal symbol and myth. For myths, as Eliade and Levi-Strauss have helped us to understand, don't explain the world, they narrate it—don't logically dissolve paradoxes or resolve conflicts but unite the two poles picaresquely, eventfully, symbolically.

Whitmont makes clear how developing a sense for the symbolic dimensions of our lives, our dreams, our impasses, brings us into a new relationship to them. Philip Rieff has suggested that what Freud gives us is the myth of the *self*, a fascination with self as a way of enduring the irresoluble and ambiguous. Whitmont seems to take this further: he enriches the meaning of the *myth* of the self by taking us beyond the language of "disease" and "symptom" and "psychopathology" into another language world, the world of "dis-ease" and "symbol" and "*therapeia*." "In a happy world all anxieties would be games."

14

Reviewing David Miller

David L. Miller's *Gods and Games* and Sam Keen's *To a Dancing God* seem to call for some response different from a critical review in a serious journal: like telling a story or making love or, for the fun of it, pretending to write a critical review for a serious journal. For both books are about theology and play; both bring into play a cluster of metaphors: play and dance, make-believe and sensuality, nostalgia and poetry, alchemy and therapy, capable of metamorphosing theology. Both are about themselves.

They have been around long enough, almost two years now, to be familiar like a song whose melody and lyrics one already knows, a dance whose rhythms and movements have come to seem natural. We no longer need to respond to these books as to a new game whose pieces and rules are strange and puzzling; we are ready to play with grace and enjoyment. We understand that playing means not repeating their moves but experimenting with our own. I don't have to choose between theology as aphorism and theology as anecdote, between etymology and personal confession, don't have to aim at being as clever as David Miller or as folksily casual as Sam Keen, don't have to lay my bets on the child Dionysos or Zorba the dancer. I can propose theology as reverie, pay my homage to Persephone—because we are "playing play" with one another not a game against one another. As David Miller says, "The language-form of a theology of play is not a word of dichotomous and schizophrenic nay-saying in opposition to other words...It is not the language of noisy gongs and clanging cymbals; it is, rather, the language of love, of yea-saying."

His distinction between *game* and *play* seems central to any appreciation of the playfulness appropriate to theologizing. It lays open the close tie between game-playing and the process of socialization, the initiation into the world of rules and competing and winning. We see that theology all too easily becomes a game, how hard it is to truly *play* it. The "rules" for writing theology (or theological reviews) seem to suggest that I may celebrate David Miller's punning but not indulge in any myself, may clumsily retell Sam Keen's stories but not contribute any of my own. Yet to agree to speak as a disembodied voice issuing from an anesthetized body, to try to abstract from my response to his book the years of talking over its concerns sitting across from David Miller's dancing green eyes, to pretend to erase the memory of the self-conscious grace of Sam Keen's body when I heard him lecture once, would be to signal that their metaphors had not yet taken hold of me. Though to aim at breaking or transcending these rules is also dangerous. As David Miller warns, there is a futility in trying seriously to transcend seriousness.

Because he seems to see this more clearly than does Sam Keen, his book that at first glance may seem the more traditional, the more intellectual, may take the root metaphor, play, more radically. He imagines not only a different style and surface for theology, but a theology truly beyond gamesmanship. Sam Keen's book seems more personal and contemporary but the rhythms of "Protestant seriousness" are still very strong. The frequent repetition of words like "memory" and "discipline," "maturity," and especially "responsibility" create a powerful undertow. Several times we encounter a surprisingly orthodox reaffirmation of justification by faith: "the ultimate significance, meaning, security, value, dignity of my life is not dependent upon anything I can do, make or accomplish. Therefore, my action may spring out of what I am rather than arising out of a desperate need to establish myself. I am already founded, rooted, grounded in (depth metaphors) or contexted and encompassed by (metaphors of inclusion) that which guarantees my integrity.... Authentic life is not governed by the spirit of seriousness. It is graceful, light, and playful." It is as though the metaphor of play had not yet fully worked its magic.

Yet Sam Keen's book in its very directness and simplicity has real power to evoke memories, to stimulate fantasies, and there is something he says at the end of his book that although directed at Norman O. Brown might also be addressed to David Miller. Brown, he says, makes the one fatal mistake of finding in wordplay the most appropriate expression of Dionysian or erotic consciousness, not recognizing that words alone, even poetic words, are not enough: "It is the real, literal, carnal body which must be resensitized and educated in the sacredness which lies hidden in its feelings." Of course, David Miller has "protected" himself against this—but perhaps only in the world of gameplaying.

There is still something incomplete. We all still talk too much about a theology of play, are still too concerned to protect ourselves on both flanks, against charges of overseriousness and frivolity. There is as yet no incarnation of a theology of play.

15

Sigmund Freud and the Greek Mythological Tradition

This paper represents an overview of one important strand in an ongoing study of Freud and Jung and the way in which each related psychology and myth. In a sense it is my version of Philip Rieff's *Fellow Teachers*; I, too, look to Freud for help in recalling us to those urgencies that pulled us into religious studies "once upon a time," to a renewed appreciation of the sacred. But unlike Rieff, I want to equate god-terms not only with interdiction and prohibition, but also with celebration. Rieff seems to want to reinstate YHVH as the only true god, albeit a god constantly struggling with the Baals and Asteroths. I am more pagan and find in Freud resources for a genuinely polytheistic theology that affirms the power of YHVH *and* Astarte, Eros *and* Thanatos.

What I will put forward here is not a literal but a depth reading of Freud: a political reading, a poetic, mythic reading. Freud still has things to say to us precisely because his thinking was more dialectical and subtle than that of the movement he spawned, and because he deliberately invites us to look for latent meanings. We are all familiar with the tensions: is Freud therapist or theorist, scientist or poet, realist or romantic? Obviously, the answer is, "Both, but not in easily reconcilable ways." Freud seems to encourage readings which exploit "Freud against Freud," as Wilhelm Reich put it: readings like Rieff's which set the interdictory over against the remissive, like Herbert Marcuse's which discovers Freud the revolutionary in Freud the apparent conservative, and like Norman O. Brown's which opposes the orgiastic to the repressive, fantasy to literalism. Each of these is a reading that goes beyond Freud—they are interpretations that are truly "the other room of the dream"—yet they are fathered by him. Freud is important in part because he both allows such going beyond *and* resists it. He is someone we learn from by wrestling with. Like his YHVH he is a figure worth fighting against. Perhaps just because he had himself so consciously played the role of the son, the rebel, he is willing to take his turn as the father who does not simply abdicate. (I suspect a new vision needs to be mothered as well; in the larger study I turn to Jung as one who might be invested with this role.) My own reading will focus on Freud's understanding of the role of myth in human life; it sees in Freud's criticism and iconoclasm the manifest of resymbolization, in his atheism the manifest of polytheism. Not that we ignore the manifest. It is precisely the analysis of the death of God that makes possible an opening to the continued liveliness of the gods. The death of this loved and hated father is as creative and shattering an experience as is the death of the literal father. I hope to show how deeply Freud's whole outlook is penetrated by presuppositions which we are accustomed to associate with mythology and to look at the way in which he incorporates specific mythic motifs, especially those associated with Greek mythology, into his own thinking.

In *The Future of an Illusion* Freud proffers a critique designed to free us from domination by religious authority. He acknowledges that religion springs from "the oldest, strongest and most urgent wishes of mankind." His polemic against religion depends on his perception of its failure to deliver the satisfactions it promises. (Thus, for Freud as for Marx, the criticism of religion is a criticism of the civilization it undergirds.) Freud offers a clear critique of the false and crippling power of a now weakened idol, YHVH. He regards the father-god of the Bible as the god of dogmatism, of repression, and of an ego-consciousness dominated by the superego. Freud saw the fatal flaw of this god lay in his claim to be the only god, but he knew, too, that gods do not die, they just go underground. He did not see the gods, even YHVH, as only projections, only subjective, but as the human way of figuring our response to the deepest, most unavoidable, most universal forces we meet. That Freud loved as well as hated the biblical god is shown especially well in his essay on "The Moses of Michelangelo": he sees in that statue "a concrete expression of the highest mental achievement that is possible in man, that of struggling successfully against an inward passion, for the sake of a cause to which he has devoted himself."[1] The invocation to Ananke in *The Future of an Illusion* is clearly addressed to but another face of the same god now put into a polytheistic framework. A god whom we are not called upon to worship but to acknowledge—to accept his power means an abandonment of narcissism and a reconversion to the finite. Paul Ricoeur describes Ananke as "the name of nameless reality for those who have 'renounced their father.'"[2]

It is important also for us to note that the title of Freud's monograph refers to the future of *an* illusion. He indicates explicitly that his argument implies a more radical critique than the one developed in its pages:

> Having recognized religious doctrines as illusions, we are at once faced by a
> further question: may not other cultural assets of which we hold a high opin-
> ion and by which we let our lives be ruled be of a similar nature? Must not the
> assumptions that determine our political regulation be called illusions as well?
> And is it not the case that in our civilization the relations between the sexes are
> disturbed by an erotic illusion or a number of such illusions?[3]

In *Freud: The Mind of the Moralist*, Philip Rieff has put together a list of the
many illusions subjected to Freud's suspicious analysis during the course of his
lifework: "the id illusions of dependence, love, happiness, union; the super-ego
illusions of the good society, progress, brotherhood, fatherhood, finally, even of
health; the ego illusions of reason, energetic, independent and purposeful in a
purposeless and meaningless universe."[4] Freud always turns against the "lie of salvation" in any form. His vision of the self is polycentric; the claim to primacy of
any aspect is always both precarious and injurious. Neither id nor ego, Eros or
Logos, is immune from questioning.

  Civilization and Its Discontents may end with an invocation to Eros; *Future of
an Illusion* may pay its respects to Ananke and give praise to Logos; but none of
these is replacement for YHVH as the authentic divinity. Freud was as deeply
critical of any monotheism as of any monocentric conception of the self. His
world is filled with dualities and polarities, with the polymorphous. In *Totem and
Taboo* he emphasizes how the sacred—before it crystallizes into specific divinities—is morally ambivalent: helpful and dangerous. Freud's sense of the tension
between the primal powers expresses an intuition more sure to him, more deeply
lying, than any naming of the conflicting forces or any division of attributes and
powers. The contrast between ego instincts and object instincts may come to
require major modifications; the death instinct may seem beyond empirical verifi-
cation; but the conviction that the instincts could not all be of the same nature is
one Freud holds on to even when he can adduce no grounds. Freud's insistence
on the ambivalences present in any relationship (ambivalences whose paradigm is
the love/hate attachment to the father characteristic of the Oedipus complex)
reflects this same awareness of the irreconcilable dualities that characterize human
existence.

  Freud's psychology is from the beginning and not only in the metapsychological, cultural essays an intersubjective social psychology: both in its anthropology
which stresses the importance of the "family romance" and represents the psyche
as the scene of dramatic encounters between ego, id, and superego; and in its
understanding of therapy which focuses on the erotic relationship between analyst and patient. For Freud, we humans are inescapably embodied and so inevita-

bly find ourselves in relation to the powers of sexuality and death; we are inescapably in a world with other desiring and acting selves and so inextricably find ourselves in relation to the authority of society. These forces—sex, death, and society—act on us both from outside and from within our own soul. Of course, Freud does not call them "gods" but rather "instincts." The instincts, especially the sexual instinct, are irreducible for Freud; they are ultimate terms, self-explicable. He himself admits: "The theory of the instincts is so to say our mythology."[5]

To see through the illusions is to be freed from idolatry, freed for a conscious direct relationship with the gods, the primal eternal forces that we in all places, at all times, have had to contend with. Freud may protest the extension of the word "god":

> Where questions of religion are concerned people are guilty of every possible sort of dishonesty and intellectual misdemeanor. Philosophers stretch the meaning of words until they retain scarcely anything of their original sense. They give the name of "God" to some vague abstraction which they have cre-ated for themselves; having done so they can pose before all the world as deists, as believers in God, and they can even boast that they have recognized a higher, purer concept of God, notwithstanding that their God is now nothing more than an insubstantial shadow and no longer the mighty personality of religious doctrines.[6]

Yet he himself, in order to suggest the numinous power of these primal forces, finds it necessary to speak of Eros and Thanatos, of Logos and Ananke, to use the names of gods. Thus his reinterpretation of religion seems less a project of demy-thization than a rediscovery of the charged power of the gods. Freud hopes to help us find the courage to look these gods in the face. There is no escaping these powers. It is, however, possible to establish a new, more conscious, more con-sciously symbolic relationship to them. Freud's iconoclasm opens the paths to a non-narcissistic reconciliation with these mythically-named forces. When we get past judging these god-terms as literally true or false, recognizing that to do so would be monolatry with respect to the falsely isolated reality principle, we begin to move toward an appropriately ironic reverence. The praise of psychoanalysis offered in *The Future of an Illusion* is not directed to its therapeutic efficacy, but to psychoanalysis as representing a different way of seeing, in which we would not be taken in by our projections and yet recognize the need for god-language. He rightly insists that psychoanalysis is not a new religion because by religion he means belief, dogma, passivity—something very different from the active make-believe of mythic consciousness.

Freud's implicit polytheism correlates with his sense of the importance of mythology in the life of modern man. He shows how man must once more, but now consciously, re-enter the world of mythic apprehension and reclaim the freedom which metaphorical consciousness alone permits to human life. Indeed, we find in Freud an immersion in mythic consciousness much more deep-rooted than just occasional references to ancient gods and heroes. The characteristics of mythopoetic thought listed, for example, in the introduction to Mircea Eliade's *Rites and Symbols of Initiation*, as we shall see, all seem pertinent to some aspect of Freud's thinking.

Freud's fascination with mythology and archaeology dates back to his student days; he somewhere writes that the extinct Greek civilization to which he was introduced in the gymnasium has brought him as much consolation as anything else in the struggles of life. He was an avid collector of ancient near eastern figurines, and jokes in a letter to Fliess how these idols convince him that "the ancient gods still exist."[7] His leisure reading during the composition of *Interpretation of Dreams* included Schliemann's account of his excavations at Troy and Burckhardt's *History of Greek Civilization*, and his letters indicate how often such reading occupied him throughout his life. Already at the outset of his career he made much of the analogy between his work and that of the archaeologist, between the unconscious and the prehistoric.

Though Freud, like Max Weber, claims deafness to the mystical, his writing reveals that he clearly feels there is something numinous about the unconscious. To approach it is to enter a sacred though dark realm. Recall the epigraph from the *Aeneid* at the beginning of *Interpretation*: "If I cannot bend the higher powers, I will move the infernal regions." He responds to dreams as to revelations, revelations as ambiguous as those given out at Delphi and so as much in need of interpretation. Jung remarks on the religious quality of Freud's awe of the unconscious, particularly in its sexual aspect. Transcendence was not for Freud an in general quality but felt here, in sexuality, long before he names it Eros. From the beginning Freud's conception of the sexual was transliteral; sex is never just genitality; it is polymorphous, metamorphic. Indeed, to put it most provocatively, sex is to Freud the equivalent of the human capacity for symbolization. Human sexuality means mythmaking. Because there can be repression of immediate and direct satisfaction without energy loss and, thus, redirection of the sexual instinct, there can be substitution, that is: sublimation, symbolism. Freud's awe of the sexual is, thus, also awe of our imaginative mythmaking capacities.

Freud's mythic bent comes out perhaps most visibly in the fascination with beginnings that marks all of his work and which he sees as characteristic of the human as such. To be Oedipus means to Freud to be fascinated with the search for one's own creation. The myth of Oedipus is, as Peter Homans put it, a myth about the origins of the human capacity for imagination, for fantasy, for myth-making.[8]

The interest in myth, the recognition of the numinosity of the unconscious, are there from the beginning, but Freud recognizes more explicitly in his later work that to speak adequately of the human is to speak of our interaction with the realm described in myth. Already in 1908, Freud writes to Jung of a new pull to the study of mythology. He regards *Totem and Taboo* (1912)—the first book directed to an analysis of primitive mythology and the one whose preparation provokes the break with Jung—as the climax, the turning point of his career. It marks the move from a focus on individual psychology before World War I to a focus on culture, especially myth and religion, afterward. Northrop Frye suggests that "every developed mythology tends to complete itself, to outline an entire universe in which the 'gods' represent the whole of nature in humanized form and at the same time show in perspective man's origin, his destiny, the limits of his power and the extension of his hopes and dreams."[9] An apt description of Freud's enterprise in his later works, especially *Beyond the Pleasure Principle* and *Civilization and its Discontents*. Psychoanalysis has now come, he says, to have the whole human race as its patient; he admits that he has now returned to his original (and, therefore, to a mythic understanding, real) objective: philosophy.

But let us look further at some of the less obvious ways in which elements of mythopoetic thought are present in Freud's work. There is, for example, the notion that myth leads us into a world that cannot be described, but only narrated. In his first book, *Studies on Hysteria*, Freud says, "It still strikes me as strange that the case histories I write should read like short stories...Detailed descriptions of mental processes such as we are accustomed to find in works of imaginative writers enable me...to obtain at least some kind of insight."[10] Long before he won the Goethe Prize, Freud voiced his awareness of the power of esthetic form to seduce us into accepting what we otherwise would not, be the form that of the secondary elaboration of the dream or the artful skill of wit or poet. He was concerned always to find the right form for his own saying: "Somewhere inside me there is a feeling for form, an appreciation for beauty as a kind of perfection"[11] which the clumsiness of the dream-book offends. As he writes his case histories, he is very aware how much the shape of the telling informs what is told. He deliberately rearranges facts, not only to conceal identities but to reveal meanings. Henri Ellenberger's research and the letters to Jung reveal how different true telling is, in Freud's mind, from journalistic accuracy.

Of course, Freud did not write only case histories, he also wrote papers on psychological theory, papers which he came to call essays in "metapsychology." He knew, however, that these projects, too, have a mythical, "as if," "let's pretend" quality to them. Indeed, he regarded his theoretical work as speculative, as visionary, and spoke of it as his play in contrast to his work as a therapist. Freud could tolerate the coexistence of several different models of the psyche. The various versions do not really replace one another any more than Lear replaces Hamlet. (Nor does it seem possible to specify what might verify one or another.) Within even these essays there is a characteristic and tantalizing fusion of mechanistic language with language drawn from another realm: Narcissus and Oedipus will not stay away. In an open letter to Einstein in 1932, Freud wrote: "It may perhaps seem to you as though our theories are a kind of mythology.... But does not every science come in the end to a kind of mythology like this? Cannot the same be said today of your physics?"[12]

It seems strange, indeed, that Freud is so often regarded as a reductionist because of his willingness to give names to these forces as the mythmaker must, to personify. For the names are not drawn from the realm of positivist science: they come from mythology or literature, from the human body (oral, anal, genital), from the language of everyday intercourse (*Ich* and *Es*, not *ego* and *id*). Even words like "normal" and "perverse," "masculine" and "feminine" are, especially in the later writings, always at least implicitly in quotes.

Freud was well aware of the danger of hypostatization. The discovery of the unconscious was the discovery of a dark, unfathomable realm. What he writes in *Interpretation* of this "navel" of the dream suggests his sense of the infinity of the unconscious, of its numinous quality. He used the word "unconscious" to suggest its not-being and, yet, its power; the unconscious is the not which does not exist and yet somehow is. In *Studies on Hysteria*, Breuer speaks for Freud also when he writes: "It is only too easy to fall into a habit of thought which assumes that every substantive has a substance behind it—to forget the metaphorical character of our spatial language.... Our mythology is then complete."[13] Such mythization is inevitable; the trick is to remain conscious of it as metaphor. In *Civilization*, Freud wrote, "The conceptions I have summarized here I first put forward only tentatively, but in the course of time they have won such a hold over me that I can no longer think in any other way."[14] The power these visions had over Freud himself may help explain why it is difficult for us to relate to them as "make-believe" rather than as literal propositions.

It is true that Freud spoke forcefully, but his "always"es and his "everywhere"s are the exaggerations of the storyteller, not the arrogance of the dogmatist, at least to my ears. If we do not hear them thus, it is indeed difficult for us to receive his naming as a storytelling, which invites us to retell rather than to believe or reject. Yet, it seems so obvious to me that the identities he proposes are metaphorical ones. His whole hermeneutic, his conception of symbolization and sublimation, is committed to the notion that this means this and also that. The second member of the metaphor is never fully an adequate substitute for the first. It is not a complete replacement; the original meaning as well as the secondary manifest meaning is still intended. The cat is a burglar in the night but still a cat. Sexual energy is transmuted into poetic creativity but is still sexual.

The recognition of the factually nonexistent, that which cannot be corroborated empirically, comes out also in Freud's fascination with "once upon a time." Eliade speaks of myth's focus on a paradigmatic time that lays the foundation for how things came to be. Basically, we humans are what we are because, at the dawn of time, certain things happened to us, the things narrated by the myths. Everything took place in the beginning and all new acquisitions are projected into the primordial time. Freud, too, speaks of a primordial determinative period in the life of the individual and of the race. In his early trauma theory of the etiology of hysteria he identified this determinative moment with a literal event. But as he came to ask more deeply about the meaning of the accounts of childhood seduction reported by his patients, he discovered that these were fantasy events, events that had happened in the imagination, in a mythic not an historical time, and yet were perhaps even more powerful than most actual childhood experiences. Likewise, the primal parricide put forward in *Totem and Taboo*, "the great event with which civilization began," may never literally have occurred and yet is nevertheless for Freud the most adequate "explanation" of human culture. Freud is so deeply impressed by the reality of such events that he himself has difficulty admitting that their reality is of a different order from that of everyday. Still, in *The Wolfman*, in *Totem and Taboo*, even in *Moses and Monotheism*, he betrays his longing for an objective historical correlative that would account for their convincingness.

Freud's oft-used analogy between his work and that of the archaeologist articulates his recognition that both involve excavation and reconstruction. Already in the 1899 essay on screen memories, he sees that the reconstructions may, indeed, be constructions: they are memories not *from* childhood but memories *of* childhood that help us adults make sense of our present. Although Freud sometimes speaks of these "original" events as the "causes" of later events, it is clear that for him the connection is not so much causal as typological. We discover the meaning of the moment in the present by seeing the way in which it recapitulates (and fulfills) an earlier moment. There is, however, no way of predicting from the first what it will lead to: this is a retrodictive hermeneutic. The earlier moment only reveals its meaning in retrospect, or as Fingarette proposes, is only given this meaning then.

Freud also adopts myth's cyclic understanding of time. Or rather, he takes seriously both modes of temporality, the mythic and the historical, the cyclic and the linear. He sees our life as repetitious and as developmental. The child becomes an adult but continues to live in the adult; polymorphous sexuality becomes genitality and remains multiform. In the unconscious, as in the realm of the gods, nothing ever dies.

Freud's understanding of therapy is to ritual as his theory of the psyche is to myth. There is a deep appreciation of the whole-making power of re enactment. It is not enough simply to have heard the story; I must re-experience its emotional impact. This is what led Freud first from hypnosis to dream interpretation and then to the focus on transference. The "interpretation" of a dream is not a causal explanation but a retelling, a fuller description arrived at together by analyst and analysand, one that unpacks the too tight allusions of the manifest version. Freud believes that not the dream itself but telling and retelling it have therapeutic effect. In the playspace of the therapeutic hour the fantasies are allowed free rein as imaginative products: they are neither repressed nor "acted out," but are relived verbally, symbolically. The focus is not on logical but on "free" associations, on the symbolic connections suggested by analogies of feeling. The interest is not in what a thing is in itself, but in the associations it provokes. There is a parallel here to the retrogression into chaos that in initiation-myths precedes rebirth. In the erotic encounter of the therapeutic hour we patients finds ourselves back in primordial times, in the time-space of re-creation. As Freud begins to take transference more seriously, it is because he sees that the relation between analyst and patient is a "replay" of the relationship between the patient and his parent. Yet, it is a ritual replay, a consciously metaphorical one, which becomes important precisely because both moments are taken seriously, the moment of childhood and the moment in the present.

Freud seems to believe as surely as any primitive that "in order to become a man, it is necessary to resemble a mythic model."[15] To be a self is to be others; thus Freud describes the child becoming a self through a series of fantasized identifications with others. We know, of course, how important it was in his self-analysis for him to discover himself in relation to the mythical prototype, Oedipus, and how he came to believe that all of us as human beings discover who we are as we come to admit this identification. We are all Oedipus, but we are all also Narcissus and Prometheus and an endless series of prototypes. As Freud was not just Oedipus but just as importantly Moses and Joseph, Leonardo and Dostoevski, Goethe and the Nietzsche he feared to re-read, so strong was his sense of their psychological empathy. As we read Freud we discover that not only the obviously mythological figures become part of his own life-story, but that this is so for every character whose inner life he tries to understand. Dora and Leonardo, Richard II and the Wolfman all become part of Freud's self-analysis.

Freud never expected much from therapy. Early on his hope was to reconcile neurotics to common unhappiness, not so much through the cure of symptoms as through the introduction to a different way of being in the world. Later he speaks of his aim in terms of the ability to work and play, to work and enjoy, to work and love. Health means being free of the longing for an impossible satisfaction and learning to take delight instead precisely in our capacity to invent substitutes, to sublimate, to symbolize. He saw in the delusions of Dr. Schreber not his illness but an attempt at recovery. Liberation comes from recognizing and celebrating the mythological universal dimensions of our manifestly banal and troubled lives—a very different liberation from the solipsistic one of Rieff's "psychological man."

I have tried to suggest some of the most significant ways in which Freud's thinking issues from a mythopoetic perspective, despite the manifest obeisance to a mechanistic and rationalistic outlook. As we read Freud we cannot help but notice how regularly it is Greek mythology that compels his imagination. The other mythological tradition centrally important to Freud is, of course, that explored in David Bakan's *Freud and the Jewish Mystical Tradition*. The interplay is subtle. On the one hand, Freud sets Greek polytheism over against Hebrew monotheism, and the Greek recognition of myths as esthetic forms over against the dogmatic literalism of the Hebrews. (That Greece represents the overcoming of the father to him is suggested by his poignant account of the guilt that seized him on the occasion of his first visit to the Acropolis.) On the other hand, although in both instances Freud directs most of his overt attention to the orthodox versions—Homer and the Torah—he comes to a slow-dawning recognition of the importance of the underlying Mycenaean and Canaanite mythologies, and his own retellings suggest some striking affinities to Orphism and the Kabala.

Freud's explorations of mythologies other than the Greek and Hebraic were occasional and heavily dependent on the research and scholarship of others. Because he shared his generation's assumptions concerning the universality of mythological motifs, he did not feel apologetic for this parochialism. These "foreign myths" seem never to have entered into his own imaginings. Even the primal parricide of *Totem and Taboo* is really a Greek myth, a retelling of Zeus' murder of his father, Cronos. Knowing about myths is very different from participating in them, as Freud does with those from Greece and Israel. N. O. Brown says that it is a fundamental law of Hesiod's mythological structure that divinities cannot die, at most they are condemned to impotence. Freud discovered that indeed, the ancient Greek gods and heroes had never died "underground" in the unconscious. He brought them from "the infernal regions" into the sunlight.

Because it was Greek mythology that Freud knew most deeply, it immediately suggested itself to him when he reached for metaphors. His insights came embodied in these figures and we miss much of what they mean to Freud if we try to disengage, try to substitute a prosaic account of narcissism or the Oedipus complex. These figures are much more than illustrations or convenient terminology. Freud does not really use them to formulate a scientific hypothesis, but to put forward a new version of the myth (as Levi-Strauss' discussion of the various recensions of the Oedipus story recognizes).

Ernst Jones, Ellenberger, and others have traced the history of Freud's exposure to Greek mythical traditions, have laid out for us what he read as a student and what books are referred to in his letters or are to be found in his library. We can compare Freud's accounts with Hesiod's and Plato's, with that of Heraclitus and Empedocles, with Homer's and Sophocles'; we can try to see what he has learned from contemporary classical scholars whom we know he read carefully, such as Jakob Burckhardt and Theodor Gomperz. We should, however, not be misled by such researches. Freud very rarely gave explicit references; he deeply resented the scholarship involved in preparing the historical survey that introduces *Interpretation*; he knew his primary gift to be intuition. Perhaps the freedom he felt to retell, almost reinvent, the Oedipus story or the story of the interplay between Eros and Thanatos is due to his not having the scholar's precise sense of a "real" version. Nor does Freud himself have one version to offer. The story of Oedipus he tells again and again and each time discovers more in it to tell. It becomes not just the story of every man's journey to manhood, but the story of the origin of religion and of culture. Likewise, to know Freud's Eros means more than looking up the scattered references to Eros even in some very early works and the more elaborated accounts in *Beyond the Pleasure Principle* and *Civilization*. It means listening also to what Freud wrote of sex and love all along the way, which has as much to do with how he saw Eros as has what he may have read in the *Theogony* or the *Symposium*. Similarly, the figure of Death announces her presence in Freud's work from very early on; *Interpretation* is written in her shadow. Death and Love are figures who have their own history—a new incarnation—as they interact again and again in this work of Freud's and in that. At first they seem to relate only to individual experience; later they come to be cosmic principles not because Freud had reread his sources but because he continued to read his life. In Freud this god Eros and the goddess Death are clearly figures in one story, a story much like that of Baal and Mot. Freud does not look upon them as moral categories: "Neither is any less essential than the other: the phenomena of life arise from the operation of the two together, whether acting in concert or in opposition."[16] It is not even possible to divide up the world between them; each penetrates the whole.

Freud's project was to reawaken us to the mythological memories still alive in our unconscious, and also to that capacity for mythopoetic thought reflected in the form of unconscious processes. Oedipus and other archetypal figures live in us. There are symbols in our dreams whose meaning seems not to derive from our own personal history nor to be accessible through free association, universal symbols which mean in my dreams what they mean in yours and what they meant in the myths of long ago. Like Jung, Freud toyed for a time with the notion of some kind of biological inheritance of cultural acquisitions to explain the presence of such "archaic contents," though he never really found an explanation that satisfied him. Explanation in any case seemed less important than recognition.

But Freud was interested not only in the recovery of buried facts from our own childhood or the childhood of the race, but also in the recovery of a buried mode of psychic functioning, the playful imaginative consciousness of the child. As we read *Interpretation* we encounter Freud's amazement at our human capacity for symbolization and his sadness at its distortion and enfeeblement. The logic and language of dream is an intimation of this power, even though somewhat distorted by dream's need to accommodate itself to the censoring repressive attitude of ego consciousness. Yet the parallels between the logics of dream and of myth, of the child's play and the poet's art, suggest something of what an unrepressed symbolic consciousness might be like. Freud sees that we are as repressed in our imagination as in our sexuality. The playspace of therapy is intended as an arena in which to exercise this unused capacity, to help us recover the primacy of play and pleasure. Freud's writings on wit and poetry hint at his recognition of the delight that comes from simply exercising our psychic capacities for giving esthetic form, for frolicking with images.

He speaks sometimes of a transformed reality principle, of a metaphorical consciousness that would not be a return to the participation mystique of primitive and dream because it would be knowingly symbolic—it would recognize its projections as projections. It would take delight in the exercise of these projective powers as an authentic response to our situation. Such a response would transcend the narrowly "realistic," utilitarian, and rational response of the untransformed reality principle, but would bring us into a genuinely erotic not narcissistic relation to the world.

Yet, there are *only* hints, only suggestions, only occasional allusions. Despite Freud's deep immersion in the world of myth, his description of mythological consciousness is not wholly satisfying. Mythically, the difficulty seems to arise in relation to Freud's relationship to the realm of the mother-goddesses. This is a realm whose pull he feels but resists. In his earlier works he stresses the central importance of the relation to the father, but in his late essays he acknowledges that the early preOedipal love of the mother is central for both men and women, the first love and the most repressed. He speaks of the difficulty of unearthing the Minoan-Mycenaean relics that for so long had been obscured by the patriarchal overlay of classical Greek mythology.

Clearly, Freud was more at ease in exploring the ambivalence of the relation to the father than to the mother. The iconoclasm directed against the father might seem to lead naturally to a reunion with the mother, but does not. Freud feels he was given strength for the battle with the father by the mother's nourishing love, but he also knows her devouring aspect and is fearful of it. In his essay on "The Theme of the Three Caskets," he refers to the three forms taken on by the figure of the mother as life proceeds: "The mother herself, the beloved who is chosen after her pattern, and finally the Mother Earth who receives him again." He concludes by saying, "It is in vain that the old man yearns after the love of woman as he once had it from his mother; the third of the Fates alone, the silent goddess of Death, will take him into her arms."[17] The mother means womb and sex and tomb, but somehow the deepest meaning to Freud is that of the mother as Thanatos: Death but not rebirth. He focuses on the regressive, not the recreative, features of the relation to the mother. This is the puzzle. It is almost as though the words about the murderous sons in *Totem and Taboo* have come back to haunt Freud. The sons' guilt at the murder of the father inhibits their having the mother, which had been the point of it all. So Freud finds himself in a double bind—wanting and not wanting, acknowledging and not acknowledging. We feel this in the opening pages of *Civilization* where Freud recognizes the pull of primary narcissism, the power of the longing for the return to the womb, and then seemingly takes it all back.

Freud's fear of the feminine side of his own psyche, of homoeroticism, of the pull of the deep unconscious, of matriarchal religion, of death, all coalesce. The strength of the resistance is a measure of the power of the pull. He identified the longing for the feminine with castration, passivity, and death. The Mother means the pull to the undifferentiated, mythically speaking to pantheism not polytheism. Freud calls upon Eros, discriminating love, to protect him from absorption by Aphrodite. Without the father, the masculine, the power of the mother-goddess seems overwhelming. Kierkegaard calls us to remember that Abraham did not have the benefit of knowing how the story turns out. Perhaps we should remember that Freud, too, was a pioneer, and that Hölderlin and Novalis and Nietzsche had gone under. Even Jung warns us. "It happens all too easily that there is no returning from the realm of the Mothers."[18]

Myths, Francis Fergusson tells us, have the power to "generate new forms…in the imaginations of those who try to grasp them."[19] As Sophocles' Oedipus generated Freud's, so perhaps Freud's mythmaking may in turn stimulate ours—and, indeed, fails as myth unless it does. Thus we may be helped by Freud to tell a myth he does not tell, a myth that acknowledges the power of father and mother. An exclusive relation to the father produces a theology dominated by the objectifying rationalism of ego-consciousness. A theology evoked by the mother comes out as a sheer pouring forth of images and aphorisms. When we turn instead to speak of the intercourse between father and mother, we find ourselves telling a story…. In his essay on "The Acquisition of Power over Fire," Freud suggests that myths are always about the mythic imagination: the perennial theme of myth is the defeat of the instinctual life, of the imagination, and of its imperishability. This was Freud's theme; it is mine.

Notes

1. Sigmund Freud, "The Moses of Michelangelo," *Character and Culture* (New York: Collier Books, 1963) 103.

2. Paul Ricoeur, *Freud and Philosophy* (New Haven: Yale University Press, 1970) 328.

3. Sigmund Freud, *The Future of an Illusion* (New York: Anchor Books, 1964) 55.

4. Philip Rieff, *Freud: The Mind of the Moralist* (New York: Anchor Books, 1961) xxii.

5. Sigmund Freud, *New Introductory Lectures* (New York: W. W. Norton, 1965) 95.

6. Freud, *Future of an Illusion*, 51-52.

7. Sigmund Freud, *The Origins of Psychoanalysis* (New York: Anchor Books, 1957) 289.

8. Peter Homans, *Theology after Freud* (Indianapolis: Bobbs Merrill, 1970) 198.

9. Northrop Frye, "Myth, Fiction and Displacement," *Daedalus 90* (Summer 1961) 599.

10. Sigmund Freud and Josef Breuer, *Studies on Hysteria* (New York: Avon Books, 1966) 201.

11. Freud, *Origins of Psychoanalysis,* 300.

12. Sigmund Freud, "Why War?" *Character and Culture*, 143.

13. Freud and Breuer, *Hysteria*, 271.

14. Sigmund Freud, *Civilization and its Discontents.* (New York: Anchor Books, 1958) 71.

15. Mircea Eliade, *Rites and Symbols of Initiation* (New York: Harper Torchbooks, 1958) xiv.

16. Freud, "Why War?" 141.

17. Sigmund Freud, "The Theme of the Three Caskets," *Character and Culture*, 78-79.

18. C. G. Jung. *Symbols of Transformation* (New York: Pantheon Books, 1956) 310.

19. Francis Fergusson, "'Myth' and the Literary Scruple," in John B. Vickery, ed., *Myth and Literature* (Lincoln: University of Nebraska Press, 1966) 140.

16

The Silent Goddess of Death and Two Who Paid Her Tribute

As we turn to the psycho-logics of Freud and Jung and listen to their recording of the soul's speech about itself, we discover a constantly recurring theme: the intrusive presence of death.

Each seems to have become even more attuned to the central importance of the psyche's relationship to death at the time of the "death" of the intense friendship between them. The working-through of the meaning of this ending coincided for both with the need to come to terms with the shocking, unprepared-for manifestation of the reality of death and human destructiveness represented by World War I. During the immediately following years Freud had also to endure several anguish-bringing deaths in his own family and the discovery of the cancer with which he was to live for the last sixteen years of his life. In Jung's case the break with Freud provoked a fearsome though deliberately undertaken exploration of his own psychic depths, an exploration that he experienced as a letting-die of all that by which he had hitherto identified himself.

For both, as we shall see, the confrontation with death meant a confrontation with the numinous, a confrontation of mythic proportions. For both, reflection on their own experience led to an expression of the meaning of death for us humans as such. This ability to recognize the universal dimensions of their personal struggles was in itself, of course, a kind of transcendence of their finitude.

I have been impressed with how important mythology is in the psychologies developed by both these men. Both find that deep self-understanding involves the recognition of our relationship to such mythological figures as Oedipus and Narcissus, Hermes and the Great Mother, Eros and Ananke—and, perhaps most importantly of all, to Persephone, or as Freud quite rightly speaks of her, since her name was traditionally left unspoken when she was addressed in her role as Queen of Hades, "the silent goddess of death."

For both Freud and Jung this divinity exists within a polytheistic context, in relation to other gods and goddesses whose claims on us are equally undeniable. Both see the rejection of the Biblical god's claim to be the only god as what made possible the rediscovery of the numinous, which had become congealed or petrified in dogmatism and objectification. The death of god, they believed, issues in the rediscovery of the liveliness of the gods. Each hoped to help awaken that in us that enables us to recognize, respond to and honor the sacred. This does not mean making an idol of our own imaginative capacities nor substituting an inner god for the rejected outer one. Neither calls us to worship the unconscious as god but rather with its help to rediscover the age-old gods to whose presence our reliance on rationality, on ego consciousness, has blinded us. They sought, through reanimation of a neglected mode of consciousness, to move toward the recovery of a transutilitarian and transrational relationship to the world, the discovery of the wonder-fulness of the world. Freud called this other mode "primary process," and saw it as representing the free play of the psyche. To him as to Jung the gods and goddesses of mythology are not subjective but the figures of our response to the most majestic and inexorable forces humankind confronts. Neither Freud nor Jung were calling upon us to worship these forces but simply to acknowledge them, give them due consideration. Freud asked his contemporaries to recognize as the ancients had the "homage" due to these "uncontrolled and indestructible forces," to their "daemonic power." Jung said that just such attention was indeed the original meaning of *religio*.

There are many such powers; each represents a particular perspective on the world. In focusing on the peculiar spirit of the illumination provided by the goddess of death, we are introduced into a different vision of the world than that provided by Eros or Zeus or Apollo or Aphrodite. This perspective, as already noted, became increasingly important to both Freud and Jung after 1913, the year of the break in their relationship. Their recognition of death's power over the psyche was deepened still further during the many years each lived with a continual awareness of the oncomingness of his own death—for Freud from 1923, the year of his first cancer operation, for Jung from the time of his first serious heart attack in 1944. During their final years each seemed to move from looking at death from the perspective of life—where death seems fearsome, though sometimes fearfully attractive—to looking at life from the perspective of death—where the deepest prayer is the one voiced by the Chorus at the end of *Oedipus at Colonus*: "I pray you, let the descent be clear."

Freud

Freud's letters to Fliess, written during the years immediately preceding the publication of *Interpretation of Dreams*, frequently give expression to his dread of a premature death and his hope that through this book he would achieve a kind of immortality: "One does not wish to die either immediately or completely."

The writing of *Interpretation* was itself a kind of coming to terms with death, an articulation of what Freud had learned about his own unconscious processes under the impetus provided by his father's death. This death, when Freud was already 40, served as his initiation into the unconscious. Freud found himself pulled by it into an intense involvement with his own dreams; he experienced something close to a breakdown; he found himself suddenly his own most important and most difficult patient. His dreams forced upon him the recognition that the father whom he had so dearly loved had also been the object of his hatred and resentment. The death of one's father, he came to believe, is the most important event in a man's life. In his own case he felt he owed to this event his two most important discoveries: that dreams are wish fulfillments and that each of us is Oedipus. These discoveries became the inspiration of the book.

Interpretation is written on the plan of a journey to the underworld, and Freud like Dante before him invokes Virgil as his guide. Dreams, he claims, provide the *via regia* to the unconscious, to an unknown, uncanny realm. The unconscious seems for Freud from the beginning of his acquaintance with it to have been fearsome, associated with death and with the feminine. The unconscious is the realm of the dead for in it nothing ever dies; it is inhabited by the lost parts of our own lives—wounded, fragmented, distorted, ugly parts—that crowd bloodthirstingly, life-searchingly, around the visitor, as the shades in Hades crowded around visiting Odysseus. The unconscious is inhabited also by ancient, long-forgotten daemonic forces—fearful but numinous. Although Freud is only slowly able to differentiate particular gods or goddesses within this realm, he intuits already that what has been most deeply repressed and what is therefore most powerful is connected with our embodiment: our sexuality and mortality. As he writes Fliess in 1900, it is a "hell, layer upon layer of it, with everything fitfully gleaming and pulsating; and the outline of Lucifer-Amor coming into sight at the darkest center." Only years later will Freud speak more explicitly of the two primary powers as Eros and his twin, Death.

At the time of *Interpretation* Freud sees the unconscious as the realm of the dead, as tomb, but also as the source of recreation, as womb. He sees it as the realm of the Mothers in *Faust*. The unconscious is "uncanny" and for Freud *the* epitome of the uncanny; what is long unknown yet at once familiar, is the mother's womb. Entrance into the unconscious is forbidden, incestuous. The dream of Irma's injection, which teaches Freud the secret of dream interpretation, is a dream of entry into the womb. There is a "navel" to every dream, one spot at which it is unplumbable, its point of contact with the unknown. But womb and tomb are closely associated. Freud's own mother figures importantly in two dreams he reports in the book and in both she is associated with death; in one she is dead, surrounded by Egyptian divinities, and thus the goddess of death; in the other she is one of the three fates, reminding him of his own mortality. In the section in the book on symbolism Freud recognizes that death and rebirth are over and over again represented by the same images. Thus, already in Freud's early work, there are intimations that the encounter with death pulls us toward the realm of the unconscious, of symbolic consciousness, and that death which literally means cessation seems at the level of primary process thinking to be somehow associated also with renewal. Nevertheless Freud's focus during the early years of psychoanalysis was more on overcoming the repression of sexuality than of death, more on moving beyond a literalistic identification of sexuality with genitality than beyond a literalistic identification of death with the end of physical functioning.

A full recognition of the awe-ful power of death doesn't come to Freud without a second initiation, an initiation that occurs when he discovers death within as a constant companion, in the guise of his cancer. Henceforward he sees the reconciliation with death as the soul's primary task, not only for himself but for us humans as such (at least in our later years) and regards the overcoming of its repression as a cultural and not just an individual necessity. He finds death not just within but seemingly all about him as well—in the conflicts within the psychoanalytical movement, especially the breaks with Adler and Jung, in his increasing recognition of the limits of therapy, in the war, in the death of his daughter and grandson. Freud's father's death had been an easy one; it meant release for him and in a different sense for Freud. When children die before their parents, death wears another face, cruel and absurd.

These new experiencings of death affected Freud deeply, both in the way he re-ordered his personal and professional life and in the new directions visible in his writing. He said often that the death of little Heinele had killed something in him, that after it he was never again able to invest deeply in a new relationship. The operation on his jaw led to his dependence on an artificial palate whose insertion and removal were difficult and uncomfortable; there were frequent further operations in the years that followed. He speaks of writing *Civilization and*

Its Discontents simply to take his mind off his pain, whose constant presence was an inescapable reminder of his mortality (though he refused to ease it with drugs which might diminish his mental acuity). A decade earlier, when working on his study of *Leonardo*, he had expressed his fear that aging would mean the sapping of his creative energies, but the cancer seemed rather to stimulate their redirection. After every operation, even after the forced move to London, he continued to do analysis, often for ten hours a day, though now it was mostly with analysts in training rather than with avowedly neurotic patients. He never again spoke in public; in his *New Introductory Lectures* he once more took his place in the lecture room only by an artifice of the imagination; often he sent his daughter Anna to speak in his stead.

In his writings from 1914 onward we discover a new perspective, a move from individual psychology to an interest in the interhuman: social interaction, historical continuities, the communal within which he called the *UeberIch*, the over-I, *the* superego. He now sees the whole world as his patient, calls his theoretical speculations *meta*psychology. This shift is not a turn from the realm of body to that of spirit; rather it arises out of a deep contemplation of our embodiment and finitude. He regards this period as representing a "regression" to his earliest interests, in philosophy and the arts, but he had already discovered in his patients how such retrogressions (especially the particular regression called "transference") are necessary to transformation.

Freud writes now of Eros not sexuality, of self-transcendence not just in the ecstasy of orgasm but in the erotic commitment to the extension of the communal bonds between humans. And as an ever-present undertone we sense him reminding us of the inescapable pain of human life, acknowledging honestly but without despair the unavoidable discontents of civilization and the inevitability of death. That such re-focusing is a necessity for the aging is suggested in Freud's description of how Cordelia's death means that King Lear must now renounce love, choose death and make friends with the necessity of dying. Freud speaks of

> The three forms taken on by the figure of the mother as life proceeds: the mother herself, the beloved who is chosen after her pattern, and finally the Mother Earth who receives him again. But it is in vain that the old man yearns after the love of woman as once he had it from his mother; the third of the Fates, alone, the silent goddess of death will take him into her arms.[1]

The war persuaded Freud how important it was that all of us give death the place that properly belongs to it, for only then does life regain its full significance. We must recognize that we were never as civilized as we had supposed; the war had let loose evil spirits in us which we had thought were tamed, and revealed that our deepest attitudes to death were little different from the primitive's. Freud's appreciation of our natural aggressiveness and of the strength of our unconscious conviction of our own immortality have both been deepened. He now sees the conversion to finitude as our most important task, but one that depends on our capacity to move from literalism to symbolism. The aim of analysis is no longer primarily reconciliation to common unhappiness but preparation for death. Yet as important as our response to biological death is how we come to terms with death in life—with losses, dead-ends, failures. These can issue in transformation if we can turn away from self-preoccupation, if we are willing to substitute, to accept symbolic satisfactions, but otherwise lead to morbid narcissism. The work of mourning, the mastery of absence and loss, is now seen as *the* work of maturation.

By 1920, the year of *Beyond the Pleasure Principle*, Freud had come to believe that there is something in us closely allied with death; that we both fear it *and* are pulled toward it. Here he speaks for the first time of Eros and Death as the primal drives out of whose interplay all of life arises and finds himself using the names of ancient Greek divinities to refer to those forces. He has moved to an explicit concern with "*Jenseits*," the beyond, and to speculation that looks "suspiciously mystical," especially to himself. He speaks of death as an *internal* necessity, as a drive, a longing; he means by the death drive the pull toward inertia, toward earlier states, toward the end of tension, toward peace, nirvana.

Yet Freud insisted on our conflicted relation to death. He recognized that there is in us, not only a *wish* for death, but also a deep lying *fear* of death. This fear is fear of being unloved, abandoned; it is the fear of being born, of being reborn, of being changed, transformed. The fear of death is paradoxically the fear of life; Eros and Death are *twin* brothers. The fear issues in denial, and the denial of our own death-longing results in the projection of our death wish onto others in the form of destructiveness. The death drive repressed becomes hate, sadism, destruction. It is in this derivative (distorted by repression) form that the death instinct becomes visible, whereas the death longing itself is not directly accessible or provable. It is mostly this become-aggression aspect of the death instinct that figures in *Civilization and Its Discontents*. There, though Freud nowhere involves the name Thanatos, he does speak of death as a Titan, is referring to the Death that comes after the unprepared aggressively, as Thanatos does in Greek mythology. For just as Eros and Aphrodite represent two very different aspects of love, so Thanatos and Persephone signify different experiences of death.

And the vision of death as Thanatos is one with which Freud is deeply familiar. We sense in him sometimes a withholding from death, perceive in his courageous endurance something of the hero's *hubris*. Several of his letters suggest that
this withholding is connected to his mother's living on until 1930 when she is
ninety-five. "I was not allowed to die as long as she was alive and now I may," he
writes after her death. "Somehow the values of life have changed in the deeper
layers."[2] By 1936 he can acknowledge looking forward with a kind of longing to
the transition into non-existence. It is as though until then the personal mother
had blocked his full reconciliation with the archetypal mother, the silent goddess
of death.

In the *New Introductory Lectures* written after her death, Freud for the first
time recognizes a pre-Olympian, Minoan and Mycenaean strand of mythology, a
mythology in which Demeter and Dionysos, Persephone and Hades are more
important than Zeus, as they are again in the post-heroic age of the mystery religions. What he writes now of the importance of the pre-Oedipal relation to the
mother suggests that he might no longer dismiss the "ocean feeling" and its longing for the restoration of a primal unity as less important than the longing for
paternal protection, as he had done in *Civilization*, written before her death. And
in one of his last essays, "Analysis Terminable and Interminable," he recognizes
the importance of transcending the heroic illusion. Now he can acknowledge that
the acceptance of the feminine (for men *and* women), of the feminine in oneself,
of passivity, receptivity, death-longing, is the ultimate aim of analysis and of life.
The overcoming of misogyny *is* the overcoming of the fear of death.

In this same essay he remarks that he has recently discovered (or perhaps redis-
covered) that his vision of a death drive in partnership with Eros had been anticipated by the ancient Greek healer and seer, Empedocles, in his description of the
eternal conflict between *philia* and *néikos*. Freud does not mention, however, that
in Empedocles' *Katharmoi (Purifications)* a deity who is very likely Persephone is
represented as outlining the way of release from this realm of strife. Yet Freud,
too, seems now to have fully understood what he had already expressed in 1913:
that there is an ancient identity between the goddesses of death and the goddesses
of life and of fertility.

Freud, and here I find him deeply true to his Jewish inheritance, never flies
from the reality of our embodiment and the literalness of our death; yet he seems
to say, *if* we accept this, we can also discover that death means not only cessation
but transformation, can take seriously that in the unconscious (which he spoke of
as the core of our being), in the realm of symbolic knowledge, there is no death
but only metamorphosis.

Jung

Jung's relation to the unconscious was from the beginning different from Freud's in ways that would seem closely related to differences in their understanding of the meaning of death in human life. The unconscious was never to him as it was to Freud a strange and unfamiliar, indeed unsuspected, realm into which he suddenly found himself pulled in midlife. Rather the never quite forgotten dreams and fantasies of Jung's early childhood seem to have created in him an essential trust of the unconscious. It is true that these early memories were neglected during the years of early manhood, but they were available to recall when once again relevant. Jung's return to the Unconscious in his adult years meant not a rediscovery of the wounds and fears of childhood but of its creativity and attunement to the numinous. Thus the unconscious was not so much the realm of the past but of as yet unrealized potentialities, a past with unlived life that might be reanimated.

Jung, like Freud, speaks of the unconscious as the mythic land of the dead; he saw his dreams as showing him that something dead was present that was nevertheless still alive. But what he stressed was that the soul entering this realm gives the seemingly dead a chance for renewed life. For Jung it is the neglect and consequent loss of our imaginal capacities and spiritual longings, our letting them become unconscious, that has been most wounding. He saw, as Freud had, that our dreams seem to suggest a deep preoccupation with sexuality and death, but understood both the longing for the womb and the void as expressive of our even deeper longings for symbolic rebirth, birth into symbolic consciousness. Jung stressed more the importance of the "archetypal" presences in the unconscious than those associated with forgotten or disvalued parts of our personal past. He saw the confrontation with the unconscious as making possible a moving beyond an overly literalistic and personalistic understanding of ourselves to a recognition of the collective, transpersonal, mythological patterns in which our lives participate.

His adult re-initiation into the unconscious was like Freud's provoked by the death of the father—in his case by the symbolic death of the symbolic father, by the break from Freud. Yet there were significant differences. For Jung the plunge into the unconscious was recognized as a return to a long forgotten but immediately familiar terrain. Jung's was a much more consciously chosen, deliberately undertaken exploration than Freud's had been. His descent into the unconscious was experienced as fearsome at times, he speaks of dreams and fantasies where he dreaded being swamped, crushed by enormous boulders, entangled by jungle growth, drowned in blood—and yet there was also a sense of being protected. He knew others had been this way before, Freud for one, and also those poets and mythological personages whose rituals and journeys of transformation he had already written of in his *Psychology of the Unconscious*. He knew that some, like Nietzsche, don't return from the realm of the mothers, knew that it *can* destroy, and yet saw it as essentially the life-giving matrix, and knew: the hero *must* break the taboo. So Jung knew he was participating in an age-old process, and he discovered, too, that there were inward guides, recurrent dream figures whose wisdom he came to trust. Though he had feared the descent might be bottomless, the journey endless (and indeed it *was* long: he spent almost six years pursuing his inner images before he emerged from the darkness), yet he found that it came to a natural end, with the appearance of strangely comforting shapes (which he later knew to be mandalas) that signified wholeness, and of a "big" dream that signaled completion.

When he found his way back to the world, started writing again and devoting more time and energy to his analytic practice, he found that he had now developed an understanding of the psyche different from Freud's and his own therapeutic method, one that seemed particularly effective with patients in the "second half of life." He saw analytical psychology as a school. From the beginning he understood therapy as preparation for death, as itself initiating a little death, an introduction into a stage of life whose characteristic focus was on questions of spiritual meaning rather than on the "work and love" orientation of Freud's early therapy. Jung's own experience had shown him that death does not come only at the end of life, that life cannot be understood on such a linear model but is rather a circumambulation of the same ever-reappearing central motifs. Death and life imply one another; death is the prerequisite of renewal.

Jung once said that he regarded all his work as attempts to answer the question of the relationship between the here and the hereafter. Yet Jung, too, experiences a decisive reorientation when death intrudes literally and dramatically in his own life. He suffered a serious heart attack in 1944 and in the years that followed there were further embolisms, intestinal fevers, and liver ailments. He was weaker, sometimes limping, often tired, required rest and privacy. He retired from his practice and from participation in conferences, spent a good deal of his time in retreat even from his family at his secluded tower in Bollingen. As with Freud this was a period of definite withdrawal, of acknowledged loneliness, *and* of renewed creativity. He spent much of his time reworking older papers, including the book written just prior to the break with Freud, *The Psychology of the Unconscious*, now reissued as *Symbols of Transformation*. It was important to him to bring all his writings up to date with his mature vision, important also to complete his studies of the psychological significance of alchemy, and to bring a kind of closure to his long and ambivalent involvement with Christianity as he did in *Answer to Job* and in *Aion*. (Aion, by the way, is an Alexandrian god, an aging god who is ever self-renewing and a son, so legend has it, of Persephone.)

But probably the most important expression of Jung's very deliberate preparations for death was the writing of his autobiography, *Memories, Dreams, Reflections*. It represented the discovery, in a sense the creation, of that "wholeness and oneness" to which these last years were committed and whose achievement was announced in what we have been told was Jung's very last dream. In the writing of this last book he recreated his awareness of the co-presence of his whole life, and recognized how all of it had been implicit in the imaginal experiences of his earliest years. These memoirs include only those aspects of his life that seemed to him important in the light of death and he concluded: only the visionary element really mattered. The book focuses on the childhood years, on the relation to Freud and the "confrontation with the unconscious" that followed it, and then on the visionary experiences that constructed his inward being prepared for death, and on the reflections these provoked.

He shares a vision begun when, as he later learned, he hung on the edge of literal death, a vision of departing from earth and being suspended far, far above it, and then discovering floating in the same space a tremendous stone block which had been hollowed out to form a temple. As he prepared to enter it, he had a feeling that everything he had ever aimed at or thought was being painfully sloughed away. It was an experience of extreme poverty and great fullness; he felt he existed in an objective form; he was what he had been but with no continuing wishes or feelings. He felt certain that in the temple all the people to whom he really belonged would be waiting for him—and then, before he could enter, he was called back by a delegate from earth. As Jung describes this vision, he says it was the most blissful experience he had had, yet also dark and painfully lacking in human warmth.

In the period that followed his "return," he dreamt night after night of participating in a mystic marriage, where he was both partners: ego and death. These dreams and visions deepened his sense of the kind of "objectivity" that would correlate with completed individuation, of what it would be like to really "let be." He had another signally important dream in which he found a yogi deep in meditation at the place in a church where one would ordinarily find an altar and knew that he, Jung, was being dreamt by that yogi. These experiences seem to have been experiences of death for Jung, as though in a sense the rest of his life was "post mortem."

In *Memories, Dreams, Reflections* he writes of the importance he attaches to our images and visions of an after life, visions confirmative of Freud's notion that in our unconscious we do not believe in the finality or reality of death. Jung knows such myths and dreams "prove" nothing and yet believes they may have healing power and may help us *live* right into death. Furthermore he proposes that if there is continued life and if it is psychic life, it would be a continuance in the world of images. He quotes the Biblical verse, "Your old men shall dream dreams," and suggests that attention to our imaginative capacities would thus be the most appropriate preparation for existence hereafter. Thus the cultivation of symbolic consciousness is the task of old age.

The visionary experiences of Jung's final years led him to speculate on death and on life after death. He senses that there is an after life for attending to what was left undone, unanswered, unconscious in one's most recent existence. The unconscious as he has known it is indeed a realm of the dead, though he is not sure whether the persons he encounters there are his own past lives or perhaps his ancestors. In either case he senses their needing him to help attain that share of awareness they failed to win in life. Yet, he questions: perhaps if one were really conscious, there might be no need to live again. Thus for Jung death means rebirth and yet perhaps ultimately: release, nirvana.

Jung knows that from the ego's perspective death is catastrophe, "a fearful place of brutality," and that we have no right to sidestep this cruel reality. Nevertheless, he believes that from the psyche's point of view, it is a joyful event, a wedding: the soul attains its missing half; it achieves wholeness. Here Jung makes explicit what is only suggested in Freud: that the meeting with death, which Freud recognized as a meeting with one's own femininity, is a *hieros gamos*, a holy wedding. Jung seems to believe that even we modern men and women can achieve the blessing of that reconciliation with death bestowed in ancient Greece by the rites in honor of Persephone, the silent goddess of death:

> Happy is he, who having seen these rites goes below the hollow earth; for he knows the end of life and he knows its god-sent beginning.

Notes

1. Sigmund Freud, "The Theme of the Three Caskets," in Philip Rieff, ed., *Character and Culture* (New York: Collier Books, 1963) 78.

2. Quoted in Ernest Jones, *The Life and Work of Sigmund Freud* (abridged edition) (New York: Anchor Books, 1963) 470.

17

Two Masters of the School of Suspicion: Karl Marx and Sigmund Freud

Freud once said that through interpretation one could remember a whole life from a dream fragment. My project in this paper seems almost as ambitious and as questionable an undertaking. For I would like to use the examination of the first few paragraphs of Marx's "Introduction of Hegel's *Philosophy of Right*" as the occasion for an exploration of the interrelationship between the hermeneutics of Marx and of Freud.

I choose to do this because of my agreement with Paul Ricoeur that the meaning for our time of Marx or of Freud remains in suspense until we find some way of considering them jointly. To decide what either says to us demands the recognition that what they mean for us is yet to be discovered and is different from what either had to say in his own time. Obviously, all I can do in a paper of this length is to sketch the direction a full exploration might take, keeping in mind all along the focus suggested by the passage in which Marx sets forth his critique of religion.

We do not, of course, have a standpoint on the basis of which we might effect a synthesis between Marx and Freud or might construct a unified hermeneutic. For the contradictions between them interpret us and our world as much as do their individual critiques. A harmonization would imply that our society is without the antagonisms that are its essence, that its tensions could meaningfully be resolved on the theoretical level alone. Paul Ricoeur has referred to both (along with Nietzsche and sometimes Feuerbach) as "masters of the school of suspicion"—as good a rubric as any I know for a joint consideration.

Sartre, speaking of those philosophies that become "the humus of every particular thought and the horizon of all culture," says there is no going beyond them so long as we have not gone beyond the historical moment that they express.[1]

Marxism and psychoanalysis are such philosophies for us. Both are products of 19th century bourgeois culture, a culture of which we are the epigones. But as participants in a much later moment in that culture's life, our situation is somewhat different from Marx's or Freud's, and it is that difference which makes bringing their perspectives together so necessary a part of our making sense of what they have to say.

Our very focus on this early text of Marx is a clue to that. Interest in the early "humanistic" Marx seems again and again to manifest itself along with the project of relating Marx to Freud: in Germany after the collapse of revolutionary hopes at the end of World War I and during the early years of the Nazi rise to power, in France after the Second World War, and here in America during the last decade as part of our response to the developments in the anti-war, civil rights and feminist movements. When revolutions fail or when institutional changes turn out to be disappointingly superficial, Marxist analysis alone seems insufficient. The "delay of the eschaton" provokes the turn to Freud. Wilhelm Reich wrote in 1934 that the forces inhibiting the development of class-consciousness, the forces that lead a large strata of the oppressed class to support the exploiters, could only be explained psychoanalytically.[2] We need a Marxism capable of understanding the subjective as well as the economic conditions of revolution. As Sartre suggests, psychoanalysis supplies the needed mediation which explains how the general social determinants present themselves as the traits of single individuals;[3] and as Juliet Mitchell believes, through its demonstration of how deeply outmoded assumptions and values, hopes and fears, are embedded in our psyches, it explains why significant cultural changes are so damnably difficult.[4] (And in the face of fascist threats, even Marxists have found some reassurance in Freud's positing a part of us, the libido, out of reach of total social control).

The ways in which psychoanalysis in turn needs the Marxist corrective are implicit in Ricoeur's turn to Hegel and structuralism after his work on Freud. For without the emphasis on teleology that Hegel represents to Ricoeur, without the recognition of the objective collective determinants of human consciousness that Levi-Strauss insists upon, one vector in Freud's hermeneutic tends to dominate. We are left with the over-familiar caricature of Freudianism as "archaeological," subjectivistic, atomistic. When it ignores the Marxist critique psychoanalysis also too easily becomes an instrument of social adaptation and loses sight of the particularism of this culture's "reality principle." Freudians then are pulled to substituting therapy for revolution, though Freud himself never confused them. He diagnosed the general sickness (the discontents of us civilized humans) and practiced therapy (which promised no more than the transmutation of neurotic misery into everyday unhappiness). He recognized the contradiction and valued his theoretical contributions much more highly than his therapeutic efforts: "My discoveries are the basis for a very grave philosophy."[5]

This outline of the supplementary character of their critiques is not intended to vulgarize the differences between them. It would be a gross misunderstanding to identify Marx with a social view of humankind and set him over against Freud as holding an individualistic view. Freud recognizes the importance of the social dimension even in his earliest writings where "social" means primarily "familial," and this element becomes increasingly important in his thought after the First World War. Marx, especially in his early work, is concerned with our alienation from ourselves and not only with our alienation from one another.

Freud had believed that Marxism tended to minimize the importance of the superego (his name for the internalized collective past) and how slowly it yields to the influences of the present. He resisted the Marxist rhetoric concerning the inevitability of the revolution and its unilateral focus on economic determinants, though he respected "its sagacious indication of the decisive influence the economic circumstances of men have upon their intellectual, ethical and artistic attitudes." He believed Marxists tend to forget that the economic situation can only bring into play universal instinctual impulses such as self-preservation, aggressiveness, the need to be loved, the drive for pleasure. He expressed his sympathy for "the Soviet experiment," though he thought it might be premature in that the success of communism might depend on a post-scarcity technology. Yet he clearly does not say that communism could never succeed; he warns only of "an incalculable time of wrestling with the untamable elements of human nature."[6] In a letter written in 1937 Freud indicates that he has come to learn that the differences between his views and Marx's are not as central as he had earlier thought: "I have since learned—rather to my satisfaction—that neither [Marx nor Engels] has denied the influence of ideas or super-ego factors. So that invalidates the main contrast between psychoanalysis and Marxism which I had believed to exist."[7]

Nevertheless, Marxism without the Freudian reminder seems to "forget" such factors, as Freudianism without the Marxist revision tends to ignore the realm of possibility. Adorno once remarked that in psychoanalysis only the exaggerations are true. I believe we need the exaggerations of both Freud and Marx—as we also need the critique of these exaggerations created by their being brought into a dialectic engagement with one another.

The Criticism of Religion as Prolegomena to all Criticism

The opening paragraph of Chapter 7 of Freud's *Future of An Illusion* shows that like Marx he recognizes that the criticism of the religious illusion inevitably leads to the criticism of politics, sexuality, and science. Thus for both Marx and Freud the criticism of religion serves as prolegomena to a criticism of cultural institutions generally. Both acknowledge that religion arises in response to real needs and real oppression. They take the appearance, the phenomenon of human religion, seriously, but also see it as an illusory gratification of those needs. They are not so much against religion as against the self-alienation that it expresses and particularly the conditions that seem to restrict us to only illusory satisfactions. They are fascinated by our power to create a world through the exercise of our imaginations and then to be trapped within this self-created world. Religion is seen by both as the epitome of this irony.

Freud's critique of religion seems at first glance pre-Marxist, a reprise of Feuerbach. For he does not relate particular religious forms to particular eco-social situations, though he does take into consideration that religion may be used by some to manipulate others as Feuerbach does not. (Of course, in this sense, the Marx of the essay on Hegel is also "pre-Marxist.") Yet actually the Freud of *Future of an Illusion* is post-Marxist, after all. Freud begins with the economic explanation and finds it insufficient; he has consciously, not ignorantly, decided to stress the universal psychological needs that give rise to religion and not just those connected to a particular form of economic oppression. He believes that to free us from religion's power over us means changing consciousness not just external structures, and that this means changing upbringing in a truly radical sense. By 1929, one had after all to come to terms with nearly a century of "delay," and Freud was thus perhaps more aware than Marx could have been of how deep-rooted religious belief is in us. His vision is thus at the same time both less historical and less eschatological than Marx's, because, oddly, he is more aware of the social limits on human change, more skeptical concerning human malleability. Nevertheless, the criticism of religion seems to inspire utopianism even in Freud. In this book more than any other we catch him wondering, "What would we be like, if..."

Fully to understand the critique of religion put forward by Marx or Freud means paying attention to the place of this criticism in their lifework. To adhere to the strictures of the "new criticism" of the forties and study our texts without regard for the biographical and cultural context out of which they emerge and which they both express and transcend, would be to show that we have not after all learned anything from Marx or Freud about interpretation. To take biography and history into account does not need to mean reducing the meaning of our texts to their author's conscious intentionality, nor substituting context for text.

Marx's "Introduction to Hegel's *Philosophy of Right*" marks his transition from a primarily philosophical orientation to a new focus on economic factors and on *praxis*. But this transition is still in process; this essay is still, after all, instigated as an interpretation of Hegel. Though in it Marx for the first time refers to the proletariat, his vision of the proletariat at this point seems more dependent on the biblical image of the suffering servant than on empirical data. In the *Theses on Feuerbach*, written very soon after, the importance of concrete social and historical determinants has become explicit. This discovery of his own perspective leads Marx into a period of intense productivity (paralleling the period in Freud's life immediately after the writing of *The Interpretation of Dreams* during which the books on sexuality, wit, the psychopathologies of everyday life and Dora appear in quick succession). *The German Ideology, The Paris Manuscripts, The Holy Family*, written during this moment in Marx's career are all clear and impassioned articulations of his revolutionary vision. But after the failure of the 1848 revolutions, by 1852, Marx's exalted dream of release seems to have dimmed. Thus Marx, too, had to confront the problems of "delay"; in his case this seems to issue in a loss of faith in the proletariat and a retreat from overt political activity. His later writings are less confident, less utopian; his understanding of the mechanisms of social change becomes more mechanical, more unilinear. There is more focus on technical economic analyses, a more deterministic reliance on automatically working historical factors, little reference to ideology or religion. In 1863 after rereading a book by Engels first published in 1844 he writes a letter to Engels expressing his own recognition of this change:

> Reading your book again has sadly made me feel my age. With what freshness and passion and boldness of vision and freedom for learned and scientific scruples you have handled the subject here! And the illusion that tomorrow or the day after tomorrow the result will spring to life as an historical reality before our eyes gives the whole a warm and spirited humor—with which the later "gray on gray" makes a damnably unpleasant contrast.[8]

Thus in Marx the "completion" of the criticism of religion leads naturally into the call to human liberation so important in his early writings, but that humanistic vision is much less evident in his later years.

Whereas in Freud's case the criticism of religion (which begins in 1913 with *Totem and Taboo*) comes at a late point in his career; it is associated with his turn away from a central emphasis on *praxis* and the technical aspects of therapy to a concern with the social and cultural. Henceforward he sees the whole world as his patient. Freud's coming to terms with what he calls the death instinct, that in us that opposes liberation and transformation, issues in a skeptical though deeply concerned humanism. It is at this point that Eros becomes an important theme in his writing. The criticism of religion issues not in a paean to sexuality but in an invocation to Eros, the force that pulls us to bond together communally. It is worth noting that in the last book Freud published, *Moses and Monotheism*, he is still explicitly involved with the question of religion.

From the Critique of Heaven to a Critique of Earth

In both instances, however, the critique of religion is what Ricoeur calls a "critique of recovery"; it represents a decisive positive transcendence of religion, is undertaken for the sake of liberation. A beginning in this direction is made, both seem to believe, when oppression is supplemented by consciousness of oppression. Freud said:

> Not in any beyond but here on earth most men live in a hell: Schopenhauer has seen that very well. My knowledge, my theories and my methods have the goal of making men conscious of this hell so they can free themselves from it.[9]

Marx says his critique is directed not towards sponsoring disillusion but for the sake of "the living flower." Criticism is not an end in itself. In Marx its pathos is indignation; its essential task denunciation. For him the criticism of religion ends with a call to overthrow the conditions in which we are degraded, enslaved, neglected. Freud's rhetoric is less impassioned, his invocations less revolutionary, but to him also it seems time to move beyond interpretation.

For both the real focus is on the critique of earth; they see the present as a time for us to re-order this world in a truly human way. Both stress the interrelationship of theory and practice, the move from interpretation to action. Both too see the danger of surrogate religions: Marx sees capitalism in this light; Freud, soviet communism. Both ask not only what has the biblical god made of us but also what have these other gods, Money and Dialectical Materialism, made of us. Secularization in itself is not enough. Freud even recognized how easily psychoanalysis too can be converted to a religion; one of his central criticisms of Jung is that Jung encouraged this conversion.

Both have a thoroughly historical perspective that leads them to protest all supra-historical fulfillment as illusory. Both, too, have an historical understanding of the relationship between past, present and future. Marx acknowledges that capitalism was a necessary stage because it made possible the material accumulation requisite for the success of communism; Freud recognized the necessary connection between repression and ego development. These particular pasts are the necessary preludes to the futures to which they look forward.

Their criticisms show both Freud and Marx to be materialists, sensualists, in a subtle rather than a vulgar sense. They share a vision of a society based on a true consciousness of human needs which our material acquisitiveness and distorted sexuality blocks. Marx's criticism of capitalism seems much less inspired by a concern for distributive justice than for a non-alienating lifestyle. The materialism of both Freud and Marx is closely connected to their taking human embodiment seriously. They regard a clear distinction between material and spiritual needs as mystification; they recognize how a focus on spiritual satisfactions can be palliative, and thus repressive. Nevertheless both also are tempted to a more trivial form of materialism; both express nostalgia for objectivity. Freud clearly wishes he could establish that there were objective events undergirding our primal fantasies; Marx insists on calling economic factors substructure, even though his formulation of dialectics doesn't really allow this privileged a role to one class of determinants.

The Dialectics of Criticism

Marx's version of dialectic, unlike Engels, is taken not from Hegel's historical writings but from the *Phenomenology*: he means by dialectic not the necessary progression thesis/antithesis/synthesis but simply the interplay of contradictions. He applies his dialectic primarily to the interaction between subject and object, which he recognizes as more than simply reciprocal action. Like Freud he sees how society comes into being as the objectification of human perception and wish and how society is in turn internalized in individual consciousness. Neither regards this dynamic interplay between us and our creations as an abstract fixed relationship, but as something that happens uniquely in each practical instance. The point is *specific* criticism: for Freud, how are conscious and unconscious factors related *here?* for Marx, what is the relationship between ideological and economic factors in *this* situation? There is no *a priori* application of the dialectic but rather a careful detailed reading of particular cases, as in Marx's study of the Eighteenth Brumaire and Freud's case studies. Both recognize the reality of the immediately appearing and its underlying meaning; the appearances are revealing and concealing. They acknowledge that the distortions and deceptions are usually not deliberate, not conscious. Both deliberately introduce into their rhetoric the tension between mechanistic and intentionalistic languages to express their vision of us as victims and as actors; both hope to widen our capacity for self-direction.

Marx recognizes that simple economism is but a new idealism, as Freud likewise seeks to avoid a monistic pan-sexism. Yet both Freud and Marx tend toward an essentializing rhetoric and toward a polemically inspired overemphasis on those factors their cultures have ignored. Thus both make a distinction between "base" and "superstructure" (Marx's language), between "primary" and "secondary" processes (Freud's). Marx speaks of economic structures as basic; Freud of the unconscious, the id, as the primary mode of psychic activity. Both Marx and Freud stressed these neglected and denied forces to a degree that makes it possible to read some of their texts as implying a mechanistic deterministic vision; this is especially true of the later Marx. Yet in the texts of the mid-1840s where he deals most explicitly with this issue, it is life, *praxis*, human activity that "determines consciousness"; the shaping structures are themselves the products of real persons. Freud asserted that everything in psychoanalysis depends on the extension of the literalistic definition of sexuality; similarly everything in Marxism depends on moving beyond a literalistic economism. The equations that Marxist analysis discerns are as complex as those of psychoanalysis. The relationship between an economic phenomenon and its ideological "correlate" is not predictable, because the latter is neither simply the effect nor the mirror of the former; the superstructure is not autonomous but it is more than epiphenomenon. The relationship, like that between sexual instinct and cultural expression in Freud's system, is rather a metaphorical one. The relevant 1844 texts speak of "interweaving," "effluxes," "echoes," "sublimates." They suggest a mutual interpenetration.[10] Granted, this is less the case in Marx's later writings; but just as Freud acknowledged that his early emphases had been politically, humanly, necessary exaggerations, so Engels in 1890, after Marx's death, could admit to his and Marx's exaggerations and come to speak as he had never done earlier of the interplay between the economic and the cultural, of how indirectly the former influences the latter, and to acknowledge as well the significance of the interactions between the now differentiated aspects of the superstructure.[11]

Even more important is that what Marx calls "base" is not his real base—as becomes apparent in his utopian reflections. For the economic substructure in Marx is parallel to the repressed unconscious and to the superego in Freud's system rather than to what Freud calls "primary process" or to the id. It is equivalent to the part of the unconscious created by alienation that now has unrecognized power over us. Indeed, strangely, the greed and acquisitiveness, the compulsion of material motives, may seem less real, less inevitably characteristic of us humans-as-such to Marx than to Freud, since for Marx they have been culturally acquired and he can imagine a society in which we are freed from them.

Thus Marxist criticism cannot properly be confined to an analysis of economic structures and their determinative force; when it is, it tends to become ideological, dogmatic. The critique of earth means not only a critique of economics and politics but of law, philosophy, art, literature, a disclosure of how the values and norms embedded in these facets of the "superstructure" bind and restrict us in ways we have come to take for granted. To recall these dimensions of Marx's criticism is to recover its dialectical aspect, to rediscover a theory that helps us transcend our short-run visible interests, which calls us to live by our imagination not our senses. To focus on the superstructure may be as reactionary and evasive as the revisionary psychoanalytic focus on ego psychology often seems to be. Yet to neglect what Freud and Marx have to say about culture is to distort what they tell us about sex and economics. Their dialectical vision insists that we consider both realms.

The Critique of Art as Consummation of the Critique of Religion

In trying to understand the full implications of Freud's and Marx's criticisms of religion it is important to pay special attention to their criticism of art because both are sympathetic to this expression of oppression and hope, as they are not to the expression represented by religion—though from the perspective of Marxist and psychoanalytic theory art and religion are in many ways equivalent illusions.

Both Marx and Freud were genuinely and spontaneously appreciative of art, especially literature. Their writings display their deep knowledge and love of the classics, especially Greek tragedy, Shakespeare and Goethe. Thus Marx could acknowledge the universal appeal of Greek art, even though this universality seemed incommensurate with his esthetic theory. His own responses protected him from a simplistic *a priori* sociological reduction of art. Like Freud he understood that it is not just the contents of a work of art that gives it power, but that the poetic form helps make acceptable what otherwise would seem a too threatening criticism. Form yields real "fore-pleasure" because esthetic form speaks to something deep in us. It is fore-pleasure because it is proleptic of true fulfillment. Marxist and Freudian criticism at its best is therefore to a perhaps surprising degree attentive to formal as well as thematic elements. Thus just as psychoanalytically inspired literary criticism is highly sensitive to the subtlety of poetic mechanisms and not just to the presence of Oedipal themes, so Marxist criticism has been particularly attuned to genre studies (*e.g.*, the way in which novelistic forms express bourgeois culture).

Art is a sign of both alienation and liberation. To Marx art expresses and surpasses the economic situation; for Freud it both expresses and surpasses repression. Although they agree that some so-called art, escapist or conformist art, may only enslave, they value what they regard as great art because it shows that reality can be transformed, mastered, turned into play. Freud sees art as an alternative to neurosis; rather than reducing Leonardo's paintings to the infantile experience he finds revealed in them, he marvels at the transformation of that experience. Both see art as a natural fulfillment of humankind, yet believe that art in our culture is inevitably distorted by repression and materialism. Artists both negate and confirm their and our alienation. Their work has power for others because it betokens freedom from such alienation.

It is noteworthy, too, that both Marx and Freud seem to value universality in art. They esteem art that transcends particular social or personal factors, art that resists reduction to the reflection of an historical period or of a personal wound or wish. Good art sees the contradictions, the tensions, in society or the individual more precisely, more concretely than even the theorist can; it gives us what Merleau-Ponty calls the "differential," the way in which a class situation, a neurotic impasse, is concretely, particularly embodied. Yet both Marx and Freud value also the art that suggests a surpassing of the contradictions that define our everyday existence. They recognize in such visions a kind of truth.

Indeed, Marx and Freud express their own hopes for humankind in esthetic terms. Both have a vision of what we would be like in a non-repressive, non-scarcity world. Both regard work as a natural human activity and see us as fundamentally productive. But work as we know it is not creative work; the dichotomy between work and play, work and leisure, which characterizes our society is a distortion. In a less repressive, less materialistic society art would be a less specialized form of activity; the distinction between "producers" and "consumers" of art that we almost take for granted would be overcome, as would the hierarchical relationship between physical and mental workers. For both Marx and Freud see us as in essence artists, symbol-makers, constructors of imaginary worlds. Each acknowledged a strong personal identification with Prometheus, and saw in his endless rebellious striving to modify the world by crafty inventiveness the immortal prototype of humankind.

They articulate an erotic appreciation of art—imagine an art made with others and for others. Freud's two therapeutic aims, to enable us to work and to love, belong closely together. As his appreciative comments on Popper-Lynkeus' *Phantasms of a Realist* indicate, he believes that the unrepressed too would dream and make art. Though we can only dimly imagine such an art, we can recognize that it would come into being for the sake of the interhuman, for Eros, not for narcissistic self-fulfillment. Art provides those vicarious extensions of our individual experience, those identifications with others, which are a necessary basis for human re-unification. Marx dreams toward a society of fulfilled sensuality, a festival of the senses, "complete emancipation of all human senses and aptitudes" in which "seeing, hearing, smelling, tasting, touching, thinking, observing, feeling, desiring, acting, loving" would all be recognized as means of enjoying reality.[12] The critique of heaven which leads into a critique of earth issues in a celebration of what human life on earth could become:

> Suppose we had produced things as human beings: in his production each of us would have twice affirmed himself and the other. (1) In my production I would have objectified my individuality and its particularity, and in the course of the activity I would have enjoyed an individual life; in viewing the object I would have experienced the individual joy of knowing my personality as an objective, sensuously perceptible and indubitable power. (2) In your satisfaction and your use of my product I would have had the direct and conscious satisfaction that my work satisfied a human need, that it objectified human nature, and that it created an object appropriate to the need of another human being. (3) I would have been the mediator between you and the species and you would have experienced me as a re-integration of your own nature and a necessary part of yourself; I would have been affirmed in your thought as well as your love. (4) In my individual activity, I would have immediately confirmed and realized my true human and social nature.
>
> Our productions would be so many mirrors reflecting our nature.
> What happens so far as I am concerned would also apply to you...
> My labour would be a free manifestation of life and an enjoyment of life...
> Furthermore, in my labour the particularity of my individuality would be affirmed because my individual life is affirmed. Labour then would be true, active property. Under the presupposition of private property my individuality is externalized to the point where I hate this activity and where it is a torment for me. Rather it is then only the semblance of an activity, only a forced activity, imposed upon me only by external and accidental necessity and not by an internal and determined necessity.[13]

Even in Marx such an articulation is rare; we cannot expect to find the like in Freud. Yet he, too, upholds the claim, the longing.

The critique of religion issues in both from their care for humankind; it leads in both to their expression of what we may rightfully hope for here on earth with due acknowledgement of Ananke. Freud's hope runs very deep; we hear it in the invocation to Eros at the end of *Civilization and Its Discontents* but it is mingled with a profound skepticism. We need Freud's insistence on the difficulty of change to protect us from a too innocent version of Marxist eschatology. But we need also Marx's reminder that the point of dreams is to act on them.

Notes

1. Jean Paul Sartre, *Search For A Method* (New York: Vintage Books, 1968) 7, 8, 30.

2. Wilhelm Reich, *Sex-Pol* (New York: Vintage Books, 1972) 64.

3. Sartre, *Method,* p. 61.

4. Juliet Mitchell, *Psychoanalysis and Feminism* (New York: Pantheon Books, 1974) *passim* but esp. 413ff.

5. Quoted by H.D. in *Tribute to Freud* (New York: McGraw-Hill Book Company, 1975) 18.

6. Sigmund Freud, *The Complete Introductory Lectures on Psychoanalysis* (New York: W. W. Norton, 1966) 531, 640-5.

7. Quoted in Ernest Jones, *The Life and Work of Sigmund Freud,* Vol. 3 (New York: Basic Books, 1960) 345.

8. Quoted in Edmund Wilson, *To The Finland Station* (Garden City: Doubleday Anchor, 1940) p. 308.

9. Quoted in Russell Jacoby, *Social Amnesia* (Boston: Beacon Press, 1975) 119.

10. Lloyd D. Easton and Kurt H. Guddat, *Writings of the Young Marx on Philosophy and Society* (Garden City: Doubleday Anchor, 1967) 414, 415.

11. Peter Demetz, *Marx, Engels, and the Poets* (Chicago: University of Chicago Press, 1967) 139-47.

12. Easton and Guddat, 307.

13. Easton and Guddat, 281 (emphases omitted).

18

Towards an Erotics of the Psyche

Each mythical tradition, each mythic personage, suggests a unique mode of self-awareness. Carl Kerenyi suggests that the imagination truly sensitive to mythology is able to "perceive realms of human existence in their dominant figures" and "to enter into these figures."[1]

There are many different mythical illuminations of the psyche: A psychology visioned in relation to Zeus might be a hierarchical one that stressed the value of the ego's ordering power. A psychology imagined from Aphrodite's perspective might be one that lured us to fascinated absorption in the images produced by the fecund unconscious. Each god represents a different aspect. Walter Otto conveys with great beauty how each of the Greek divinities is a totality, a whole world:

> None of them represents a single virtue, none is to he encountered in only one direction of teeming life; each desires to feel, shape and illumine the whole compass of human existence with his peculiar spirit. Its special characteristic is always the signature of a world complete in itself. Each represents a wholly different, but a whole world.... In the case of each deity we find anew that it is most intimately bound up with the things of this earth and yet it never denotes one single facet but is an eternal form of existence in the whole compass of creation.[2]

The peculiar spirit of Eros's illumination can he discovered through attending to the importance attached to this figure in the work of Carl Jung and Thomas Mann. I do not purpose here a Jungian archetypal reading of Mann's fiction but rather an exploration of their shared commitment to the perspectives opened up by Eros. I find in both resources for what we might name an erotics of the psyche, quite different from the logics of the psyche with which we are more familiar.

Thus I want to do more than demonstrate that Eros is a dominant theme in their writing and have no intention of suggesting that the presence of Eros could in any sense serve as a touchstone of good literature. He is not the only god to inspire poets. This is not primarily an exercise in literary criticism nor the proposal of an interpretative method. I turn to Mann and Jung because I believe they may help us become aware of Eros's presence among us, as Nietzsche helped us to recognize the continued liveliness of Apollo and Dionysos. Eros is a much more powerful god than the insipid child many of us first think of when we hear his name. Mann and Jung recall us to the full range of his significance, as it was known in ancient Greece.

The notion of an erotics of the psyche is, of course, related to Susan Sontag's call, in *Against Interpretation*, for an erotics of art in place of a hermeneutics. She meant thereby commentary that would "serve the work of art not usurp its place," that would "supply a really accurate, sharp, loving description of the appearance of a work of art."[3]

Loving regard for what appears in the psyche's self-presentations is among Freud's most significant contributions to psychology. He turns away from the objectifying language of the physician to the patient's own speech, focuses his attention on the minute details of the patient's dream images and associations and on the peculiar structures of primary process language: condensation, displacement, fusion, juxtaposition, concretization, over-determination. From him we learn an appreciation of the precision of the psyche's image language. Freud's dream reports and case histories are erotic also in being "speech that leads to participation…a speech of stories and insights which evoke in the other who listens new stories and new insights…. It evokes, calls forth, and creates psyche as it speaks."[4] Yet we find in Freud also a commitment to interpretation. He takes on himself the task of translating the phenomenal, the imaginal, into the secondary language of directed, rational thought.

A less compromised love for the appearances is suggested in Jung's way of responding to the images brought forward in dream and fantasy and myth. His focus is on the manifest and its many meanings rather than on a particular latent meaning. Having rejected Freud's emphasis on repression, he does not accept the disguise theory of dreams. Dream images do not refer to something known but repressed that interpretation, analysis, can discover but to something unknown, something not directly expressible, for which the image is the most telling equivalent available. Understanding emerges neither from decoding nor through free association that (in Jung's view) leads away from the specific image to the life concerns of the patient that almost any other image might just as well have elicited. Jung believes in "amplification"—as distinguished from interpretation—because he is persuaded that meaning is revealed by staying with the image and *its* associations, those analogues which familiarity with mythic and literary traditions makes available. Such a piling up of mutually illuminating analogies creates a meaning not translatable into conceptual terms. It is having the dream, attending to it, which enriches us.

Jung's recognition that the truths of the psyche are best communicated in image and event rather than through theory or interpretation is most powerfully conveyed in *Memories, Dreams, Reflections*. "What we are to our inward vision can only be expressed by way of myth."[5] Therefore this memoir, singularly poor in outward events and interpersonal texture, focuses on inner experiences, dreams and visions. It recreates Jung's sense of his life as a continual circumambulation of a few central images, images that appeared first in childhood, reappeared with transformative power during the radical crisis of midlife and again at the end as he sought to name the signs of wholeness and oneness. It does not seem irrelevant that this book with its immediate power to evoke our memories and dreams should have been written erotically, prepared through literal dialogue with his friend and editor, Aniela Jaffe.

Freud ended *Civilization and Its Discontents* with an invocation to Eros: "Now it may be hoped that the other of the two heavenly forces, eternal Eros, will put forth his strength so as to maintain himself alongside of his equally immortal adversary."[6] It seems almost inevitable that Jung's book would also climax in a tribute to this god—as though Jung now, at the close, knew explicitly how all along he had been creating an erotics of the psyche:

> At this point the fact forces itself on my attention that beside the field of reflection there is another equally broad if not broader area in which rational understanding and rational modes of representation find scarcely anything they are able to grasp. This is the realm of Eros. In classical times, when such things were properly understood, Eros was considered a god whose divinity transcended our human limits, and who therefore could neither he comprehended nor represented in any way. I might, as many before me have attempted to do, venture an approach to this *daimon*, whose range of activity extends from the endless spaces of the heavens to the dark abysses of hell; but I falter before the task of finding the language which might adequately express the incalculable paradoxes of love. Eros is a *kosmogonos*, a creator and father-mother of all higher consciousness.[7]

We have shifted somewhat from what was implicit in Sontag's sense of "erotics" to that "initiation to Eros" which is the central theme of Esther Harding's *Woman's Mysteries*.[8] For her this means initiation into imaginal consciousness, into a mode of perception that is not literal nor objectifying but symbolic, associative, personal, feeling-toned. Sontag used "erotics" to refer to a critic's approach to literature; Harding suggests the extension of that kind of loving regard for the appearances to the realm of experience, particularly to that aspect of it which Jung calls "psychic reality." It is perhaps because Jungians generally have been sensitive to the deep connections between the erotic and the psychological, that so many of them have felt the fascination of the myth about Psyche and Eros, and have recognized how different is the psychology implicit in it from the psychology correlative with the myth of the hero. Erich Neumann sees this myth as representing the female's journey toward individuation. Marie Louise von Franz believes it is about the male's initiation into his own psychological femininity. James Hillman finds in it the recognition that psychic life needs the encouragement of another's love and that human love is directed toward the psychic life of self and other. Yet all three recognize that to tell the story of Psyche is to tell a story which necessarily includes Eros.[9]

Eros is the obvious sponsor of an archetypal psychology for he is "the friendliest of all gods to men" and indeed perhaps, as Socrates maintains, really more *daimon* than god, an intermediary who connects us to the gods, the individual to the transpersonal.

Eros is clearly of a radically different character from the well-defined Homeric gods: shape shifting, elusive, of questionable parentage, as fluid as the theophanies of our dreams. Robert Graves says that Eros was not considered serious enough for Olympus and yet both Hesiod and Orphism regard him as a more ancient and a more significant god than any of the Olympians, who are in no sense Creators, sources of life. Freud felt this too: his Eros is Titan not child or irresponsible youth. Jane Harrison tells us that the worship of Eros is "worship of the real mysteries of life, of potencies (*daimones*) rather than personal gods (*theoi*)." She quotes from the *Symposium*:

> Reason is great but it is not everything. There are in the world things, not of reason, but both below and above it, causes of emotion which we cannot express, which we tend to worship, which we feel perhaps to be the precious things in life. These things are God or forms of god, not fabulous immortal men, but 'Things which Are,' things utterly nonhuman and nonmortal which bring man bliss or tear his life to shreds without a break in their own serenity.

She goes on to say, "It is these real gods, this life itself, that the Greeks, like most men, were inwardly afraid to recognize and face, afraid even to worship." And again quotes Plato's Aristophanes: "Mankind would seem never to have realized the might of Eros. For if they had really felt it they would have built him great sanctuaries and altars and offered solemn sacrifices and none of these things are done."[10]

Perhaps Eros is more important in cosmogonic speculation than in cult because he is not so much an object of love or devotion as the one who provokes it—and yet just because of that is "the one supreme object of worship to those who know."[11] In Orphism Eros is regarded as the creator god; he is *Protagonos*, the first born, thus the eldest of all the gods and as first-born, primordially new born, primordially child. He is the god of beginnings, or origins, of the possibility of new beginnings for us.

Eros in this first-born aspect is also known as *Phanes*—the god who appears and thus the god of appearances, phenomena, of theophanies and fantasies, of just those psychic manifestations to which Jung and Mann devote most of their attention. He is the god who appears and who causes to appear, who reveals.

This vision of Eros as revealer seems clearly different from the image of Hermes as interpreter. Yet in the fluidity of the pre-Homeric understandings these figures interpenetrate one another as the more distinctly defined Olympian representations cannot. Hermes is the god whose tutelage Mann most often acknowledges, yet his Hermes is not so easily distinguished from Eros. Kerenyi, in his essay on the divine child, speaks of the primordial child, "the best known of whose many names is Eros."[12] Perhaps because he is the firstborn of the gods, Eros remains in some sense the divine child and so is assigned many parentages. Often Hermes is named as father—and as child of Hermes Eros is also Hermes in child form, shares with him the role of intermediary, of psychogogue and guide to the underworld. In response to Kerenyi's essay Mann wrote: "I could not help being pleased to note that the psychopompos is characterized as essentially a child divinity: I thought of Tadzio in Death in Venice"[13] (the same Tadzio in whom Aschenbach recognized Eros).

When Hermes is the father, Aphrodite is often named as mother (though Eros is also her attendant from the very moment of her emergence from the sea). Eros is then perhaps to be understood as but another name for their other son, Hermaphroditos. This would fit in with the Orphic tradition that regards Eros as bisexual "since he is to create the race of gods unaided."[14] Jung's somewhat confusing choice of the name Eros to designate the feminine principle receives at least some validation here, though it may not sufficiently bring into view the difference between the love associated with Aphrodite and the love inspired by Eros. For Aphrodite represents the pull toward the undifferentiated union of lover and loved, the longing for reunion with the mother that Freud called primary narcissism and identified with death. And Eros, as Freud had learnt from Plato, is the god of object-love, of relationship, who binds all things together without merging them into one, the god who releases us from the prison of isolation and subjectivity. In classical Athens Eros was often represented as the god of homosexual love—a love looked upon as more spiritual than heterosexual, reproduction-directed love—creative, imaginal love.

The fable attributed to Aristophanes in the *Symposium* suggests that Eros (here the son of *Penia*, need) represents our desire for a lost wholeness. In Jung's essay on "The Spiritual Problem of Modern Man" he suggests that psychology arose towards the end of the Enlightenment out of just such nostalgia, or perhaps desperate need, for wholeness at a period when we humans came to experience acutely the pain of self-division. Thus psychology is from its birth Eros-inspired.

Eros is also closely associated with Dionysos. In Orphic theology Eros and Dionysos are but two names for the same divinity, swallowed by Zeus as Eros and reborn as Dionysos.[15] But Eros is not Dionysos as defined in opposition to Apollo. For if we take our stand in the daylight world of Apollo, in ego consciousness, then the psychic world which emerges from the depths will appear as ultimately fearsome, though perhaps fearfully attractive. We will then see Dionysos as meaning only orgy, dissolution, chaos and death, though perhaps a death we might be ready to embrace.

Mann's *Death in Venice* begins with Aschenbach's vision of a primeval wilderness world and a fearful crouching tiger in the thickets. Venice is from the moment of his arrival palpably a place of disease and death. When Aschenbach first glimpses the godlike beauty of Tadzio he is reminded of an ancient marble head of Eros. The sight of Tadzio emerging from the sea conjures up myths of the birth of the gods. Aschenbach dreams one afternoon of conversing with Tadzio as the aging Socrates might have spoken with one of his young admirers. Yet there is from the beginning a frenzied, morbid, excessive quality to his devotion. All along the vision of the orgiastic ritual to the stranger god into which he feels himself irresistibly drawn has been prepared. The abyss from which he had too carefully protected himself, the mysteries from which he had too deliberately turned away, the instinctual too long denied, overwhelm him. Tadzio becomes the summoner to death. Perhaps the most important moment in this story is when Aschenbach refuses the opportunity to make an actual overture to Tadzio and thus acknowledges his unwillingness to "realize" the images that swirl through his head. "Dreams, inscapes and visions," Hillman reminds us, "are not creative; they are but aspects of reflection until they cross the threshold of erotic involvement."[16]

Serenus Zeitblom (the narrator of *Dr. Faustus*) feels in his friend Adrian Leverkuhn an exaggerated purity that represents a deep aversion to the instinctual and so a dangerous susceptibility to it. Adrian deliberately ignores the harlot's warning of her infectiousness and thus expresses that same "deep, deeply mysterious longing" for chaos and death which also enthralled Aschenbach. In *Dr. Faustus* the unconscious, at least as Adrian experiences it, is the devil's realm. "Genuine inspiration, immediate, absolute, unquestioning, ravishing," his stranger visitor confides, comes only from the devil. God leaves the understanding too much to do.[17] The devil grants vitality and passion, an intensity closely related to diseased sexuality—but the price is an exclusion from the love that warms. Aschenbach's and Adrian's passions are deeply narcissistic. The pain this brings to Adrian is poignantly, and terrifyingly, presented in his anguish over the death of his young nephew, Echo, which prefigures his own being overcome by madness. Yet there is love in this novel: Zeitblom's impotent, uncomprehending, pedantic and yet unwavering care for his friend. And there is in Mann the hope that the terrors of *Dr. Faustus* might "still be lighted by a glimmer of art and thus *after all* of gaiety."[18]

Adrian Leverkuhn is, as Mann admits, in part modeled on Nietzsche, for whom Mann all his life felt "reverence and pity." He saw Nietzsche as:

> A delicate, fine, warmhearted soul in need of love, formed for noble friendships and not at all made for solitude. And upon this soul deepest, coldest solitude, the solitude of the criminal, was imposed.... His life was inebriation and suffering—a highly artistic combination. In mythological terms, it was the union of Dionysos with the Crucified One.

His overleaping had:

> none of the acrobatic gay virtuosity, none of the dancer's joyousness. All the "dancelike" elements in his conduct were paroxysms of the will and entailed pain. In overleaping himself he was bodily cutting his own flesh, practising flagellation.

Mann, who had loved Nietzsche in his youth, came to recognize the dangers in his celebration of the aesthetic and instinctual:

> Nietzsche's major premise, which contains within itself his Dionysiac pessimism—namely, that life can be justified only as an aesthetic phenomenon—applies exactly to himself, to his life, his thinking, and his writing, these

can be justified, understood, honored, only as an aesthetic phenomenon....
Anyone who takes Nietzsche "as he is," who believes him and takes him at his
word, is lost.[19]

Jung saw this aspect of Nietzsche's Dionysian consciousness much earlier. He,
too, read *Zarathustra* in his student years and immediately recognized its morbid
quality and feared, therefore, that perhaps his "other" personality, his No. 2,
might also be morbid. In Nietzsche, he felt, the Philistine and the ecstatic were
tragically, fatally, dissociated and so he fell—"into depths far beyond himself."
Nietzsche's fearful example slammed a door shut for Jung, a door he remained
reluctant to open for a long while.[20]

But for Eros, too, and not only for Dionysos, the close relationship to death is
inescapable. Freud spoke of Eros as twin brother to death; in Hesiod Eros
emerges from chaos and is brother to Tartarus and Night. In Apuleius' tale
Psyche's last task is her journey to the underworld. There are countless myths of
mothers making that journey in search of lost sons or daughters, of lovers pursuing their loves. The journey of love seems to be the journey to the realm of the
dead. I have spoken of an erotics of the psyche but perhaps we need also acknowledge a *psychotics* of eros. Eros (who is also sometimes son to Ares, the stirrer up of
strife[21]) is Lord of Misrule and Disorder. Love, as Plato taught, is a divine madness. The original meaning of psychosis is: I give life. It is profound, psychotic
disturbances—abductions, betrayals, separations—that bring renewed life. A
common affinity with disease and a shared recognition of its productive power
are, so Mann believed, among the most important bonds between psychoanalysis
and his own creative impulse.[22]

In *Symbols of Transformation*, Jung seeks to have us recognize the creative
potentiality in a regression that goes through the longing for mother-reunion "to
a discovery of the immemorial world of archetypal possibilities where slumbers
the divine child."[23] Such regression leads to the primordial child whose most
familiar name, as we have already learned, is Eros. In *Memories, Dreams, Reflections* Jung shares with us his own experiencing of this process when at last he was
ready to let the door slammed shut by *Zarathustra* reopen. He talks of the
moment—which he can still date over forty years later—when he let himself
drop, and was confronted by the terrifying images of the stone spurting blood
and of Siegfried's death. As he tells us how close he came to being lost in the
darkness, as he describes the threat of being strangled by the jungle's creepers, of
being crushed by the gigantic tumbling blocks of stone, we are reminded of
Aschenbach's visions. It was only his *daimon*, Jung tells us, that saved him, and

that enabled him to find in these psychotic experiences the source of all his later creative activity.

Eros-love is transformative and all serious transformations involve death. Eros-love implies the encounter with the dark but not abandonment to it. In Mann's *Magic Mountain* Hans Castorp's vision in the snow has much in it reminiscent of Aschenbach's Dionysian nightmare. It begins with an incredibly beautiful Grecian scene that Hans finds uncannily familiar—sunlit, filled with an aura of dignity, serenity and happiness. But then in the temple that he enters only with dreading reluctance and with anguish he sees a sight as bloody, as horrifying, as vilely obscene as the orgy in *Death in Venice*. And it echoes closely an experience that Nietzsche suggests all of us might have if we were ever, "if only in a dream" to be:

> carried back into an ancient Greek existence. Walking under lofty Ionic colonnades, looking up at a horizon that was cut off by pure and noble lines, finding reflections of his transfigured shape in the shining marble at his side, and all around him solemnly striding or delicately moving human beings, speaking with harmonious voices and in a rhythmic language of gestures—in view of this continual influx of beauty, would he have not to exclaim, raising his hand to Apollo: "Blessed people of Hellas! How great must Dionysus be among you if the god of Delos considers such magic necessary to heal your dithyrambic madness!"
>
> To a man in such a mood, however, an old Athenian, looking up at him with the sublime eyes of Aeschylus, might reply: "But say this, too, curious stranger: how much did this people have to suffer to become so beautiful! But now follow me to witness a tragedy and sacrifice with me in the temple of both deities!"[24]

Hans feels his to have been "a lovely and horrible dream."

> In a way, I knew it all beforehand. But how is it a man can know all that and call it up to bring him bliss and terror both at once? Where did I get the beautiful bay with the islands, where the temple precincts, whither the eyes of that charming boy pointed me, as he stood there alone? Now I know that it is not out of our single souls we dream. We dream anonymously and communally, if each after his fashion. The great soul of which we are a part may dream through us, in our manner of dreaming, its own secret dreams, of its youth, its hope, its joy and peace—and its blood-sacrifice. Here I lie at my column and still feel my body the actual remnant of my dream—the icy horror of the human sacrifice, but also the joy that had filled my heart to its very depths, born of the happiness and brave hearing of those human creatures in white. It is meet and proper, I hereby declare, that I have a prescriptive right to lie here

and dream these dreams. For in my life up here I have known reason and recklessness, I have wandered lost with Settembrini and Naptha in high and mortal places. I know all of man. I have known mankind's flesh and blood. I gave
back to the ailing Claudia Chauchat Pribislav Hippe's lead pencil. But he who
knows the body, life, knows death.[25]

But Hans' vision takes him beyond this knowledge of death to a recognition
of Eros' superior power:

> I have made a dream poem of humanity. I will cling to it. I will be good. I will
> let death have no mastery over my thoughts. For therein lies goodness and
> love of humankind, and in nothing else. Death is a great power. One takes off
> one's hat before him, and goes weavingly on tiptoe. He wears the stately ruff
> of the departed and we do him honour in solemn black. Reason stands simple
> before him, for reason is only virtue, while death is release, immensity, aban-
> don, desire. Desire, says my dream. Lust, not love. Death and love—no, I can-
> not make a poem of them, they don't go together. Love stands opposed to
> death. It is love, not reason, that is stronger than death. Only love, not reason,
> gives sweet thoughts. And from love and sweetness alone can form come: form
> and civilization, friendly, enlightened, beautiful human intercourse—always
> in silent recognition of the blood-sacrifice. Ah, yes, it is well and truly
> dreamed. I have taken stock. I will remember. I will keep faith with death in
> my heart, yet well remember that faith with death and the dead is evil, is hos-
> tile to humankind, so soon as we give it power over thought and action. *For
> the sake of goodness and love man shall let death have no sovereignty over his
> thoughts....* And with this I awake. For I have dreamed it out to the end.[26]

But of course Hans cannot hold on to this vision; it begins to fade that very
evening; it is too archetypal for him to integrate. Nevertheless when this delicate
child of life returns to the flatland and the war, Schiller's song on his lips remains
as inexpressible talisman of a transformation that at some level truly occurred.
The magic mountain stimulates that same diseased intensification of life that
destroys Aschenbach and Leverkuhn. But Hans seems to have the "talent" of getting well through getting sicker. The mountain made possible the "development
of inner space, time, and imagination," through which, Hillman tells us, "the
psychic world comes into actuality."[27]

Mann's Joseph is transformed by his experiences in a much more festive, complete sense than Hans. Twice he finds himself forced into the underworld, into
the pit, which he is blessedly able to recognize consciously as the deep, deep,
almost bottomless well of the past. On the first occasion it is his narcissistic prov-
ocation of his brothers' jealousy that leads to his being imprisoned in an aban-

doned well. He acutely feels the discomfort and desperateness of his situation and its inevitability. He comes to understand how he had himself created it, was the giver of the given, and that somehow it was supposed to happen thus. He both gives up, knows he cannot return to his former life, and yet finds something hopeful, joyful in his situation. In the midst of the worst he never stops dreaming and playing, always knows with some part of him, a part deeply attuned to the prototypicality of his situation, that like Tammuz and Adonis and Christ he will emerge, newborn. Years later it is again a failure in loving, his rejection of the consuming love of Potiphar's wife (which Mann presents as transforming her into a frenzied Dionysos-possessed maenad) that returns him to the pit. Again he comes to feel a rightness in his being there and again his sense of the correspondences between his situation and that of many another mythical personage enables him to live his despair and to hope. Joseph represents "the mythical view become subjective," the loving identification with the realities of his own situation achieved through loving identification with the others into whose pattern he has slipped.[28] From this second pit Joseph emerges as provider and nourisher—not as one immersed in self-love nor the object of another's boundless desire but as the source of love.

Which brings us to Felix Krull, that other giver, whose trickery brings joy not harm to those it touches, and who, in his final encounter with Dona Maria, gives and receives love.

That healing love is mutual love, that Eros is accompanied by Anteros, responding love, is the central theme in Jung's later writings, especially in *The Psychology of the Transference* and in *Mysterium Coniunctionis*. There he uses the image of brother-sister incest to suggest a love as numinous as the incestual union of mother and son but more truly recreative. Eros-love is not narcissistic love but love between one and another. "The psyche wants the human connection." "Even the hermaphrodite needs the human other."[29]

It is this that distinguishes an erotics of the psyche from a poetics or an aesthetics. The erotic perspective does open us to the beauty of psychological events, to a kind of psychic sensuality;[30] it suggests "a poet's utopia," but it does not mean the narcissistic aestheticism of an Aschenbach or a Leverkuhn. It pulls us to love our lives even when we cannot understand them. It means imagining the real, realizing our images, intertwining the realistic and symbolic as intimately as Mann does in *Death in Venice*. It means fourfold vision, imaginal consciousness. Eros is, in the words of an ancient hymn, "He of the fourfold eyes, beholding this way, beholding that way."[31]

Notes

1. Alexander Gelley, trans., *Mythology and Humanism: The Correspondence of Thomas Mann and Karl Kerenyi* (Ithaca and London: Cornell University Press, 1975) 7.

2. Walter F. Otto, *The Homeric Gods* (Boston: Beacon Press, 1964) 160-62.

3. Susan Sontag, *Against Interpretation* (New York: Dell Publishing Company, 1966) 22.

4. James Hillman, *The Myth of Analysis* (Evanston: Northwestern University Press, 1972) 206.

5. C. G. Jung, *Memories, Dreams, Reflections* (New York: Pantheon Books, 1963) 3.

6. Sigmund Freud, *Civilization and Its Discontents* (New York: Doubleday Anchor, 1958) 105.

7. Jung, *Memories*, 353.

8. Esther Harding, *Woman's Mysteries* (New York: Bantam, 1973) xiii (and 32 where she disclaims connection between Jung's Eros and the Greek god).

9. Erich Neumann, *Amor and Psyche* (New York: Harper Torchbook, 1962); Marie Louise von Franz, *A Psychological Interpretation of "The Golden Ass" of Apuleius* (New York: Spring Publications, 1970); Hillman, *Myth of Analysis*, Part 1.

10. Jane Harrison, *Prolegomena to the Study of Greek Religion* (New York: Meridian, 1957) 57-58.

11. Otto, *Homeric Gods*, 101; W. K. C. Guthrie, *Orpheus and Greek Religion* (New York: W. W. Norton, 1966) 54.

12. C. G. Jung and C. Kerenyi, *Essays on a Science of Mythology* (Princeton: Princeton University Press, 1969) 55.

13. Gelley, *Mythology and Humanism*, 21.

14. Guthrie, *Orpheus*, 80.

15. Guthrie, *Orpheus,* 23.

16. Hillman, *Myth of Analysis,* 85.

17. Thomas Mann, *Dr. Faustus* (New York: The Modern Library, 1948) 55, 237.

18. Gelley, *Mythology and Humanism,* 169.

19. Thomas Mann, "Nietzsche's Philosophy in the Light of Recent History," *Last Essays* (New York: Alfred A. Knopf, 1966) 42, 158, 159, 172, 173.

20. Jung, *Memories,* 103.

21. H. J. Rose, *A Handbook of Greek Mythology* (New York: E. Dutton, 1959) 58.

22. Thomas Mann, *Essays* (New York: Vintage Books, 1957) 106.

23. C. G. Jung, *Symbols of Transformation. C.W.5* (New York: Pantheon Books, 1956) 330.

24. Walter Kaufmann, ed., *The Birth of Tragedy* in *Basic Writings of Nietzsche* (New York: Modern Library, 1968) 144.

25. Thomas Mann, *The Magic Mountain* (New York: Alfred A. Knopf, 1949) 495.

26. Mann, *Magic Mountain,* 496-7.

27. Hillman, *Myth of Analysis,* 71.

28. Mann, *Essays,* 318.

29. C. G. Jung, "The Psychology of the Transference," *The Practice of Psychotherapy, C.W.16* (New York: Pantheon Books, 1954) 234, 243.

30. Hillman, *Myth of Analysis,* 101.

31. Harrison, *Prolegomena,* 648.

19

Jealousy:
A Depth-Psychological
Perspective

The phrase "depth psychology" refers to that way of understanding human existence introduced in Sigmund Freud's *Interpretation of Dreams* (published in the first year of this century) and elaborated by him and others, both followers and dissidents, who find the notion of the "unconscious" necessary to their description of human behavior and experience. There are, they believe, "depths" to human beings' wishes and fears and memories of which they are not immediately or easily self-aware. Every conscious feeling is likely to be accompanied by its unconscious opposite. We tend to be ambivalent: to hate those we love, to desire what we fear. In every present, and in ways likely to be surprising, our whole past is active and influential; and perhaps not only our own literal lived past but in some strange way the accumulated past of countless human generations. Such a psychology is inevitably a deep one also in the more obvious sense of the word: It is subtle, complex, and easily misunderstood.

The psychologies that derive from Freud are sometimes also called "insight therapies." This designation suggests that they focus more on extending insight than on cure. Psychoanalysis represents a different way of looking at our experience. With respect to jealousy, for example, it would hope to be able to extend our understanding of the meaning of human jealousy, by showing what intentionalities are expressed in it, rather than to teach us how to eliminate it. The assumption is that jealousy is not a self-evident phenomenon, that it calls for interpretation. Psychoanalytic interpretation claims to offer us a self-understanding that uncovers some common self-deceptions. It calls upon us to recognize our finitude—that is, our mortality, our limitation by the needs and desires of others, and the impossibility of the fulfillment of some of our deepest longings.

Jealousy is a pervasive theme in the psychoanalytic explorations because it refers to this central human dilemma: the necessity of coming to terms with "reality" in all the aspects just named and the inevitability of our resistance to such limits, denials, and frustrations.

Indeed, jealousy is so central to Freud's image of humankind that it hardly occurs to him to focus on it explicitly, except in one disappointingly condensed essay written in 1922. Thus, to discover his understanding of jealousy, we must pay careful attention to the many allusions and, occasionally, to the more extended discussions scattered throughout his work. It soon becomes apparent that we cannot disentangle what he has to say about jealousy from the other most important, typically Freudian, themes: the Oedipus complex, bisexuality, ambivalence, repression, regression, displacement, and narcissism.

Freud's discussions of jealousy are in the first instance discussions of jealousy as it is experienced by *males*. Because his understanding of what distinguishes female from male sexuality changes significantly during the course of his work and would lead us into an enormously complicated issue, I am deliberately, throughout this essay, using masculine pronouns as a way of indicating that some of it would need to be modified if applied to women.[1]

Jealousy is, from Freud's perspective, not innate, and yet it is inevitable. It has its origins for each of us in our earliest familial experiences. Freud calls the whole complex of events and feelings associated with the child's relations to his parents "the oedipal situation." He means thereby to denote not only the character of the child's desire for his mother and his resentment toward his father, but the universality of these feelings. This universality, and the intensity of the emotions, suggests to Freud that something more than the imprint of actual childhood experiences is at work here. Somehow my memory also has an ancestral or "racial" dimension; my jealousy is in some way the re-enactment of the jealousy felt by human beings since the beginning of time.

"Normal" jealousy is competitive; it arises first in relation to rivalry with the father (and probably siblings) for the exclusive love of the mother, and it is felt again whenever the fear of losing the object of our love is aroused. The childhood experiences do not "cause" the later ones; but they are re-evoked and they help to shape how and how intensely we respond to the tensions of adult life. "There is not," Freud says in his typically offhand way, "much to be said from the analytic point of view about normal jealousy." But then he goes onto suggest that perhaps there is no wholly "normal" jealousy, no jealousy that is "completely rational, that is, derived from the actual situation, proportionate to the real circumstances and under the complete control of the conscious ego."[2]

We can understand jealousy better from its pathological manifestations because in all of us jealousy assumes some pathological characteristics. Freud does not want to eliminate the distinction between "normal" (by which he means rational and congruent with "reality") and pathological, but rather to suggest that most of us who are "normal" in our conscious orientation also harbor pathological tendencies.

In its root sense, which Freud wants to return us to, pathology means woundedness. He hopes to bring us back in touch with that in each of us that has been wounded, hurt, and abandoned, that which still cries and rages. We have all been deprived of the mother's breast; we all have had to give up our claim for exclusive possession of her. Mostly, we have forgotten these childhood longings and losses, and especially how much feeling was attached to them. We have little sense of the strength of these jealousy impulses, of the tenacity with which they persist, and of the magnitude of their influence on later life.

Jealousy is "regressive," immature; but at some level every one of us is still a child, as well as the adult we pride ourselves on having become. The memories and the over-intense feelings persist. We continue to respond emotionally in ways that are exaggerated, are not appropriate to a rational response to situations, and are perhaps not even based on a realistic assessment of them. In us, too, there is something that wants to "kill" the one who has usurped our place (as in childhood we dreamt of murdering a father or younger brother), or the one who has proven "faithless" (as the mother was when we were infants). In all of us there still lives the child's unregarding possessiveness—the longing for an absolute, certain, and exclusive love. Each of us still experiences the child's greedy passivity, his conviction that love means receiving love. The child is "narcissistic," is unquestioningly its own preferred love-object, and so are all of us.

It is these claims, these expectations, which manifest themselves anew in the jealousy that takes our adult selves by surprise. Thus jealousy is not, for Freud, in the first instance, sexual jealousy except in the extended metaphorical sense of sexuality peculiar to psychoanalysis. It relates more to the affectionate, personal, possessive side of a love relation than to its strictly sensual or sexual side. But Freud has been concerned to help us see how easily sexuality is invested with over-meanings, so that my failures or successes in this realm become paradigmatic, representative of how I most basically feel about myself. Thus sexual infidelity almost inevitably becomes a symbol for the most threatening loss we might suffer.

Psychoanalysis seeks to open us to the continued power of these old desires and hurts. Analysis of a jealousy that may, on the surface, seem only a distorted, ineffective, and perhaps destructive response to a present situation may reveal that jealousy as the way to a recovery of neglected and repressed, denied but still alive, aspects of ourselves. It encourages me to look upon my jealousy as something by which I may be taught, through which I may be made whole.

The tendency in psychoanalytical interpretations is to bypass consideration of the reality factors that may have prompted the immediate jealousy and to assume that all jealousy is to some degree delusional jealousy. Little attention is paid to the factor of literal infidelity, except sometimes to show how I provoked, in some sense desired, the very betrayal that arouses my anger and anxiety. Psychoanalysis tends to ignore what my jealousy suggests about anyone other than me. The assumption is that all jealousy is a kind of fantasy activity that both expresses and disguises some of my deepest wishes and fears. Because psychoanalysts are persuaded that jealousy has more to do with self-love than with love of others, it seems appropriate to them to view it as primarily an intrapsychic problem.

The explanations of jealousy that emerge from such an exploration are intended firstly to help me to recognize how much in my present feeling is "displaced" from earlier, never accepted experiences of loss, and particularly from a deeply ingrained sense that if I was betrayed by my mother's infidelity, I somehow deserved it, that I am not worthy of love, and so am destined to be betrayed over and over again. The further interpretations are equally subtle, deliberately farfetched, and consciously upsetting to our self-esteem. They provoke reflection and call for honest self-probing: "Can this possibly be part of what is going on here?" Freud never suggests that all of these meanings may attach to any one experience of jealousy; rather, he suggests that jealousy is not a single thing—that it may have a variety of meanings, express various intentionalities. Often, he believes, jealousy represents the disguised, transferred fulfillment of a tabooed wish. I may "project" my own longings for extramarital experience onto my spouse, and accuse him of living out what I wish to live myself but fear to, or perhaps can live because I believe he does also. Or I may be expressing my wish that he were more sexually free—with me. Or my projection of infidelity might mean anger at not being loved as completely as in my childish dreams I still imagine being loved—or it might mean a resentment of being loved in too containing or smothering a way. Sometimes jealousy may be a way of bolstering my self-esteem: "My wife is worthy of *his* attention!"

Freud also believed that delusional jealousy may sometimes be a disguised expression of an "acidulated homosexuality": "I don't love him; *she* loves him." Freud believed that we are all to some degree bisexual; that in all of us there are "masculine" and "feminine" dispositions—a longing to play the active, aggressive role and a longing to be passive, receptive. But because our acculturation often makes it difficult for us to accept this, it may be only in unacknowledged (and thus distorted) fantasies that a man can take on the feminine role. He projects onto his wife the desires he must repudiate in himself.

Another approach Freud uses to get at the "meaning" of jealousy is to look at what he calls the "secondary gain." What wish is fulfilled by my jealous behavior itself? Do I gain solicitous attention that I have been craving? Or a reaffirmation of my innocence, my victimization? Or the pleasure of indulgence in elaborate sexual fantasies? Or a self-punishment I somehow deserve?

What these various proposed explanations have in common is that they all involve the uncovering of hidden meanings—forgotten memories, unadmitted wishes, denied fears, a hurt that has its primary locus within (a wounding to my self-esteem) rather than in an outward relationship. They are strange explanations in that they can't be verified, except by our assent. There is no way of proving the pertinence of these invisible factors. What psychoanalysis does is to provide a perspective, a way of looking at jealousy—a way of understanding it that we may find provides us with a sense of how jealousy fits in with a whole way of being in the world. As I see how my jealousy is congruent with my history, it no longer seems an isolated "symptom." This perspective may appeal because it is more interesting, more subtle, more capable of unifying some particular experience with others; it doesn't in any way invalidate other perspectives. Jealousy is what Freud called "over-determined"; that is, it may be interpreted in several equally valid ways.

Freud sees jealousy as normal, inevitable, and universal; but he also sees that jealousness and particular familial and cultural forms are correlated. Jealousy is aggravated in a culture that worships a jealous monotheistic god, which holds up an ideal of monogamous marriage and of a monocentric, rational, and repressed self. Such a culture seems to encourage an expectation of exclusiveness in loving which makes it very difficult for us to come to terms with our own or another's infidelities, real or imagined. Freud understands, too, how the illusions connected with romantic love both make jealousy reprehensible and create it. Different social patterns may undoubtedly mitigate the pains of jealousy; nevertheless Freud cannot imagine a civilization in which men would be wholly freed from this "discontent."

Because all societies demand the renunciation of the child's boundless impulses toward self-gratification we can no more completely overcome jealousy than we can entirely extinguish our childhood. The recognition of the persistence of feelings and longings which are inconsistent with "reality," "rationality," and "maturity" is what makes this a *depth* psychology. Yet Freud gives us some hints as to what an unrepressed and therefore nonregressive jealousy might be like. Psychoanalysis may free us to accept the "pathological," the exaggerated, emotional, tied-to-childish-illusions, aspect of our jealousy as dangerous only if not met by a normal, reality-oriented, aspect. It may free us to recognize that in all of us love of others arises out of and remains deeply entwined with love of self. It may open us to living our jealousy with less guilt and less repression, and with more awareness of it as something that may move us forward rather than back. Depth-psychological insight stimulates a kind of jealousy of my own integrity. As Robert Seidenberg puts it:

> The turning away from one's origins, from one's history, the denial of impulses and relationships, are attitudes of deception about one's own being. They are the greatest infidelities of which we are capable.[3]

To live my jealousy as rage against another is to betray, to hide from, its most central meaning. Thus psychoanalysis itself becomes a substitute for acting-out jealousy: The suspicion is redirected towards oneself, one's own duplicity. This duplicity, this doubleness, is something all of us participate in; for we are all conscious and unconscious, mature and infantile, masculine and feminine, loving and hating, self-loving and other-loving, rational and emotional.

It is the oedipal triangle, the discovery that I cannot have my mother to myself, that moves me out of my self-absorption into recognition of the otherness of others, to what Freud called *object*-love. Sibling jealousy, Freud says in *Group Psychology and the Analysis of the Ego*, is the impetus to group feeling, to communal identification, to a concern for social justice. To learn that I cannot have any other wholly to myself is to be educated to reality and finitude; to know that the longing nevertheless persists is what energizes all my imaginative activity.

Loss initially issues in mourning; but then leads to an awakening of my capacity to love elsewhere, to love this same one differently, or to turn my love energies in a new direction, be it toward another individual or toward a cultural task. Loss means education to reality and to creativity. To know that there is, in me, a child whose longing for love is unappeasable can mean the discovery that I can love rather than punish that child without letting it become the central actor in my adult relationships. It makes no sense to expect another to satisfy that primal longing; that only devalues and perhaps destroys what we can be to one another. But the longing itself, utopian and romantic as it is, is to be cherished as the source of the wishes and hopes that underlie all my activity. The capacity to over-

invest is but the other side of the capacity for creativity, substitution, symbolization, "sublimation."

Such an affirmation of jealousy, only hinted at in Freud, is more explicitly
elaborated by Carl Jung in his depth psychology. The perspective here is even
more radically intrapsychic than in Freud. The focus is less on how jealousy inevitably arises in the interpersonal context of the family than on what my jealousy
reveals about my incompleteness, about my tendency to depend on another for a
wholeness only really to be achieved within.

The "other" in me to whom my jealousy introduces me is, in Jung, not the
child but what he calls the "shadow." The shadow is my dark other self, that part
I tend to disvalue and disown, or to use as a scapegoat. Indeed, so blind am I to
his role in my own psyche that I tend to "project" him, to see my shadow qualities not directly in myself but in others towards whom I have exaggeratedly negative feelings. Infidelity, anger, and vulnerability are all more easily seen in another
than in myself. But the upsurge of a feeling like jealousy forces upon me the recognition of the presence in me of a hitherto unsuspected person-like entity—one
who has memories, desires, and fears as complexly organized as those of my
familiar ego-self and yet radically different. The shadow is not a child so much as
it is a person who has grown up without real nurture and care, and so he is a
strangely misshapen figure. He is first experienced as ugly, disruptive, and fearsome, like the toad whom the princess must (in the unexpurgated version of the
Grimms' fairytale) take to bed. Yet Jung believes that if we can bring ourselves to
acknowledge, "This too is me," we can transform him into a new brother who
continually provides us with new energies, new perspectives. The shadow provides access to the unconscious, and thus to sources for renewal and transformation.

Freud saw in the unconscious primarily unrecognized motives. Jung sees it in
terms of mythical motifs, patterns operative in my life that connect me to the
experiences recounted in age-old, apparently universal myths. The confrontation
with the shadow is not simply the confrontation with my peculiar denied experiences and feelings but with an "archetypal" figure: the dark "other" of countless
tales and legends. The discovery of this transpersonal quality is what seems most
important to Jung. It is through my "pathology," my shadow, my jealousy, that I
am introduced into the mythic dimension of my own life. Through my jealousy I
am being pulled to live anew primordial transformative experiences, the stuff out
of which the myths and literature that most deeply affect us are composed.

Jung suggests that instead of struggling to overcome my jealousy, I should let
it teach me how to move from "single vision" to an imagination that is attuned to

symbolic repetitions. I can learn to proceed from a focus on the literal situation that provoked my jealousy to a recognition of how, through it, I participate in Aphrodite's jealousy of Psyche, or that of Psyche's uglier sisters, or perhaps in Hera's jealousy of Zeus. Jung then wants us to learn how consciously to exploit what Freud called the delusional aspect of jealousy: its capability of stimulating our propensity to fantasy. Jealousy releases daemonic energies that can be creative as well as destructive.

It may even be possible to enter this transpersonal imaginal realm with the others who are part of the jealousy-provoking situation, so that we can celebrate together the archetypal as well as the personal dimensions of our mutual involvement. To be released from the illusion that this is just our problem, and to see it as a perennial human experience, may open us to see, by means of jealousy, what otherwise we were blind to. Jealousy is thus an initiation into the depths of our psychology.

Notes

1. For a useful study, see Juliet Mitchell, *Psychoanalysis and Feminism* (New York: Pantheon, 1974).

2. Sigmund Freud, "Certain Neurotic Mechanisms in Jealousy, Paranoia and Homosexuality," in Philip Rieff, ed., *Sexuality and the Psychology of Love* (New York: Collier, 1953) 232.

3. Robert Seidenberg, "Fidelity and Jealousy: Socio-Cultural Considerations," *Psychoanalytic Review Vol. 54* (Winter 1967) 37.

20

Poetically Dwells Man on this Earth

I found Medard Boss's book, *The Analysis of Dreams*, by chance one day when as a graduate student I was working on a paper on Jung. I found its critique of Freud's scientism and Jung's mysticism exciting and felt some of my own uneasiness about their ways of working with dreams confirmed. I was immediately sympathetic to a response to dreams that seemed to help us stay close to the particular, concrete and often-mundane images of the dream as dreamt. Boss seemed to follow more faithfully than Jung himself the hermeneutical implications of the latter's affirmation that dreams were not distorted messages requiring unciphering, but rather directly revealing expressions presented in a different mode of apprehension than the one which dominates in waking life. But that was then. My response now, almost twenty years later, is somewhat different.

Since then I have read Freud carefully for myself and am no longer as dependent on Jung's view of him as I once was; and returning to Jung from Freud, I have come to read him differently as well, for I understand now how much Freud remains the counted-upon over-against of his own speaking. I no longer find Boss's criticisms of them as justified as I did then. I am no longer persuaded that having the "right" philosophical grounding is as important as I once considered it. I now find an idolatrization of the literal in that focus on the concreteness of what appears which I once celebrated. I am less sure that Boss's redescriptions of dreams are any less abstract, any less tied to his philosophical presuppositions than are Freud's or Jung's. I still value Boss's insights, still find myself learning from him, and being re-minded anew by him of what caring for our dreams requires of us. But there are *depths* in the psychologies of Freud and Jung which I do not find in Boss and which I believe are integral to a full honoring of our dreaming.

Boss, of course, acknowledges his dependence on Freud and Jung. In his book, *Psychoanalysis and Daseinsanalysis*, he claims that what he offers us is a positive critique of Freud: he hopes to recover the original meaning of Freud's concrete and brilliant observations which, he believes, are distorted in Freud's own theoretical formulations by being forced into a natural-scientific philosophical framework. Boss suggests that Freud "secretly shared" the central daseinsanalytic insights into human existence, that he knew intuitively what Heidegger later explicates in the form of his fundamental ontology. Thus Boss sees his own project as the liberation of Freud's essential discoveries through a Heideggerean re-evaluation of the basic theoretical concepts of psychoanalytical theory.

I agree that phenomenology (as articulated in Heidegger's "sublimation" of Husserl) does offer us a better philosophical basis for the articulation of Freud's and Jung's anthropologies than the Cartesian positivism which Freud is alleged to have adopted so uncritically from his scientific mentors or than the rather unsophisticated Kantianism which Jung claims to espouse. Yet Freud and Jung were not entirely ignorant of the existential phenomenological option; though their rejection of it may in some respects seem mistaken, it was deliberate.

Husserl and Freud were near contemporaries; both studied under Brentano and each in his own way sought to overcome the idealist, subjectivistic understanding of the human dominant in their time. Freud was familiar with the attempt, begun as early as 1922, of his close friend, Ludwig Binswanger, to explore how Husserl's phenomenology might be related to psychiatry. He was also aware of Binswanger's later reliance on categories derived from Heidegger's analysis of being-in-the-world to help him reconstruct the life-world of mental patients. In one of his letters he testifies to his respect for Binswanger's work, says how much he enjoys his beautiful style, his erudition, the breadth of his horizon, and his tact in contradicting him; but he adds, "Of course, I don't believe you." Binswanger had recognized from the beginning of their friendship how little need Freud felt for philosophy, how irrelevant he found those questions which most interested Binswanger.[1]

Of course, Binswanger's appropriation of Heidegger differs significantly from that of Boss, as Boss is quick to remind us. For Binswanger being-in-the-world becomes an attribute of the subject; the genuinely phenomenological overcoming of the subjectivist perspective is not realized, and so (as we can see in the diagnostic section of "The Case of Ellen West") the therapist is not freed from an objectifying stance toward his patient. But Jung was directly acquainted with Boss's own adaptation of Heidegger, and he seems even less sympathetic to it than Freud had been to Binswanger's. (Jung doesn't think much of Heidegger himself either; he calls him a master of "complicated banalities," and says, "his *modus philosophandi* is neurotic through and through and is ultimately rooted to his psychic crankiness.") Jung writes Boss, "I do not comprehend your existential philosophy. I have tried seriously to form some picture of your philosophical concepts but found myself step by step entangled in contradictions. I am just no philosopher." He feels that Boss has fundamentally misunderstood him, has ignored his own rejection of Freud's causalistic interpretations, has failed to see that Jung's "Self" is entirely different from the subjectivistic ego and indeed is Jung's way of representing the connection between subject and world. He criticizes Boss's belief that he has discovered something entirely new with the invention of a new phrase, "pre-given world pattern," which Jung believes means just what he means by "archetype." But most important to Jung is not that Boss has misread his own work but that he overvalues what Heidegger's philosophy can contribute: "In spite of all existential philosophy the opposition between ego and world, subject and object, is not annulled. That would be too simple."[2]

We shall need to return to the question of why both Freud and Jung believe something essential to their discoveries is lost in a Heideggerean re-interpretation of them. But first we must acknowledge how sincerely and urgently Boss believes that much is gained. He found (as have many others who believe they understand Freud and Jung) that psychoanalysis and analytical psychology left him in an objectifying relation to his patients and to the dreams and fantasies they shared with him—whereas Heidegger showed him another possibility.

Boss is not only persuaded that Heidegger offers "an explicit articulation of that understanding of man which has always guided our therapeutic actions...although secretly only and without our awareness," but also that the conscious appropriation of this understanding makes possible a different attitude towards one's patients and the therapeutic process. "Analysis of Dasein urges all those who deal with human beings to start seeing and thinking from the beginning so that they can remain with what they immediately perceive and do not get lost in 'scientific' abstractions, derivation, explanations and calculations estranged from the immediate reality of the given situation." Existential philosophy, he believes, changes not just our thinking but our way of being in the world. The therapist informed by it will now "really be able to accept as genuine all the new possibilities for communication which grow 'on the play-ground of transference' without mutilating them through his own intellectual and theoretical prejudices and his personal affective censure."[3] Boss's accounts of his therapeutic interventions suggest the same enormous confidence in the transformative power of being presented with a new way of understanding one's life situation. Such a high valuation of the effect of our philosophical choices is obviously appealing to philosophers and theologians—but, as Jung cautioned, it may be too simple.

Contrary to Boss's view of him, Freud does not really fit snugly into a positivist schema even in his theoretical formulations. In his papers on metapsychology we find a characteristic, tantalizing symbiosis of mechanistic language with language drawn from the realm of myth and poetry; his insights come embodied in the figures of Oedipus and Narcissus; Freud acknowledges that his theories are a kind of mythology. Jung can imagine himself a Kantian only because he feels free to reinterpret Kant. Both really invent their own language to communicate their own vision; there is no given mode of discourse, no recognized literary genre, no established philosophical option, which is wholly adequate. Their fusions of the languages of myth and of science are not confusions but conscious and deliberate undertakings. Because they are writing out of their own unique and overwhelming experiences—Freud out of his discovery, "I am Oedipus," precipitated by his father's death; Jung out of his six-year-long deliberately chosen "confrontation with the unconscious"—they could not borrow another's language to render them. To them their own speech was alive, pregnant, avowedly metaphorical. They realized the danger of literalization and hypostasization, and knew how easily we are bewitched by language; but they could not prevent their metaphors from being understood as clichés.

Boss does experience their metaphors as clichés (or at least he misses the way in which their metaphors are attempts to transcend a natural-scientific ontology). So his liberation came not so much from a depth psychological experience of his own as from the discovery of Heidegger. For him it was the new language that opened the door to new experience rather than the other way around. Yet I suspect that Boss's over-literal reading of Freud reveals not only how easily one may take the positivist side of Freud for the whole, but a tendency on Boss's part to be overly literal. As we shall explore in more detail later, Boss seems to be attuned to the "like" of simile and analogy but deaf to the "is" of metaphor. He says he sees no need for a metapsychology, for a depth psychology, no need to go beyond the appearing (and its similitudes). His tendency to focus on Heidegger's analysis of Dasein in *Sein und Zeit,* rather than on his later meditations on how poetically man dwells on earth, points in the same directions: the call to Being is interpreted moralistically rather than as meaning a respectful caring for what is (including our-selves).

The consequence is that, somewhat surprisingly, Boss is closer than we might at first imagine to those other denigrators of Freud's metapsychology, the ego psychologists. His image of therapeutic health ("being a masculine, mature, selfless, helpful fellowman") is very much like theirs, as is his conviction that we see more while we are awake than while dreaming. Freud's shattering discovery that we are not master in our own house is suppressed. Boss's reasons for dismissing Freud's "Unconscious" and Jung's "archetypes" as unnecessary entities have merit; but when he relinquishes these notions, he comes perilously close to losing as well the central insights they express.

As Heraclitus observed, "You could not discover the limits of psyche even if you traveled every road to do so; such is the depth of its logos." No philosophy, no language game, protects us from the idolatries, the subjectivism and the objectifications which Boss protests in Freud and Jung. Rather than criticizing Boss for taking Freud and Jung too literally, we might ask instead what it means about us as human beings that we resist the metaphorical and are pulled to literalize it, that we evade the concrete and are pulled to mystify it.

It is Boss's bringing *this* question to our attention that seems important to me. He raises the question of what it means to care for the dream, for dreaming. Why do we persist in "doing violence to our dreaming?" Why do we over and over again betray and deny, rape, plunder and strangle what we dream? Surely it is not just because we approach our dreams with the wrong philosophy, but because there is something threatening about dreams. To take dreaming seriously undermines what Husserl called "the natural standpoint," the comforting assumption of an ego confronting (and controlling) the world. The pull to subjectivism, as Freud plainly saw, bespeaks much more than the inadequacy of our philosophical language. Subjectivism is not just a mistaken description of human awareness, but a deeply tempting misdirection of our awareness away from the world and thus from human be-ing. Freud called this pull "narcissism" and saw it as a kind of death; it is only as we are erotically bound to the world of others that we exist humanly. To take dreaming seriously entails a change in our whole sense of what it is to be a self, just as to take my own particular dreams seriously demands an enormous revision in my self-understanding.

The Poetics of Space

Freud and Jung and Boss are each concerned to validate dreaming as an autochthonous mode of being present, as a particular "human bearing." They regard dreams as the "royal road" to the very core of human existence, for to take seriously that and how we dream is to be forced to give up our subjectivistic illusions about consciousness. Freud and Jung use the language of psychology to try to communicate this insight; Boss, the language of existential phenomenology. Much is said more clearly in this version, but some things are left out.

Husserl's phenomenology attempts to change radically our notion of consciousness. He uses the term to refer to the being of both subject and object—the object's mode of being is being known; the subject's mode of being is knowing. We can know subject and object only in their interrelation. Consciousness is not a property of the ego but always transcends it, for it means the subject's turning toward others as its own mode of being. We can't really separate the self that has experiences from the objects that are experienced. The world is always already present (as in Freud the family is always already there). We humans are always and everywhere beyond ourselves, within a world of objects, people and meanings.

Heidegger's and Boss's way of dealing with this understanding is to refuse to use the term consciousness at all, to speak instead of Dasein, being-there, being in a world with others. They hope thereby to overcome the commonsense notion that there is any difference between the two propositions: "the ego constitutes the world in various ways," and "the world discloses itself in various ways." Yet the naive presuppositions are so deeply rooted in our language that the comprehension of this basic insight is seemingly impossible. Boss still has to ask two questions to be able to characterize any particular mode of existence: "for what givens" and "in what special way" is one present at any given moment?

Freud and Jung take a different route. They are still engaged in articulating a logos of psyche, not in Daseinsanalysis. But they mean by psyche something different than the subject of the subject-object dichotomy, and by psychology, something different than the logic of the ego. Freud comes close to returning to the original Greek meaning of psyche as the animating principle of human life, the beating in us of the wings of life, our breath-ing, our be-ing. His focus on the drives as the primary *psychic* modalities, as his god-terms, is his way of overcoming the notion that "I" "have" a body or that the psyche is a ghost in the (body) machine. Drive to Freud, as Paul Ricoeur recognizes, is need become wish, energy become meaning (though psychoanalysis has often disregarded this insight).[4] When Jung speaks of wanting to restore the psyche to psychology, he intends a vision of "soul" as encompassing "the mysterious truth that the spirit is the life of the body seen from within and the body the outward manifestation of the life of the spirit."[5] When Jung speaks of a "collective unconscious," of an "objective psyche," he is also radically putting in question the notion that psychical processes are personal possessions. For both Freud and Jung psyche means the human way of being. I do not have a psyche, but I am present in the world in a variety of ways, waking, dreaming, fantasying, but always in a characteristically human, that is psychical, way.

Yet Boss is right in noting that we are easily misled into understanding the psyche of which Freud and Jung speak as referring to some peculiar kind of inner space, to a container, and then to regarding the images of dream and fantasy as some strange kind of interior objects. Because of our prejudice in favor of one mode of psychic activity, the perception of the sensibly present, we are led to speak of that which presents itself to us in other modes as images or ideas "in" our psyches. Boss helps us see that the immediate experience of our thinking of, or remembering, something gives evidence of a completely different state of affairs. At the moment that I think of Notre Dame in Paris I am with Notre Dame in Paris and Notre Dame is with me, though "only" in my relationship of thinking of, or remembering, it.[6] "We are constantly 'out there' with the things which are present at hand and with our fellow human beings at their places in the world, even when these things and these fellow human beings are given to us only in that mode of presence in which they are brought to mind, and not in the sensibly perceptible mode of presence." Freud and Jung mean to say much the same thing when they carefully distinguish "psychic reality" from physical reality—their way of pointing to the two different ways that things can be present to us, but they say it more clumsily than Boss. Freud's affirmation that what distinguishes dreaming from being awake is not some special contents but a particular mode of ordering contents is often ignored. Many share Boss's understanding of Jung's notion of archetypes as referring to a special, universally present, kind of psychical contents, even though Jung by the archetypal means to point to an oft denigrated but always available human way of being present to the things of the world—open to their human meaningfulness and not simply to their purely utilitarian thing-ness. Jung retains the biological understanding of instinct that Freud dismissed; archetypes are his way of referring to instinct become human, imaginal, psychical.

Heidegger sometimes dramatizes the dangers connected with the hypostatization of consciousness by speaking of consciousness as Nothingness. Freud and Jung take a closely related route: they speak of the Un-conscious. They accept the traditional equation of consciousness with conceptual awareness and then posit an Un-conscious to account for the non-conceptual aspects of awareness. This is an enormous risk, of course, for it seems to compound the problem: it defines what is not conscious by what is, and instead of questioning one entity seems to create another. Boss glimpses what is really going on, that the concept of the unconscious is the negation of the notion of a conscious-ness. He believes Freud was on the way to the discovery of concealment as such, but "as a child of his power hungry time," he was unable to let concealment be the secret it is.[7] Freud found it necessary to make subjectivistic, psychologistic objects out of conceal-ment in order to be able to drag it into the light and make it usable.

But Freud is up to a familiar trick: he insists on using the notion of conscious-ness, just as he insists on speaking of "sexuality," of "normality," of "death," pre-cisely to bring us to recognize the limitations of our everyday understanding. As early as *Studies on Hysteria* Freud was puzzled about how one speaks of a reality that has no substantive existence. He resorts to negative description; like the god of the *via negativa*, the unconscious is defined by what it is not. The unconscious is the not that doesn't exist and yet somehow is. He makes use of analogies drawn from electricity and physiology, architecture and optics, to remind us that the descriptions are necessarily metaphorical. He fears his metaphors will be taken lit-erally. "It is only too easy to fall into a habit of thought which assumes that every substantive has a substance behind it...to forget the metaphorical character of our language."[8]

By the time of *Interpretation of Dreams* Freud had come to regard the uncon-scious mode of psychic activity as primary. Now the mode of being present that is to be accounted for is the one that governs our lives while we are awake; con-sciousness is now explained as a redirection, a diversion of the original mode of psychic activity. He says we must abandon the overvaluation of being conscious, must recognize the unconscious as the true psychical reality. Freud again uses metaphors drawn from physics, from mechanics and electricity, and from biology to communicate his understanding of the psyche as a process rather than a struc-ture. He uses water metaphors: dams, channels and icebergs. There are many political metaphors, mostly referring to underground movements and to the eva-sions and subterfuges to which they resort. There are metaphors drawn from eco-nomics: references to sacrifices, balances, and investments. Military struggle—battles and the movement of armies, heroic exploits and strategic retreats—is a frequent theme. The psyche is like a theatrical company, each of whose members is from time to time given the starring role. This last image sug-gests the new conception of self that emerges in *Interpretation*. There are connec-tions that constitute our existence other than the causal, chronological ones perceived by rational consciousness. All through the day, mostly unbeknownst to us, the unconscious is at work making connections in its primary-process way, along lines suggested by the recognition of analogies and responsive to feel-ings—without regard for temporality or the distinction between the factual and the fantasized. To notice concretely, visually, animistically, is one of our natural modes of perception. The unconscious is not inner experiences but a different way of perceiving, ordering, remembering (which indeed denies the importance of the inner-outer distinction so important to rationality).

For Freud the unconscious is a mode of psychic presence. At first his focus is on the unconscious as one of the ways in which the subject responds to the world; later, when he comes to speak of *das Es* (the id) instead of the unconscious—at the same time that he comes to speak of our inescapable involvement with the transpersonal powers he calls Eros and Death—he emphasizes rather that what he has called unconscious is given to us, not made by us. His *Es* is closer than Boss seems to suspect to the "*Es*" of "*Es traumte mir.*" The unconscious thus serves to refer to a mode of being of both subject and object—much like Husserl's consciousness. Though his theoretical formulations may often seem heavy and coarse, they nevertheless can never quite obscure Freud's sense of the unconscious as a realm where the mystery of Being discloses itself.

Freud recognizes the danger of spatial metaphors—and their inescapability. They continue to dominate his own rhetoric. The most pervasive image for the unconscious is now the underworld, the realm of the dead and the invisible. But he also turns often to metaphors from archaeology, speaks of the psychic layers as a series of cities built each on top of the ruins of previous cities; he draws from geology, speaks of strata, of digging shafts and tunnels. The psyche is a series of rooms, a nature preserve, a tribal relocation.

Freud uses spatial metaphors to convey the interplay between self and world, self and other. "Transference," "projection," "introjection" (though Boss sees them as mechanistic terms) suggest the poetic creation of self and other: "I am who I am because I am this one and that one; you are who you are to me because you are also another and also myself."

To be in the world psychically, intentionally, humanly (not just physically) leads us naturally to speak of psychic space, and so of psyche itself as a space. Heidegger, too, speaks of the human person as a clearing. We should not dismiss such language too quickly just because it is misleading if understood literally: we should rather try to respond to its poetry as Gaston Bachelard does in *The Poetics of Space*. Just as we need to care for our dreams, so we should also care for the language that comes to us to explain our being here. Bachelard helps us appreciate the full resonance of the terms "outside" and "inside," to discover how "at the slightest touch, asymmetry appears.... No one can live the qualifying epithets attached to inside and outside in the same way."[9] To speak of consciousness as inside, of the unconscious as even deeper inside, of Jung's collective unconscious as somehow deeper still, is to point to the invisibility of the psychical—it is not in the head but further within, ever further. It is not any place, but in-ness expresses its mode of being. It is not to be seen but is a way of seeing—yet a way of seeing that has regard not for what shows on the surface, but for meanings that are not immediately apparent, that are within (not added by interpretation), though this "within" too is only metaphor. (And it is indeed true that emphasis on within-ness may lead to neglect of with-ness.)

Freud and Jung were drawn to speak of the unconscious precisely by their concern to attend faithfully to all psychic phenomena. They would agree with Boss that to free ourselves of our prejudices regarding what constitutes psyche means attending to whatever appears as it appears. Boss explicitly aims at a pure phenomenological description which approaches the given without abstractions or presuppositions, which sets aside the reality question and the question of causality and origin. Attention is not to be directed to an "I" who makes my dreams or perceptions or thoughts, or to the world that is their presumed source, but, subtly and carefully, to the dream, the perception, the thought. Daseinsanalysis "asks us for once just to look at the phenomena of our world themselves, as they confront us, and to linger with them sufficiently long to become fully aware of what they tell us directly about their meaning and essence."[10] But such loving regard for what appears in the psyche's self-presentations is among Freud's most important contributions. He turned his attention away from the objectifying language of the physician to the patient's own images and associations and to the peculiar structure of primary-process language. It was his achievement to have discovered as meaningful what had hitherto seemed gibberish: neurotic symptom, error and dream. Openness to whatever appears as it appears is the rule of psychoanalytical therapy, as Boss freely acknowledges.

Yet Boss believes that Freud does not linger long enough, that he rather moves from perception to inference, description to explanation. I see this judgment as a failure to discern that Freud's "causes" are really prototypes, that his explanations are really fuller descriptions, the cooperative creation of a more coherent version of a dream or life-story than the patient was able to give initially. The criteria of meaningfulness are poetic: does the version arrived at through interpretation enable us to discern a meaningful pattern in what has seemed to be only chaotic fragments? As Wittgenstein recognized, Freud does not present a hypothesis on the basis of a dream report, but helps fit the dream "into a context in which it ceases to be puzzling. In a sense the dreamer re-dreams his dream in surroundings such that its aspect changes."[11] Boss misinterprets Freud's search for the wish that creates the dream as a search for a mechanistic cause, whereas I take it to be Freud's equivalent for Brentano's notion of "intentionality." Freud's deliberate mixing of the language of force and of meaning, of causality and of intentionality—as his way of suggesting the dynamic interplay of self and world, mind and body—may seem clumsier and less elegant than speaking of Dasein, but it has the advantage of suggesting both the sense in which these two phenomena are not one (because of our pull toward objectification and egoism) as well as the sense in which they are.

Jung calls himself a phenomenologist, though he does not mean thereby to associate himself with Husserl; he simply means to emphasize his care for the manifest and its many meanings, and his rejection of Freud's notion of latent meaning. Dream images as he understands them do not refer to something known but repressed which interpretation can discover; they refer instead to something unknown, something not directly expressible, for which the image is the most telling equivalent available. Understanding emerges neither from decoding nor through free association (which he believes leads away from the specific image to the life concerns of the patient, concerns that almost any other image could just as easily have elicited). Jung believes rather in "amplification"—as opposed to interpretation—because he is persuaded that meaning is revealed by staying with the image and its associations, those analogues which familiarity with mythic and literary traditions makes available.

Boss is right that both Freud and Jung find that describing what appears as it appears is not enough—that there is more than appears. What appears discloses the Undisclosed from which it appears. Boss says something like this too, but he does not approve of Freud's and Jung's way of saying it. Their naming of the Undisclosed appears to him as reification.

The Poetics of Dream

Truly to regard dreaming as a particular way of being able to be in the world means to consider carefully what distinguishes this way of existing from the mode of being awake. When Boss undertakes this project, he finds that the givens of dreaming seem more metamorphic and fleeting than those of waking life, and that what is given to us in the dream appears in only one mode—that of immediate presence. The dream only seems more open and less inhibited. There is no past or future, thus properly speaking no remembering or wishing. There is no distance between ourselves and the objects of our perception, no relief from their oppressive given-ness and no opportunity for insight or reflection. There is only perception. There is, however, the possibility that the reawakened individual might discern in the dream-givens analogies to his life situation.

Freud gives us a more detailed analysis of the peculiar structure of dreaming. Freud's speaking of psychic activity as work recalls the original meaning of *poesis*:

making. Freud is interested in bringing into view the processes involved in dream-work, mourning-work, and artistic work. The fascination that he and Jung have with the peculiar shaping of content displayed in the dream leads them to speak as though there were a creative agency shaping the dream—though both also know that for the ego the dream is a given. Boss dismisses as a mechanics of dream-ing Freud's analysis of the elements of dream-work (condensation, displacement, reversal, the absence of negation, the omission of syntactical conjunctions, the replacement of the abstract by the concrete); in contrast Lionel Trilling recognizes that what psychoanalysis offers us is a "science of tropes." Jung extended Freud's poetics in his early studies of psychotics; his work enabled him to distinguish more clearly the operation of primary-process thinking undiluted by compromise with secondary-thought processes.

Boss says that the dream in itself means only what is directly, literally represented, what it means to the dreamer during the dream—though upon awakening we may be able to discover similarities between the dream situation and our present day-light way of being. Both Freud and Jung understand the relation between the dream-world and the waking one more subtly. Freud discovers not only analogies but also antithesis, metonomy, synedoche, periphrasis, hyperbole. Jung speaks of "complementarity," but shows that this takes many shapes. Boss seems to have a real antipathy for metaphorical conjunctions, a need to translate them into the prosaic flatness of similes. He might "transfer" his father-love onto his analyst, yet he is perfectly comfortable saying, "His human condition is still so child-like and undeveloped that...he is open to the perception only of the father-like aspects of all the adult men he encounters. Thus, he behaves toward the analyst as if the latter were like his father."[12] Freud felt it possible to say that the analyst is the patient's father and also the immediately present analyst.

Boss's claim that our dreams are address to us, calling for our answering, is one to which both Freud and Jung would accede—though they do not say it as well as he. Freud believes that dreams call for interpretation, for re-membering, that they are completed by the response of the waking self. He, too, would "grant the highest rank to our most fully awake way of existence." "Where id was, let ego be," he asserts, though the point for him is that the most fully awake way of existence is one genuinely open to the world of dreaming. "A total severance of the two systems is above all what characterizes a condition of illness."[13] (And he seems to understand better than Boss why the limitation to the mode of immediate presence may be experienced as openness rather than as privation, for he discerns its similarity to the "oceanic feeling" of mysticism.) Freud's interpretations are sometimes reductive and forced, but the point of free association is to teach us to "dream awake" as poets do, to release the plurivocity of meaning in the given images. H. D., the Imagist poet, praises Freud's ability to effect this release, to "charm the very beasts of the unconscious mind, enliven the dead sticks and stones of buried thoughts and mind."[14] Freud resorts, too, to what he calls "symbolic" interpretation, because he found that our dreams tend to point to what are perennially the most urgent and fearsome concerns of human life: parents and children, birth and sex and death. Freud knows that interpretations move beyond the manifest dream to a new creation, which he perversely calls the latent dream.

Jung says more clearly that what he gives us is amplification not interpretation. He deliberately brings into relation to the dream analogies that are taken not from the dreamer's idiosyncratic life situation, but from religious and mythological traditions. He hopes thereby to help us discover that images perceived in the full range of their possible meanings can free us from an egotistical focus on our own lives and from a purely utilitarian relation to the world we find ourselves in. Boss says we speak of the "symbolic" meaning of a thing only if we have "previously mutilated the meaning-content of this thing and reduced it to its purely utilitarian aspects of an isolated object."[15] It is because they consider a naive focus on the appearing to be a participation in such mutilation that Freud and Jung feel the need of depth interpretation. A Jungian would be willing to see a mythological savior figure in the surgeon who appeared in the dream of one of Boss's patients not only because there are mythological analogies to cures accomplished in this way, but more importantly because healing has a magical and mysterious quality to it, a human importance which is lost in Boss's own interpretation which reduces the figure to that of "a tall, strong, white-haired man of ordinary flesh and blood, albeit possessed of an unusually mature, selfless ability to love a fellow human being who is ill to the point of death."

Boss's own sense of what answering the address of our dreams might mean sometimes seems to entail an overly moralistic understanding of our responseability. He says, "This call from conscience and this guilt feeling will not abate until man has taken over and responsibly accepted all those possibilities which constitute him, and has borne and carried them out in taking care of the things and fellowmen of his world."[16] This "taking care," too, seems more heavy-handed than that imagined in Rilke's "Ninth Elegy." Dreams seem to be approached as pointers for a redirection of the patient's life in accordance with the analyst's vision of authentic Dasein. It is the therapist who comes up with the abstract redescription of the dream situation and then asks the dreamer what analogies from his waking situation come to mind. The therapist feels free to "point out to the dreamer" the "unbelievable predominance" she concedes to her mother, to express "his astonishment" at her submission. The therapist puts himself forward as someone who is fully responsible, who "has gathered his existence into a self-owning way of being himself." Despite the greater restrictedness of the dream-world, Boss admits that new life possibilities sometimes dawn for a patient for the first time in a dream situation—though he does not even try to explain how this might be possible. He does, however, seem to have tremendous confidence in the transformative power of the discovery of the possibility of a completely different bearing.

My suspicion about using our dreams primarily as pointers that guide us in our waking life is shared by James Hillman. "When we take the dream as a corrective to the leftovers of yesterday," he says, "or as instruction for tomorrow, we are using it for the old ego. Freud said the dream is the guardian of sleep...Perhaps the point of dreams is that night after night, year after year, they prepare the imaginal ego for old age, death and fate...Perhaps the point of dreams has very little to do with our daily concerns."[17] Perhaps a depth interpretation of our dreams leads us to a fuller recognition of the ambiguity and mystery inherent in life rather than to a resolution of our perplexities. Perhaps the point of dreams is to dream.

In the cases to which Boss refers he seems again and again to find passivity and dependence to be the problems the patients need to overcome, and he voices what to me is a too easy assumption that this possibility is realizable. I am more in tune with Freud's admission: "My discoveries are no cure-all. My discoveries are the basis for a very grave philosophy." I value Freud's recognition of how much in us is pulled to passivity, and the luminous insight of his last years that accepting our dependency is the most difficult of all life tasks and a necessary part of our preparation for death.

Notes

1. Ernst L. Freud, ed., *Letters of Sigmund Freud* (New York: Basic Books, 1960) 431; Ludwig Binswanger, "My First Three Visits with Freud in Vienna," in Hendrik Ruitenbeek, ed., *Freud As We Knew Him* (Detroit: Wayne State University Press, 1973) 367.

2. Gerhard Adler, ed., *C. G. Jung: Letters* (Princeton: Princeton University Press, 1973, 1975) Vol. 1, 330, 331; Vol. II, xl-xliv.

3. Medard Boss, "Daseinsanalysis and Psychotherapy," in Hendrik Ruitenbeek, ed., *Psychoanalysis and Existential Philosophy* (New York: Dutton, 1962) 82,

86; Medard Boss, *Psychoanalysis and Doseinsanalysis* (New York: Basic Books, 1963) 29f.

4. Cf. David L. Miller, "Spirit," in Daniel C. Noel, ed., *Echoes of the Wordless Word* (Missoula: AAR/SBL, 1973) 93-110; Paul Ricoeur, *Freud and Philosophy* (New Haven & London: Yale University Press, 1970) 59-158.

5. C. G. Jung, "The Spiritual Problem of Modern Man," in Joseph Campbell, ed., *The Portable Jung* (New York: Viking Press, 1971) 479.

6. Boss, *Psychoanalysis*, 95.

7. Boss, *Psychoanalysis,* 101.

8. Sigmund Freud and Josef Breuer, *Studies on Hysteria* (New York: Avon Books, 1965) 651.

9. Gaston Bachelard, *The Poetics of Space* (Boston: Beacon Press, 1969) 215.

10. Boss, *Psychoanalysis*, 30.

11. Ludwig Wittgenstein, "Conversations with Freud," in Richard Wollheim, ed., *Freud: A Collection of Critical Essays* (New York: Anchor Books, 1974) 4.

12. Boss, *Psychoanalysis,* 124.

13. Sigmund Freud, "The Unconscious," *General Psychological Theory* (New York: Collier Books, 1963) 141.

14. H. D., *Tribute to Freud* (New York: McGraw-Hill, 1975) 106.

15. Boss, *Psychoanalysis*, 129.

16. Boss, "*Daseinsanalysis*," 86.

17. James Hillman, *The Myth of Analysis* (Evanston: Northwestern University Press, 1972) 187.

21

Re-Visioning Autobiography:
The Bequest of Freud and Jung

"One never discusses other men's dreams innocently."[1] To read Freud's *The Interpretation of Dreams* and Jung's *Memories, Dreams, Reflections* as contributions to a poetics of autobiography is at some level to put forward an autobiography of autobiography. For these two have parented my vision of myself, as I believe they have done for all of us who, willy-nilly, are their heirs. They have changed our very sense of what it is to be a self; after Freud and Jung we cannot tell our stories in the same old way. Between them they have transformed the genre created by Augustine far beyond the radical reshaping already accomplished by Rousseau.

Both Freud and Jung seem to have taken for granted the archetypal significance of their lives. To understand Freud means grasping the connection between his two discoveries: "I am my most important patient," and "The whole race is my patient." The entire lifework of each is really autobiographical; even their most theoretical writings represent the psyche's search to understand itself. Freud's self-analysis is pursued in everything he writes, as is Jung's project of individuation.

There is a continual interplay between what Freud learns from his own analysis and what he learns from his patients. The protagonists of Freud's case histories become figures in his story. We are intrigued by the only half-admitted countertransference Dora inspires in Freud. The "Wolfman's" own account of his life has almost no intrinsic interest; we read it only because we have come to care about him as one of Freud's "characters." Freud's essays on the Moses of Michelangelo, on Leonardo and Dostoevski each reveal his own involvement: his struggle not to be overwhelmed by the defections of Jung and Adler, his fear of the waning of his own creative powers, his hope of becoming a teacher and liberator of humanity and not one of the jailers. The metapsychological essays of Freud's later years are ultimately related to his "working through" of the new recognition of death and human finitude forced upon him by the horrors of the world war, the deaths of his daughter and favorite grandson, the discovery of his own cancer. Nevertheless the autobiographical concern is more clearly visible in *The Interpretation of Dreams* than anywhere else in Freud's work. Despite its overtly didactic form, we must accustom ourselves to reading this book as an exercise in autobiography. It is a much more self-revealing book than *An Autobiographical Study*; it is the public version of that process of self-discovery earlier articulated in Freud's letters to Fliess.

Though in a letter written during their period of intimacy Jung had criticized Freud for withholding the deeper, more personally painful layers of the interpretation of his own dreams,[2] he is not himself ready to risk as personally disclosing a publication as *Interpretation* at the very beginning of his mature career as Freud had done. His own most explicit autobiographical work, *Memories, Dreams, Reflections*, was written at the end of his life with the stipulation that it not be published until after his death. Characteristically, it is more a work of synthesis than of self-analysis, of discovering (or creating) the wholeness and oneness implicit in the almost completed life.

Both *Interpretation* and *Memories* are self-consciously formal innovations; Freud and Jung were conscious that there was no given form appropriate to their projects. Each recognized that in discovering the form for his telling he was at the same time discovering himself. James Olney calls such autobiographies "duplex" and says: "In the great autobiographers...consciousness of this continuing creation of the self accompanies the creation" of the autobiography. Freud recognized that in writing *Interpretation* he was continuing his self-analysis; Jung understood that the composition of *Memories* represented a process of transformation and objectification. Each understood his book as a "metaphor of self" which enabled him to body forth his hitherto unknown meaning.[3]

Both were well aware of the poetic or mythic dimensions of these works. In his prologue Jung writes: "I cannot employ the language of science to trace this process of growth in myself...What we are to our inward vision...can only be expressed by way of myth" (p. 3).[4] Freud says in his original preface that he has consciously submitted to the necessity for a kind of self-exposure usually demanded only of a poet not of a writer who is a man of science (p. xxiv).[5] He acknowledges, too, the importance of his identification with the biblical Joseph, the archetypal interpreter of dreams (p. 522). The figure of Oedipus possessed Freud not only because of its association with the incest theme but because Oedipus' relentless search for the truth of his story prefigures the work of psychoanalysis (p. 295). Self-analysis means dismemberment and re-membering (cf. the dissection dream, p. 491); it inevitably evokes the myths of Osiris and Orpheus. Robert Scholes suggests that mythic patterning is an inevitable correlate of the focus on the inner life: mimesis dissolves into mythos when the narrator penetrates the labyrinth of the psyche.[6]

The discovery of the unconscious leads to a new sense of the form and content of autobiography. The usual chronologically ordered arrangement of outward events misses the point. There is a center to us beyond our direct knowledge and control (which Freud called "the core of our being" and Jung, "the undiscovered self"), which we know only through its manifestations, especially dreams. Dreams and other imaginal events (like the seduction fantasies of Freud's hysterical patients and the play-rituals of Jung's early years) are often more important to us than most of the literal, objective events in which we participate. The recognition that our dreams create us as much as we create them suggests autobiography as a dream series. The focus on dreams is "wonderfully suited" to a vision "poised between the mythic and mimetic for we can refer them to divinities or to mental processes."[7] The requirements for writing such an autobiography seem to be those Freud put forward for conducting one's own dream analyses; being honest, normal and a good dreamer, being initiated into the "secret" that dreams express our deepest wishes and mean more than at first appears. It does not depend on the illusion that we can ever fully consciously circumscribe the meaning of our life any more than we can ever fully interpret a dream.

The "plotting" of an autobiography written to take account of the importance of the unconscious is also determined by the recognition that the usual focus on profane events is superficial. We are not surprised that Jung understands his autobiography as a history of numinous experiences and so begins it with his childhood dream of a ritual phallus. But in Freud's book, too, the encounters with the uncanny, with "the 'daemonic power' that produces the dream wish" (p. 652), dominate; even in this early work the numinosity he discovers in sexuality and death is evident.

The awareness of an aspect of myself radically other than my conscious ego implies also that autobiography emerges as the expression of a divided self. Id, ego, super-ego are Freud's terms; persona, ego, shadow, anima or animus are Jung's. Either way autobiography has become dramatic rather than lyric or epic: His Majesty the Ego can no longer assume that his voice will be the only one. Rousseau had already offered us a hero who could criticize his own heroic illusions, but now that heroic project too is undermined. *Interpretation* and *Memories* both reflect an acknowledgement of the fictiveness of the unity of the self.

Recognition of the unconscious also suggests that the conventional notion of a discrete individuality as subject of the autobiography misses the point. For Jung, "the only events in my life worth telling are those where the imperishable world irrupted into this transitory one" (p. 4). I discover myself as I discover the transpersonal archetypes to which I am most deeply related. In Freud's view the child becomes a self through its inevitably ambivalent involvements with others, particularly parents and siblings; we adults discover who we really are as we learn that we are Oedipus and Narcissus. Thus autobiography becomes a series of identifications, and a discovery of mythical prototypes. That both *Interpretation* and *Memories* offer us psychologies developed in what Jung calls "the second half of life" seems pertinent to their appreciation of the necessary interpenetration of mythology and any depth psychological understanding of the self. "While in the life of the human race the mythical is an early and primitive stage," Thomas Mann tells us, "in the life of the individual it is a late and mature one."[8]

Freud is convinced of the prototypicality of his childhood, and thus of its mythical significance. His memories are not his alone; they are every man's. All of us, he believes, resent our fathers and desire our mothers for ourselves; all of us feel love and resentment toward our brothers or sisters; all of us carry infantile patterns of feeling into the relationships of our adult lives with substitute parents and siblings; all of us are who we are in large measure because of those upon whom we have modeled ourselves. As surely as any primitive, Freud believed that he had found himself in relation to a mythical prototype, Oedipus, and he came to believe that all of us as human beings discover who we are as we come to admit to this identification. Later he discovers that we are not only Oedipus but also Narcissus and Prometheus, and that each of us is the reanimation of particular other mythical figures just as he is the reanimation of the biblical Joseph and of Moses. He sees, too, how we project mythic identities upon the actual others in our lives.

It is recognition of the inescapable patterning of our lives by such archetypes that leads Jung to focus so much of his attention on what he calls the collective aspect of the unconscious (in contrast to its historical or personal aspect). Freud's myth (Oedipus) seems to have come to him unsought; Jung went in deliberate search of his when he recognized his ignorance of what myth might be ordering his life without his knowledge. This search began shortly after the break with Freud and after completing his *The Psychology of the Unconscious*, which explores the continued presence of archaic images in the contemporary psyche. It was the search for that myth which prompted his plunge into a six-year period of conscious introversion. His quest was initiated by a strange mythical dream in which he was somehow responsible for the death of the hero Siegfried. He understood this dream as a call to a different kind of heroism, modeled on Parzival's. Parzival's destiny is very different from that of Oedipus—his task is to heal the wounded and aged king through his slowly maturing compassion; he is engaged in an explicitly spiritual quest that does not, however, call for the abandonment of earthly love. Jung sees this as one of the myths that is living him; he recognizes more explicitly than Freud the plurality of archetypes that inform the life of any one of us. To tell our story truly is to take them all into account.

"All genuinely creative writings are the product of more than a single motive and more than a single impulse in the poet's mind and are open to more than a single interpretation." Thus Freud (p. 299); both he and Jung recognize that their autobiographies will reveal both more and other than they had consciously intended. They know, too, that their structures and their metaphors "tell" as much as do their ostensible contents. Both are "unreliable narrators"; both are tricksters. When first person narrative appears in Western literature, it is as the traveler's tale. As Bachelard reminds us, "The man who comes back from afar lies with impunity."[9] Jung says explicitly, "Whether or not the stories are 'true' is not the problem. The only question is whether what I tell is my fable, my truth" (p. 3). Freud cares more than Jung about our acceptance of "the reality principle," but he, too, recognizes the importance of "psychic reality." He hopes that we will learn not to take our fantasies literally, but to recognize them as fantasy and celebrate them as such.

Despite the many agreed-upon revisions of the genre there are significant differences in form between *Interpretation* and *Memories*, differences correlative to different understandings of the unconscious, different views of dream.

The Interpretation of Dreams

Like Augustine and Rousseau before him Freud intends his "confessions" as an invitation to us to repeat the author's experience, to "transfer" our identities onto him. The dream of Irma is not only Freud's initiation, but is intended to become ours as well.

Even the manifest shape of *Interpretation* is provocatively ambivalent. The title, *Traumdeutung,* suggests a popular fortune-telling work; the table of contents and the introductory chapter prepare us for a work of careful scientific exploration. Yet the inner structure of *Interpretation* is constituted through the interplay of three closely related metaphors: the book is ordered to suggest a dream, but also follows closely the pattern of the hero's journey to the underworld, and represents an incestuous return to the mother's womb. There are thus three different orderings of time operative in the book: the dream's interfusing of time present and time past, the quest's linear progression through time, the archetypal timelessness of the ritual reunion.

The dream-like quality of the book is suggested by its apparent fragmentation and incompleteness. The dreams and their interpretations become elements of one all-inclusive dream: the component parts, which seem to reveal so much, exasperatingly seem also full of concealment. We do not even know in what order Freud dreamt the dreams he here reports. There are confusing transformations, disappearances and reappearances. Pregnant but isolated moments from Freud's childhood flash into view. We are introduced to many of the characters presently involved in Freud's life who then turn out to be reincarnations of earlier intimates. There are many clues but no coherence; the meaning is latent.

The motif of the journey is suggested by the epigraph from the *Aeneid* and its reference to a journey to the infernal regions; Freud like Dante goes with Virgil as his guide. The many references to Faust suggest that he too serves as prototype. Dreams are spoken of as the "royal road to the unconscious" (p. 647); analysis is typically represented in dreams as a journey, often into sub-terranean regions (p. 445).

Freud's journey follows the age-old pattern. "At the time of my birth an old peasant-woman had prophesied to my proud mother that with her first-born child she had brought a great man into the world" (p. 225). And yet when he was seven or eight he remembers his father warning, "That boy will come to nothing" (p. 250). A few years later, after watching his father capitulate meekly to a Christian, he felt so ashamed of this unheroic conduct that he replaced him with a father more in harmony with his own heroic destiny: Hamilcar Barca, sire to Hannibal (p. 229). But it isn't until the literal father has died that this hero is called to his task. Then in the middle of the journey of his life he comes to himself in a dark wood where the straight way was lost:

> The whole thing is planned on the model of an imaginary walk. First comes the dark wood of the authorities (who cannot see the trees), where there is no clear view and it is easy to go astray. Then there is a cavernous defile through which I lead my readers—my specimen with its peculiarities, its details, its indiscretions, and its bad jokes—and then, all at once, the high ground and the prospect, and the question, "Which way do you want to go?"[10]

The journey begins with the death of the father and with the break with tradition. The dream of Irma is the initiating revelatory experience. The interpretation of this dream suggests how Irma serves in the dream as a collective image for the feminine. She is his Diotima, his "She." (Freud speaks later in the book of Rider Haggard's novels in which a woman typically serves as guide for a perilous journey into an undiscovered region, p. 491.) The dream, even more in Erik Erikson's[11] interpretation than in Freud's own, justifies his vocational commitment to psychotherapy and his reliance on intuition. Then with the way into the unconscious opened up by this dream, Freud encounters all the other threatening and helping figures who live in this underworld realm. He speaks of the abandoned wishes encountered there as being "like the shades in the Odyssey, which awoke to some sort of life as soon as they had tasted blood" (p. 282). The figures who appear are strangely familiar, some associated with long-forgotten childhood experiences, others with the prosaic happenings of his everyday life—familiar and yet magically transformed. None of the taken-for-granted assumptions about time and space, causality and logic, seem to apply in this other world.

And then suddenly Freud finds himself back in the daylight world and discovers that "the easy and agreeable portion of our journey lies behind us" (p. 549). The return, the communication of his *theoria*, his vision, persuading others that his discovery is a boon, offers the most difficult challenge of all—particularly because he understands well that it is subversive of his culture's dominant assumption: the overvaluation of consciousness and rationality (p. 65). How bring the new insights into the old world? For Freud had discovered that the essence of dreaming is a particular form of thinking, and that this form represents the original, primary form of human consciousness: "These processes which are described as irrational are not in fact falsifications of normal processes…but are modes of activity of the psychical apparatus that have been freed from an inhibition" (p. 644). "It is essential to abandon the overvaluation of being conscious…the unconscious is the larger sphere which includes the conscious; the unconscious is the true psychical reality" (p. 651).

Freud returned, hoping to teach his contemporaries not only to value their most disparaged dreams, but even more to appreciate this form of expression as responsible for most intellectual and artistic production. Primary process thinking is not confined to dreams; it is the form of the uninhibited activity of the psyche: its play. We are all in touch with it in our daydreaming; the poet knows how to dream awake and share his dreams with us. Freud's method of dream interpretation, free association, is an attempt to introduce primary process activity into waking life. He developed this method to help his patients gain access not only to the facts of their lives but to the feelings and connotations associated with those facts. He invited them to enter an uncanny realm, unfamiliar and yet in some way deeply familiar. He taught them to appreciate how deep is the pull to fantasy within them and how cut off from themselves they are when this capacity is only unconscious.

A radically new conception of self emerges in *Interpretation*. There are connections in us different from the causal, chronological ones perceived by rational consciousness. All through the day, mostly unbeknownst to us, the unconscious is at work making connections in its primary process way, along lines suggested by the recognition of analogies and responsive to feeling—without regard for temporality or the distinction between the fantasized and the factual. To notice concretely, visually, animistically, is its natural mode of perception—this mode does not represent translation from abstract, conceptual thought. The unconscious organizes these perceptions on the basis of the particular patterns, the associational complexes, which are its version of the self's history and also in response to phylogenetic memory-patterns. The unconscious is not inner experiences but a different way of perceiving, ordering, remembering (which indeed denies the importance of rationality's inner-outer distinction). Because it pulls all new experience into a complexly organized whole where everything that has ever been part of one's life persists, any particular image or event can lead us into the whole. Thus from even a dream fragment a whole life can be reassembled—if we are willing to trust our intuition in following these complicated associational paths. One cannot get to these meanings by using rational logic. "Accepting the hypothesis of the unconscious paves the way to a new orientation in the world." The dream leads us to a remembered self—but it takes *poesis* to discover it. Primary process thinking gives expression to our deepest wishes, "the core of our being" (p. 642). Freud's discovery is, as he recognizes, ultimately rediscovery: "The respect paid to dreams in antiquity" indicates that the ancients knew "the homage" due "to the uncontrolled and indestructible forces in the human mind, to the 'daemonic' power which produces the dream wish" (p. 652). As his letters to Fliess reveal, Freud's journey, like that of the ancient heroes, was undertaken as a search for the secret of immortality. The secret of dreams with which he returns is his equivalent of Gilgamesh's magic plant.

As pervasive as the archetype of the journey is the incest motif and its three dominant moments: battle with the father, intercourse with the mother, conception of the child who is oneself. The "passage through the dark woods" in the first chapter can in relation to this mythic pattern be seen as a battle with the fathers, the authorities. The entrance into the "cavernous defile" which follows is the entrance into the forbidden realm of the mother who (as Goethe put it in that essay on nature which directed Freud toward the study of medicine) allows her favorite children to explore her secrets. All investigations are, so Freud proposes in his writing on childhood sexuality, transmutations of the child's curiosity about sex and its own origins. The theme of the exploration of the mother's womb appears in the dream that occasioned the discovery about the wish-fulfilling function of dreams, the dream of Irma's injection. The interpretation of dreams leads to conflict with the father; dreams themselves return us to the mother. Dreams are the "via regia" to the unconscious. Every dream has a "navel," a central image that resists full interpretation, which connects it to the deep unfathomable unconscious.

In *Interpretation* the first explicit reference to the incest theme arises in connection with wishes in dreams for the death of a parent. Throughout Freud's work incest provokes the notion of parricide as much as of intercourse, but the theme of conflict with Freud's own literal father is especially prominent in *Interpretation*. As he discovers when he comes to write *The Psycho-Pathology of Everyday Life* almost all the errors in *Interpretation* are connected with the father motif. Freud presents himself as one struggling to challenge his father's prophesy: that boy will come to nothing. He wants desperately to "overcome" his father, to be more of a hero than the Jew who had allowed the Gentile passerby to shove him off the sidewalk. The lifelong persistence of this ambition shows itself in one of his last writings, an essay that centers around the guilt Freud experienced on his first visit to the Acropolis at having fulfilled in his own life a wish left unfulfilled in his father's. The guilt is there because, as *Interpretation* makes clear, the father is not only the resented father but also the deeply loved one.

A similar ambivalence shows itself with respect to the mother. She is not only Jocasta but also Medusa. She is the object of his desire, the one who transmitted to him her own conviction of his future greatness, who calls him to heroism. But she also means death: abandonment, betrayal, seduction, castration. Womb and tomb are closely associated. Freud's mother figures importantly in two dreams he reports in the book, and in both she is associated with death. In one she is dead, surrounded by Egyptian divinities, and thus, the goddess of death. In the other she is one of three fates, reminding him of his own mortality. There is a deep fear of woman manifest all through Freud's writings as well as a deep pull towards her: intercourse means death. The flaccidity that follows intercourse provokes the fear of being feminine oneself. The reunion with the mother, so deeply longed for, is at the same time an expression of one's longing for death, peace, passivity, the end of all desiring.

There is, however, also the recognition (in a passage added to *Interpretation* in 1914) that dreams about life in the womb, which often come up at the beginning of analysis, may be rebirth fantasies. The penetration into the womb in the Irma dream, as Erikson suggests, has to do with Freud's "conception" of psychoanalysis. The theory about psychic structure which Freud outlines in Chapter 7 can be understood as the boon with which the hero returns or as the child conceived as a result of the son's intercourse with the mother—the child who is himself. At the core of our being, Freud found, is the child in us who never dies: the child's wishes and the child's primary process mode of thought. Freud's autobiography is intended to help us see that the relation between the child and the adult cannot be understood chronologically; the child is co-present with the adult. "In the unconscious nothing ever dies."

Memories, Dreams, Reflections

Interpretation was written in the middle of Freud's life, yet he revised it almost every time it was reissued in order to incorporate his later discoveries. Nevertheless, it is always still written from the perspective of midlife; there is no attempt later to provide the synthesis not given in the original. Our sense of our lives, in Freud's view, remains incomplete. In *Dora* he says that the completion of an analysis would create a consistent, unbroken, case history out of the contradictory, disordered bits and pieces with which one begins. Yet there, too, he gives us a "fragment" of an analysis—a fragment which is a whole; and there, too, he conveys the process of discovery and remembering, not its potential end. Analysis is interminable.

Memories, by contrast, is composed toward the end of Jung's life as part of his conscious preparation for death. (Jung's *Psychological Types* is in some ways the equivalent of Freud's *Interpretation*: it marks his emergence from the period of deep introversion into which he was plunged by the symbolic death of his symbolic father, *i.e.*, by the break with Freud. In it he presents the psychological theory by which he comes to terms with the conflicts between them.) A few days before he died Jung is reported to have seen in a dream a stone inscribed, "This shall be a sign unto you of wholeness and oneness."[12] We sense that *Memories* served as such a sign as well.

Jung's autobiography, like Freud's, consists primarily of a series of dreams, but for Jung the world of dreams is a realm he has been closely in touch with from earliest childhood—not a world suddenly discovered at midlife—and so his "dream book" is very different from Freud's. Dreams to him are not ciphers that conceal as much as they reveal; they are symbolic expressions that reveal more and more as life unfolds. He includes not only the dreams contemporary with the composition of the book, but those associated with the three most significant, most dream-filled periods of his life: his childhood, the years immediately following his break from Freud, the period initiated by his nearly fatal attack in 1944 within which he still finds himself as he writes *Memories*. Most important of all, he believes, are the childhood dreams that reappeared with new power and new meaning at each of these subsequent times. Freud recognized the importance of our adult dreams of childhood, which show that in some sense the child we were is still present. But Jung is speaking here of something else: the child's own dreams as the adult remembers them. Like Dante, who said that childhood presents us with the symbols whose understanding we only receive at midlife, Jung believes that in those earliest images the whole life is implicit. The adult we become was already in some way present in the child.

What childhood means to Jung is not primarily forgotten, dynamically repressed wounds and terrors, but imaginative presence, spontaneity, renewal. This is said more explicitly in his essay on the child-archetype: childhood means the mystery of new beginning.[13] His vision of childhood is similar to that of Bachelard who sees it as providing "reserves of enthusiasm which help us believe in the world, love and create our world." To return to our childhood is to "re-enter into contact with possibilities which our destiny has not [yet] been able to make use of."[14]

When Jung's early dreams reappeared in mid-life, they served to energize and channel the development of his own psychology; when they once more became important toward the end, it was to bring into view the hidden wholeness of Jung's life.

We are given the dreams but no "interpretations." Jung simply tells them in such a way that we too "catch" their meaning and sense its direct presence in the dream-images. We are guided into an appreciation of what Jung means by "amplification" as we discover, seemingly for ourselves, how the dreams comment on one another and how naturally the dream images suggest parallels in myth and folktale. Dreams introduce us into the transpersonal, the collective; they release us from the narrow confines of subjectivity; of ego-orientation, into the archetypal. As Jung recounts his dreams, his stories, most of us find ourselves recognizing them or remembering dreams or other fantasy experiences of our own which we had long since forgotten. With no overt invocations to effect such appropriation, Jung's story becomes ours.

Dreams were determinative in Jung's decisions to study medicine, to break with Freud, to emerge from his period of focused introversion, to retire from his practice and teaching. As we see how the dreams help shape Jung's outward life, we understand also Jung's stress on their teleological aspect, their formative power, in contrast to Freud's emphasis on their power to bring new illumination to the past. Both bring into view the unsuspected multidimensionality of the present—but Freud emphasizes the dead past's liveliness and Jung the future's stirrings in the womb of the present. We learn, too, what Jung means by "realization" as we see how the dreams are given expression in the delicate yet powerful watercolors of the Red Book, in the impressive towers and intricate stone carvings of the Bollingen retreat, and in these autobiographical reflections.

Though their atmosphere is magical and "otherworldly," and the figures that appear in them often archaic or legendary, Jung's dreams, as he reports them, have a narrative coherence not found in Freud's. The autobiography as one long dream—perhaps the dream of the yogi deep in meditation in a small wayside chapel of whom Jung dreamt after his illness in 1944 (p. 323)—has the same quality of a harmoniously unfolding whole. Yet as we reflect on this quality we realize that this wholeness has a fictive aspect. As we contrast Jung's autobiography with Freud's, we recognize how much it lacks the dense interpersonal texture that in *Interpretation* give us a sense of the conflicts and tensions inherent in life.

Like *Interpretation*, *Memories* suggests that the relation of the unconscious to time is different from the ego's, and that a sensitive autobiography will find some way of including these several temporalities. Jung achieves such inclusion by adopting the typical pattern of the *Bildungsroman*, where the focus is on attained vision not completed action. He counterpoints to this focus the continual recircling of the same primary, ever recurring images: "There is no linear evolution; there is only a circumambulation of the self. Uniform development exists, at most only at the beginning; later, everything points toward the center...one could not go beyond that center" (pp. 196-98). The self is constructed by this interplay between historical and cosmological, linear and cyclical, time. *Memories*, written as part of Jung's conscious preparation for death, seems to emphasize the cyclical aspect, the Self's perspective rather than the ego's.

Myths of the Self

Interpretation and *Memories* suggest new ways of telling one's life-story. We should expect that accounts by Freud and Jung of the life-stories of others, their "case histories," would include many of the same elements.

Freud was highly conscious of the formal problematic involved in the composition of his case studies.[15] Partly it was a question of not betraying confidences, of not giving away identities, and nevertheless somehow demonstrating the close attention to detail demanded by the psychoanalytical method. To provide a satisfactory description of an analysis, he says, "One would have to be unscrupulous, give away, betray, behave like an artist who buys paints with his wife's housekeeping money or uses the furniture as firewood to warm the studio for his model."[16] But the concern for form only begins here. He sought a way of recognizing fully the kind of unity given in a human life by the weavings of the primary process as well as by the outward sequence of events. This meant a form that would combine history and poetry. It was important to try to communicate the feel of the inner life, the dreams and fantasies, the secret wishes and strange associations of his subjects. Freud overtly disavows any literary intentions and yet makes use of highly sophisticated literary devices: flashbacks, hints, the careful building up of suspense, and (especially in the case of *Dora*) the blind and misleading narrator. What makes Freud's cases interesting is the way he tells them. We value them for essentially literary reasons—because there is more present than is directly given, because the story is completed by our responses. Freud appropriates something he learned from his therapeutic practice: intellectual knowledge is not enough; we must collaborate in the discovery if it is to affect us significantly.

Freud's case histories teach us the importance of how a story is told. We come to see how much it matters which version one chooses. For how one imagines one's life shapes deeply how one lives it. Freud understands the point of analysis to be the creation of a good story. He makes this explicit in his study of "Dora." The aim is to help her move from her initial version of her life, with its omissions, uncertainties and false connections, to a coherent narrative—though, of course, this aim is not achieved. Ideally, therapy issues in the imaginative, collaborative creation of a better version: a rich complex whole which will reveal the subtle connections and the over-determined multiple meanings of both the events in the patient's life and also the images in her dreams, and will discover the typological correspondences which make her childhood prefigural of her adult experiences. The new story that therapist and patient seek to create together will not be just an agglomeration of events, but a *mythos*. It will have a plot, and will show the prototypical elements hidden in the tale of confusion and suffering. It will be organized both linearly and a-temporally, to show developmental unity and a symbolic associational whole. Since the wish is what makes the whole, the focus is on what seemingly is the individual's creation of his or her own story, the creation even of what happens to us and thus our complicity in our own unhappiness. This kind of plot, the focus on the single organizing wish, sometimes seems to impose a false, forced unity. In the case histories much more than in *Interpretation* Freud appears to assume, or pretend, that there is one plot to a life, though that plot has a rich, dense structure.

Freud's case histories all stem from a particular period in his life, from the decade prior to the publication of *Interpretation* through the decade that follows. Thus the autobiography can be seen as his own case history, differing from the others in that here, of course, teller and subject are ostensibly one, and so the tension between them is not part of the manifest content. During this period Freud was focusing on *mythos* as meaning life-plot, and was still very much under the power of a particular myth, Oedipus. He was intrigued at this point by the interrelationship of the historical and the mythopoetic, the factual and the imaginal, in human lives. After World War One, when the myth that compels his imagination is the one about the battle between Eros and Death, case history no longer appeals as a way of describing the human situation. But even in his earlier works, long before he comes to understand humankind as the scene of the struggle between the primal powers, he recognizes the power of *pathos* in our lives. We suffer from the intrusion of alien elements, the gods. Although the heroic plot is introduced, it is ironically deflated. The patients mostly don't get anywhere. Dora revolts, the Wolfman settles into his lifelong role as Freud's famous patient, the Ratman dies soon after his case is "closed." There is no all-redeeming vision. As in *Interpretation* there is tension between that which remains fragmentary in a life and the imposed plot which holds it all together.

As we might expect, Jung's case studies are as different from Freud's[17] as *Memories* is different from *Interpretation*. His letters reveal what a very different story he would have made out of the "raw material" of Dr. Schreber's memoirs (which he had been responsible for bringing to Freud's attention). He would have made more of the fact that Schreber was a psychotic and not a neurotic, that his fantasies were not compromise formations but the direct expression of the archaic level of the unconscious. Jung felt that Freud put too much emphasis on Schreber's latent homosexuality and thus missed the fact that his deepest longing was to create.

But in fact Jung did not write this case nor, indeed, write anything immediately recognizable as a case history subsequent to his "Freudian period." *The Psychology of the Unconscious* is based on the fantasies of "Miss Miller," whom Jung knew only through her memoirs as published by Flournoy; the associations are Jung's not hers. He wants to show how spontaneously produced fantasies recapitulate age-old mythic and poetic fantasies and how the meaning of the modern fantasy is illuminated by showing parallels in ancient sources with which the patient could not have been familiar. The study of the extensive dream series included in the 1935 essay, "Individual Dream Symbolism in Relation to Alchemy," is again based on the dreams of someone personally unknown to Jung, and he explicitly treats them as if they were his own! We learn almost nothing of the personal historical context of the dreams discussed in careful detail in *Psychology and Religion*. Jung clearly has no interest in communicating to us the dreamer's outward history of the progress of a Jungian analysis. The focus is on the spontaneous psychological expressions, on the dreams and fantasies and their archetypal meaning—not on their meaning for a particular life, nor on the interaction between inner and outer events, nor on their relation to some developmental progress. Past, present and future are not to be related on the basis of the "illusion" of causality. There is even less recognition of such elements in these other works than in *Memories*. Dreams are not to be made the basis of a story or history but of "reflection." Dreams are image-sequences not verbal narratives. To impose a plot would mean to reduce a life to one story, one myth, one archetype. Jung implicitly calls into question the notion that plurality should be interpreted as fragmentation, as a contradiction of unity rather than as one of its forms. His analyses suggest that more important for depth understanding of the self than relating dreams to history is understanding "outward" events as all having an "inner" or metaphorical significance.

Attention to their ways of telling the stories of others deepens our appreciation of what is innovative in Freud's and Jung's ways of telling their own stories. The discovery of the unconscious implies that to communicate the truth of any life, more attention must be given the imaginal than the historical, the numinous than the profane, the archetypal than the idiosyncratic. It means that some way must be found to express the co-presence of the different ecstasies of time, the interpenetration of past, present and future, of phylogenetic and ontogenetic. Above all, it means recognizing that such tellings involve poesis, conscious shaping, the kind of attention to form we have traditionally associated with fiction.

The revisioning is even more significant in the case of autobiography, for to adopt a poetic attitude toward one's own life means not only discovering a different way of telling one's story but a different way of living it. Both Freud and Jung suggest that we have not lived our lives if we have lived them cognizant only of their outward and singular aspects. A depth psychological perspective releases us from the spell of literalism and historicism, opens us to an appreciation of our dreams and their formative power, and of our participation in age-old mythic patternings. It is this vision, life as fictive, as myth, that Thomas Mann seeks to articulate in his essay, "Freud and the Future." There he describes what it would be like for the mythical point of view to become subjective, to "pass over into the active ego and become conscious there, proudly and darkly yet joyously, of its recurrence and its typicality.... The myth is the legitimization of life; only through and in it does life find self-awareness, sanction, consecration."[18]

Mann, like Freud and Jung, knows: Life in the myth is a kind of celebration. Perhaps it is only fitting for us to turn to Mann, a novelist, at this point, for Freud's and Jung's examples seem to put in question the conventional distinction between autobiography and fiction. When we look for other works embodying their understanding of how one tells one's story, we find ourselves looking primarily at writings we have been accustomed to read as novels, Proust's *Remembrance of Things Past*, Joyce's *Portrait* and *Ulysses*.

Notes

1. Jeffrey Mehlman, *A Structural Study of Autobiography* (Ithaca: Cornell University Press, 1974) 18.

2. William McGuire, ed., *The Freud/Jung Letters* (Princeton: Princeton University Press, 1974) 392.

3. James Olney, *Metaphors of Self* (Princeton: Princeton University Press, 1972) 44, 47.

4. C. G. Jung, *Memories, Dreams Reflections* (New York: Pantheon Books, 1963). Page references will be given in text.

5. Sigmund Freud, *The Interpretation of Dreams* (New York: Avon Books, 1966). Page references will be given in text.

6. Robert Scholes and Robert Kellogg, *The Nature of Narrative* (Oxford: Oxford University Press, 1966) 202.

7. Scholes and Kellogg, 176.

8. Thomas Mann, *Essays* (New York: Vintage Books, 1957) 317.

9. Gaston Bachelard, *The Poetics of Reverie* (Boston: Beacon Press, 1969) 11.

10. Sigmund Freud, *The Origins of Psychoanalysis* (New York: Doubleday Anchor, 1957) 292.

11. Erik Erikson, "Freud's Dream of Irma," *Identity, Youth, and Crisis* (New York: W. W. Norton, 1968) 197-207.

12. Miguel Serrano, *C. G. Jung and Hermann Hesse: A Record of Two Friendships* (New York: Schocken Books, 1966) 104.

13. C. G. Jung and C. Kerenyi, *Essays on a Science of Mythology* (Princeton: Princeton University Press, 1969) 70-100.

14. Bachelard, 124, 112.

15. Cf. Stephen Marcus, "Dora: Story, History, Case History," *Partisan Review*, XLI:1 (1974) 12-23, 89-108.

16. Sigmund Freud/Oscar Pfister, *Psychoanalysis and Faith* (New York: Basic Books, 1963) 38.

17. Cf. James Hillman, "The Fiction of Case History: A Round," in James B. Wiggins, ed., *Religion as Story* (New York: Harper & Row, 1975) 127-73.

18. Mann, 317.

22

Visions and Re-Visions: A Response to James Hillman's ReVisioning Psychology

About ten years ago I found myself at a dead-end. A relationship between myself and another had been broken by a third who felt injured and threatened, indeed violated, by it. She summoned the Furies and they descended on me. They tore from me all that I had loved and trusted in myself, that which had been cherished by the other and that he had experienced as life-giving. Laughingly they turned it upside down and revealed it as ugly and scabrous, decaying or poisonous. A friend, hoping it might "speak to my condition," gave me a pamphlet called "Betrayal." It didn't help, and in some ways it was too simple, for it didn't speak of how in a situation like ours each one of the three of us was betrayer *and* betrayed. But though it didn't help me find a way out, it seemed to help me find a deeper way *in*—and thus eventually *through*.

Then several years later my oldest son suffered a psychotic break, a trial much more painful for him and more fearful for me than the persuasive pieties about "transcendent breakthroughs" I had earlier embraced seemed to have promised. I found myself wrestling with what it means to let another go mad, perhaps even to die, to have whatever experience his soul is pulling him to, to have his own life. There was clearly much in me that feared this kind of going down, that was ready to "treat" it as were those around me who were so confident that true concern would mean shock and heavy tranquillization. At that time I came across, seemingly by chance, a book by the same author, *Suicide and the Soul,* that confirmed the part of me that wanted to trust that serving soul means following where it leads.

The pamphlet and the book were both, of course, by James Hillman; what I had found in both that was most important to me is what animates also his more recent *ReVisioning Psychology,* and what leads me to want to urge it upon others.

In this book he communicates even more clearly (and more passionately) his love for everything psychological, his care to discover the meaning for soul of all the symptoms or emotions or traumas that visit or besiege us. As I first read it I kept thinking of some lines from Auden's poem in honor of Freud:

> He would have us remember most of all
> To be enthusiastic over the night
> Not only for the sense of wonder
> It alone has to offer, but also
> Because it needs our love.[1]

What I value most in Hillman is this remembering. He speaks of "saving the appearances," attending to what appears rather than seeking to cure or deny it, because he believes something essential for the psyche's very life is being expressed here and can only be expressed thus. Falling ill, being wounded, going mad, dying are each among the psyche's fundamental themes—each represents the stirring of dark forces in the depths. Hillman suggests there is always a god at work in my afflictions, and that staying in my messes but looking for their deeper, hidden significance means looking for the god who wants something from me. To discover the god, the story, the myth that is active here is to find a way of experiencing my dis-ease more precisely and more subtly, but not of resolving it. The events become more mysterious, not less so.

This is a perspective toward our more painful experiences that experience itself has taught me. Yet how easily I forget. How easily I fall back into literalizing and see my wounds and my destructiveness only negatively. How easily I am taken over again by the developmental fantasy that values the dark times only because they lead toward enlightenment: the way down is the way up; death means rebirth. I value Hillman because he remembers when I forget, and reminds...

Saying "death-and-rebirth" in one breath is something I have often castigated Jungians for doing, perhaps just because it is such a temptation for me. Though Hillman acknowledges Jung as his immediate ancestor, I find him often including in his re-visioned psychology themes that I have tended to associate with Freud, perspectives that I could not find in Jung and had to go to Freud to find. The acknowledgement of pathology as the necessary starting-point for any *depth* psychology is such a theme. For I remember Jung's explicit disparagement of Freud's inability to free himself from his initial focus on psychopathology, his asking: "Freud still suffers. How can he help?" But Hillman has discovered a Jung who recognizes the importance of failures and disruptions, separation and death in our lives.

Hillman's finding within his very dialogue with Jung the clues to a psychological vision that includes aspects that Jung on a surface reading seems to disparage or ignore reminds me of Lou Salome's relation to Freud. I find very beautiful the sense of the friendship between Lou and Freud in their old age as this is communicated in their published correspondence.[2] She could say to him things that no one else could and stir him to responses that reveal his tender appreciation of her, his openness and vulnerability, his understanding of his gifts and their limits. She could tease him about the over heavy coarseness of his language, his reluctance to give scope to his pull to fantasy, the tendency of many to treat his writings as though they had canonical authority. Early in their friendship he speaks of his amazement at her talent "for going beyond what has been said, for completing it and making it converge at some distant point," and some fifteen years later announces his delight that "nothing has altered in our respective ways of approaching a theme. I strike up a—mostly very simple—melody; you supply the higher octave for it; I separate the one from the other, and you blend what has been separated into a higher unity." Though Freud was to Lou "the father face that has presided over my life," she was moved by their interchanges to voice insights that we might rather have expected to arise within a Jungian provenance. Alongside Freud's Narcissus she names another, who gives birth to himself from the water, and a third Narcissus, who is the discoverer of himself, the self-knower. What Freud writes of the "oceanic feeling" leads her to affirm how such feelings represent not only wishes but a "dim memory of things having been different once upon a time," and insists that infantile elements are closely "allied to those powers of imagination which form part of all creative activity." She takes what Freud has to say of Eros and death and responds, "death and life stand in a mutual relationship.... just as the invisible half of the moon forms a mysterious integral part of our total lunar concept."

Lou once wrote a paper called "What Follows from the Fact that It was not the Woman who Killed the Father"; the title suggests that it may not be accidental that it was easier for a woman to gain access to Freud's more poetic side, to disagree and re-vision without having to rebel or defect. It makes sense to me that in the case of Jung it would be one of the "sons" who finds this same freedom. In the circle that surrounded Jung the danger seems to have been more absorption than revolt. In many ways it was the "World of the Mothers" that came alive again in Zurich, yet somehow Hillman received from Jung not the Great Mother's binding blessing but the impetus of Eros's creative spark.

This spark has led him to lay beside Jung's words other words whose "belong-ingness" I think Jung would have recognized, though many Jungians might not. For some of them are, as I have already said, words once spoken by Freud—and I believe that all his life long Jung was aware of continuing the dialogue with Freud literally broken off in 1913. There is much that Jung leaves out, much that he feels free to exaggerate, because he knows the other part is being spoken for, and powerfully so, by another. As *Memories, Dreams, Reflections* attests, the break with Freud still provoked hurt and anger toward the very end of Jung's life. As Hill-man helps us remember: where there is a wound, there is a god and a message. Hillman has clearly not set out to heal that breach, but he seems to have been addressed by whatever daimon it was that Freud wrestled with as well as by Jung's familiar spirit.

But that he is touched by both changes things. When Hillman plays with Freudian themes they are deepened, more clearly freed from literalization, more clearly brought into relation to soul-making. Nevertheless both Hillman and Freud are deeply attuned to our finitude and fragmentation and deeply suspicious of a psychology that overleaps them. Both remind us of the inescapability of giv-ing and receiving wounds—and of dying. Both recognize how easily we are tempted to deny our embodiment; both know that "concrete flesh is a magnifi-cent citadel of metaphors." Both insist that other persons are inextricably involved in my soul's inmost processes. "If others are instruments of the Gods in bringing us tragedy," Hillman says, "so too are they the way we atone to the Gods." Hillman also recognizes the importance of the triangular pattern in Freud's central metaphor (Oedipus): the intrusion of a third person always acti-vates immense psychological energy. This is one of the reasons he keeps returning (as Freud did) to the role of the father and to the dangers in the Jungian tendency to focus exclusively on mothers (and their sons). He has learned (as Freud also eventually did) that the psychology of the female is not a simple mirroring of the males'. Freud came to see that for women as for men the relation to the mother is primary and that for both the negative evaluation of their own femininity is the most difficult psychological task. Hillman has come to understand that it is not only men who have to be pulled from the persona to interiority, to establish a relation to the *anima*. And where Jung seems sometimes pulled to value the visual image over the word, Hillman is persuaded of the special relation between soul and word, psyche and logos: "Their union is our field, psychology. Psychology initially means giving soul to language and finding language for soul."

Hillman also knows that when we speak most deeply of our souls, Hermes, who is god of equivocations as well as guide of souls, is inevitably present. To tell the truth about soul means taking a circuitous and deviant path. I sense Hermes at work in his words, as I also sense Hades who pulls us down to the depths.

Notes

1. W. H. Auden, "In Memory of Sigmund Freud," *Collected Poems* (New York: Random House, 1976).

2. Ernst Pfeiffer, ed., *Sigmund Freud and Lou Andreas-Salome: Letters* (New York: Harcourt Brace Jovanovich, 1972).

23

The Subliminal Presence of the
Goddess in Hebrew Tradition

My present concern with Hebrew goddesses is connected to an interest I have had for a long while in the role of myth in Hebrew tradition. I did my dissertation almost fifteen years ago on Martin Buber and at that time I found myself intrigued by his conviction that the history of Judaism is not, as we often suppose, the history of the triumph over myth, but rather the history of the continual struggle between rational rabbinic religion and mythical folk religion. To really understand Judaism, we have to see it as continually engaged in this tension between mythical religion and rational religion. In an essay that he wrote in 1918 Buber alleges that despite the apparent victory of the rabbinic perspective, the mythical tradition has never been completely eliminated from Judaism; it continually reemerges in times of threat, whether that threat takes the form of outward menace or of inward disintegration. Some fifty years later in his book *After Auschwitz*, Richard Rubenstein, reflecting on the meaning for Judaism of the Holocaust, confirms Buber's view. Neither prophet nor priest, neither the call to justice and mercy nor the emphasis on the cultic, says Rubenstein, has won the day in traditional Jewish practice. Each has founds its place in a tradition wise enough to endure the tension between them, rather than falsely choose one in preference to the other.

I have, as I suggest, long been interested in the importance of recognizing the function of myth within the total thinking of Israelite culture. To do that means several things. First, it means trying to get as full an understanding as we can of the role of myth within the Hebrew spiritual tradition; that is, within the Tanakh, or as Christians call it, the Old Testament. In the Tanakh, we discover a conscious use of Mesopotamian mythic traditions which from the perspective of the writers of scripture are seen as broken myths: myths which are no longer regarded as being true tales, but nevertheless are familiar tales which can be reworked in the service of articulating a radically different theology. Such retellings represent a process of reinterpretation, or (to use a phrase that was very popular in Christian theology a few decades ago) of demythologizing.

Brevard Childs' *Myth and Reality in the Old Testament* explores in careful detail how passage after passage in the Tanakh is a reworking, a modification, a reformulation of various ancient near-Eastern mythic traditions. For instance, he looks at the Genesis accounts of creation and shows how the first story of creation is very closely connected to the Babylonian creation account, *Emuna Elish*. Yet if we weren't familiar with the comparative religious traditions, the dependence on this pagan mythical narrative would be masked for us. The Genesis account, as we have it, does not really look at all like a myth: there is not the plurality of divine beings, the immanence of the divine in the natural, the tension between creative and destructive forces, that we associate with the mythological. Yet comparative analysis discloses that the chaos with which God finds himself beginning his work of creation is closely related to the Babylonian conception of a primordial matriarchal being, Tiamat, who is overcome by the divine creative agency and whose body actually becomes the very material of creation. Childs also shows how in the second creation story of Genesis, the Adam and Eve story, the serpent on the surface level is clearly simply an agent of evil. Yet if we read the story with care, we recognize that it is related to ancient traditions about the serpent as an occult source of hidden wisdom. "Behind the figure of the serpent shimmers another form still reflecting its former life." Childs goes through the Tanakh and shows how frequently ancient mythical traditions have been reworked to present a perspective very different from the perspective of the original source. Yet, "even in the final stage, the mutilated and half digested particle struggles with independent life against the role to which it has been assigned within the Hebrew tradition."[1] Another way in which mythic traditions are used in Hebrew scripture is as poetic imagery. We can see in the beautiful account of paradise in Isaiah 11 metaphors that were drawn from ancient myths but which are now serving simply as fanciful description; here there is no tension between the mythical motif and its new setting.

One could also show how we have in Hebrew scriptures the creation of a different kind of myth. Buber calls this different kind of myth the myth of I and Thou. He suggests that perhaps we ought to call this new form "legend" rather than "myth" to distinguish it from myths in which a cyclical conception of time dominates, for this new kind of myth, the myth of history, introduces a linear conception of time. It is not aspects of the natural world but rather historical events that are perceived as religious truth. On this view, what we have in the

Tanakh is not the absence of myth but rather the creation of a unique form of myth. Biblical history is mythical because it is a presentation not simply of history as fact but of historical events as wondrous, as revealing divine activity, as paradigmatic, as having meaning not just for the time in which they happened but also as somehow illuminative of what is the case at other moments in history. These events are presented as having significance for our understanding of our present situation. The biblical myth, if we want to call it that, is a myth about a god who speaks in the unique events of history rather than in the repetitive patterns of the natural world, about a divine being whose word, whose activity is incomplete without human response.

Another way in which the Hebrew scriptures give evidence of myth is their recognition of the continued hold of unbroken myth among the people. I have been talking initially about the way in which the writers, in order to articulate their own perspective, which is very different from that of traditional myth, make use of myth as material, as a source of metaphor. But the Tanakh also gives frequent evidence of the degree to which myth continues throughout the biblical period to be important in the life of the people. The prophets' protestations make this clear. In order to get a full sense of the religious life of the ancient Israelites we have to attend not only to the official version, not only what is given to us in canonical scripture, but also to oral tradition. It is important for us to recognize that the decision about the constitution of the canon was not made until the first century of the common era, until after the destruction of the second temple; although, of course, it was made in line with what had come to be a kind of consensus about which texts did have some definitive authority. Yet we know that the texts that were recognized as having that kind of special authority at that time by no means comprise the whole of Israel's national literature. It is also not to be forgotten that there is a real bias involved in thinking that the only sources for learning about the religion of a people are texts, are scriptures. We must also take into account all kinds of other evidence, particularly the findings of archeology.

There are several collections of Hebrew folk traditions that suggest how popular religion differed from the official religion: Louis Ginsburg's *The Legends of the Jews*, and *Hebrew Myths* by Robert Graves and Raphael Patai. Both of these depend a good deal on legends and tales that are included in the Talmudic literature, and also in even later Hebrew literature, but which give evidence of having originated in a much earlier period although not given written form until the Talmudic period. There is also an enormous book by Theodore Gaster called *Myth, Legend and Custom in the Old Testament* in which he surveys some of the same literature and also takes the trouble to include comparative material from

Canaanite and other ancient near-Eastern sources. As one begins to look at traditions assembled in these books, and also in Raphael Patai's *The Hebrew Goddess*, one comes to discover that the strict ethical monotheism of the prophets and rabbis is not at all the perspective that is communicated in this folk literature. Rather over and over again it expresses recognition of other divine powers in addition to YHVH, both divine powers that support him or serve as his intermediaries and also divine powers that oppose him and with whom he finds himself in continual conflict.

These divine powers include goddesses as well as gods. There is a good deal of evidence to suggest the real importance that goddesses had in the life of Israel during the whole period from the arrival of the Hebrews in Canaan until the destruction of the first temple. It is obvious, of course, that the Canaanite goddesses, Asherah, Astarte and Anath, are much more ancient that what we might call the young upstart god YHVH, and it is probable that the ancestors of the Hebrews themselves had for many hundreds of years been worshipping these goddesses long before they began worshipping YHVH. Contemporary biblical scholars now seem pretty much agreed that not all those who eventually became the twelve tribes of Israel participated in the Exodus journey from Egypt through the Sinai into Canaan. They believe that the assembling of all the tribes just before Joshua's death may represent the making of a covenant between the descendants of those who had participated in that journey and indigenous tribes; through this compact they were now joined together to become one nation. If that is the case, then obviously the forefathers and foremothers of many of those who at that point acknowledged their common allegiance to YHVH had been worshipping Canaanite goddesses like Asherah, Astarte and Anath for many, many generations.

In any case, the scriptures show the continued importance of those goddesses among the Israelites, among those who also acknowledged their devotion to YHVH. Indeed, they portray those goddesses as a source of constant temptation throughout the biblical period. I find it intriguing that the Tanakh has no word for "goddess," and thus when it is speaking of these divine beings generically, refers to all of the divinities that are seen as in some kind of conflict with YHVH as "other gods." Although there are specific references by names to the goddesses, some 40 odd references to Asherah and a dozen or so references to Astarte, such references are always condemnatory and usually purposely pretty vague. We would not know nearly as much as we do about the character of these goddesses if the only basis for knowledge that we had available to us were the biblical texts. But we are in a position to be able to supplement what the biblical texts tell us by archeological research which has discovered, for instance, that Hebrew graves very often contained figurines of the goddesses. We can also obtain much more detailed information about the divine beings that are referred to so vaguely in the biblical text by examining how these same goddesses are spoken of in the literature of neighboring peoples and in the Hebrew folk literature to which I have already referred.

There is general agreement among contemporary biblical scholars that the monotheism which we tend to identify with Hebrew religion does not go back anywhere near as far as the canonical texts would have us believe it does. And even those texts suggest the patriarchs, Abraham and Isaac and Jacob and Joseph, were not really monotheists but something that scholars call henotheists: to believe that our god is more important than anybody else's god does not mean that we think our god is the only divine being that there is. Genesis tells us how, when Jacob had finally gotten the wife that he had really wanted all along and had decided to move way from the father-in-law whom he served for fourteen years to get first the wrong wife and then the right one, he and Rachel took off with her father's household gods—I think it is pretty clear that those household gods were also household goddesses. The Mosaic period is often identified as representing the time when the Hebrews did become monotheistic; yet we have in the Bible acknowledgement that over and over again, during that period and later, there was defection from a strict worship of YHVH alone. As soon as they had crossed the Red Sea, those who were following Moses began to murmur that they would really rather be back in Egypt with their garlic and their onions. The very first moment that Moses lets the people out of his sight, they start dancing around the golden calf—and from comparative sources we know that in the ancient near-Eastern world the golden calf is a central element in goddess rituals. Such stories about the pull of the Hebrews to worship of the goddess recur during the period of conquest and throughout the monarchial period. Ezekiel, writing immediately after the razing of the first temple, recounts a vision of finding himself in that temple just prior to its destruction and seeing why it deserved to be destroyed. In his vision as he enters the temple he sees it filled with women weeping over the death of Tammuz—Tammuz, as those of you familiar with ancient near-Eastern mythology will remember, was the consort of Ishtar (or Astarte). That indicates how goddess worship had penetrated into the temple itself.

Indeed, a central theme in the prophetic literature is the protest against the way in which the people are continually turning from YHVH back to the Baals and the Asteroths. It is intriguing that there is a good deal more emphasis in the texts on the importance of exterminating the Baal cult, a cult dedicated to a masculine god, than on extinguishing the worship of the female divinities. That there are so many more references to Baal than to Astarte or Asherah is strange because the comparative material makes it clear that in the cult the female deity was much more important than the male divinity and that the worship of Baal and Asherah or Astarte was very closely intermingled. Baal and the goddess were figures in the same myth. There was one story, one cult. Baal was the consort of the goddess, the real emphasis was on her; his role was clearly a subordinate one. Perhaps the biblical texts tend to emphasize the importance of the conflict between Baal and YHVH because Baal was seen as a competitor of YHVH, whereas the goddesses may often have been regarded less as competitors than as counterparts to the worship of YHVH. It is evident that for the people the worship of YHVH was not seen as contradictory to the worship of the goddess. The biblical tradition itself shows that for most of the people, most of the time, worship of the goddess and worship of YHVH were felt to be compatible. Among the reasons for this might be that actually the cultic elements of the worship of Baal and the worship of YHVH were not really all that different, and ritual plays a central role in popular religion. In fact, archeologists testify to the difficulty of deciding, with respect to a particular shrine, whether this shrine was one where YHVH was worshipped or where the local Baal was worshipped. The difference between YHVH and the "other gods" lay not in the cult, but rather in the ideology and morality articulated by the prophets. Amos protested against the Yahwistic cults, its feasts and solemn assemblies, its burnt offerings and its cereal offerings, its songs and its harps, because he understood that the ritual transformed YHVH into a Baal by another name. Rituals are generally more resistant to change than myths and, although their meaning may be open to reinterpretation, the original significance may still persist. Thus, Passover and Succoth, for example, although celebrated as historical commemorations, never entirely lose their association with the seasonal cycle and the rhythms of vegetal fertility. It is likely that for many of his worshippers, YHVH was viewed as the victorious rival of Baal, as a recently arrived consort of the goddess. During the time of the monarchy it is probable that strict Yahwism was really only a prophetic fantasy, shared by a few kings, but not really the religion of court or temple, much less of the people.

The temple built by Solomon, as the description in I Kings reveals, was modeled on typical ancient near-Eastern patterns, and for at least one biblical tradition the very building of the temple was itself a betrayal of authentic Yahwism. Solomon himself, scripture attests, "was not whole with YHVH his god." He "did what was evil in the eyes of YHVH and went not fully after YHVH." Solomon's son, Jeroboam, who became ruler in the northern kingdom after his father's death, set up calves of gold to be worshipped at several northern shrines to insure that his people would not divert their allegiance to his brother in Jerusalem. At the same time his brother, Rehoboam, set up an image of the goddess, Asherah, in the temple itself. Many of the later kings of Israel and of Judah also gave their devotion to goddesses. The most notorious, of course, is Manasseh who rebuilt "the high places," the biblical euphemism for the places where the goddesses were worshipped. As the chronicler reports it, "He rebuilt the high places which his father Hezekiah had destroyed; he set up altars for the Baal and made them an Asherah, as did Ahab King of Israel, and he bowed down to all the host of heaven, and served them. And he built altars in the House of Yahweh...for all the hosts of heaven.... And he made his son to pass through the fire, practiced soothsaying, used enchantments and appointed them that divine by a ghost or familiar spirit; he wrought much evil in the sight of Yahweh to anger Him. And he set the statue of the Asherah that he had made in the house of Yahweh." Patai, in his book, *The Hebrew Goddess*, after a careful reading of Chronicles concludes that for almost two thirds of the time that Solomon's temple stood it contained a statue of Asherah. That may be an exaggeration (Patai relies more than I am sure we can on omission as negative evidence and on the Chronicler's historical accuracy) but there is no doubt that much of the time goddesses were being worshipped, not just on the high places, not just out in the country, but right in the temple itself.

Another telling indication of the importance of the goddess comes from the book of Jeremiah. When Jeremiah tells the people to shape up and worship YHWH single-heartedly if they are to have any hope of preventing the overtaking of Jerusalem, they answer him thus:

> As for the word which you have spoken to us in the name of Yahweh, we shall not listen to you. But we shall without fail do everything as we said: We shall burn incense to the Queen of Heaven and shall pour her libations as we used to do, we, our fathers, our kings and our princes, in the cities of Judah and in the streets of Jerusalem. For then we had plenty of food and all were well and saw no evil. But since we ceased burning incense to the Queen of Heaven and to pour her libation, we have wanted everything and been consumed by sword and famine.

There is thus a good deal of evidence that the goddess and worship of the goddess continued to be important for the people of Israel throughout the monarchial period. Why was that suppressed? And by whom? As we try to answer that question, we discover that the focus on YHVH as the only god can be related to the desire to validate a new social order and a new psychology in mythic terms. The attempt to establish the monotheistic cult is related to the attempt to establish a society in which father right predominates and in which fealty to the central monarchy takes precedence over tribal loyalty. Yahwism becomes part of the endeavor to break the importance of matrilineal bonds and to break the allegiance to the clan. Yahwism represents a national political cult in conflict with what are primarily local fertility cults. YHVH is presented to us as a god who claims to be the only god but who, as evidence we have already pointed to establishes, is always still defending himself against other gods (though in the prophetic tradition, other people's gods are seen as demons or idols).

During the time when there were kings in Israel, the attempts to suppress the other gods, and particularly the attempts to suppress worship of the goddess, were infrequent and ineffectual. It is really only in the later, post-exilic period that the suppression becomes effective, but when that happened monotheism was read backward into the earlier period. The suppression of the goddesses became operative in Hebrew life during the period of the second temple because then being a Hebrew (or, more accurately now, a Jew) is defined by religious criteria, by meticulous participation in the worship of YHVH, whereas earlier being a Hebrew had really simply meant being a member of the political community. According to Rabbinic tradition itself, "the instinct of idolatry" was eradicated in the days of Mordecai and Esther, or, so it is sometimes said, not until the days of Nehemiah. Strict monotheism becomes even more important after the destruction of the second temple and the dispersion of the Jews from Palestine because at that point Judaic faith comes to be defined not by cult but by law. The leaders of the community are no longer the priests but the rabbis and Judaism truly becomes what we call aniconic, that is, without any images of the divine. From that time onwards, also, Judaism is the religion of a landless people, whereas goddesses are associated with a people who live on the land and who relate to the divine through the natural world.

My guess is that all of us are likely to take over the later official view much more than we realize. We tend, for instance, to buy into the retrospective definition of which kings of Israel were the good kings and which the bad, perhaps without fully taking into account that the one criterion that the later historians used for defining what makes a good king is a religious one. The good kings were those who gave all their religious devotion to YHVH. We also may too easily take over the rabbinic reduction of goddess cults to fertility cults. We thereby ignore the fact that the most frequent title that is given to the Canaanite goddess is not earth mother but queen of heaven. The goddess is associated not just with fertility, whether agricultural or human, but also viewed as creator of all that is; she is spoken of as prophet, as inventor, as healer, as warrior. We may, perhaps, also, be inclined to take over the identification of the followers of the goddess as harlots, as the prophets over and over again refer to them. This identification may then lead us, almost unthinkingly, to adopt the prophetic view that to follow the goddess is somehow to epitomize every kind of sin there might be.

If we thus ignore the importance, the longevity, and the complexity of goddess traditions, we inevitably misunderstand the persistence of those traditions and fail to appreciate their reemergence at various periods in subsequent Jewish history. As the Shekinah, for instance, the goddess is very important in Jewish Gnosticism and particularly in the Kabala. We may be unprepared for the importance some contemporary Jewish theologians, particularly Richard Rubenstein to whom I referred earlier, see the goddess as having for 20th century Jews, nor will we readily understand the importance that ancient goddess traditions have for some contemporary Jewish feminists who long for a religious tradition that takes into account feminine experience and yet is related to their Jewish heritage.

To underestimate the persistent power of the goddess may also blind us to how much the patriarchal monotheistic tradition is reactive and defensive and thereby oppressive. Theoretically, the god of the Hebrews, YHVH, is neither male nor female; nevertheless, he is spoken of in the Hebrew scriptures in exclusively masculine terms, referred to with masculine pronouns and described as king, as lord, as shepherd. The message that is conveyed by that reliance on masculine pronouns and attributes enters deeply into our primary naïve assumptions about the divinity. We absorb the concrete image of god as male long before we are at a point where we can recognize that something more subtle, more transcendent, more abstract, is intended to be conveyed through that language. Nor should we too quickly discard the biblical image of god as father. The biblical god is a god who in a very profound way answers the longing for god as father, a longing that, as Freud showed, corresponds to a deep and universal psychological need.

Comparative religion suggests that there is an equally deep need in all of us as human beings for god as mother. Thus worship of the goddess among the early Hebrews persists because there is something YHVH does not provide that nevertheless feels essential. It is important for us to remember that the goddess cults were not cults just for females but were cults in which both men and women participated. It is also crucial for us to acknowledge that those who turned to her did not turn to her just for the sake of being perverse but rather because there was some really deep and primary religious need which YHVH did not fulfill. One way of naming that need would be to say that the prophetic emphasis on the moral and intellectual implies a relative neglect of the emotional and ritual. One of the most important ways in which goddess religion differs from Yahwism is that it is a religion of participation. Patai tends to stress the importance of the goddess in relation to psychological needs and that is a valid perspective, but it is also important to recognize that the goddess also serves what we might call communal or social needs—and which kind of need is most significant may vary at different times. (We can see something comparable in Greece where at an early period the worship of Demeter and Persephone was primarily related to the concerns of an agricultural community whereas later, in the mystery cults, Demeter and Persephone were associated with more explicitly spiritual longings.) To understand the role and meaning of the goddess in ancient Israel, we should remember that initially the arrival of YHVH in Canaan meant havoc and destruction; it meant battle between the indigenous peoples and the invading peoples, meant tremendous turmoil. Throughout the early period, YHVH was seen as the god that you turn to in times of national political crisis. But in times of peace, when most of your energies are given to life sustenance activities, to hoping that the crops would grow, that you would have children and that they would survive, in such times the ancient goddesses were turned to because from time immemorial they had been associated with these aspects of human life. The Book of Judges suggests that there was a kind of cycle in Israel's history. In times of peace the Israelites turned to the worship of the goddess; then they would be threatened from outside and would return to YHVH for help. He would come through; there would be peace again and then they would turn back again to the goddess. YHVH did not seem to have within his province the central concerns of everyday life that have to do with agricultural fertility, with the continuation of the family, and with death.

But to fully understand the power of the goddess cult, we must not delimit it as a fertility cult. The goddesses also answered to the longing for divine beings whose presence could be made visible, who would allow themselves to be imaged, to be represented in statue. The kind of austere aniconic worship that YHVH seemed to demand ("Thou shalt make no graven images") left frustrated that yearning for an imaginable faith. The goddess cults also did not denigrate the desire for an experience of religious enthusiasm, of feeling oneself being overwhelmed by the immanent presence of the divine. YHVH presented himself ever again as the god of the living, whereas the goddesses were connected not only to life but also to death. That ascetic denial of any kind of individual immortality that characterizes ancient Yahwistic faith may well have been too demanding for most of the people, whereas the goddess cults affirmed that there is some kind of immortality, some kind of continued life of the dead. The goddesses seem also to have been connected to that longing that human beings in many times and places have expressed to be able to know the future, to be able to know what is coming. Thus the goddesses were associated with oracles and particularly with consultation of the dead. Remember Saul, who at the most desperate moment of his life, when he has been utterly deserted by YHVH, goes to the witch of Endor because she might be able to tell him what is still to happen. The goddess cults recognized that the divine sometimes speaks to us through our dreams, again something that tends to be denied within Yahwistic faith.

The goddesses seem also to have been connected with the recognition that the divine does not appear only in the realm of history, but that we may also experience the numinous in connection with the natural world. This acknowledgement of the divine in the natural world makes permissible the recognition of the sacred dimension of childbirth and sexuality. The different relationship to nature also entails an appreciation that nature itself is somehow divine, that it has intrinsic meaning and importance, is not simply there as material for human projects. The goddess cults may also have spoken to a sense that there is something inadequate about a purely linear conception of time and the correlative notion that all meaning, all fulfillment comes in the future, comes at the end of time. The goddess cults were connected with the more cyclical notion of time that characterizes mythological consciousness, and with a valuing of the alternating rhythms of waxing and waning, growth and decay, waking and sleeping, activity and receptivity, extroversion and introversion. There is at least one other thing: that is that the goddess cult did not explain all of the evil in the world by referring it to human sin and guilt. The stubborn reality of pain and suffering is a difficult problem in monotheism which stresses the goodness of the divine and which then tends to lay the responsibility for all the suffering and evil that there is on human sinfulness. In the goddess cults the divine is seen as source of both good and evil, of both gratification and deprivation, as the source of all that is. The goddesses are associated with life and death, with giving and taking away, with creative and destructive energies.

There is a long period in Jewish history during which the goddess seemed to disappear, yet her subliminal presence remained and as the Shekinah she re-emerged in the Kabala. The Shekinah is already named in the Aramaic Targum as YHVH's presence in the world. Though not yet a distinct person, this presence is referred to as an emanation of the divine and in the feminine gender. Gradually, as in diaspora Judaism YHVH becomes more distant and more abstract, she becomes more important.

It is she who accompanies the exiled and brokenhearted, she who manifests divine compassion. According to medieval kabalistic tradition, Sarah is jealous of Abraham's journeying in her company—and for the sake of being always available to her, Moses separates from his wife. For the sophisticated exponents of the Kabala, the references to the Shekinah were no doubt compatible with a theoretically maintained monotheism, but the importance of Kabalism in Jewish history lies not in what it meant for the select few but in how it was understood by the people. The deep emotional attachment of the simple and unlearned to the Shekinah is comparable to the Mariolatry of Spanish or Italian peasants. The motherly, passionate and compassionate female divinity satisfied many of the same deep-seated religious needs that the Hebrew goddesses had answered centuries earlier.

Those same needs make themselves felt today. In *After Auschwitz*, Rubenstein speaks of the importance that remembrance of the ancient goddesses might have in a contemporary world:

> After the death camps, life, in and of itself, lived and enjoyed in its own terms without any superordinate values or special theological relationships becomes important for Jews. One cannot go through the experience of having life pulled so devastatingly and radically into question without experiencing a heightened sense of its value, unrelated to any special categories of meaning that transcend its actual experience.... Life need have no meta-historical meanings to be worthwhile....
>
> Once again, we have come in contact with those powers of life and death which engendered men's feelings about Baal, Astarte, and Anath....
>
> The priests of ancient Israel wisely never suffered Jahweh entirely to win his war with Baal, Astarte, and Anath.... That is why Jews were never puritans, cut off from their inner life and the powers of earth which engendered it. Paganism was transformed but never entirely done away with in Judaism. Canaanite agrarian festivals were transformed into celebrations of Israel's sacred time, but their inner connection with nature's fertility was never lost. No element, pagan or monotheistic, in the formation of the Jewish religious consciousness was ever entirely repressed in the Torah. In the twentieth century we have learned much concerning the futility of repression in personal matters. The Torah instinctively and intuitively understood this futility long ago in religious matters. Nothing within the domain of human experience escaped its attention. It understood the paradoxical truth that one can best overcome atavisms and primitivisms, insofar as they are destructive, by

acknowledging their full potency and attractiveness and channeling their expression to eliminate their harm.[2]

Notes

1. Brevard S. Childs, *Myth and Reality in the Old Testament* (London: SCM Press, 1960) 45.

2. Richard Rubenstein, *After Auschwitz* (Indianapolis: Bobbs-Merrill, 1966) 69, 70, 124.

24

Goddess-Sent Madness

Some five years ago I had a dream that I have not been able to shake off. In the dream I found myself confused and despairing. I decided to drive into the desert alone, hoping there to rediscover the still center I had lost. I drove and drove, on unfamiliar and seemingly rarely traveled byways, far into the night. Then, in the middle of nowhere, a tire went flat and I remembered I had no spare. It seemed unlikely that anyone would come by soon to offer help, but far in the distance I saw a light that might mean someone available to assist me, or at least a telephone. I set out toward it and walked and walked. It was some time before I realized the light was no closer and that I was no longer sure it was there at all. I turned around, thinking it might be better after all to wait by my car; but it had vanished, as had the road.

At that point a figure appeared from behind some sagebrush in the strangely moonlit desert night, the figure of a wizened but kindly appearing old man. "Can I help?" he asked. "No," I said, "you and I have been through this before. This time I need to go in search of Her."

So I set out across the desert, seeming now to know in what direction to proceed, though there were no marked ways and I knew I had never been here before. Hours later I found myself at the foot of some steeply rising sandstone cliffs. I made my way up the cliffs, heading straight for a deep small cave just large enough for me to lie down in. Still seeming to know exactly what I must do, I prepared myself to sleep there, as though to fall asleep were part of my way toward Her.

While I slept there in the cave I dreamt that within the cave I found a narrow hole leading into another cave well beneath the earth's surface. I sat myself down on the rough uneven floor, knowing myself to be in Her presence. Yet, though She was palpably there, I could not discern Her shape. Though I waited and waited, expecting to be able to see Her once my eyes grew accustomed to the darkness, that did not happen.

When I returned to waking consciousness, I was aware that, though I did not know who She was, it was indeed time for me to go in search of Her. My way of doing that was to return to the goddesses of Greek mythology to whom my mother had introduced me as a child but to whom I had paid little conscious attention in the intervening years. I discovered that they had nevertheless been actively present in my life all along and that attending to their presence yielded a hitherto unknown depth to my own experiences, particularly some that had earlier seemed meaningless trivial or unredeemably negative.

I began to understand why She had appeared to me in the dark underground cave. For each of the goddesses is in her own way intimately connected with some of our darkest and most difficult moments. Each shows herself most forcibly in moments we would prefer to circumvent or quickly transcend: occasions of intense grief or desperate loneliness, of ugly, possessive rage or all-consuming lust, impotence or failure. Among the most fearful of the ways in which the goddesses manifest their power is in the experience of madness. Yet just as grief or jealousy, abduction or abandonment, are suffered differently when we recognize them to be divine mysteries, so madness, too, changes its meaning when we understand it as goddess-sent.

That madness may sometimes be more gift than curse is suggested by Socrates when he tells Phaedrus that it is not "an invariable truth that madness is an evil; in reality, the greatest blessings come by way of madness, indeed of madness that is heaven-sent." When due to divine dispensation, madness is a valuable gift; in fact, Socrates holds heaven-sent madness to be superior to man-made sanity. Yet as anyone who has seen or read Aeschylus' *The Eumenides*, Sophocles' *Ajax*, or almost any of Euripides' tragedies knows, the Greek apprehension of madness is in no sense romantic. I would not want my exploration of madness as in some sense divine to encourage an evasion of the ugliness and misery, the terror and often cruel destructiveness that accompany insanity. I remember too well the pain one of my sons experienced during a psychotic break seven years ago. I do not expect ever to forget his fear of being overwhelmed or his sense of isolation. Nor can I deny the panic I have felt in those moments when my own most ominous nightmares seemed to become my only reality. The same anger that I feel when someone seems able to say "death and rebirth" in one breath is stirred by those who can too glibly compact "madness and transformation." To die is really to come to an end; rebirth has meaning only when it happens where it had seemed impossible. Madness is really being taken out of one's everyday mind—and that is terrifying

Jung knew its terror, as any reader of the "Confrontation with the Unconscious" chapter of *Memories, Dreams, Reflections* discovers. The dreams of bloody tides, crushing boulders, strangling jungle growth that he describes as part of his lengthy *nekyia* communicate this terror unforgettably. The psychosis-like experience of those years was not voluntarily self-induced. It followed the traumatic break from Jung's surrogate father, Freud, and was spontaneously initiated by the Siegfried dream. Yet the original meaning of psychosis, "I give life," was here realized, because Jung was able to acknowledge the visitations rather than resist them. His attitude was consonant with his own definition of religion: careful, scrupulous consideration and observation of the dangerous or helpful numinous "powers" that act on a subject independent of his or her will.

To go mad is terrifying, in part because (as Jung felt he had learned from Nietzsche's example) not everyone returns. Yet he would also affirm that one is different for having gone through such experience. Jung says, too, that he believed he had risked a greater shattering and thereby achieved a greater wholeness than had Freud. The "greater-ness" of the wholeness on the other side of madness seems to be that one knows, as one could not have before, the parts that constitute the whole.

Nietzsche's contemporary, Erwin Rohde, was impressed by the degree to which "Greek religion at the height of its development regarded madness (*mania*) as a religious phenomenon of wide-ranging importance." It understood madness as "a condition in which the self-conscious spirit is overwhelmed, 'possessed' by a foreign power." This madness, and here he quotes the *Phaedrus*, "comes not from mortal weakness or disease, but from a divine banishment of the commonplace." To the Greeks (as Walter Otto demonstrates in his book on Dionysus) madness was a mystery in the deepest religious sense of that term.

What is divine about madness is that it introduces us to the gods and goddesses. The gods reach us through our afflictions, because we moderns are no longer attuned to their presence when unafflicted. In Jung's words: "The gods have become diseases."

Madness is different, though, if we can perceive it as heaven-sent, as a mystery, as a religious phenomenon. Again Jung says it well: "It is not a matter of indifference whether one calls something a mania or a god. To serve a mania is detestable and undignified but to serve a god is full of meaning." Yet, as Socrates saw, simply to speak of madness as divine is insufficient. One needs to be able to distinguish between different types of madness and to do so means being able to know which god one is serving. One needs to ask, "Who? Who is at work here?" Thus Socrates speaks of four types of divine madness and ascribes them to four gods:

the inspiration of the prophet to Apollo, that of the mystic to Dionysus, that of the poet to the Muses, and the madness of the lover to Aphrodite and Eros.

Socrates' list does not single out female divinities as instigators of divine madness, nor would I for my part want to suggest that it is only goddesses who drive us mad or provide us with models of divine madness. Yet of the nineteen instances of mortals driven mad by Greek divinities analyzed by Philip Slater in *The Glory of Hera*, the agents are all either goddesses or Dionysus (who, Slater reminds us, was himself first driven mad by the goddess Hera). Though my perspective is somewhat different from Slater's, I too believe that to know what the Greeks meant by calling madness divine necessitates examining why heaven-sent madness should be especially associated with female divinities. Slater's conclusion (buttressed by analyses of the dominant attitudes toward women and their social position in classical Greece) is that the Greeks were already picking on mothers as schizophrenogenic, just as Freud and many who followed him have done.

Yet Slater's failure to deal seriously with the difference between attributing madness to the personal mother and to a goddess is, I believe, misleading. It is not our mothers but something divine, archetypal, transpersonal that drives us mad. Nor are only mother goddesses guilty—the virgin goddesses, Artemis and Athena, are just as often culpable.

Perhaps the goddesses are more implicated in human madness than the gods because they are generally more involved in the full range of human affairs than the male divinities whose connections with mortals most often take the form of sexual liaison. That the interventions of the goddesses are as likely to be creative as destructive is suggested by the singular dependence of the heroes of Greek mythology on the support and encouragement of one female divinity or another: Jason and Achilles on Hera, Odysseus, Perseus, Heracles and Bellepheron on Athene, Aeneas and Paris on Aphrodite.

The goddesses represent the forces essential to human life upon which the ego depends. To be receptive to their intervention is to experience their helpfulness. To ignore them or to deny their divinity is to court madness. It is only when a mortal believes it possible to evade paying one of them homage that the goddesses become pathogenic. Thus when Hippolytus assumes immunity to Aphrodite's persuasions she drives Phaedra, his stepmother, mad with a lust for him so passionate that it ultimately brings about his death. Previous veneration provides no protection if the goddess believes that devotion has been compromised. Artemis displays no pity for Callisto when she learns of her seduction by Zeus. Mortals who implicitly deny a goddess's divinity by claiming power or beauty in equal measure are also apt to be struck mad—as is Arachne who challenges Athene's

skill at weaving or Myrrha who claims to be as lovely as Aphrodite. Such infla-
tionary conflation of ego and archetype inevitably leads to the mortal's becoming
less than human. Arachne is changed into a spider, Myrrha into a tree. The goddesses also will not tolerate being objectified; to look upon a goddess naked as
Actaeon does with Artemis is a violation quickly punished. The crime most inevitably associated with an eruption of madness is matricide, for this is the most
heinous offense against the feminine realm, the epitome of the attempt to deny
one's dependence on a feminine source, to cut oneself off from one's origins.

Though I am particularly interested in how the goddesses relate to the ways in
which women are and go mad, I do not want to suggest that only the madness of
women is goddess-sent. Indeed, Slater's reading is that the relation between agent
and victim is predominantly contra-sexual: the goddesses mostly drive men mad,
whereas women are driven mad by Dionysus. Because his working definition of
madness in Greek mythology is narrower than mine, I cannot accept that conclusion. But I do agree that men may go mad because of their dealings or misdeal-
ings with each of the goddesses: Athene is responsible for the madness of Ajax,
Artemis for that of Broteas. Furthermore I believe that men, too, may experience
the kinds of madness the goddesses model: they too may be consumed with grief
like Demeter's or with jealousy like Hera's—and these visitations may be particularly difficult and mad-making just because the victim may feel he is behaving
like a woman.

My focus is on the goddesses. As always, I begin with Persephone, the goddess
who initiated me into the realm of the goddesses and their ways with women. I
first knew Persephone as the innocent maiden who is abducted as she plays with
her friends and taken into the underworld; I knew that (though she is eventually
allowed to return to earth and is joyfully reunited with her mother) she was destined to return to the underworld each year. I felt close to Persephone because I
felt I too knew what it is like to be periodically pulled away from myself into a
dark place, into depressions that felt like death, and to long to return to life. The
sense of being abducted, taken away from myself, and having to endure passively
until some Hermes-like rescuer arrived, was the earliest form of madness I knew.
Yet because I had a sense of its periodicity, of how the down times were part of a
cyclic pattern, I could understand them as analogous to the time that a seed rests
in the earth, gathering the nourishment that will allow it to come forth as grain
when spring returns. Thus the association of these times with Persephone light-
ened them for me.

But the Greeks knew a darker truth about Persephone, a truth I too eventually
came to know. For Persephone is not only the maiden who passively endures her

time in Hades; she is herself the queen of the underworld, who comes to love her dark consort, and whose real home is there. (There are no myths that tell of anyone arriving in Hades and finding her absent.) Thus Persephone leads us to something more difficult than the acceptance of periodic cycles of depression. She represents a willingness to embrace being pulled away from self as having its own meaning, a life-giving meaning rather than time out from real living. All the fears we have of genuinely transformative experience are constellated in her. Recognizing this permits us to let go of our fears of the underworld and our negative evaluation of underworld experience. The Eleusinian rites in honor of Persephone (as Sophocles described them) represented an initiation into the underworld which transforms one's relation to it: "Thrice happy are those mortals who having seen these rites depart for Hades; for to them alone is it granted to have found life there; to the rest all there is evil." But we who live in a world where that ritual initiation is no longer available will probably only discover the life-giving quality of Hades in a more traumatic, fearful, involuntary way (more as Persephone herself does than as her Eleusinian devotees did). Only an abduction into Hades finally brings us to realize that it is more mad to resist, more deadly to be transfixed by the fear of dying. To choose Persephone's realm will always seem mad to those who have not experienced this transvaluation.

It is important to remember that for the uninitiated "all there in Hades is evil." The other valuation, that of the initiate, is hard won. I feel the need to warn against sentimentalization: Persephone as queen of the underworld is not a romantically beautifully maiden—she is austere and awesome.

It is always easier to romanticize the goddesses and so avoid their darkness. Thus when we turn to consider Demeter (the other half of the mythologem of the two goddesses who are one) it is tempting to see in her only the beautifully devoted mother grieving her daughter's disappearance. There is nothing pretty in Demeter's grief. She is overwhelmed by it. She has suffered what feels like an unendurable loss. She perfectly exemplifies Freud's description of melancholy: "an exclusive devotion to mourning which leaves nothing over for other purposes or other interests." She refuses to accept the loss and is completely ready to let the world die. "In grief the world becomes poor and empty," as indeed it does when Demeter mourns:

> And she made this
> the most terrible year
> On this earth
> that feeds so many,

and the most cruel.
The earth
did not take seed
that year.

And in fact
she would have wiped out
the whole race
of talking men
with a painful famine
and deprived
those who live on Olympos
of the glorious honor
of offerings and sacrifices.

Her mourning is truly divine in its extravagance—and mad. Demeter's madness is one easily recognized by those of us who have given ourselves so totally to a loved other that we have lost our sense of who we are apart from that love. Her sense of unendurable and meaningless loss issues in a felt loss of self and, paradoxically, in unceasing self-indulgence.

The madness of Hera has some of the same extravagance attached to it. She longs for a deep, fulfilling committed relationship with another and cannot bear to have this longing unfulfilled. Thus she is defiled in her very being by her rage at Zeus's betrayal of that longing—a betrayal as mythically inevitable as Persephone's rape or Demeter's loss. We know Hera's madness when we feel ourselves consumed by an unremitting jealousy that aims to destroy all that reminds us of our unfulfillment. It is not even Zeus himself who most bears the brunt of her jealousy, which is directed instead at the women he seduces (Leto, Semele, Ino) and at their sons (Herakles, Dionysus), and at her own sons and daughters. The effects of Hera's possessiveness are evident in the heroic madness of Herakles, endlessly performing one impossible task after another at her behest. Ares and Hephaistos represent the madness she imposes on her sons: one, the self-defeating aggressive delighter in violence for its own sake who is hated by the gods; the other, the gentle and skillful but impotent and crippled artisan whom they mock. She consumes Hebe and Eilythneia, too—daughters who are little more than shadow versions of herself. We also live touched by Hera's madness when the Furies of another woman's jealousy are directed against us. To experience that and thereby to discover how—unwittingly—that is, unconsciously—we have so destroyed another's well-being that she has gone mad may send us mad ourselves and may force a confrontation with sides of ourselves we cannot bear to see.

Remember, I am not saying that pathology is all there is to Hera. Every archetype has its creative and its pathological aspects. I am stressing the importance of recognizing their dark sides because it may help us toward a better understanding of our own wounds and destructiveness. To see the mythological representation may perhaps make possible a vicarious experiencing of the madness implicit in these archetypal patterns and thus a release from having literally to be taken over by it. The Greeks believed that to see, as the audience at the Dionysian theater sees or as the participants in the mystery cult rituals see, is to be pulled so deeply into pity and terror that a catharsis may occur. Hera may carry some of our jealousy for us—rather than forcing us to carry hers.

It is easy to see the madness of Hera because our culture has difficulty in admitting her other more creative side. It is less easy with Athene, "about whom few if any unworthy tales are told." Yet surely there is something mad about a father-bondedness which leads her to deny all dependence on feminine origins: "There is no mother anywhere who gave me birth and, but for marriage I am always for the male with all my heart, and strongly on my father's side." It is not so difficult, after all, to discern in Athene that form of madness labeled "identification with the aggressor." When we observe Athene more carefully, we discover another more profound relation to madness. Her other face, the one she wears on her breast, is that of the Gorgon Medusa whose terrifying visage turns those who see it into stone. When Athene wears the gorgon-head, it conveys the dark sources of her power but does not destroy or petrify; indeed, she uses the blood caught from Medusa's dripping neck to heal. In Athene a power that is potentially destructive is presented in its creative transformed aspects. She may strike Teiresias blind when he comes upon her naked, but she then gives him supernormal powers: second sight and the capacity for creative thinking even in Hades. She deludes Ajax into thinking that the cattle he slaughters are the fellow Greeks (Agamemnon, Menelaus, and Odysseus) he seeks to murder because he feels they have treated him unfairly; she drives him mad in order to prevent the killing. Athene represents the possibility that a way of seeing things which seems delusionary, blind, even petrifying, may in actuality provide a necessary safeguard, may represent a more penetrating insight than that vouchsafed to ordinary seeing or may even bring life back to that which had been given up as dead.

The madness of Artemis is integrally connected to the singular purity of her chastity. She has no patience with those who violate her privacy nor with those who allow themselves to be violated. Artemis, the fleeing one, is inevitably a goddess who slays those who pursue too relentlessly or those who allow themselves to be caught. The punishment she imposes is loss of self, since it is in-one-self-ness that is in question. Actaeon who comes upon Artemis bathing is transformed into a stag; Callisto who succumbs to Zeus's seduction, into a bear. Both lose the power of human communication. Artemis is the solitary wilderness she inhabits. To stay sane in such radical solitude, instead of becoming animal, is tricky indeed—something perhaps only a goddess can accomplish.

Aphrodite, too, is connected to divine madness, though the temptation is to emphasize the sunny joyous side of being taken over by love. Helen of Troy knows the ambivalence inherent in being possessed by this goddess who pulls us away from all other commitments and allegiances. Though Helen often expresses delight in the gifts the goddess bestows, she also laments: "I grieved for the madness that Aphrodite bestowed when she led me there away from my own dear country forsaking my daughter, my bedchamber, and my husband." It is Aphrodite who inspires Pasiphae with love for a bull and leads Myrrha to seduce her own father. She fills Phaedra with a passionate longing for her stepson, Hippolytus, a longing Phaedra knows is madness but which she cannot resist:

> O, I am miserable! What is this I've done?
> Where have I strayed from the highway of good sense?
> I was mad. It was the madness sent from some God
> that caused my fall.
> I am unhappy so unhappy! Nurse,
> cover my face again. I am ashamed
> of what I said. Cover me up. The tears
> are flowing and my face is turned to shame.
> Rightness of judgment is bitterness to the heart.
> Madness is terrible. It is better then
> that I should die and know no more of anything.

The madness of a goddess is always balanced by a mode of health, of creative being. Each of the goddesses represents a way of being mad as she represents a way of loving, a way of knowing, a way of fighting. As Walter Otto showed us, each of the Greek divinities represents a whole but singular world:

None of them represents a single virtue, none is to be encountered in only one direction of teeming life; each desires to feel, shape and illumine the whole compass of human existence with his peculiar spirit…. Its special characteristic is always the signature of a world complete in itself. Each represents a wholly different but a whole world.

What can co-exist simultaneously in goddesses is experienced sequentially by mortals. A goddess is at all times all that she is—infant and adult, virgin and mother, mad and sane.

When humans are struck with divine madness in Greek mythology the story is different: their madness excludes sanity although sometimes the madness is so fully lived that sanity is recovered. Thus in Aeschylus' trilogy Orestes is finally released when Athene intervenes and in Sophocles, years of lonely wandering bring Oedipus to a point where he can at last die in peace. Both stories represent the transformation of the Furies into the Eumenides—the consoling ones—and suggest that if one stays with the inflicting agents long enough, their transformative power may be released. The "cures" (like the madness itself) are divine mysteries.

Mostly, however, there are no cures. In the myths about those who suffer from Hera's jealousy, Artemis's merciless judgment, or Aphroditic passion, there are no reprieves. As Roheim once observed, though Eros may triumph in fairy tales, in myths it is Thanatos who prevails. This is real madness that Greek mythology describes, not just the bad trip that we know will soon wear off, the bad dream out of which we can awaken. The divine power that inflicts madness is a power that can enter human lives creatively, but is here shown working destructively because too long denied or taken too lightly.

Though in the myths mortals are represented from the perspective of a linear temporality and thus are youthful or mature, mad or sane, we know that there is a sense in which for us too, and not only for the gods, it is possible to be both at once. We know that in the unconscious there is no time. The child we were co-exists with the adult we are, in our dreams we may be mad while in waking life we appear sane—and the fears and fantasies of nightmare sometimes appear unexpectedly but inescapably during the day. Not all of us go certifiably mad, yet (as James Hillman says) all of us experience the fear of going mad as primally as we do fantasies of growth and health. All of us have moments when we know we are mad and we tend to experience such moments mythologically—that is, we imaginally transform them into their worst potential. Such moments introduce us to dark forces in the depths that seem ready to overwhelm us forever. All of us have some experience of madness. But, once more: I am talking about our most fearful, really terrifying moments, the moments when we really feel we have lost it all, moments when we believe *that* is the real truth.

Divine madness attacks us in a variety of ways, because there are different goddesses at work. It may be that at different times a different one will keep reappearing because we still have not learned to pay attention to her. The fear of loss of control is very strong. Madness is scary. Even when we think we have learned how much we constrict, how much we lose, how much we risk, by being too much in control—my guess is that most of us try to reinstate control. We choose the madness of Zeus, the illusion that the Titans or the giants or the goddesses can be subdued for eternity.

Yet I believe we can learn to bless those appearances of the goddesses that remind us that they are always present, that the ego is never really master in its own house. The illusion of ego-mastery, and the constriction of self it represents, is what Socrates meant by "man made sanity," an always fragile and inherently inferior mode of consciousness. To see madness as a gift of the gods and goddesses is not to abrogate responsibility for our lives. Rather, it brings us to acknowledge the importance of learning to attend to those powers that work in and through us, powers that can bring creation or destruction. For the Greeks it was not a sign of psychosis to see divine beings intervening in our psychic life: rather it was felt to be madness to ignore their presence. The gods intervene not only in our boundless jealousy or mindless grief; they are also the source of energy, strength, courage, insight, restraint, of every fateful decision and every inner transformation. For Socrates reason, too, was "an active manifestation of deity in human being." The point of divine madness is to teach us that these divine beings are always present. We seem to learn that only when forced to—and we seem to need to learn it over and over again. Madness introduces us to the "Who"s at work in our soul. Socrates could see madness as blessing because he knew the "Who"s—and so prophecy could mean insight rather than sophistic babble; ritual ecstasy could mean creative release from egoistic isolation rather than orgiastic frenzy; the Muses would inspire poetry, not a formless outpouring of imagery; Aphrodite and Eros could lead toward an appreciation of harmony and beauty, not a wallowing in bestial lust.

The real madness, so he taught, is not to know oneself—one's selves, all the "Who"s at work within.

References

E. R. Dodds. *The Greeks and the Irrational.* Boston: Beacon Press, 1957.

Sigmund Freud, "Mourning and Melancholia." In Philip Rieff, ed. *General Psychological Theory*. New York: Collier, 1963.

James Hillman. *ReVisioning Psychology*. New York: Harper & Row, 1975.

C. G. Jung. "Commentary on the Secret of the Golden Flower." *Alchemical Studies, C.W. 13*. Princeton: Princeton University Press, 1967.

Walter F. Otto. *Dionysus*. Boston: Beacon Press, 1964.

Philip E. Slater. *The Glory of Hera*. Boston: Beacon Press, 1968.

25

Your Old Men Shall Dream Dreams

A human being would certainly not grow to be seventy or eighty years old if this longevity had no meaning for the species. The afternoon of life must also have significance of its own and cannot be merely a pitiful appendage of life's morning.[1]

These words of Carl Jung invite us to consider the creative process in relation to the image of the wise old man and not only as we usually do in relation to the child. So often we identify the creative with characteristics associated with youth—originality, spontaneity, play, narcissism—and ignore the work of art, the discipline, the ordering, the recognition of limits. All our tribute is given Dionysos or Eros; we forget the sacrifice due Apollo and death. Even when we recognize the conjunction of creativity and death, we may well have in mind the "romantic" premature death of a Keats or a Novalis. "He whom the gods love dies young," we say. But death, too, is viewed differently from the perspective of the morning of life than from its afternoon. Perhaps there are insights about the creative process, about what sustains it and brings it to maturity and not only about what gives it birth, to be gained from the contemplation of the late works of those writers who do grow to be seventy or eighty years old.

This would be especially true of late works consciously understood by their creators as part of their own preparation for death and as in some sense works of self-completion, works in which old man and youth are rejoined. Thus last works which are obviously completions of projects begun much earlier are of particular interest. Though I intend here to focus on Sophocles' *Oedipus at Colonus* and Thomas Mann's *Confessions of Felix Krull, Confidence Man,* the most obvious example of such a last work is probably Goethe's *Faust,* of which Mann wrote:

A life so abundant and manifold that there was ever present danger of its being squandered, here asserts, by the power of memory, its essential unity. *Faust* is the representative achievement, the symbol of Goethe's whole life. He himself said of it:

> Man's life a poem similar to this;
> It has, of course, beginning, has an end too—
> But yet a whole life it does not come to.

It is touching to see how his mind, in the later, elder, time, reaches back to give to the fragmentary and illimitable work the unity that in his deepest heart he craved. "He is," he said, "the most fortunate man who can bring the end of his life round to its beginning again."[2]

In his study of Leonardo da Vinci, Sigmund Freud suggests such a reunion of *senex* and *puer* as integral to the creativity of the mature. He believes that when the aging artist's creativity was waning, it was through regression to his infantile experience, with "the help of his oldest erotic energies," that he found renewal. The mysterious smile of the Mona Lisa inspired Leonardo because it awakened in him the earliest memories of his mother.

Mann seems to invoke this presentation of Leonardo as prototype of the artist renewed by contact with youth in several of his own "studies" of the artist. Mona Lisa's smile may well lie behind the enigmatic smile of Tadzio which stirs Mann's aging artist, Gustav Aschenbach, in *Death in Venice*, written shortly after Freud's study. Is not Felix Krull's becoming Louis de Venosta (L. d. V.), sketchpad in hand, a not too subtle indication of Mann's recognition, when he has himself become an aging artist, of his bond with Freud's Leonardo—a bond mediated through his youthful protagonist Felix, who is also thus "the fortunate man" whom Goethe described?

Such connections seem legitimate because Mann has made explicit acknowledgement of his indebtedness to Freud, his conviction that Freud, particularly in his late works (the works from the time of *Leonardo* and *Totem and Taboo* onward), points the way to "a relation to the powers of the lower world, the unconscious...productive of a riper art."[3] In these meta-psychological works in which Freud self-confessedly returns to his long-neglected philosophical interests, to "the early passion of his youth," he offers us a psychology particularly appropriate to the second half of life. As his earlier more therapeutically-oriented works pertain primarily to the concerns of the young, work and love; so, in the later writings Freud recognizes the coming to terms with death as the central task of life and posits the discovery of the mythopoetic dimensions of our lives as an essential part of this preparation.

The beautiful essay Mann wrote in celebration of Freud's eightieth birthday indicates that the reconnection with the past that inspires the mature artist is not just a recovery of personal infancy and youth but "a penetration into the childhood of mankind, into the primitive and mythical." For, "while in the life of the human race, the mythical is an early and primitive stage, in the life of the individual it is a late and mature one." Mann speaks of the "curious heightening of his artist temper," the "new refreshment of his perceiving and shaping power," that comes when an artist acquires "the habit of regarding life as mythical and typical." He relates this to the transition in his own career (which he identifies with the beginning of the *Joseph* cycle) from "the bourgeois and individual to the mythical and typical."[4]

Freud, says Mann, helps us to understand what it means for myth to "become subjective," to pass over into "the active ego, becoming conscious there proudly and darkly, but joyously, of its recurrence and typicality."[5] For Freud maturity means becoming conscious of our participation in mythic patterns and thus discovering a kind of freedom in relation to them. This is the significance of his putting the working-through of the transference at the center of the psychoanalytical process. For when we come to understand the degree to which all our experiencing is the reliving of ancient patterns and to recognize how much we shape our present on the basis of imaginal (not literal) versions of our past, we can become aware of the symbolic and thus make the move from repetition to recognition, from myth to mythopoetic.

The move to mythopoesis is also a move beyond the monomyth of the hero; the heroic illusion persists only as long as one is still caught in an ego-identification with the myth. That identification represents what Jung calls "inflation": taking the myth literally, not yet recognizing myth as myth. As we transcend the confusion of the literal and the symbolic, we become conscious of the multidimensionality of what happens between us and the others intimately implicated in our lives and learn to celebrate our capacity to transfer onto those we love our deepest longings—knowing exactly what we are up to. Mann calls what is gained "a smiling knowledge of the eternal," a release from bondage to the identification of the real with the unique and unitemporal. Freud suggests that the capacity to distinguish between the literal and the symbolic is integrally related to our conversion to finitude, our acceptance of Ananke and Death. Trying to repress myth, like Oedipus trying to evade the oracle, is what gets us into trouble—but participating in the myth knowingly is utterly different from unknowing compulsion.

Thus the cultivation of mythic consciousness becomes the primary challenge of old age.

We might expect then that in the artistic works of old men we might find evidence of this more subjective, more conscious relation to myth. It is not so much the presence of mythical themes that distinguishes youth from maturity as a different relation to myth. There is more freedom for creative response to the inherited patterns rather than simple determination by them, more awareness that we are implicated in a plurality of myths and not wholly defined by any one, and that our participation in mythic patterns is not just a matter of seemingly accidental and superficial parallels but of the basic structures of our being. Mann's conviction that the move to this deeper appreciation of the mythical characterizes the mature artist suggests that when Sophocles returns to Oedipus after a twenty year lapse, when he himself returns to Felix Krull after an interval almost twice as long, we might look for a different approach to the same material—both the return to the beginning which Goethe commends and the transformation which *Faust, Part II* exemplifies.

Thus we should not be surprised if the Oedipus of *Oedipus at Colonus* and the Krull of Parts II and III, are more aware and more accepting of their participation in mythic patterns than was true of them in their earlier appearances. The mythopoetic logic of the psyche that Freud articulated in his later years suggests some other themes we might look for in literary works written by those engaged in coming to terms with age and death. Whereas in youth the heroic stance is appropriate, in later years the overcoming of egoic illusions, the recognition that life is *poesis* and *pathos*, doing and suffering inextricably intertwined, is crucial. Thus the focus shifts from the quest of the hero to the battle between the Titans, Eros and Death. And with the yielding of the heroic there comes an end to the exaltation of the tragic; in its place there appears the recognition (long ago voiced by Socrates at the end of the *Symposium*) that the tragic and comic visions do not exclude one another. The more mature relation to myth means not only the transcendence of the heroic but also the end of the hyper-masculinity so often correlative with it. In "Analysis Terminable and Interminable" Freud suggests that the overcoming of misogyny, the subversion of our repudiation of our femininity (be we men or women) is the most difficult task of analysis. The full acceptance of self includes the discovery of our psychological bisexuality, in mythological terms of our hermaphroditism. The new perspective also implies release from the hero's mother complex, from his seeking everywhere for a reanimation of his literal mother and from his obsessive longing for rebirth, his nostalgia for innocence. It is now understood that the realm of the mother means death as well as rebirth, that mother means tomb and not only womb. In his essay on "The Three Caskets" Freud speaks of

> The three forms taken on by the figure of the mother as life proceeds: the mother herself, the beloved who is chosen after her pattern, and finally the Mother Earth who receives him again. But it is in vain that the old man yearns after the love of woman as once he had it from his mother; the third of the Fates, alone, the silent goddess of death will take him into her arms.

He shows how Cordelia's death means that King Lear must now renounce love, choose death and make friends with the necessity of dying. Paradoxically, the radical acceptance of death entails the realization that it does not mean the end, does not mean resolution or completion. There are no tidy ends; in Freud's terms, analysis is interminable.

Send Us Back Then To Ancient Thebes

Even at the time of *Interpretation of Dreams* Oedipus meant to Freud not only patricide and incest but the long and painful process of self-discovery. This myth represented the pull each of us experiences toward being our own father, toward denying our separation from our mother, and the recognition that we cannot get away with either. "Resolution" of the Oedipus complex entails the move toward a different kind of seeing, toward transliteral, sacred understanding. Freud understands the significance of the fact that in *Oedipus Tyrannos* only the blind see; literal blindness, blindness to the literal, makes possible imaginal, metaphorical perception. But some twenty years later Freud, now painfully cancer-ridden, recognized even more profoundly that the story of Oedipus does not end in Jocasta's bed but in Demeter's grove outside of Athens. As throughout his years of wandering Oedipus' eyes were his daughter, Antigone, so now Sigmund's mouth is his daughter, "my Anna/Antigone." There is more to being Oedipus than at first appears. Freud had discovered early: I am Oedipus; you, too, are Oedipus. As his longing and guilt are ours, so, Freud seems now to suggest, could be his death, "wonderful if ever mortal's was."

When Sophocles returns to Oedipus some twenty years after the composition of *Oedipus Tyrannos,* he portrays Oedipus as dying at Colonus, his own birthplace. Thus he conveys that this, his last play (which he probably did not live to see performed), represents a homecoming. Although this is not sheer invention on Sophocles' part (there were ancient Attic traditions in its support), our familiarity with Sophocles' version may blind us to how much more freely Sophocles has reworked received versions of the myth here than in the earlier play. There are widely varying accounts of what happens to Oedipus after his downfall. The most popular seems to have said nothing of banishment at all: Oedipus was simply shut up in an inner room of the palace at Thebes. According to Homer he dies in battle at Thebes as befits a hero. Another ancient tradition has him exiled and after years of aimless wandering dying in the wild wastelands near the place where he slew Laius. In Euripides' *The Phoenician Women* Oedipus, long a prisoner in Thebes, does not leave the city until after he has witnessed the horrifying fulfill-ment of his curse: his sons have slain one another and only after witnessing that has Jocasta in her grief killed herself. In Apollodorus as in Sophocles, Oedipus dies at Colonus, but whereas according to Sophocles, "the underworld opened in love the unlit door of earth,"[6] according to Apollodorus he is hounded to death by the Furies.

It is clear that Sophocles felt free consciously to rework the story in the light of his own vision of a death appropriate to an Oedipus who has lived long enough to understand the meaning of his own story. The more conscious relation to myth is thus also reflected in the protagonist's own self-understanding. This Oedipus is aware that he is living a myth, is a living myth. As the chorus tells him, "Old man, your name has gone over all the earth" (305); "Your story is told everywhere and never dies: I only want to hear it truly told" (517-8). Oedipus himself has come to recognize how all of his life has been lived in accordance with the oracle. Trying to evade living out the mythic pattern only intensified its power over him:

> The bloody deaths, the incest, the calamities
> You speak so glibly of: I suffered them,
> By fate, against my will. (962-4)

But he trusts that the rest of Apollo's prophecy is also to be fulfilled, and soon:

> For when he gave me oracles of evil,
> He also spoke of this: A resting place,
> After long years, in the last country, where
> I should find home among the sacred Furies:
> That there I might round out my bitter life,
> Conferring benefit on those who received me. (87-92)

The blind Oedipus who has come to Colonus has now himself become the possessor of that clairvoyant insight which earlier (because he could not bear to see) had been carried by Tiresias. Oedipus has now become Tiresias in another sense as well. Though Tiresias remains the only mortal to have experienced life both as male and female, Oedipus—in a less literal sense—has during his years of exile lived as a woman. His blindness is a kind of castration; he has had to come to terms with a dependent status conventionally associated with the feminine, has had to surrender the heroic masculine notion of being able to make the world conform to his wishes. He has also learned how little gender determines our psychological orientation and how multiple are the confusions of object-love and identification-love in any primary relationship. He recognizes that Antigone who is not only his daughter but also his sister is also at times his son. She and Ismene "are not girls but men in faithfulness" (1368), while their brothers "sit by the fire like home-loving girls" (342).

Oedipus in this final scene of his life re-enacts the mythic pattern that is so indelibly associated with his name. He is still Oedipus—and yet, because he understands now what he is about, the meaning is utterly different. His readiness to enter the forbidden grove of Demeter is a repetition of his earlier readiness to enter the forbidden womb of Jocasta. But now (as Slochower has noted)[7] there is this crucial difference: "This return to the mother takes place, not on a literal, but on a symbolic level." Oedipus has learned now that literal incest is beside the point.

The importance of the recognition that the return to the mother is to be enacted symbolically is a major theme in the writings of Carl Jung. This theme is boldly articulated in *Symbols of Transformation*, the work that both he and Freud understood as a consciously patricidal attempt to free himself from domination by Freud and establish his own unmediated relation to the unconscious. Jung found Freud's understanding of incest too literal and too biological; he was persuaded that incest longing, properly understood, is always symbolical. It represents the longing for spiritual rebirth, for renewal at the source of life. The forbidding of literal incest, the taboo, forces the move toward symbolization and spiritual transformation. The point of regression is introversion, the relation not to the parents but to the collective psyche. The prohibition (or in Oedipus' case, the punishment of its violation) forces further regression to the mother as nourisher and not as sexual object. Thus it is his blindness that represents the introversion that brings Oedipus to the Demetrian grove.

The pull toward the mother and the taboo that says, "not the literal mother, not literal sex," moves us toward spiritual transformation. Jung's interpretation suggests the necessity of the kind of symbolic incest that Oedipus commits at Colonus. "The fear of incest must be conquered," the hero is the one who yields to the incest wish.[8]

> Therapy must support the regression and continue to do so until the "pre-natal" stage is reached.... The regression leads back only apparently to the mother; in reality she is the gateway into the unconscious, into the "realm of the Mother."[9]

(It seems pertinent that in the preface to this book Jung should acknowledge his identification with Theseus. He is to Theseus as Freud is to Oedipus. Theseus' daring of the labyrinth is the equivalent in his life of Oedipus' entry into the grove, but at a much earlier point in his life. At Colonus Theseus is the only one to witness Oedipus' descent and the one to whom Oedipus' secret is passed on—an image clearly consonant with Jung's understanding of his relation to Freud.)

At Colonus Oedipus' return to the mother is symbolic, and is a return to her in her role as the silent goddess of death. Having in the violent act of self-blinding had a preliminary experience of death as the hero typically encounters it, Oedipus is now ready for death as it is understood in Demeter's realm. Here death means reunion with Persephone ("Veiled Persephone lead me on," 1548.) Death is now blessing not curse, initiation not termination—like the death offered to participants in the Eleusinian mysteries. Of which Sophocles said elsewhere: "Thrice happy are those mortals, who having seen these rites depart for Hades; for to them alone is it granted to have found life there; to the rest all there is evil."[10]

At Colonus everything is turned around. What had been a source of difficulty has become a blessing to be celebrated. The grove is a place of many reversals and transformations. The gods have not forgiven Oedipus nor has he been brought to accept his sinfulness. But he has suffered long enough to have come to accept his life as it has been—without trying any longer to argue a distinction between "so it was" and "so I willed it."[11] The years of wandering serve as the equivalent of participation in the preparatory outwardly visible phases of the Eleusinian initiation. The burial place of one whose presence during the years of exile had been perceived as curse will be a source of blessing. The Furies who haunt violators of the mother so mercilessly now appear as the Eumenides, "the gentle all-seeing ones." Blind Oedipus long led by Antigone, now becomes the guide.

These resolutions do not depend on Oedipus' story now being explained; the mystery that has surrounded his life is not dissolved:

> Now the finish
> Comes, and we know only
> In all that we have seen and done
> Bewildering mystery. (1675-8)

The lines describing Oedipus' end are utterly beautiful:

> But in what manner
> Oedipus perished, no one of mortal men
> Could tell but Theseus. It was not lightning,
> Bearing its fire from God, that took him off;
> No hurricane was blowing.
> But some attendant from the train of Heaven
> Came for him: or else the underworld
> Opened in love the unlit door of earth.
> For he was taken without lamentation,
> Illness or suffering: indeed his end
> Was wonderful if ever mortal's was. (1655-65)

Yet this wonderful end does not betoken the end of human tragedy. Sophocles does not offer us a world that after Oedipus' death is restored to harmony. The last lines of the play communicate a vision of the interminable quality of the troubledness of human existence. The curse Oedipus visited upon his sons is still to be fulfilled; Antigone and Ismene, grief-shattered, confront a "wide and desolate world," with no way clear before them.

Nevertheless in his last tragedy Sophocles offers us his vision of a wonder-full, creative death—a death in which a "bitter life" is transformed into something that "confers benefit."

Hole! Heho! Ahe!

As Sophocles returned in his last tragedy to a figure whose story he had begun to relate some twenty years earlier, so Thomas Mann returned at the end of his life to continuing the narration of the adventures of a character who had made his first appearance more than forty years earlier. Mann began "Felix Krull" in 1910 and already guessed then, "It will probably be my strangest work."[12] He put it aside, so he thought temporarily, to work on "Death in Venice," and then published the completed fragment in 1912, having discovered that he was not ready to take it further after all. He came to regard it as a youthful expression, "belonging to an outmoded bourgeois-artist period" in his history as a writer. This relatively early phase of Mann's life is perhaps comparable to the one in Freud's during which he wrote his case histories. After World War I both Freud and Mann had moved to a view of life so deeply attuned to the shaping power of mythic forces on individual existence that the earlier focus on individual quest no longer seemed an appropriate vehicle. "Felix" seemed to belong to that outgrown period.

Yet in late 1945 after finishing *Joseph and His Brothers*, Mann found himself picking up the fragment again, as though there were after all something to be finished here. He had an intuition that the completion of "Felix Krull" might in some way be meant to be his last work. Again another project became more immediately compelling and Mann soon found himself completely immersed in the writing of *Dr. Faustus*. But then in 1950 he returned to "Felix," still uncertainly ("perhaps it will only be mischief"), and on this occasion found it was indeed time to take up the old tale once again. It was finished in 1954 and was, after all, his last work.

The return to "Krull" is continuation—and transformation. As Mann wrote Carl Kerenyi:

> I was not aware, God knows, of undertaking a Hermetic novel when I began with this forty years ago. I had no other intention than yet another impersonation and parody of art and the artist. It was only in the course of the subsequent continuation that certain associations, undoubtedly induced by the proximity of the Joseph, found their way in, and the name of the god arose.[13]

It is an important part of Krull's acceptance of himself as a "confidence man" that his trickery brings joy not harm. The recognition of the identity between blessor and violator lies at the heart of *Felix Krull* in its final version and is central to Mann's identification with Felix as archetypal artist: creator and thief in one. (Perhaps *Oedipus at Colonus* is also a hermetic work in Mann's sense. Certainly Oedipus invokes Hermes as well as Persephone to guide him to his death, and the reversals whereby the violator becomes the bringer of blessings have a decidedly hermetic flavor.)

Mann has in the later parts of his novella come to see Krull in mythic terms not consciously included in his earlier conception. He writes of his delight that once again as so often before he and Kerenyi should have been engaged quite innocently in such parallel projects; he on his "hermetic novel" and Kerenyi on the trickster figure in mythology. Of course, a mythological element is visible in Mann's fiction long before *Joseph and His Brothers*. The difference between earlier works, like the initial version of "Krull" and "Death in Venice," and the final parts of *Felix Krull* is not that myth is present in the latter and absent from the first—but rather in how myth is present. Aschenbach is destroyed through being possessed by the mythic, taken over by one mythic pattern and not having any creative freedom in relation to it. Whereas Felix, "favored by fortune," is like Mann's Joseph aware of the many mythic roles in which he participates. Therefore he can celebrate the mythic as source of rebirth rather than destruction. He takes delight in his many impersonations, sees them as providing the means for "renewal of my worn-out self."[14] He believes that it is the attitude which underlies one's performances that gives one's activities their meaning: "For my part I am in agreement with folk wisdom which holds that when two people do the same it is no longer the same" (112). It is his ability to see his life as an artistic creation, in symbolic terms, that underlies his self-enjoyment. His spurning of Strathbogie's adoption offer expresses his rejection of "a reality simply handed me" (215). He can take as much delight in passing as less than he is when he is a waiter, as in passing for a marquis. He gives voice to his most deeply held conviction when he says, "to be allowed to live symbolically spells true freedom" (101). As befits one thus attuned to the mythic aspect, he knows how impossible it would be to disentangle the "good luck" in his life from his own contribution.

Felix adopts an artistic, mythopoetic attitude toward life without, however, being consciously informed about the particular classical mythological roles that he is reenacting. He is quick to appreciate the pertinence of the Hellenic motif when another suggests it, as when Diane Philibert calls him a Hermes figure, but in large measure the explicit parallels are conveyed to the reader indirectly. They are not part of Felix's conscious self-understanding. Thus when Louis asks him, "Are you strong on mythology?" Felix answers, "Not very, marquis. There is, for instance, the god Hermes. But aside from him I know very little" (230).

Yet Felix, as we come to recognize, participates in many myths. Though he might not be able to name his classical counterparts, we see him not only as Hermes but also as Adonis, Actaeon, Eros, and Proteus. Felix's own way of explaining this polymorphism is to say, "He who really loves the world shapes himself to please it" (61).

The Hermes identification is, nevertheless, the central one; not only because Felix as confidence man is Hermes as trickster nor because Felix as waiter is Hermes as servant, but because of Hermes' primal connection with Aphrodite and thus with the image of the hermaphrodite. Much is made in the novel of Krull's slender and delicate beauty and of his being someone with whom both men and women fall in love. His own eroticism has a definitely feminine aspect, particularly in its pronouncedly passive orientation. He speaks of "eccentrics who were seeking neither a woman nor a man but some extraordinary being in between. And I was this extraordinary being" (104). And he himself feels the pull toward what he calls a "double creature": the brother/sister pair on the balcony of the Frankfurt hotel, Andromache the very masculinized female acrobat who arouses his worship.

But Felix's "penchant for twofold enthusiasms" (281) is particularly evident in his attraction to mother-daughter combinations, beginning with his own mother and his sister, Olympia, in the Rhine valley town of his childhood years and ending with Senhora Kuckuck and her daughter, Zouzou, in Lisbon. Though the story of Felix's encounter with the latter pair is comically and joyfully told and has none of the awesome power of Sophocles' drama, here too the climax takes place in "Demeter's grove," that is, in the garden of the Senhora's house. Here, too, Krull is brought to recognize that it is in vain that he turns to the female who most directly arouses his sensual interest, the virginal daughter. For suddenly there stands her mother.

> And yet I ask you to believe that I was less cast down by this maternal apparition than one might have thought. However unexpected her appearance, it seemed fitting and necessary as though she had been summoned, and in my natural confusion there was an element of joy (376).

Both Felix and the Senhora recognize that she has come to lead him "back to the right path." It is time for him to encounter "the graciousness of maturity." He had turned to the mortal daughter when he should have turned toward the archetypal mother. As his coming to Lisbon represented his discovery of an "older geological strata in the earth's history," so the Senhora appears to initiate him into primordial, mythical mysteries. He had recognized from the beginning that she was not one to be trifled with. The preceding scene during which Felix becomes aware of the connection between the Senhora's surging bosom and the violence of the bullfight below had made fully manifest the bond between the Mother and death. Now as the novel ends, Felix is aware of "a whirlwind of primordial forces" bearing him "into the realm of ecstasy." Again he sees "the surging of that queenly bosom." The Senhora is clearly the Great Mother and, as Jung says, the hero is the one courageous enough to commit incest.

Perhaps an entirely just appreciation of Mann's own last "confessions" would demand our looking at both *Dr. Faustus* and *Felix Krull*—together they represent a profound honoring of the tragic and comic perspectives on human sufferings. But, that of the two, Krull should be the very last seems highly appropriate. Mann in his own old age deliberately chooses Felix, an archetypal *puer aeternus*, to represent artistic creativity. Yet without romanticizing the play-ful and narcissistic aspects of the creative. Felix is well aware that his career is "based on imagination and self-discipline," and that the "great joy"—the experience of love given and received—is what redeems his trickeries. Because of Felix's youth his turn to Dona Maria is inevitably ambiguous. Is he still caught in a too-literal pull toward the mother or is he, indeed, aware that in turning to the Senhora he is moving into the transformative realm of the Mothers? That ambiguity is, I believe, intentional. Mann does not want to dissolve the mystery of the discovery of the mythical within the actual. And after all, we are by no means at the end of Felix's adventures.

The novel ends—and yet what we have are still only fragments of Felix's confessions. They could theoretically continue interminably. We know that much else is to follow; that at some point in the future, for example, Felix will find himself in prison. Accepting these fragments as all we have is accepting the finitude of life—and recognizing that our fragments nevertheless serve as symbols of wholeness.

Consent to mortality and celebration of the mythical are profoundly intertwined in both *Oedipus at Colonus* and *Felix Krull*. Through this conjunction, Mann and Sophocles in their last works communicate their "smiling knowledge of the eternal."

Notes

1. C. G. Jung, "The Stages of Life," in Joseph Campbell, ed., *The Portable Jung* (New York: Viking, 1971) 17.

2. Thomas Mann, "Goethe's Faust," *Essays of Three Decades* (New York: Alfred A. Knopf, 1971) 19.

3. Thomas Mann, "Freud and the Future," *Essays* (New York: Vintage, 1957) 323.

4. Mann, "Freud," 317.

5. Mann, "Freud," 318.

6. Sophocles, "Oedipus at Colonus," in David Grene and Richard Lattimore, eds., *The Complete Greek Tragedies, Volume II*, 150. Hereafter line references in text.

7. Harry Slochower, *Mythopoesis* (Detroit, Wayne State University Press, 1970) 90.

8. C. G. Jung, *Symbols Of Transformation* (New York: Pantheon, 1956) 294.

9. Jung, *Symbols*, 329.

10. Quoted in George E. Mylonas, *Eleusis: The Eleusinian Mysteries* (Princeton: Princeton University Press, 1974) 284.

11. Cf. H. D. F. Kitto, *Greek Tragedy* (New York: Doubleday, 1954) 419, where he brings in Nietzsche's definition of redemption.

12. Hans Burgin and Hans-Otto Mayer, *Thomas Mann: A Chronicle of His Life* (Alabama: University of Alabama, 1969).

13. Alexander Gelley, translator, *Mythology and Humanism: The Correspondence of Thomas Mann and Karl Kerenyi* (Ithaca: Cornell University Press, 1975) 210.

14. Thomas Mann, *Confessions of Felix Krull* (New York: Vintage, 1969) 252. Hereafter page references in text.

Acknowledgements

"Dear Chris...Love, Christine," in Mary Jo Meadows and Carole Rayburn, eds., *A Time to Weep, A Time to Sing*, Minneapolis. Winston, 1985, 48-63.

"Such Stuff as Dreams Are Made On," term paper for graduate seminar on Dante's *Commedia* at Drew University, Spring 1961.

"What is Theology?" *Quaker Religious Thought*, Fall 1964 (shortened).

"All Real Living is Meeting," *Inward Light*, Fall 1966.

"How Can We Hope and Not Dream? Exodus as Biblical Metaphor," *Journal of Religion*, January 1968, 35-53.

"It Pleased God to Save the World: Heinrich Boll's *The Clown*." Paper read at annual meeting of The Society for Religion in Higher Education, August 1968.

"Theology as Make-Believe: A Response to the Theology of Hope," paper read at American Academy of Religion, annual meeting, Dallas, October 1969.

"Guilt and Responsibility in the Thought of Martin Buber," *Judaism*, Winter 1969.

"Abraham and Orpheus Be With Me Now," paper read at Earlham School of Religion, October 1968; Lafayette College, March 1969.

"God Made Man Because He Loves Stories: Martin Buber's Retellings of the Hasidic Tales," paper read at a symposium on Religion and Literature, Wilson College, April 1970.

"Daydream," in Daniel O. Noel, ed., *Echoes of the Wordless Word*, Religion and the Arts Series, #2, American Academy of Religion.

"The Three 'Incarnations' in Hesse's *Magister Ludi*," paper read at Hartford Seminary lecture series, November 1972; American Academy of Religion annual meeting, Boston, September 1972.

"Symptoms and Symbols: A review of Edmund C. Whitmont, *Symbolic Quest*," *Inward Light*, Spring 1972, 42-45.

"Reviewing David Miller," a review of David Miller, *Gods and Games*, and Sam Keen, *To a Dancing God*, *Journal of the American Academy of Religion*, September 1972.

"Sigmund Freud and the Greek Mythological Tradition," *Journal of the American Academy of Religion*, March 1975, 3-14.

"The Silent Goddess of Death and Two Who Paid Her Tribute: Sigmund Freud and Carl Jung," paper read at a USC-NEH Colloquium on The Symbolism of Aging, April 1976.

"Two Masters of the School of Suspicion: Karl Marx and Sigmund Freud," paper read at a Symposium in honor of Paul Ricoeur, University of California at Santa Cruz, April 1976.

"Towards an Erotics of the Psyche: A Tribute to Thomas Mann and Carl Jung," *Journal of the American Academy of Religion,* December 1976.

"Jealousy: A Depth Psychological Perspective," in Gordon Clanton and Lynn Smith, eds., *Jealousy,* Prentice Hall, 1977.

"Poetically Dwells Man on This Earth," *Soundings*, Fall 1977.

"Revisioning Autobiography: Freud's *The Interpretation of Dreams* and Jung's *Memories, Dreams, Reflections*," *Soundings,* Summer 1977, 210-228.

"Visions and Revisions: A Response to James Hillman," *Inward Light*, Spring 1978.

"The Subliminal Presence of the Goddess In Hebrew Tradition," paper read at Jewish Studies Symposium, San Diego State University, Spring 1979.

"Goddess-Sent Madness," *Psychological Perspectives*, Fall 1981.

"Your Old Men Shall Dream Dreams," in John Raphael Staude, ed., *Wisdom and Age*, Berkeley: Rose Books, 1981.

978-0-595-35431-3
0-595-35431-9

Made in the USA
Lexington, KY
09 August 2013